AF593672

The Swagger Portrait

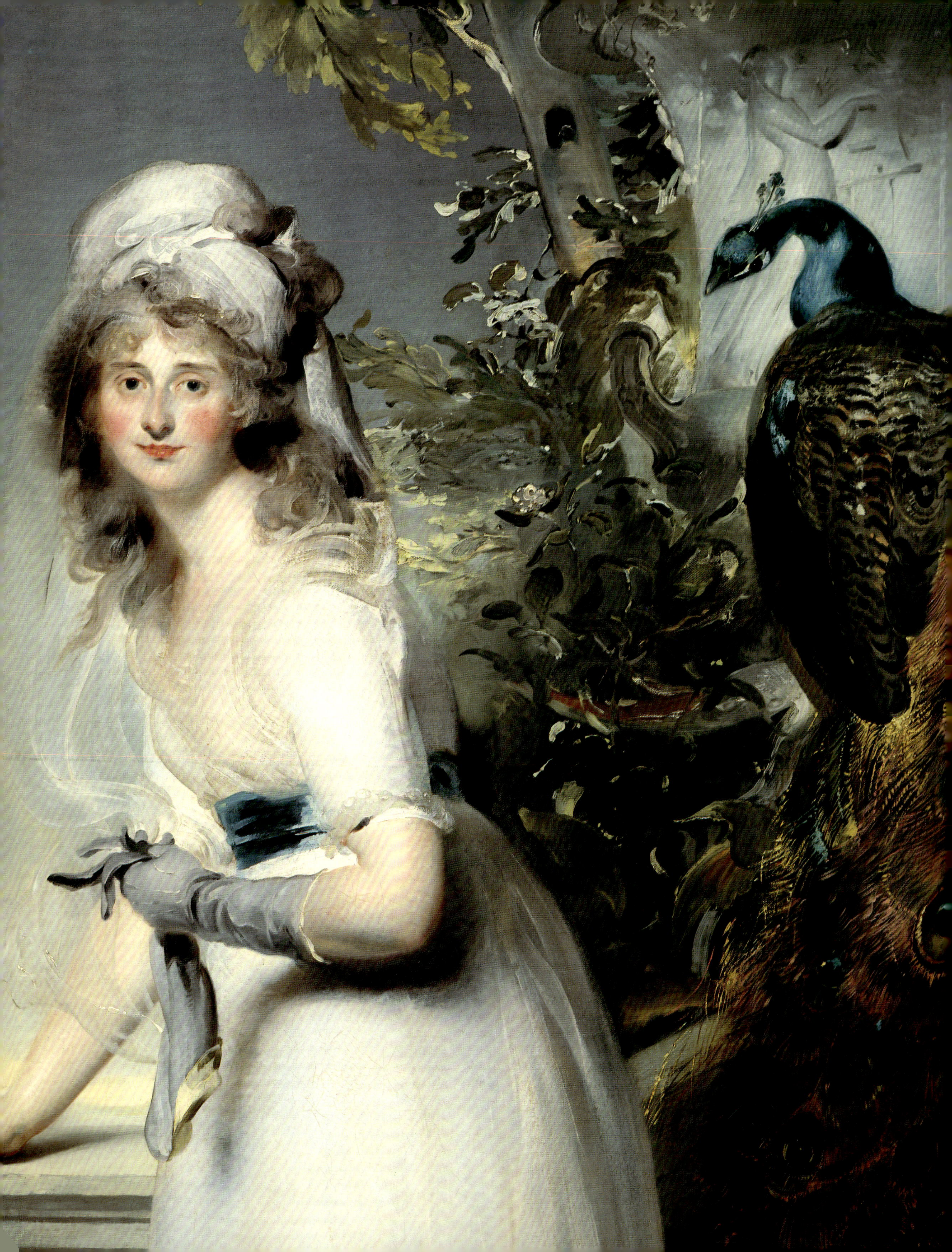

ANDREW WILTON

The Swagger Portrait

Grand Manner Portraiture in Britain

from Van Dyck to Augustus John

1630 – 1930

TATE GALLERY

front cover/jacket:
Sir William Orpen 'Mrs St George' *c.*1912
(detail, no.73)

frontispiece:
Sir Thomas Lawrence 'Catherine Gray, Lady Manners' 1794
(detail, no. 51)

ISBN 1 85437 105 3 paper
ISBN 1 85437 106 1 cloth

Published by order of the Trustees 1992
for the exhibition at the Tate Gallery
14 October 1992 – 10 January 1993

Designed by Caroline Johnston
Published by Tate Gallery Publications, Millbank, London SW1P 4RG

Typeset in Garamond by August Filmsetting, St Helens
Printed in Great Britain by Balding + Mansell plc,
Wisbech, Cambridgeshire on Parilux matt white 150gsm

Contents

Foreword

One of the principal ideas underlying this exhibition is that the British national character has always found the art of portraiture particularly congenial. It is appropriate, therefore, that the Tate Gallery, as the National Collection of British Art, should examine the subject in some depth. The National Portrait Gallery has, over the years, mounted many fine exhibitions devoted to individual painters – one remembers among others those on Van Dyck in England, Dobson, Lely, Kneller, Lawrence and Winterhalter. But if the National Portrait Gallery tackles particular artists, it seems fitting that the Tate should survey the subject more broadly as a distinct area within the field of British art. We are very grateful on this occasion to our colleagues in the National Portrait Gallery who have agreed so readily to our trespassing on their specialist area, and cooperated so generously.

The purpose of the present show is not simply to display British pictures; it is to place those pictures in the context of certain types of portraiture brought into this country from Europe from the time of Van Dyck onwards, and to assess the reactions of British masters to those stimuli. At the same time, it aims to define more exactly the characteristics of British portraiture and the social and psychological conditions that moulded it. In doing so, the exhibition reflects a growing concern among historians of British art to place the national school in a wider, international context. That theme will be taken up again later in the decade when the Tate mounts an exhibition devoted to the European roots of British sixteenth-century painting.

We are aware that the term 'Swagger Portrait' is not necessarily familiar to everyone; but as Andrew Wilton, Keeper of the British Collection and curator of this exhibition, explains in the Introduction, it is a phrase that exactly conveys the mood of those grand manner likenesses that have always been the greatest challenge to a portrait painter's imagination, and the most revealing of the social aspirations of his sitters. There is much bombast, glamour and dressing-up, and not a little unconscious humour. The exhibition will, it is hoped, be entertaining as well as instructive, and will carry the visitor with gusto over its three-hundred-year span.

The difficulties associated with bringing together so many large works are formidable – so much so that some of our initial choices had regretfully to be abandoned, as their removal would have required the virtual demolition of the houses in which they have lived since they were painted. Even that prospect did not deter some owners from offering us the opportunity to try. In view of the great sacrifices which they have made in lending such pictures, the many owners who have generously lent to the show are particularly deserving of our thanks. Without their generosity this exhibition would never have been mounted. We offer them our heartfelt gratitude.

Nicholas Serota, Director

Acknowledgments

In addition to the owners of the works, we also thank all those who have taken such trouble in allowing us to inspect pictures in awkward places and to arrange for their removal in the face of considerable physical problems. We have encountered enthusiastic interest on all sides, and are indebted to many people for their information and ideas. Sir Oliver Millar was an initial source of innumerable valuable suggestions; and the following have helped in many ways: the Countess of Airlie, Timothy Bathurst, Michael B. Ball, Margie Christian, Michael Clarke, Elizabeth Conran, Jane Cunningham, Lindsay Errington, the Viscount FitzHarris, James Holloway, Jeremy Howard, Alastair Laing, Emily Lane, the Hon. Sandra de Laszló, David Learmont, Christopher Lloyd, the Lady Amabel Lindsay, Norma Lytton, Colin Menzies, James Miller, Christopher Newall, Hannelore Osborne, Michael Preston, Simon Reynolds, Francis Russell, Douglas Schoenherr, David Scrase, MaryAnne Stevens, Stephanie Tasch, the Hon. Michael Tollemache, Pieter van der Merwe, Peter Watson, Christina Wilton, Sarah Wimbush, Christopher Wood, and Antoine Xuereb. Several members of the Tate Gallery's British Collection staff have contributed advice and read portions of the text. Among them, David Fraser Jenkins and Robert Upstone contributed substantially to the later catalogue entries. Helen Sainsbury compiled the Biographical Details of Artists which appear on pp. 225–233. To all these people the organisers extend their grateful thanks.

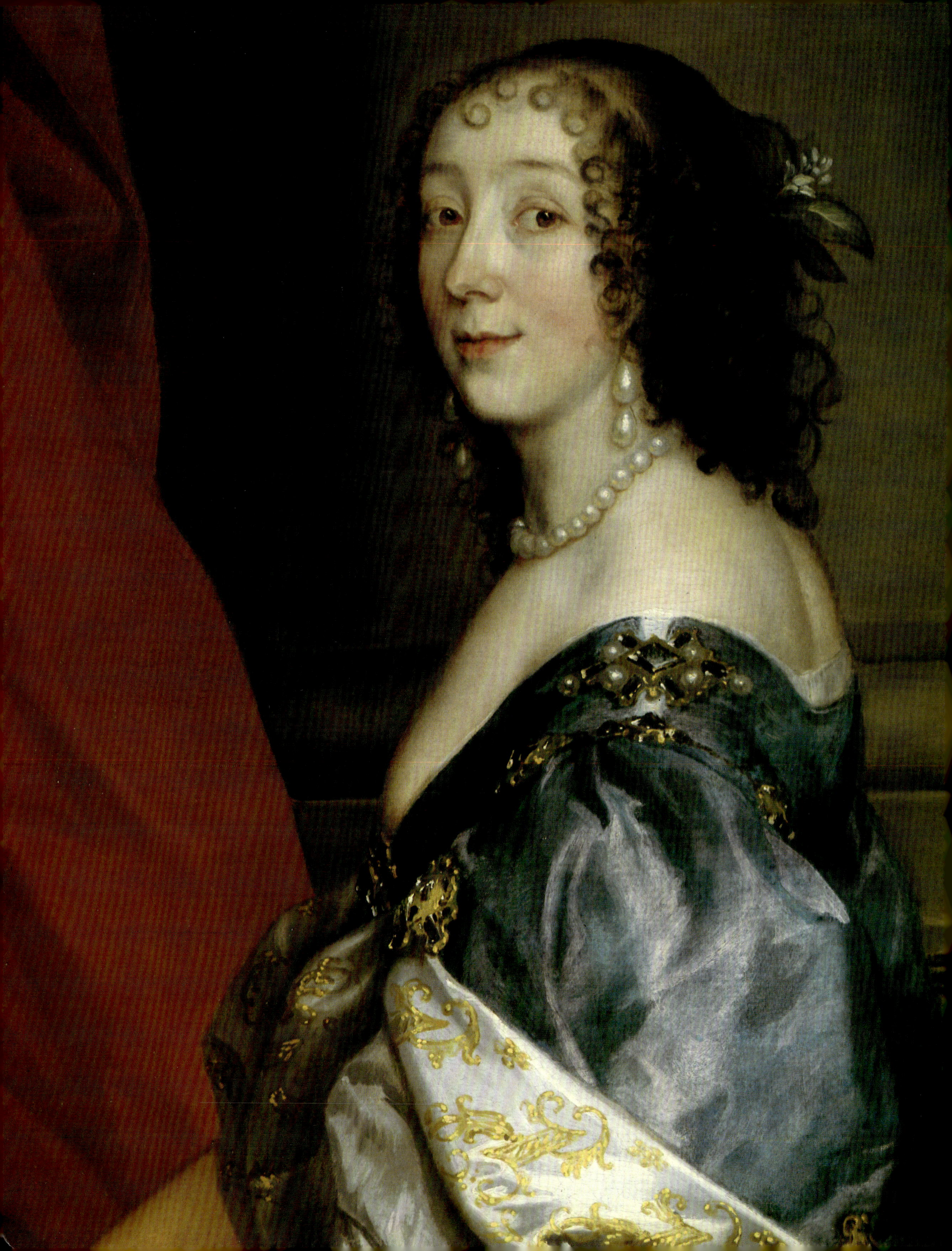

Introduction

At the head of the Serpentine in Kensington Gardens the Victorians laid out, in the late 1850s, an ornate Italian water garden. It boasts fishponds and fountains, balustraded terraces with huge urns, and an extravagant little pavilion or summerhouse. The atmosphere is Mediterranean, recalling the Baroque park furniture of Rome, Naples or Madrid. In those cities the whole design would culminate in a splendid sculpture of nude figures – Neptune, Tritons and Nereids – disporting among dolphins and plumes of spouted water. In London, the sculptural component consists of a larger-than-life bronze seated figure of Charles Jenner by Calder Marshall, looking wise and benevolent in an academic gown.

The statue is placed, not in a central position, but in the middle of one of the long sides of the layout, positioned like a tennis umpire as if to supervise swimmers in the pond from the best vantage point. It is a solemn moral footnote to the garden, a reminder that the enjoyment of healthy water by Londoners was due to the enlightened discoveries of men like Jenner, whose smallpox vaccine marked an epoch in the march of modern medicine. The entertainment value of the garden is qualified by an object-lesson.

In designing and building the Serpentine water garden the Victorians demonstrated their pre-eminence in the equipment of the capital with appropriately metropolitan developments. But they could not resist tempering ostentation with practicality. The English are embarrassed by show for its own sake. This is why the pomp associated with royalty occasions controversy. Those who are not persuaded that it is strictly functional demand that it should be dispensed with, while those who approve it argue that it is a very necessary aspect of the constitutional system. When dealing with questions concerning the display of the human form, this trait of the national character takes on fascinating complexity. The notion of a morality based on function is fundamental to the traditional national temperament. That is to say, it is rooted in a Protestant code of values which has interacted with the prevalent character of the islanders to produce a system of thought from which frivolity was rigorously excluded. Art must serve a social purpose, or it is useless.

This is puritanism, a legacy of Calvin and, ultimately, of St Paul, whose great church has dominated London for a thousand years. We take much of the argument about puritanism with a pinch of salt nowadays; we know that the Protestant ethic has inculcated guilt and a sad inability to enjoy ourselves; but we hardly ever follow these propositions to their logical conclusions. It is often asserted that the English are philistines; the term was invented by an Englishman, after all. But it is perhaps truer to say that the English are art-lovers under particular sets of circumstances. Of course, being Protestant, they abhor religious painting; as Hazlitt said,'Pictures for Protestant churches are a contradiction in terms' (Hazlitt, p.133). There is little room for myth or allegory in English lives. But portraiture is another matter.

Sir Anthony Van Dyck
Lucy Percy, Countess of Carlisle
(detail, no.4)

England is perhaps the last remaining country on earth where portraiture is a flourishing practice. Company boardrooms and college dining-rooms still require that their inherited rows of likenesses should be regularly topped up with pictures of their great and good. Although portraits have ceased to occupy quite so much space at the Royal Academy's Summer Exhibitions (a development first apparent when photography came in), there are still a fair number; and every year the National Portrait Gallery – the first institution of its kind in the world – runs a competition to which young painters contribute portraits in a range of styles and moods. The Royal Society of Portrait Painters continues to provide both exhibition space for professionals, and a membership whose talents are available for commission.

The reason for this remarkable activity is that, in a land where art is not generally perceived to serve any useful purpose in itself, the portrait continues to demonstrate its functional relevance. It is clearly of value in establishing status, in conferring dignity and confirming worth. The picture as metaphysical statement has never appealed to the practical, pragmatic national character; but the portrait as propaganda has always seemed both useful and necessary. It was an essential part of that propaganda that the image should carry with it the values attributed to works of art – permanence, intellectual respectability, technical skill – and so, despite the prevalence of photography in almost all walks of late twentieth-century visual life, the painted portrait has endured.

The tradition extends back, of course, long before the invention of photography. It is rooted deep in the national character, and has formed an essential part of civilised life here since the time of Henry VIII, when Hans Holbein the younger (1497/8–1543) effectively introduced it from the Continent single-handed. Thereafter, portraiture was practised in England by immigrant artists for about a hundred years before native talent managed to assemble itself into the beginnings of a national school. And it was another Continental figure who gave that process its kick-start: Anthony Van Dyck (1599–1641).

As we look more closely at portraiture in Britain we see that the whole story can be told in terms of a dialogue between native artists and visitors from abroad. There are the great Britons who develop and punctuate the narrative: Dobson, Hogarth, Reynolds, Gainsborough, Raeburn, Lawrence, Millais; but there is another way of construing the sequence of events. Taking as a pattern the primary impact of Holbein on a succession of later and lesser artists, repeated with Van Dyck and his followers, we can interpret the entire history of the genre in terms of foreign influence and native imitation, variation and deviation.

The most important foreign portrait painters after Van Dyck, from the British point of view, are Lely, Batoni and Sargent. To these names one may add, with some provisos, that of Winterhalter. Each of these artists established an idiom which a significant group of the portrait-commissioning classes seems to have agreed, at a certain moment, was the ideal, the *ne plus ultra*, the infinitely-to-be-desired. In each case, what was provided was a vision of that group as supremely glamorous, dashing, glossy and sophisticated. What the work of all these painters has in common is sex appeal.

Like Holbein and Van Dyck, Lely, Batoni and Sargent led in their train a number of lesser figures, who benefited more or less from the inspiration supplied by their example. But the cases of these artists are not precisely parallel.

For one thing, the British School was in a state of continuous and quite rapid development throughout the three centuries from Van Dyck to Sargent, increasing its technical and conceptual capacity to meet external stimuli in progressively more creative ways. For another, the foreigners in question brought their gifts to bear on very different sections of the market.

Pompeo Batoni (1708–87), for instance, never set foot in Britain, but operated very effectively from his base in Rome. There he was sought out by every visiting milord, in order that a dashing likeness of the grand tourist might accompany him home to England. A recent count suggests that, out of a lifetime's output in portraiture of about two hundred and sixty-five works, as many as two hundred show Britons (Clark, p.43). The travellers that Batoni painted were for the most part young, at a stage of life when swagger and bravado were entirely appropriate. Whether intellectually inclined or not, they could only be gratified if they were presented to the world as knowledgeable and elegant. Batoni achieved this to perfection. The polish of his canvases was a physical embodiment of the refinement that a year in Italy could instil; the easy nonchalance of his poses was a flattering encapsulation of the lifestyle of the sitters. His formula was irresistible, and his ability to capture a likeness was considered almost miraculous. If he was thought by some to be 'the best portrait painter in the world', that may have been for much the same reasons that Pietro Annigoni was held in such esteem in this country in the 1950s and 1960s: he was an Italian Master.

It would be grossly unfair to suggest that the British painters who worked in and after Batoni's lifetime could only follow where he led. In some respects Reynolds, Ramsay, Gainsborough and the rest were not attempting the same thing – Sir Joshua Reynolds (1723–92) heartily disapproved of Batoni – and all could, for different reasons, be argued to be greater artists. But in another sense they could hardly compete with him. Effortlessly, he provided models of ease and facility combined with refined finish which few Britons could emulate, and which, indeed, it would have been inappropriate to copy. Not all those who wished to have their likenesses taken wanted to look like idle young aristocrats.

Likewise there was only a limited market for the portraits of Franz Xaver Winterhalter (1805–73) when he was summoned to Windsor by Queen Victoria in 1842. His extravagantly glossy Biedermeier version of Batoni's bravura seems to have appealed particularly to the European royal houses of that period, and it is hardly surprising that he was so deluged with commissions to paint the highest in the land that his ambitions as a painter of 'serious' subjects were largely frustrated. This was a blessing, as it is clear from those he did manage to produce that he had little, if anything, to say.

While Batoni had been working in an age when British portrait painters of genius were plentiful, Winterhalter struck a barren patch so far as grand portraiture was concerned. Although much was produced, very little was distinguished; or rather, the distinction lay in fields so remote from Winterhalter's type of portraiture that it can hardly be compared: the small, intimate works of the young John Everett Millais (1829–96) or William Holman Hunt (1827–1910) catered to a wholly private clientele, worlds removed from the public show of the court. Public face-painting was in the hands of a generation preoccupied with the sober and respectable ambitions of the Victorian administrative classes, and, even at its best in the hands of, say, George Frederick Watts (1817–1904), did not often aspire to glamour. Even when, later, Millais had stepped into Winterhalter's shoes as the fashionable portraitist of the 1870s, his brilliant talents were rarely directed to subjects in which there was scope for glamour, and seem almost to have been suppressed in the interests of a more down-to-earth view of the British.

It is, at first sight, a mystery that so gifted a technician as Millais should have eschewed, for the most part, the flamboyant portrait. It was not that demand was limited to the circle around Victoria and Albert – though during Victoria's long mourning for her Consort (who died in 1861) there was an understandable decline in the demand for celebratory portraiture. A decade or so later another foreigner, John Singer Sargent (1856–1925), was able to demonstrate that many people in England were glad to be portrayed as dashing and overwhelmingly glamorous. Two other visitors of that period, Boldini and, soon afterwards, de Laszló, achieved a similar success in what Walter Sickert (1860–1942) was to call the 'wriggle and chiffon' school of portraiture (Emmons, p.80); and there were, as usual, plenty of native artists to follow suit.

But, once again, the native artists rarely achieved that particular kind of brio, the sheer bravura, that had come so naturally to Sargent. When we contemplate his work, and that of Van Dyck, Batoni and Winterhalter, there is apparent a qualitative difference between it and that of the British artists. For them glamour seems to be the principal and perhaps the sole object; for the British, almost any other quality takes precedence. Sex appeal is, as a rule, strictly excluded.

Of all great native British artists, Sir Thomas Lawrence (1769–1830) is possibly the only one for whom the mere feel and texture of paint embodies a sensuous power capable of evoking the physical attractiveness of his sitters. In his day Lawrence was famous for his meltingly lovely female portraits, and for emphasising the erotic charm of women: 'Phillips shall paint my wife, and Lawrence my mistress', one commentator suggested (Cunningham v, p.159). So prevalent was this view of his work that his often equally glamorous men were given less favourable attention. That was partly because womenfolk were required to be beautiful and little more, while men were expected to embody all the Protestant virtues. Lawrence, despite his natural penchant for luscious paint as a means of presenting human beings as desirable objects, was repeatedly forced by the national preference for solid worth to rein in his sensuousness in favour of something more sober, more bourgeois. Impasto and sex appeal alike were foreign, aristocratic and Catholic; England was, by the early nineteenth century, essentially the middle-class 'nation of shopkeepers' that Napoleon identified so clearly – and it had been for more than two centuries profoundly Protestant.

The religious distinction is the clue to the problem. English pragmatism did not require portraiture to be decorative: it needed only a reassurance that the sitter was worthy, upright and reliable. During the eighteenth century the principle was enunciated by theorists and, more significantly, in hundreds of pictures: they showed their subjects as family men or as able functionaries, as responsible landowners or successful horse-breeders. These were in essence the old-fashioned Calvinistic virtues of prudence and industry which Protestantism, with its plain churches and vernacular liturgy, elevated to a means of salvation. Catholicism, which vested spiritual salvation in the Church alone, granted absolution from sin by means of ritualised confession, and emphasised in its services the material splendour of God's creation, had built into it a liberal permission for material indulgence and display. The difference between the Catholic and Protestant aesthetic is repeatedly demonstrated: that is why this survey begins with Van Dyck. It was he who broke into the Protestant hegemony that had been established in England by a century of northern painters, bringing with him an art founded in the Baroque of the Catholic Counter-Reformation, fed in Venice and Genoa and nurtured in Catholic Flanders. The contrast between Van Dyck and his contemporary from the Protestant Low Countries, Rembrandt (1606–69), makes the point. Rembrandt never presents his sitters as 'stars', but invariably as all too mortal human beings. His self-portraits in oriental dress, with turbans, plumes and sashes, always point up the incongruity of such finery on a clumsy and inconsequential little man. If we think of Frans Hals (1584–1666) as a painter of swaggering sitters, he is so only within the narrow confines of the unassuming Haarlem bourgeoisie, more boisterous than bravura (see fig.18 on p.53). But even he, if we look closely, is preoccupied with the vulnerable humanity of his subjects, and if some of his men are glamorous, he certainly rarely, if ever, showed a female sitter in that light.

The British inherited this very northern approach. The predominantly Dutch artists who came to work in Britain in the late sixteenth and early seventeenth centuries reinforced what the new Protestant church was in the process of establishing: a practical, dignified but decidedly undemonstrative view of greatness and public responsibility. Van Dyck in one sense continued and enlarged the tradition; in another he shattered it. He was not the first Catholic painter to have worked for the Stuarts – Rubens (1577–1640) had already been involved at Whitehall – but his presence as chief image-maker for the ruling class was only possible because Charles I's court was hovering on the brink of Popery; the Queen, Henrietta Maria of France, was in any case a Catholic – a source of huge suspicion and resentment in the country at large.

But if Van Dyck brought an entirely new quality to bear on English portraiture, his own art was radically affected by what the English brought to him. He responded with exquisite artistic tact to the cultural differences he experienced in London by creating a different kind of portrait, which suited the English temperament and at the same time introduced a Baroque energy and panache that was new in this country. It was a brilliant, seminal moment. British portraiture would never recover from the experience – not, at least, for the next three hundred years.

There exists then, and has existed for centuries, a polarisation in British portraiture between the practical and Protestant, and the ornamental and Catholic, or at least the foreign. The native suspicion of frippery, of sexuality and ostentation, has ensured that for the most part face-painters have served purposes other than those of celebrating their sitters' glamour. Yet glamour has, at the same time, exerted an appeal which the British have secretly responded to and occasionally found irresistible. These tensions between revulsion and attraction have been responsible for some of the most creative moments in British art.

Equally interesting is the question of how native British painters themselves responded to these Continental influences. Many of them were capable of painting grand portraits, sometimes of real splendour. But it is surprising how rarely their work vies for sheer bravura with the foreigners we have been discussing. That is not because they were incapable of such technical flights; or if they were, it was because their training was directed towards a different kind of technical ability. They – and the social institutions that trained them – were inhibited from developing in that direction by an unstated imperative: that of the Protestant ethic. Even the 'great style' of Reynolds takes on a new meaning when it is seen, not as an attempt at Continental dash but as a means of substantiating glamour with intellectual earnestness. Gainsborough who, like Lawrence, had a natural proclivity for panache, confines this quality to his brushwork while almost invariably treating his sitters as old friends. His work is imbued with an intimacy and familiar charm that often militates against true 'swagger'. The Scots, ever practical and more deeply Calvinistic than the English, could not be expected to produce 'swagger' portraiture. Raeburn, it is true, was the master of a technique as virtuoso, in its own way, as that of Lawrence; but he usually subordinates it to the needs of a singularly restrained art. When he gives it full rein, he usually does so because he is not painting Scots of the dour Lowland breed, but Jacobite Highlanders, and eccentrics at that, who may be said to belong to a quite different culture. And there are many English painters who do not appear here – Riley, Wright of Derby, Romney, Richmond – because their work is almost invariably too intimate – domestic, even. It lacks the rhetoric that is essential to swagger. The British have, in the end, opted for the private rather than the public statement in their portraiture, and it is that aspect of the form that is practised almost exclusively today.

Swagger portraiture, insofar as it existed in England, was coeval with the grand country house. The convulsions of the twentieth century, and especially the economic changes that came with the Second World War, effectively destroyed both, and while there is a generation of grand society portrait painters that parallels the house-building of Sir Edwin Lutyens and Sir Herbert Baker in the 1920s and 1930s, there is none after 1945, just as there are no significant stately homes from the post-war period either. The state portrait survives but, as in every age, fulfils a rather different function. The best modern portraiture is informal, experimental and personal, with – a telling development – as strong an emphasis on the character of the artist as on that of the sitter.

The extent to which the artist paints his own portrait when painting someone else's will vary according to the temperament of the painter. But the literal self-portrait has remained a common theme of painters since the Renaissance, and was imbued with special value by Rembrandt's demonstration that it may become, in inspired hands, one of the most poignantly expressive of all types of subject matter. Rembrandt was fond of dressing himself up in exotic costumes, and it has been observed that painters, like actors, tend to make flamboyant sitters, especially when they depict themselves. It might seem inevitable that self-portraits should form a part of this survey. But Rembrandt's ultimate concerns were not with social display, and the relationship between the artist and his own self-image is a separate matter from that between the (quite different) sitter and his. However bold, even grand, an artist's self-portrait may be, it does not, by definition, involve a dialogue between two individuals. That dialogue is a microcosm of the artist's relationship to society and acts as the essential catalyst for those inventions that are here designated 'swagger'. This is to some extent an arbitrary distinction, but it is useful as a reminder of the primarily social function of this class of portrait.

Since the term 'swagger' is being used here in a quasi-technical sense that it has not hitherto been required to bear, some clarification and definition is due before the argument is taken any further.

'What hempen homespuns have we swaggering here?' enquired Puck in *A Midsummer Night's Dream* (*c.*1595), having very early resort to the word. In its first uses, 'swagger' carried with it rather pejorative connotations, of pretension, even of insolence. By the early nineteenth century it was often associated with grandeur, sometimes of an unimpressive kind, but by the late nineteenth century it had acquired a colloquial meaning that was unequivocally admiring, and strongly suggestive of social superiority. In this sense it conveyed showiness and ostentation, but these qualities were tolerated, if not actually admired, as amusing and entertaining. It could be applied to high life or to handrails, provided the thing it qualified was a splendid example of its kind. There are two very clear parallel connotations: one of social snobbery, the other of showy excellence. The term is therefore quite apt for the kind of portraiture that is the subject of this catalogue.

'Swagger' implies a degree of self-consciousness on the part of the artist, if not of the sitter (though often the two will coincide), which causes the portrait to transcend the private statement (in which the sitter communes with a single viewer), and address itself to the public at large. There is therefore an element of rhetoric in it, even of challenge – the 'insolence' that was always inherent in the meaning of the word. That challenge can often be erotic: swagger nearly always demands sex appeal. It is in its element in the theatre, and the interrelationship between theatrical and other kinds of ostentatious portraiture is an important facet of the subject. It lends itself naturally to expanded compositions involving groups of figures, though it is very different from that most English of genres, the conversation piece. In these, the participants converse; in swagger group portraits, they are linked by grand movements and gestures, festoons of flowers and fruit, or even supernatural beings. A common device for this purpose is billowing drapery: the wind often blows in swagger portraits; it rarely does in others.

The groups often include children – may sometimes consist only of children. The treatment of the young in this context is, again, a subject that must be counted as a sub-theme. In an age like the period around 1700 when adults were often portrayed as almost excessively sober and virtuous, children could be made the excuse for a more light-hearted, less moralising work. Some of the most decorative pictures of the period show children, and because they frequently deal with groups rather than individuals they avail themselves of a wide range of Baroque pictorial devices to create an atmosphere of youthful innocence and charm. Children could be treated as glamorous objects because their sexuality is harmless: it can be dismissed as morally irrelevant and simply enjoyed for its decorative value. Children carry with them no threat of the kind that obvious sexuality in adults inevitably does. To compare the children of Closterman with those of Sargent is to learn much about changing attitudes to them as glamorous objects. For in the end swagger is a question of glamour, and its extraction from (or application to) whatever subject matter the artist has to paint.

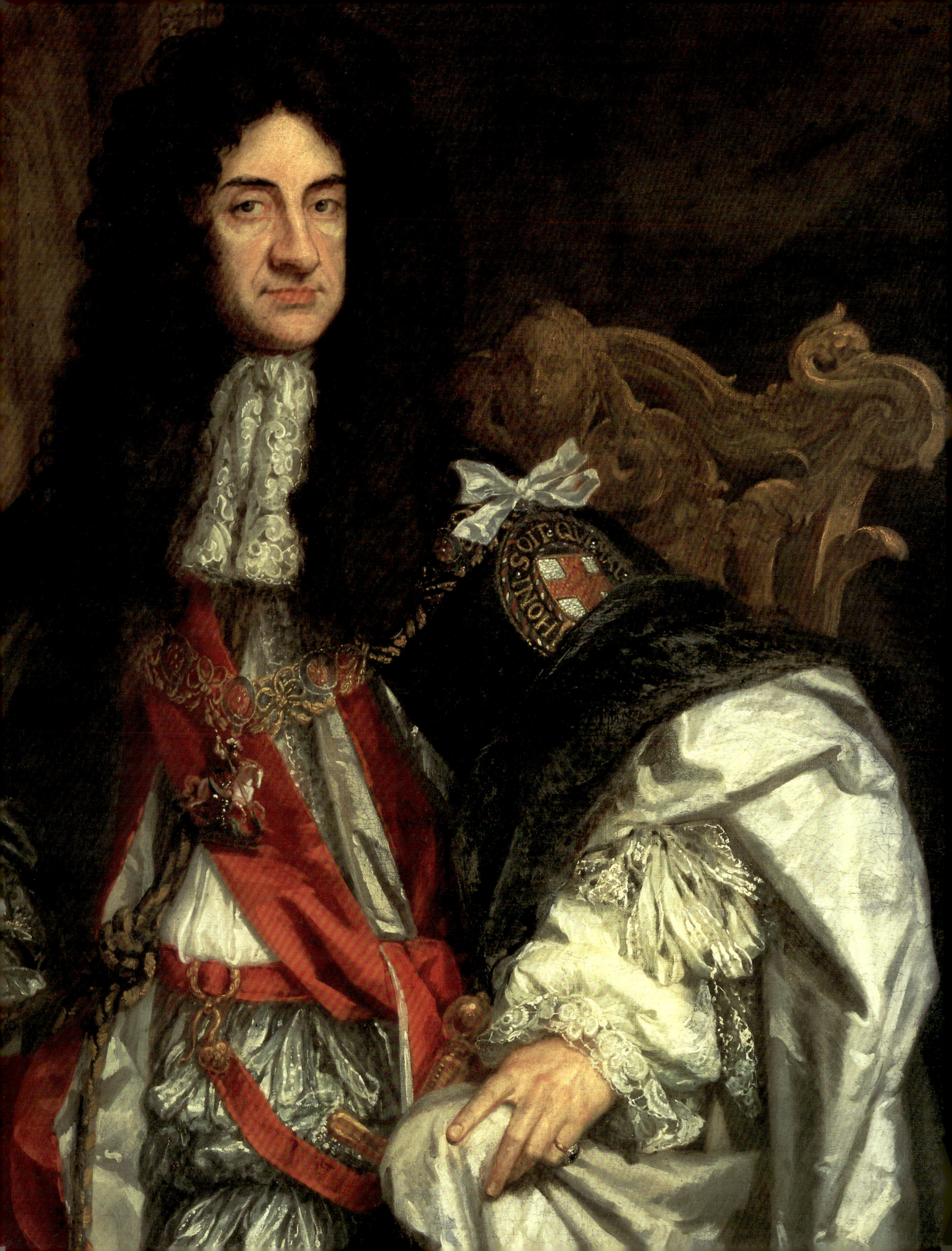

One striking exception ought to be mentioned concerning the basic generalisation that is being made here about religions. Spain is alone among the Catholic countries in having produced great portrait painters who instinctively, and with some consistency, avoid the grandiose. Considering the importance of the Counter-Reformation for Spain this is surprising. Both Velásquez (1599–1660) and Goya (1746–1828) are preoccupied with character almost to the exclusion of special 'grand' effects. But the Catholicism of Spain is very different in kind from the Catholicism of Italy, France, Germany or Flanders, embodying as it does a strain of almost masochistic puritanism which puts it in a special category.

A Portraiture of Display

The primary impulse towards a portraiture of ostentation was political. Exalted sitters demanded exalted portraits. There has always been a market for likenesses of national leaders – monarchs and their families, the highest dignitaries of government – which seek only to establish the authority of the sitter. These are state portraits. Because they are intended to invoke and reaffirm a right – the right to rule – they lay great emphasis on the outward trappings of authority, and favour a uniformity of approach which embodies the continuity of legitimate power. State portraits are therefore usually distinguished by their sameness rather than their individuality, and they tend to militate against the display of imaginative talent by particular artists. The reiteration of red plush and ermine, columns and swags of damask, itself an assertion of institutionalised pomp, subordinates individual characteristics and suffices to create an icon in which people can conveniently believe. Typically, such portraits are fully frontal, or almost; they can relate closely, like the portrait by John Michael Wright (1617–94) of Charles II (fig.6 on p.29) for the City of London (now at St James's Palace), to the image on a state seal. Elizabethan royal portraiture was either frontal or nearly so, with much emphasis on splendour of raiment. Poses tended to be simple, with the arms held at the sides, or slightly lifted if the sitter carried objects such as sceptres and orbs. If Van Dyck deviated from this pattern – and he often did – that was because he had his own ways of making people seem important. Because these ways were not dependent on state formalities but, instead, on an inherent sense of style, they were adaptable to use in the portrayal of other people with public reason to be perceived as important, and hence became the model for a more flexible grand manner portraiture that could be put to the service of all who could afford it.

There is then a distinction to be drawn between state and swagger portraiture; but it would be wrong to exclude state portraits entirely from a survey of the subject, since much of the language of social swagger derives from and deliberately alludes to the paraphernalia of state portraits. This raises the question of how the most gifted British artists respond to the challenge offered by the state

Sir Godfrey Kneller **Charles II** (detail, no.17)

portrait. On the whole, they behave like poets laureate confronted with the need to produce a poem for a solemn national occasion – they resort to formulas and become dull. There is not much scope for original invention, though there is always the possibility that an exquisite technique will save the day, as Allan Ramsay (1713–84) and Lawrence, in their very different ways, can show. But Lawrence can also contradict the convention of the state portrait by refusing to generalise the likeness itself, as in his early masterpiece, the portrait of Queen Charlotte (no.50). On the other hand, Reynolds can often solve the problem by the sheer energy and subtlety of his mind, as in his commanding and convincing manipulation of largely conventional elements in the portrait of the Duke of Cumberland (no.34). The restraint of this approach is apparent if Reynolds's solutions are compared with heroic military portraits by Continental painters like Nicolas Largillière (1656–1746) or Hyacinthe Rigaud (1659–1743), who treat such subjects with an altogether more uninhibited brio.

We are bound, then, to take state portraiture into account as a particular challenge to the English. But we are justified in discriminating between it and the more varied and emancipated portraiture that results when the intention is not to reinforce a political structure but to impress us with the *personal* superiority of the sitter. The elements of show that are commonplace in this class of picture bear a strong resemblance to the kinds of effect that were sought in dramatic presentations as the stagecraft of the Baroque theatre developed in the seventeenth century. The Aristotelian principles on which Renaissance drama was based – that is, the rule that dramatic actions, to be significant, must be those of people who are of exemplary significance in society – ensured that most plays were concerned with high-born or even divine characters. Since actors are not, as a rule, themselves kings and princes, the theatre depends very largely on a heightened language of gesture and expression to convey the majesty of office or the weighty import of tragic action.

Actors themselves were hardly of enough importance to warrant representation. The powerful studies made by Velásquez of actors at the court of Philip IV of Spain are somewhat exceptional. A few scattered likenesses survive from early seventeenth-century England. But the court masque which was an important feature of life in the highest ranks of society during the reign of Charles I introduced the possibility of persons of rank and distinction being shown in theatrical terms. Masques had come to England via France from Italy and had been fashionable court entertainments through much of the sixteenth century. In the early Stuart period they were the product of a strongly classicising movement in English cultural life: both Ben Jonson, who after 1603, when he succeeded as court poet, was responsible for writing many of them, and Inigo Jones, their designer, were steeped in things Italian, and deliberately modelled their work on Italian examples. After Jonson's departure from the court in 1634, Jones continued to produce masques, if anything still more elaborate for being unshackled by Jonson's literary ideas.

Enter, to this fantastic Italy on the shores of the Thames, the thirty-three-year-old Anthony Van Dyck. He had already visited this country briefly in 1620, but in 1632 came from his native Antwerp to live in London for most of the rest of his life. He at once established himself as painter to Charles I and his court, and beyond comparison the leading master of the day. Deprived in England of

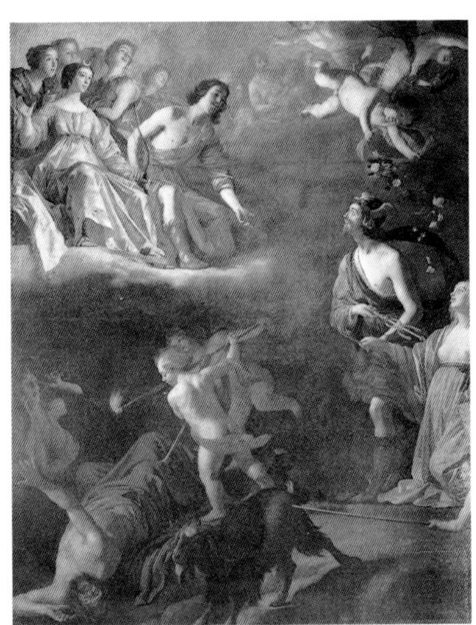

fig.1 Gerrit van Honthorst **Mercury Presenting the Liberal Arts and Sciences to Apollo and Diana** 1628 (detail) Oil on canvas *Her Majesty The Queen*

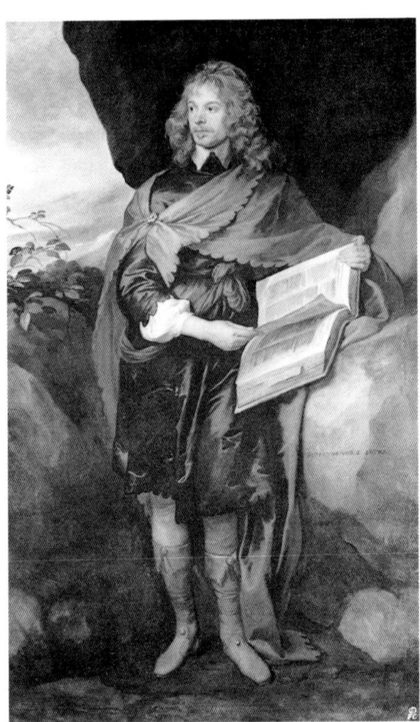

fig.2 Sir Anthony Van Dyck **Sir John Suckling** 1637 Oil on canvas *Frick Collection, New York*

any opportunity to exercise his talents as a religious painter, he transferred the rhetoric of Counter-Reformation religious art to portraiture. Immediately, the possibilities for compositional invention were multiplied, and the notion of an internal dynamism in the structure of the picture was developed in ways previously undreamed of.

But religious painting was not Van Dyck's only source. He must have been impressed by the masques presented at the English court and their imagery seems to have entered his visual vocabulary. A surprising number of his English portraits include elements, not encountered elsewhere in his work, that seem to be associated with the masque. Sometimes, as in the portrait of the Countess of Southampton as Fortuna (no.7), they enabled him to give full rein to his innate Baroque energy: the stage *dea ex machina* is combined with the cloud-strewn vision of some Italian altarpiece to create a many-layered image in which the religious and the spectacular are brought together for an entirely secular purpose. Here, Van Dyck may well have been inspired by the work of a slightly earlier immigrant painter: Gerrit van Honthorst's great canvas, painted in 1628 for the Banqueting Hall at Whitehall, showing Charles I and his Queen as Apollo and Diana (fig.1; collection Her Majesty The Queen), appearing on clouds exactly as in one of Jones's masques. In the portrait of Olivia Porter (no.5) the influence is more suppressed, though there are still reasons for guessing that he had actually witnessed the sitter in some theatrical role and used that as the starting-point for his design. The craggy rock that acts as a backdrop seems to have been taken directly from some 'wild scene' designed by Jones (see fig.27 on p.72). This type of background became the favoured model for Lely in the next generation. Although he and countless later artists have made the edge of rock a commonplace of portrait composition, it was not used by Van Dyck himself in the context of portraiture before he painted English sitters and it occurs hardly at all in works by earlier artists. The closest parallel to 'Olivia Porter' is Titian's half-length 'Penitent Magdalen' (versions in Naples and St Petersburg), but it is clear that Van Dyck intends no allusion to that subject. When he employs the rock motif, it is often in a literary context: his portrait of the poet Sir John Suckling (fig.2; Frick Collection, New York) is one of the most striking examples.

Masques did not figure in the entertainments of the court after the Restoration, but the theatre enjoyed a renewed popularity and began to develop rapidly. Its value as a means of overlaying the simple likeness with layers of complex meaning came to be recognised by artists and sitters alike. John Michael Wright's portrait of a lady in masquerade costume (no.15) illustrates the pictorial value of theatrical dress and even, possibly, stage-setting. If the subject is indeed Dido, as suggested here, and not Diana as has been supposed, the picture marks a departure in seventeenth-century portraiture. The attributes of Diana, notably her chastity, were directly referable to the sitter, and intended to be read as such. Dido was not a heroine celebrated for that virtue; it is unlikely that any lady would have wished to be associated with her character as a woman passionately in love with a man who ultimately betrays her. The picture would then be a record of a theatrical occasion, a role, a performance worthy of memorial in its own right. The sitter is nevertheless in all probability a court lady rather than an actress. The way is prepared for the eighteenth-century love of 'play-acting' – the temporary assumption by the sitter of a role which has significance purely in terms of that one picture. It is often rash to read more durable interpretations into the ad hoc and essentially visual fictions devised by Reynolds and his contemporaries.

The important changes that occurred in the late seventeenth-century theatre included greater recognition for the performers. Actors – and actresses, for the Shakespearean boy actors were now a thing of the past – enjoyed markedly higher social status, and their portraits were in consequence more ambitious. In about 1670 John Michael Wright painted a full-length triple portrait of the actor John Lacy in three different roles (fig.3; collection Her Majesty The Queen) which anticipates the depictions of actors in character that remained popular through the later eighteenth century and well into the nineteenth. That convention relies on direct reporting, on the assumed accuracy of the transcription. Even at its grandest, in the hands of Hogarth painting Garrick as Richard III (fig.4; Walker Art Gallery), it remains a true record, rather than the evocation of an extrapictorial atmosphere. It required an approach from the standpoint of a renewed admiration for Van Dyck to revive the long-buried links with masque. Reynolds, who, following Van Dyck, maintained close contact with the art of the Italian Renaissance and Baroque, was perfectly capable of conceiving a society portrait in terms of a Bolognese altarpiece, and it is in such terms that he reinvents the kind of grandiose portrait that Van Dyck developed in his picture of the Countess of Southampton (no.7). If there is a direct successor to the Countess in British art it is Mrs Siddons, throned on clouds as the Tragic Muse in Reynolds's presentation of her (no.37). The idea of the actor as divinity reaches its apogee here, and so brings together the two worlds of theatre and Grand Style painting that had circled round each other for so long.

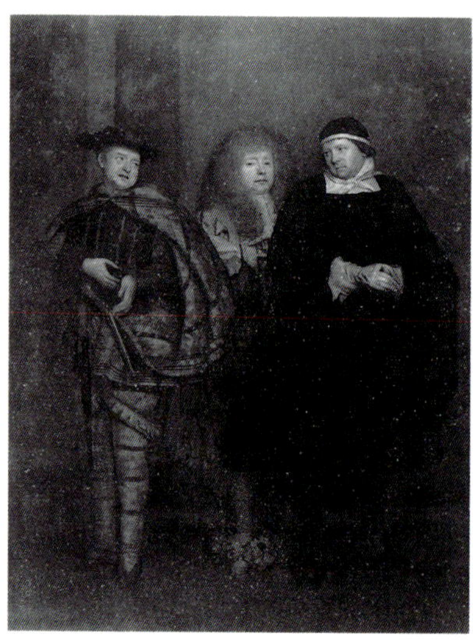

fig.3 John Michael Wright **John Lacy in Three Characters** *c.*1668–70 Oil on canvas *Her Majesty The Queen*

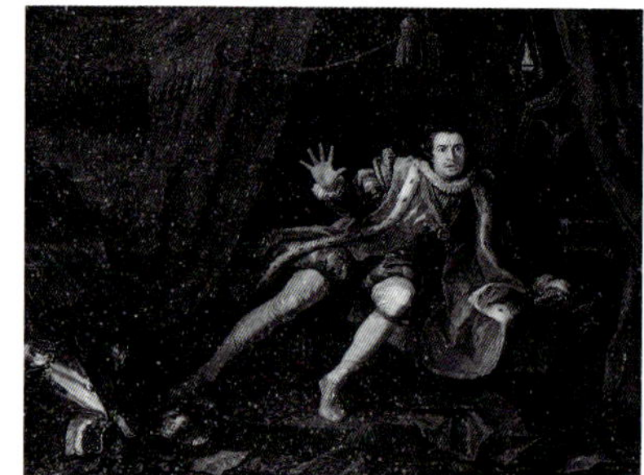

fig.4 William Hogarth **Garrick as Richard III** 1745 Oil on canvas *Walker Art Gallery, Liverpool (The National Museums and Galleries on Merseyside)*

Reynolds's 'Mrs Siddons' is not the record of a performance, as Hogarth's 'Richard III' is, but it borrows from the theatre not only a sitter but two important devices which are frequently encountered in grand portraiture: dramatic lighting, and a low viewpoint. The development of lighting techniques in the theatre during the eighteenth century coincides with the emergence of romantic lighting schemes in the portraiture of Reynolds and, later, of Raeburn and Lawrence. The requirement that the viewer should look up at the subject of the picture can be traced back, once again, to religious art. Altarpieces were raised above the congregation partly for greater visibility and partly to inspire awe. State portraits demanded similar treatment, for not dissimilar reasons, and the habit of hanging whole-length portraits above eye level in rooms of state was well established by the eighteenth century. By then, Reynolds and his generation were adopting the low viewpoint almost as a matter of course for many of their most important works, as a compositional means of increasing the grandeur of their sitters. In his series of portraits of John Philip Kemble in character (no.52), Lawrence repeatedly does this. The tricks of the theatre could invest the component elements of portraiture – background, gesture, pose, lighting – with a more immediate and popular glamour than ever before.

If some painters have seen the portrait as a kind of theatrical event, it is also true that what takes place in the picture needs to be presented as it were through a proscenium. The very nature of state portraiture often ensured that it was framed in a grand architectural casing, carved and gilded in accordance with the decoration of the surrounding room. Indeed, many such pictures are as much a part of the fabric of an interior as the panelling or mouldings. They were installed when the house was built – or redecorated – and to remove them now would involve taking away essential fittings: they serve instead of wallpaper or hangings to cover bare plaster or, sometimes, bare masonry. Some are so large that they cannot be removed without demolishing the building.

Although great size is not essential to the swagger portrait, which can on occasion be found on a small scale, it is an intrinsic property of any grand picture, which accordingly requires corresponding scale and elaboration in the frame. Sequences of royal or family portraits were often conceived as uniform series; some were deliberately created by employing artists to paint replicas of works scattered in many collections; at some period in the history of their accumulation the sequence would aquire a set of matching frames, often distinguished by some ornate trophy or coat of arms which appears on all alike. The heraldic significance of the pictures is manifest in the way that the central image is generally bold, presenting the sitter as confronting the world with direct self-assurance. The trappings of drapery and tassels that so often accompany that image are not only a reflection of regal grandeur, but also have the function of heraldic mantling, which surrounds the central image as if it were a coat of arms, and embellishes it. The habit of painting heraldic devices in the corners of portraits died out in the early seventeenth century at precisely the time when the paraphernalia of the Baroque throne was taking the place of the plain or emblematic backgrounds of Elizabethan portraiture. Frames are sometimes conceived as extensions of that drapery, carved and gilded folds and scrolls that fall like mantling round the edges of the canvas. The so-called 'Sunderland' frames (see no.7) that became common in seventeenth-century England have a formalised character that is suggestive of heraldry.

If the painted coat of arms disappeared from most family portraits, the inscribed title, name and dignity of the sitter did not. Throughout the seventeenth and eighteenth centuries, and into the nineteenth, family portraits often incorporated inscriptions, usually in gold paint, which provided a ready means of identification. These inscriptions are often valuable but frequently misleading; the notion of identity is sometimes more important than the accuracy of the information. If the ubiquity of these verbal glosses is a particularly, if not exclusively, British phenomeon, that is perhaps further indication of the special interest the portrait has in these islands as a record of political, social and family history.

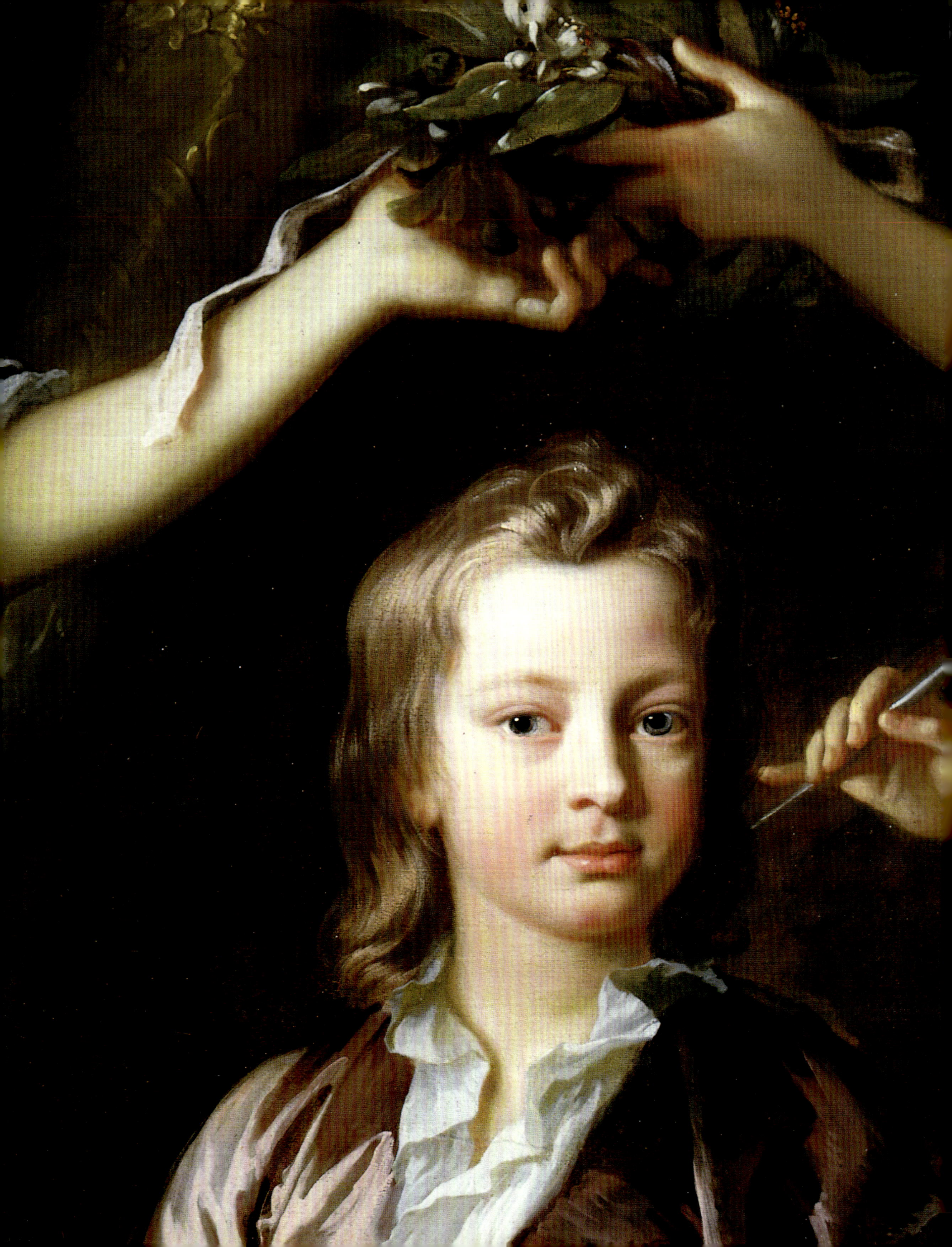

The Seventeenth Century

The court of Charles I, 'the greatest amateur of paintings among the princes of the world', as Rubens described him, was psychologically the right milieu for the introduction of new ideas about grand portrait painting. Charles was the first of the (rather meagre) line of great royal collectors of art in Britain; he and his entourage were characterised by a natural aesthetic sense and an innate narcissism. His passionate belief in the divine right of kings ensured that the life of the court was underpinned by an ideology that stressed the hierarchical nature of society and its relation to the deity. This was expressed in a religion closer to Rome than to Canterbury, coexisting with a highly literary neo-Platonism that saw the world as a paradigm of a divinely appointed order, in which the images and objects of daily reality were the symbols or shadows of eternal and universal truths. The friction that exists almost automatically between such attitudes and the English national character quickly manifested itself. The fall of Charles I to a puritanical and broadly philistine, if much more realistic, regime was of symbolic as well as practical significance.

Van Dyck's achievement was to realise in paint the aesthetic yearnings of an idealistic class who were shortly to pay the penalty for having set themselves apart from the hard political and social realities of the world about them. His qualifications for performing this task were extraordinarily apt. He had been trained in Antwerp, the hub of a newly prosperous mercantile state, where the solid bourgeoisie, not having adopted Protestantism like their Dutch cousins, could still appreciate the benefits to vanity of finery and feathers. The natural ebullience of the Flemish culture was expressed supremely in the work of Van Dyck's master, Peter Paul Rubens, who himself worked in England for a short while, but whose whole artistic personality resonated with a great love of the Italian – and especially the Venetian – Renaissance. Rubens interpreted the art of Titian, Tintoretto and Veronese for the Baroque age, and his young pupil, brilliantly gifted both as a draughtsman and as a manipulator of paint, rapidly evolved his own distinctive version of the style.

It came to be accepted, even in England where Holbein had wrought such important changes, that the *fons et origo* of portraiture was Titian – 'the father of portrait-painting', as Fuseli said; 'of resemblance with form, character with dignity, grace with simplicity, and costume with taste' (Pilkington, p.577n.). This definition of the successful portrait is valuable as being all too rare. Few writers have taken the trouble to state specifically what are the criteria by which portraiture is to be judged. This is probably because it has always seemed self-evident that it exists to show likenesses as convincing yet as flattering as possible, and the inherent contradiction in that recipe has been accepted as natural and necessary. While landscape, say, has been subject to changes in aesthetic fashion – the topographical, the sublime, the picturesque – portraiture has remained the truly practical art form, and in so far as it has been judged by independent aesthetic standards they have been those of History – the most prestigious category of painting. ('History painting' comprehended all serious subject matter, religious, literary and mythological, as well as historical.) The

John Closterman **The Children of John Taylor of Bifrons Park, Kent** (detail, no.21)

greatest masters of the portrait – Titian, Rubens, Van Dyck – were indeed equally celebrated as exponents of history; small wonder that Reynolds, despite his success in portraiture, always felt the need to prove himself in the grander branch of art.

Van Dyck was able to absorb the crucial influences at first hand: he came to London briefly in 1620–1, returned to Antwerp and then went to Italy for several years. There his already well-established splendour of manner was further developed, notably during his stay in Genoa, where he painted portraits of the city's patrician class. The sumptuousness of these canvases has hardly ever been equalled; they were quite unknown to the English not only at the time but for two hundred years afterwards. When Van Dyck arrived in England for a second and much longer stay in 1632 he did not attempt to recreate the atmosphere of those portraits. He knew that he was back in the north, among a very different people. The grandeur, the sensuousness of his painting had to be remoulded for a new audience.

It is hard to define in what ways the English – and especially the upper-class English sympathetic to Catholicism – were different from their Italian counterparts. The first thing to be said about them is that they already belonged to a more fluid, mobile society than any on the Continent. Macaulay points to the role of Parliament in the Middle Ages in ensuring that a constant interchange between nobility and middle class is built in to the English system: 'our democracy was, from an early date, the most aristocratic, and our aristocracy the most democratic in the world; a peculiarity which has lasted down to the present day, and which has produced many important moral and political effects' (Macaulay 1, pp.19–20). More recently, John Barrell has emphasised a contrast between an essentially 'republican' view of the national history in England, and a much longer-lived feudalism on the European mainland (Barrell, p.34). The Tudors had emerged from the ranks of the landed gentry only a hundred years or so before, and much of the aristocracy had been newly created from the successful entrepreneurial classes of Elizabeth's and James's reigns. Their closeness to the business of making, rather than spending, money linked them with the Netherlanders and this no doubt gave Van Dyck an important clue as to how they wished to be portrayed. Certainly the mercantile aristocracy of Genoa, ensconced in a profoundly authoritarian culture with all the visual awareness that is unique to the inhabitants of the Italian peninsula, and no great distance from the great artistic centres of Venice, Milan and Bologna, called forth an entirely fresh response. In the same way, the style that Van Dyck evolved for his English sitters is distinct from that of his Flemish portraits, and thanks to its overwhelming influence on subsequent portraiture has come to be identified with a pure Englishness which it cannot originally have claimed. He accomplished for portraiture in the seventeenth century what Claude did for landscape: he established its pictorial essence in a form that was to remain valid for over two hundred years.

Van Dyck had the advantage of knowing well both the northern and the southern portrait traditions – the art that had evolved in Bruges, Antwerp and Nuremberg, and that of Venice and Genoa. His task was to bring these to bear on the English tradition which was a reflection of the German, Flemish and Dutch styles that had survived the sixteenth century. Despite his overwhelming

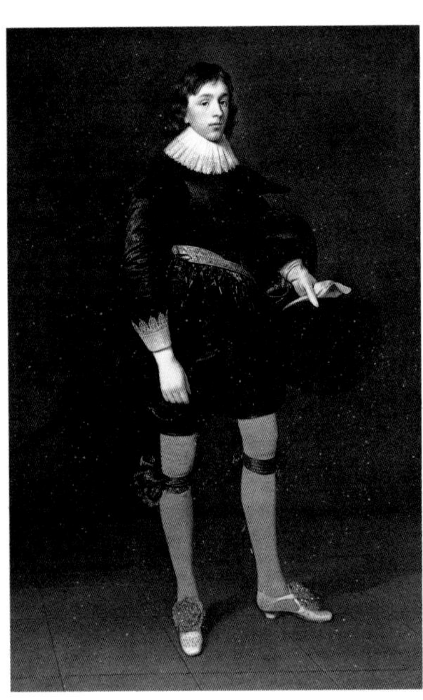

fig.5 Daniel Mytens **The 1st Duke of Hamilton as a Boy** 1624 Oil on canvas *Tate Gallery*

superiority to any of his predecessors, he introduced less of a disjunction than might first appear. The portraiture of Daniel Mytens (*c.*1590–1647), his ablest precursor, who worked in London from 1618, already possessed a dignity and directness that suited the English well (fig.5). The standing figure, soberly or splendidly clad against a draped background, with a table or some other unobtrusive property, was a standard formula that could be traced back to both Holbein and Titian, though the English were for the most part used to something less exciting. Mytens lacked both variety and bravura – qualities with which Rubens was, however, superlatively endowed, and which Van Dyck had flaunted in his Genoese portraits. He adopted the format common to many portrait painters of the time, including Mytens, but invested it with a new verve and fluidity, substituting these qualities for the traditional formalities of stance and gesture which were often reinforced by coats of arms, emblematic devices, and other extraneous tokens of rank and status.

Much of Van Dyck's fluidity is attributable to something precisely indicative of national character: clothes. In the early seventeenth century, fashions among the European upper classes continued as they had been during the preceding fifty years, highly ornate, with fabrics stiffened by quantities of metal embroidery, and heads supported on vast starched and pleated ruffs. The Hapsburg princesses painted by Velásquez in the 1650s seem to be held immovably in position by their drumlike farthingales, and Van Dyck's own Genoese are immobilised by jewel-encrusted stomachers, heavy robes and densely ornamented doublets. Even the more middle-class Flemings maintained their formality of dress, whereas the English court under Charles I had abandoned itself to flowing curls, loose open lace collars and fresh-coloured silks. The atmosphere was that of the cavalier poets, and Van Dyck unerringly sensed it and gave it visual expression.

In taking up this native quality of informality he did not simply reproduce the sartorial appearance of his sitters. He imbued the outward forms with an inner significance that was an essential part of how the English courtiers saw themselves. A graceful body denoted a graceful mind, and perhaps a soul touched with grace also. Allegory may not have been a viable art-form for the English, but neo-Platonic philosophy made it possible at this juncture for the portrait to achieve some symbolic meaning. When Van Dyck introduces emblematic detail into his pictures, it has a validity reinforced by the poetic imaginations of his sitters as well as his innate artist's instincts. He celebrates the close cultural bonds between Charles's unusual court and his own European roots.

Perhaps the single most important element in the transformation that Van Dyck effected is the painterly touch that he adopted from Rubens and developed as a hallmark of his style. This seems to achieve a natural consummation when it is used to portray the flowing dress and lively, literary minds of the English courtiers. Van Dyck's compositions are imbued with an effortless dignity, but they are made to vibrate with conviction and human warmth, invested with splendid life, simply by the power of his brushstroke. The embodiment of a grand principle in the sweep of the brush is one of the most remarkable aspects of painting as a physical act, and can be observed at its most astonishing in portraiture. A vigorous brushstroke can evoke human personality with great immediacy, and endow a simple design with vitality. The example Van Dyck set in this respect was to be taken up by a sequence of key figures in the history of English portraiture, and it is this, more than any other characteristic of their work, that enabled them to produce swagger pictures.

The significance of William Dobson (1610/11–46) lies in his exceptional ability to absorb and reinterpret the lessons offered by Van Dyck. He had been trained in the Italo-Flemish tradition, and came to prominence in the 1640s, after Van Dyck's death. He was not merely an imitator: within the conventions that Van Dyck had established he brought his own vision to bear on his sitters and, most significantly for the future development of the genre, evolved a personal style of handling paint which endows his subjects with a distinctive swagger of their own. It is noticeable that, on the whole, Dobson eschewed the full-length. Apart from two that he executed for the Earls of Peterborough and Northampton he confined himself almost exclusively to busts and three-quarter-lengths. Into the latter format, however, he compressed vivid character studies conveyed with a splendid élan.

The particular quality of these works is determined by the texture of their paint. This is handled quite differently from Van Dyck's, even though it obviously owes its essence to him. Dobson interestingly anticipates the coarse, broad treatment that was to become so characteristic a feature of English painting in the later eighteenth century – the manner of Reynolds, Wilson and their respective followers. It is a bold and practical technique derived from the need to make paint describe vividly what is seen, and not from a wish to create an elegant surface. Crusty, sinewy and unaffected, it instantly distinguishes English pictures from Continental ones. When it is absent, even an English painter seems more 'European'. It is not so much a failure to achieve Continental refinement of finish – though it can sometimes seem like that – but a robust island alternative to the academic finishes of Italy and, more particularly, of France and Germany. With this irreducible earthiness, and an almost Hogarthian curiosity about individual character, Dobson demonstrates that an identifiable 'English' quality can be discerned in portraiture long before the high period of the school in the mid eighteenth century.

Dobson's preoccupation with character led him to make substantial modifications to Van Dyck's iconographic prescriptions. Complex iconography is employed with restraint in Van Dyck's English work; the allegorical portrait of Venetia Digby (no.2) is exceptional. He more often depicts a sitter with a single emblematic motif, or if there are more, they are incorporated into the design in a natural and unobtrusive way. However introduced, they reflect in some way on the moral or spiritual qualities of the sitter. For Dobson, the symbolic accessories are a means of coming closer to the totality of the subject: his family, his allegiances, his tastes in art, literature and sport, can all be explained by the accumulation of appropriate objects. So Dobson's canvases are cluttered with evocative detail, which sometimes jostles with the sitter for pride of place in a highly Baroque ensemble.

In comparison with the vigour of Dobson, John Michael Wright seems an almost over-refined artist, with a sophisticated sense of colour and a penchant for *triste* poetic backgrounds. His work is often so decidedly Continental in character that it helps define retrospectively, as it were, the full extent of Dobson's achievement in creating an English style of painting. Wright's portraits constantly remind us, in their design, colouring and handling, of Dutch painters like Daniel Mytens the Younger (1644–88) and Caspar Netscher (?1635/9–84). The much earlier figure of Cornelius Johnson (1593–1661) has also been suggested as a Dutch influence. These echoes suggest that Wright must have spent some time in Holland, although there is no other evidence for this. He seems to have operated in Flanders as antiquary and collector of works of art on behalf of the Archduke Leopold of Austria; perhaps he used his visits to the Low Countries for a wider exploration than has hitherto been assumed. A 'curious Italian flavour' has also been detected in his work, and this would not be surprising since Wright spent some time in Rome in the late 1640s and early 1650s. Also in the 1650s he appears to have been in Paris, so that all in all he is one of the most cosmopolitan figures in seventeenth-century British painting. His work reflects this. It certainly owes little to the prevailing manner of Lely, or even to Van Dyck.

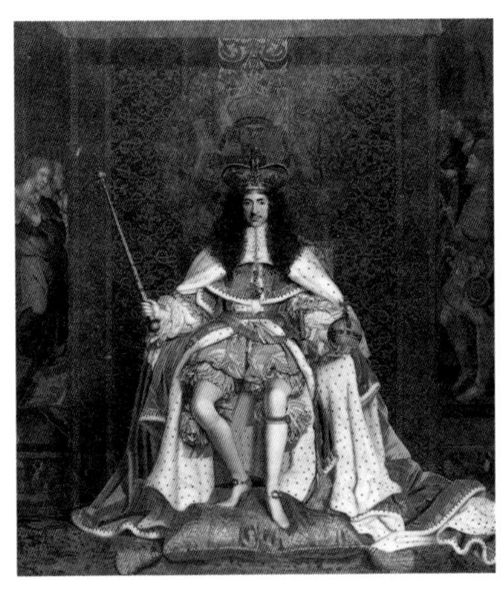

fig.6 John Michael Wright **Charles II** *c.*1676 Oil on canvas *Her Majesty The Queen*

Something of Wright's position among the portrait painters of Charles II's reign can be gathered from the splendid picture of the King in full regalia that he painted, probably in 1676, for the City of London (fig.6; collection Her Majesty The Queen). Its archaic, hieratic presentation of the monarch as though on a state seal, frontally and seated before a tapestry, makes it an archetype of state rather than swagger portraiture. It is very unlike Wright's usual somewhat informal approach to his sitters, and contrasts with the relatively relaxed convention used by Lely; but it is large and grand and celebrates the Crown in a very positive and assured fashion. The panache with which the work is carried through endows it with a presence that belies its apparently simple design, and is a tribute to the training that Wright picked up during his period in France: we are reminded more of the French court painters – Philippe de Champaigne (1602–74) in particular – than of any Italian or Flemish precedent. One obvious reason for Wright's success in the competitive British market for portraits is the technical superiority that his foreign training gave him over any native rivals; and it has been suggested that his Catholicism was a further factor (Stewart, p.16). Quite apart from the social contacts this gave him, it encouraged a temperamental appreciation of show and of rhetoric invaluable to a portrait painter. Even so, Wright is by no means as unbridled in his use of these elements as, say, Huysmans.

Jacob Huysmans (*c.*1633–96) was another son of Antwerp, and as a favourite painter to Charles II's Queen, Catherine of Braganza, took his place as an important artist in Restoration England. His Flemish bravura with its overloading of rich and decorative detail often approaches quite closely to the atmosphere of certain Counter-Reformation altarpieces; but we do not feel, as with Van Dyck's Countess of Southampton, that a refined and sophisticated visual joke is being perpetrated: Huysmans gives us the sense that this overblown language is the only one that will do full justice to his sitters' opinions of themselves. The whole style offers an interesting contrast to the methods of his principal rival, the King's favourite, Sir Peter Lely. Lely is too often seen as a lesser imitator of Van Dyck, devoid of any personality of his own. This is not the case. As a dedicated follower of Van Dyck in England he learned much from the older master, and became an accomplished copyist of his compositions. But his own original work is quite distinctive, with a sumptuous and entirely personal use of colour and a very different approach to the whole idea of grandeur.

This was in a sense inevitable, for Lely came to England from the Protestant north of the Netherlands in the early 1640s and began his career in England in the service of a somewhat less High-Church circle of patrons. His approach is summed up aptly in the full-length portrait of Sir Edward Massey (fig.7; National Gallery of Canada) that he painted in the late 1640s. Massey was a disaffected royalist who fought in the Civil War on the side of Parliament; appropriately, his portrait has a hint of Van Dyckian elegance about it, but is ultimately a more sober affair, showing the down-to-earth, honest soldier. So shorn of glamour is it that the picture has been taken for the work of an Englishman, Dobson. Lely was quite capable of suiting his style to his sitter, and when he came into contact with the restored monarchy of Charles II he was perfectly able to reflect the changed mood of the times.

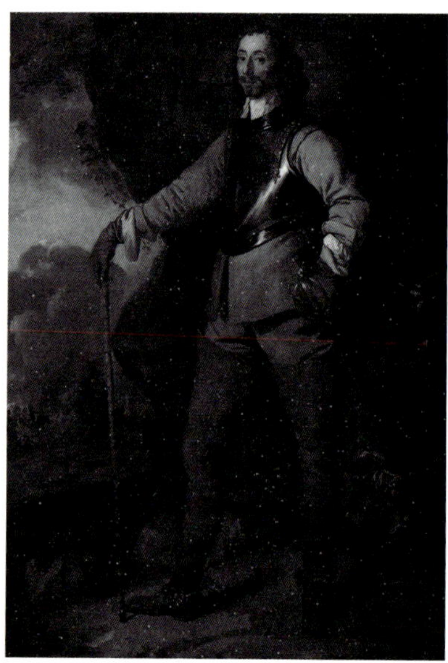

fig.7 Sir Peter Lely **Sir Edward Massey** *c.*1651 Oil on canvas *National Gallery of Canada, Ottawa*

There were already hints of a penchant for the Mediterranean, for warmth and richness, in the pastoral subjects that Lely was producing when he first arrived in England. In choosing to paint drowsy landscapes peopled by naked nymphs in the Dutch-Italian tradition, Lely aligned himself with those of his countrymen who had been most influenced by Venetian art. That trait can only have been strengthened when he came into contact with Van Dyck. He collected drawings by Italian artists of the Renaissance and Baroque, and owned an important Baroque portrait bust – that of Thomas Baker by Bernini, now in the Victoria and Albert Museum. In so far as he could, the Dutchman thus became an exponent of the high Baroque.

Straddling as it were the northern and southern traditions, Lely was able the more readily to adapt to the changed climate of the Restoration. He at once became the favourite painter of a court that was doing its best to recreate the atmosphere of the 1630s. The traditional role of portraiture as the propaganda of an establishment ordained by God was augmented by a lively appreciation of its value as the distraction and adornment of a set rejoicing, perhaps over-heartily, in its regained privileges.

Lely was not a Dutchman for nothing. His formal state portraits of Charles II are sober enough; and he was, in fact, a master of restraint in his orchestration of warm sombre colour to create a mood of mature richness, which enhances his male as well as his female portraits. But he was undoubtedly highly gifted at expressing glamour. His early exercises in the Italianate vein of Poelenburgh were supplemented by the example of Van Dyck, so that when the Restoration gave its permission, he was able to handle flesh with a sensuousness and warmth that lends all his female portraits an unsurpassed lusciousness. The juxtaposition of this glowing flesh with his marvellous arrangements of fabrics, always cunningly invented to set off the form and texture of the sitter's body to best advantage, is the aspect of his work that has most fascinated commentators. It is here, almost for the first time, that we encounter naked sex appeal as an ingredient of British portraiture. The atmosphere of the times was partly responsible: 'it was a great mode after the restoration', Vertue tells us, 'for several years for Ladies to dress naked shoulders brest and neck – as may be seen in many pictures of Lely Cooper Soest Wright &c' (Vertue IV, p.189). The strongly felt Christianity and the philosophical neo-Platonism that had permeated the culture of Charles I's court were equally disregarded now. Lely presents his beauties as sirens first of all, and everything follows from the premise that they are desirable. An eighteenth-century historian characterised his art thus: 'he had a very peculiar expression in the eyes of his female figures; a tender languishment, a look of blended sweetness and drowsiness, unattempted before his time by any master, which he certainly conceived to be graceful' (Pilkington, p.286). Whereas Van Dyck's 'Lucy Percy' (no.4) hints at a private world from the standpoint of a public position, Lely's ladies are the public manifestations of private dreams. This is the process whereby female portraiture moves from the aristocratic to the bourgeois.

As with Van Dyck, the relative informality of English costume is capitalised on; but it has been pointed out that Lely deliberately adopted a convention for dressing his sitters that went somewhat beyond the bounds of ordinary daytime attire. He chose to show both ladies and gentlemen in *negligée* at times, and his love of rich stuffs led him not infrequently to drape his women in purely decorative swathes of fabric like a window-dresser's dummy – 'a sort of fantastic night-gowns,' Walpole commented, 'fastened with a single pin'. (Walpole II, p.92). The materials are satins and velvets, and usually orchestrated in a range of browns, from apricot to chocolate, set off against pearly grey or white silk, a dull blue, or occasionally green. Dutch painting of the period lies behind these schemes, though Lely takes the physical and tactile delight of such feasts further than one normally encounters in Holland. For the true climax of this tradition of dressing the model we have to look forward to the work of Reynolds in the 1770s, when loose arrangements of sumptuous fabrics, almost wholly unrelated to real clothing, became the accepted method of presenting female sitters as transcendental beings.

Such overtones hardly figure among the ideas that Lely deploys. Allegory counts for little in his work. It was contrary to the ethos of the court to lard a likeness with moral reflection. Symbolism occupies a curiously unimportant place in his repertoire of tricks. If a lady is shown holding a lamb, the intention is primitive; charm is a more relevant criterion than chastity. If this trait marks a change of purpose from Van Dyck, it is even more a mark of how far Lely is removed from the formulas of Dutch art, where the solemn and careful use of symbols is all-pervasive. His deliberate abandonment of ulterior meaning constitutes a commentary not so much on the lives and characters of his sitters, as on the role that it was assumed portraiture might play. The formal state portraits make their own point in a fairly conventional language. In the less formal pictures colour, form and texture take the place of more direct reference. Portraiture is conceived as decoration, as entertainment, and in this Lely perfectly reflects the values of Charles II's court. It was perhaps fitting that Lely should have died in 1680, five years before that epoch came to an end.

Lely's mastery of tactile effects and subtle colour enabled him to transcend a more or less formulaic approach to the actual design of his portraits. His compositions are not remarkably varied or imaginative, and he by no means recreates the medium anew for each sitter. To that extent he is a minor painter. But the negative consequences of his system were reserved for those who came after him. Among these were several painters well qualified to continue in the Baroque idiom he had popularised, and indeed to take it still further. Huysmans particularly was by temperament and training even more inclined to the flamboyant, and others, like the short-lived William Wissing (1655–87) and John

Closterman (1660–1711), might have sustained the trend. Closterman was gifted with an exceptional talent for complex pictorial structures, and his greatest works, like the large Taylor family portrait (no.21) and the even larger Churchill family group at Blenheim (fig.8), are among the high points of group portraiture in Britain. But, as all accounts reiterate, this new generation was in fact led by Godfrey Kneller (1646/9–1723), whose work was conspicuously less flashy, yet who certainly dominated portraiture in England during several decades around the turn of the century. He came to England in 1676 and so just overlapped with Lely, taking up the dourer, more 'northern' aspects of Lely's art and extrapolating them into a system which served him – and many patrons – well into the next century.

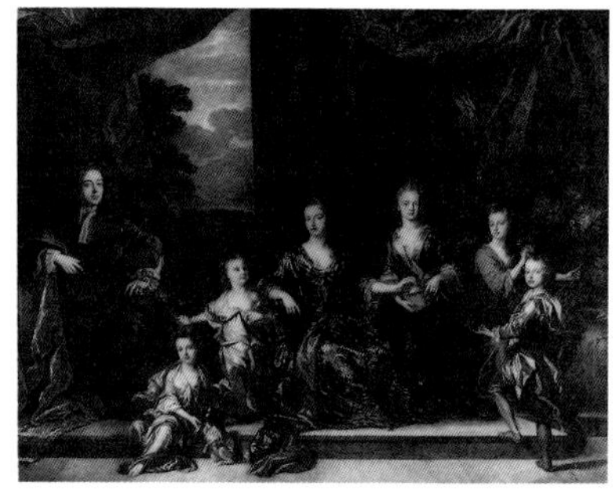

fig.8 John Closterman **John Churchill and his Family** *c.*1698 Oil on canvas *Duke of Marlborough, Blenheim Palace*

Many circumstantial reasons can be adduced to account for Kneller's ascendancy: his self-confidence and talent for business, the efficiency of his studio, the personalities of his rivals – and in several cases their short lives; but the true cause must at least partly be identified as an active wish on the part of the portrait-commissioning class to be depicted by Kneller rather than by anyone else. The fact that Huysmans, for instance, was a Catholic and much employed by Catholics leads one to the conclusion that Kneller, a Protestant from Lübeck in northern Germany, was more to the taste of most Protestant patrons. The essentially Protestant quality of his art must have been reinforced by the time he spent working with Bol and Rembrandt in Holland, whose influence is obvious enough in his early work.

Perhaps even more important, on the other hand, is the fact that Kneller studied in Italy, possibly under Carlo Maratta (1625–1713), who was himself responsible for a number of portraits of Englishmen. Maratta's example had a significant formative effect on Kneller, though one which may not have been to the long-term advantage of his art. While the Dutch had taught him to take advantage of chiaroscuro and the study of expression in creating intensely-felt groups of figures, Maratta relayed to him a more objective, restrained Baroque verging on the classical – a discipline that Kneller's naturally undemonstrative art hardly required. He was confirmed in a love of plainness and formality, virtues that remained with him throughout his career. His influence on the next two generations of portrait painters was profound. This in itself needs pondering. How did it come about that such a figure, so lacking in the kind of excitement that Van Dyck and Lely had both in their different ways supplied, could have dominated his profession not only financially but aesthetically?

It might be said that the force of his essentially unforceful artistic personality was the principal agency in the dismantling and dispersal of Van Dyck's legacy. He was evidently the man for the hour. The period he ushered in has been stigmatised since the days of Reynolds and Horace Walpole as the lowest ebb of painting in England, and it is inescapably the genre of portraiture that must take the brunt of that criticism, for it was by far the most widely practised of all the branches of art. 'The face painter himself who is in great vogues', wrote Hogarth late in his career, 'repeats the Eyes nose and mouth may be three or 4 times – may before he is thirty have drawn about a thousand faces' (Burke, p.214). The use of rigid formulas in face-painting was inevitably commonplace, and artists practised all manner of tricks to make every sitter conform to a standard pattern of execution. With such Procrustean habits among the artists, we should look for signs of a parallel social conformism that could tolerate this kind of treatment.

We can blame Kneller's temperament – Walpole, who disliked his work, said that 'he united the highest vanity with the most consummate negligence of character' (Walpole II, p.202) – and we can blame his Protestantism; we must also take into account the political background of his career. Although it began under Charles II, it extended through the reigns of James II and William and Mary to Anne and George I; Kneller died in 1723. This was a period in which the English were struggling with perhaps the most significant developments in their political history, deposing a tyrant (James) and establishing, by long trial and error, the foundations of a parliamentary democracy. The first Continental wars of the imperial expansion of the eighteenth century were being fought, and a new sense of solemn purpose was descending on the ruling classes. The excesses of the Stuarts were conspicuously set aside in favour of a more sober and responsible view of the Englishman's role, both at home and in the world at large. William of Orange set the tone of moral earnestness in which these vital matters were debated, and Anne and George, in their different ways, confirmed it, if not positively, then negatively by their lack of sparkle as personalities, and their lack of interest in the arts.

The part played by portraiture in such circumstances is perhaps best explained by comparison with another period of administrative seriousness and mercantile expansion: the mid-nineteenth century. Victoria did not, it is true, preside over a nation striving to discover its political identity; the structure of government was by then well established, although the storms over parliamentary reform were not so long past. But there was, on the other hand, greater responsiblity than ever before for nations beyond the seas, and worldwide administrative commitments that make the period of Bolingbroke and Churchill seem untrammelled in comparison. The 1850s, 60s and 70s are marked, like the years around 1700, by a sobriety of approach to portraiture that betokens not dissimilar attitudes. We should perhaps regard these periods as normative in evaluating portraiture in Britain, though Victoria's long period of mourning for the Prince Consort in the 1860s must also be taken into account – a dark night of the court that might be paralleled with the aesthetic death of George I's reign. In general, these epochs show us what is to be expected when those in authority are preoccupied with questions, whether political, social or economic, that reflect directly on their sense of their own moral status. The flowering of a more fully expressive portraiture in the later eighteenth century followed the unequivocal imperial triumphs of the Seven Years' War; the upsurge of glamorous portrait painting in the late Victorian and Edwardian periods coincided with the post-Disraelian apogee of imperial confidence. The latter is particularly interesting because it occurred at a time when the monarch was setting no example in art patronage.

Kneller's style of portrait painting was, then, well attuned to the psychology of his time. It presented men and women as they felt they ought to be presented: devoid of glamour, evidently worthy, capable and honorable. It emphasised the polite, and the political, virtues. It was a function of civic pride, and drew its justification from the need to reinforce civic values. The underlying appeal to qualities associated with ancient Rome led other artists – De Wet (no.19) and Closterman, for instance, to clothe their subjects in explicitly 'Roman' costume. In conformity with this 'antique' programme, portraits were divided into types

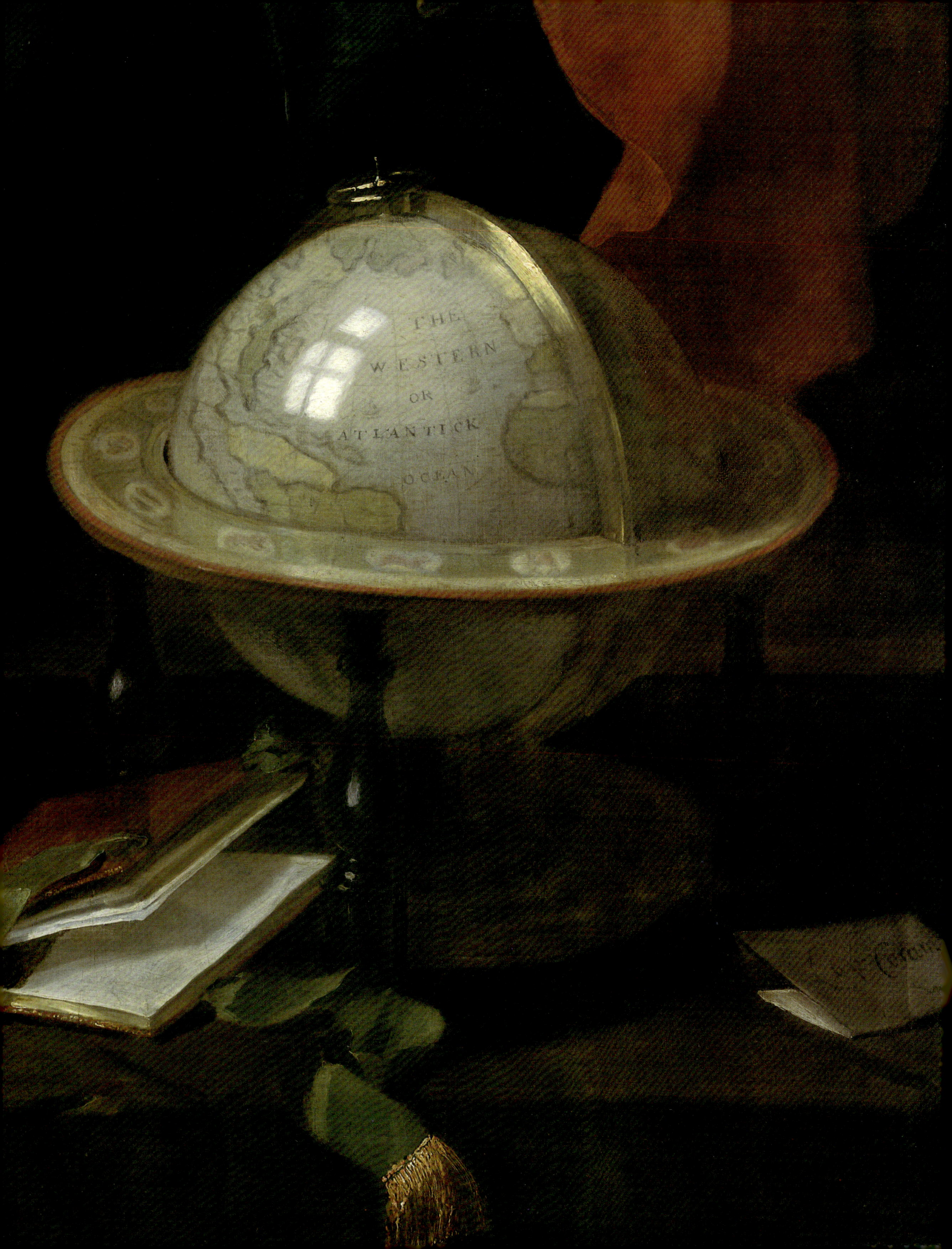
THE
WESTERN
OR
ATLANTICK
OCEAN

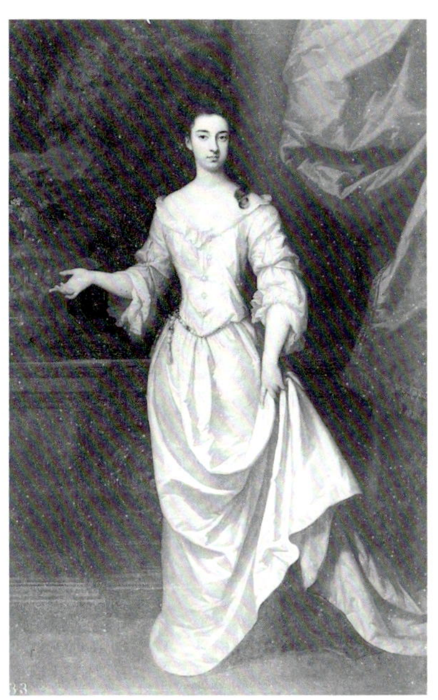

fig.9 Sir Godfrey Kneller **Margaret Cecil, Countess of Ranelagh** 1690–1 Oil on canvas *Her Majesty The Queen*

distinguishing the 'active' from the 'contemplative' life. Kneller reflects the restraint of this new Protestant classicism, but rarely embarks on the full rhetoric of an art inspired by ancient Rome. On occasion, he could rise higher; like many portrait painters, he responded well to the individual stimulus of personal friends. His portrait of Matthew Prior (Trinity College, Cambridge) is rightly regarded as an exceptional work, alive with a sinewy energy expressed in vigorously applied paint. For the most part, he does not penetrate beyond the screen of proprieties prescribed by current fashion.

His female portraits were equally subdued. When Kneller painted his famous series of eight 'Hampton Court Beauties' (fig.9), following the example of Lely a generation earlier, the Van Dyck tradition of portraying female beauty in Platonic terms as an absolute value became, in several senses, academic. Sensuality has been expelled from these pictures; love and desire are present, if at all, in perfunctory symbols of the kind – a putto, a fountain – that Lely had already drained of real meaning, while the ladies are quite unlike Lely's: remote and stiff, embodiments of the almost puritanical propriety that characterised the court of William and Mary. In obeying the dictates of contemporary taste Kneller was painting the moral portraiture that Richardson made the basis for his account of the profession at the beginning of the eighteenth century.

Eighteenth-Century Ideas

Jonathan Richardson (1665–1745) is one of the more consistently competent painters of the early years of the eighteenth century; Pilkington remarked in his *Dictionary of Painters* (1770) that 'The good sense of the nation is characterised in his portraits', an epitome that perhaps makes Richardson's own opinions useful, for the purposes of the argument advanced here, as having a central and representative value.

He judged his own time more favourably than we are inclined to do today. He attributed what he perceived as the excellence of portraiture among his contemporaries largely to the beneficent influence of Van Dyck, 'ever since which time . . . England has excelled all the world in that great branch of the art'; but also to the example of other artists and to thriving patronage: 'being well stored with the works of the greatest masters, whether paintings or drawings, being moreover the finest living models, as well as the greatest encouragement, this may justly be esteemed as a complete and the best school for face painting now in the world' (Richardson, p.21).

Notwithstanding his misjudgement on this point, Richardson's observations on portraiture, in his *Essay on the Theory of Painting* (1715), constitute one of the most substantial accounts to have come down to us of what the portrait painter himself thought he was doing. They amount, in fact, to a kind of philosophy of portraiture. How this emerges out of his discussion is itself interesting.

William Hogarth **Captain Coram** (detail, no.24)

the broader context of history painting. So he tends to allow arguments normally associated with history to apply to portraiture as well, with a consequent redefinition of what the portrait aims to achieve. While he makes no attempt to distinguish different genres of face-painting, he examines the various aspects of the subject minutely to build up an argument about the relation of artist to sitter, and of sitter to society. His first point relates directly to history, and is obvious enough as a comment on portraiture; it has become even more central to the discussion since photography. 'Painting gives not only the persons, but the characters of great men. The air of the head, and the mien in general, give strong indications of the mind ... Let a man read a character in my lord Clarendon (and certainly never was there a better painter in that kind) he will find it improved by seeing a picture of the same person by Vandyke.' There is a strong and very English propensity to treat portrait painting as a literary art, relying at least partly on verbal parallels (in this case with the character studies in Clarendon's *History of the Rebellion*, 1702–4) 'to improve and instruct us' and 'to excite proper sentiments and reflections' like 'a history, a poem, a book of ethics, or divinity' (Richardson, pp.5–6). Indeed, Richardson goes so far as to lay it down that 'to be a good face-painter, a degree of the historical, and poetical genius is requisite'.

Even for the more practical matter of sitting to the painter there is, according to Richardson, a literary parallel: 'to sit for one's picture, is to have an abstract of one's life written, and published, and ourselves thus consigned over to honour, or infamy.' The moral force of history painting is applicable to portraiture; a likeness committed to canvas is a public injunction to emulation or abhorrence. People who have their faces painted become 'monuments of good, or evil fame' and, 'secretly admonished by the faithful friend in their own breasts' may resolve to live a better life in consequence of what the artist has revealed. 'Methinks,' says Richardson, 'it is rational to believe that pictures of this kind are subservient to virtue' (Richardson, pp.7–8).

This strong sense of the moral purpose of portraiture has made it difficult for British artists to approach their subjects with a purely aesthetic interest – with a sense of the possibilities for creative design inherent in, say, the depiction of the human figure, in splendid clothes, on a large scale. The Baroque assumptions that lay behind Van Dyck's manner remained deeply alien even if Van Dyck's practical example persisted in exerting an irresistible appeal. But Richardson makes a distinction between what is permissible to the great Van Dyck and what to lesser painters. 'A flattering mercenary hand may represent my face with a youth, or beauty, which belongs not to me, and which I am not one jot the younger, or the handsomer for, though I may be a just subject of ridicule for desiring, or suffering such flattery ... my own conduct gives the boldest strokes of beauty, or deformity' (Richardson, p.8). Van Dyck, then, may be said to have succeeded with the English because he was able to convince them, Platonically, of their moral worth while presenting them as beautiful: he suggests that the beauty he finds in the face and clothes reflects an inner virtue. This would be an entirely appropriate reading of a painter who is always ranked in portraiture alongside his contemporaries Velásquez and Rembrandt, both men who conform to Richardson's dictum that 'a portrait-painter must understand mankind, and enter into their characters, and express their minds as well as their faces' (Richardson, p.12).

But this definition of a portraitist goes much further: 'as his business is chiefly with people of condition, he must think as a gentleman, and a man of sense, or it will be impossible to give such their true, and proper resemblances.' Van Dyck had clearly been possessed of this necessary talent, and it is noteworthy that social skills are particularly associated with artists who specialised in the grander type of portrait. Lely, we are told, 'was so much in esteem with Charles II, that he would oftentimes take great pleasure in his conversation . . . so extraordinary were his natural endowments, and so great his acquired knowledge, it would be hard to determine whether he was a better painter, or a more accomplished gentleman' (Walpole II, p.98n.). Kneller was 'a fine & handsome well turnd Gentleman', with 'a pleasant conversation finely entertaining when a Painting' (Vertue II, pp.120, 122). Reynolds was noted for his address in the company of the aristocracy, and Lawrence's capacity to charm his sitters, especially the ladies among them, became legendary. Sargent too had the social gift in a pre-eminent degree. There was, of course, a negative aspect of the problem. Lawrence's ease and charm did not prevent him from seeing his position from a more cynical point of view: it was part of his professional responsibility to support 'a certain Manner . . . to deal with Fashion and its thousand whims – with Power – its arrogance, meanness and injustice'. The moral dimension of portraiture as a creative medium goes, then, somewhat deeper than one might suppose. The interrelationship between grandeur in portraiture and the expectations of history painting is a function of the artist's own temperament, and especially of his social abilities.

Richardson's view of the portrait as expressing moral as well as physical qualities must be seen in the broader context of eighteenth-century philosophical discussions of 'beauty' and 'deformity'. These accidents of physical appearance were perceived as bearing directly on the chain of emotional and rational processes that constitute our response to the world, and as relating in a reciprocal manner to less visible, inward qualities. David Hume, for instance, in his *Treatise of Human Nature* (1739), brought together natural and moral beauty as agents operating similarly in giving rise to the emotion of pride, while, by contrast, deformity of body and spirit causes 'humility'. Indeed, it is the presence of these passions that gives the outward appearance meaning: beauty 'is nothing but a form, which produces pleasure, as deformity is a structure of parts, which conveys pain' (p.299). He goes further, suggesting that 'Whatever in ourselves is either useful, beautiful, or surprising, is an object of pride, and it's contrary, of humility' (p.300). A complete structure of moral values, then, rests on the notion of beauty as it is manifested in a responsible society. It was this idea that made it possible for Edmund Burke, in his *Enquiry into the Origin of our Ideas of the Sublime and Beautiful* (1757), to categorise the relationship between human physiology and the emotions in such a way that a complete system of aesthetics could be built upon it.

Burke discusses the Sublime largely as it can be used in the context of our relation to natural phenomena, so it was inevitable that his ideas should quickly be applied to landscape painting. But the Sublime had been a term of literary criticism since ancient times, frequently invoked in discussions of Homer and Milton, and by the beginning of the eighteenth century was often cited in the context of historical painting. If Richardson's quasi-literary view of portraiture was valid, then, the Sublime might be equally relevant there. Reynolds was to take up this idea and develop it notably. The old notions of kingly virtue, whereby a royal portrait embodied definite ideas about man's relationship with the social order and with divine providence, could now be extended to embrace other virtuous public figures, and as the century advances we find more and more that the phenomenology of the Burkean Sublime becomes subsumed into the language of grand portraiture.

The philosophical issues implied by such questions as the opposition of beauty and deformity were worked out by portrait painters in immediately practical terms by the process of responding to individual sitters. Under the influence of formulaic painting of the kind practised in the age of Kneller, the features that had come to distinguish male and female portraiture began to be established as conventions. Men enjoyed clear social identities which themselves provided the artist with his subject matter. Occasionally an appropriate property might be introduced to give visual point to a particular avocation – an anchor for an admiral or a horse for a general, rather as a king would be shown wearing the regalia. Women, rarely involved in professional or even artistic activity of any public significance, were simply women.

> Nothing so true as what you once let fall,
> 'Most Women have no Characters at all.'
> Matter too soft a lasting mark to bear,
> And best distinguish'd by black, brown, or fair.
>
> (Alexander Pope, *Moral Essays*, Epistle II, *To a Lady of the Characters of Women*, lines 1–4; published 1735 but written earlier)

The artist was therefore free to make of them what subjects he would, and in some cases, as often with Kneller, that meant very little. But women shared with men the moral characteristics of all humanity, and those characteristics could be demonstrated to pictorial effect, especially in the more public branches of portraiture. In composing his portraits of the women of Charles I's court Van Dyck had frequently made use of allusions to virtue and desire in forms allegorical or symbolic and Lely, as we have seen, leached this tradition of any meaning it may have had. But the habit of showing women with symbolic accoutrements remained, and the possibility of endowing them with entirely imaginary qualities for the sake of the picture itself was increasingly recognised. There grew, as the eighteenth century progressed, a tradition of showing women as the personifications of almost anything rather than themselves.

A man in even the most imaginary of costumes, like the Marquis of Atholl (no.19), or the most idealising of poses, like the MacLeod (no.27) is always himself, soldier, statesman, landowner or monarch; a women is often shown as Venus, Diana, Chastity, Patience, or Truth.

> How many pictures of one Nymph we view,
> All how unlike each other, all how true!
> Arcadia's Countess, here, in ermin'd pride,
> Is there, Pastora by a fountain side.
> Here Fannia, leering on her own good man,
> And there, a naked Leda with a Swan.
>
> (Pope, Epistle II, lines 5–10)

There tends therefore to be a stronger element of sheer make-believe in female portraiture; costumes are less likely to be those of current fashion, more fanciful or theatrical. Whereas men carry with them their own moral purpose, their own innate capacity for greatness, women, to whom, it was felt, few or no such qualities naturally attach themselves, need to be cast in the role of a moral archetype which develops and generalises the feminine virtues they are held to embody. But the sentimental identification of feminine virtues with women is exactly parallel to the (ultimately equally sentimental) assumption of manly virtues in men. The difference is that men are not required to impersonate an abstraction: their value is considered self-evident.

This distinction does not necessarily denigrate women, though it reflects their position in a society which expected them to represent private rather than public virtues. It culminated, at the hands of Reynolds and his followers – notably Hoppner and Lawrence – in an exaltation of women to the status of goddesses far more explicitly and frequently than men were ever asked to assume the disguise of past heroes. Even with actors this holds true: Mrs Siddons represents the Tragic Muse (no.37); Kemble is simply portrayed in one of his roles (no.52).

The idea of women representing something while men simply *are* (something) is one that underlies a great deal of grand portraiture. It corresponds to the literary idea of women as angels or saints or muses which is constantly encountered in the eighteenth century, and becomes even more common in the nineteenth. But while the literary conceit remained powerful until the First World War, the pictorial parallel was to die out in the Victorian period: by 1880 metaphors of virtue had been transferred to academic subject-pictures and the message of portraiture became one of overt materialism.

To return to the eighteenth century: there is a direct philosophical and aesthetic line from Richardson to Reynolds. It was in the studio of an essentially Richardsonian artist, Thomas Hudson (1701–79), that Reynolds first worked in London. But Richardson's position needs to be further defined by the ideas of another painter of the early eighteenth century: William Hogarth (1697–1762). For if most of Richardson's ideas are English only by implication, or because they cannot help it, Hogarth was determined that his art should be English unmistakably and before everything else. He was passionate in his chauvinism, and without that passion it would have been hard for the next generation to pursue their careers in the furtherance of English art, as they did, with an established assumption that the national school was an institution to be proud of. It was Hogarth who focused the many strands of concern for a national academy, by insisting in his writings and, more importantly, in everything that he painted or drew or engraved, that the prevailing preference for foreign artists was simply a prejudice that ought to be cleared away.

For the most part his campaign for a national art took the form of social satires – 'modern moral subjects', as he called them, like the 'Rake's Progress' and the 'Marriage à la Mode' – which offered a commentary that fits quite happily with Richardson's idea of a moral portraiture. Face-painting he tackled less often, and when he did found that it was misunderstood. In his own words, he 'painted Portrait[s] occationally but as they require constant practise to be reddy at taking a likeness & as the life must not be strictly followd they met with the like approbation Rembrant's did, they were said at the same time by some Nature itself by others exicrable' (Burke, p.212). This is surely a reception that any portrait painter must encounter. What is striking and new about Hogarth's portraits is their vivid immediacy of characterisation, and their elevation of an 'English' technique into the ideal vehicle for this. The vigorous application of paint, no less than the constantly moving double curve of the 'line of Beauty' that he espoused as a fundamental principle of design, ensured vitality and humour in almost every portrait that he painted. These qualities were rarely to be found in the works of his contemporaries. They were qualities not particularly conducive to grandeur, but by their means he could invest the most unprepossessing people with dignity. In doing so, he showed the next generation that humour may be called in to the service of serious portraiture; and humour is one of the ingredients that give Reynolds's work its value.

By contrast Thomas Hudson, who represents the portrait establishment of the 1740s and 50s, relied on a dead-pan execution and a drapery painter. Hogarth had no time for the drapery painter, 'a person evry [fa]ce painter in vogues is supplied with ... as much a still life painter as he that set[s] a bottle and Glass pipes and a candle upon the table [and] copies it' (Burke, p.214); but drapery men, usually from abroad like the Antwerp painter Joseph Van Aken (*c*.1699–1749), performed a valuable service during much of the century: Van Aken was often responsible for the more swagger elements in Hudson's male portraits – namely the waistcoats, often splendidly narcissistic, embroidered affairs executed with a refinement of detail quite alien to the styles of most indigenous painters (no.25). The perception that the waistcoat constitutes an essential ingredient in the composition of the male image is one that can be particularly associated with Flemish practitioners. It is related to the no less important stress on glamorous clothes that so dominates the work of another foreign artist – Batoni. The glorification of raiment that can at times almost take over as the subject matter of Batoni's portraits is unimaginable with Hogarth, who records clothes with a delight in their flow and rhythm, but with no sense that they are more important than the person wearing them.

Dispensing with the outward trappings, Hogarth plunged into the heart of his subject, the bare psychology of the sitter. His portraits are direct – they are both literally and figuratively unembroidered. But this did not mean that he would not admit the possibility of a grander form of presentation. What he had particularly to say was that the opulent forms of Continental Baroque portraiture might be applied, not only in a more 'honest' English way, but also to people from social classes which had never before been so treated. The great manifesto in which he embodies all his most ambitious ideas for an 'alternative' portraiture is the picture of Captain Thomas Coram (no.24) of 1740. With it, the great age of self-assured and consistently original British portrait painting well and truly begins.

A few years were to pass before the arrival of an institutional embodiment of the new state of affairs. What was needed was an organisation that brought together all the economic and technical concerns of the practising artists of the day; but that was not a straightforward matter. The interrelationship between patterns of patronage and programmes of training in any given society is complex and not always obvious. In seventeenth-century England young practitioners would generally acquire their training directly by joining the studios of established artists, as was the normal state of affairs in Europe since before the

Renaissance. But from the end of the sixteenth century onwards it became increasingly common for capital cities to set up institutions that embodied both a corporate professional identity for artists, and a system of practical study. England was relatively late in establishing an Academy of Art, although various artists, mostly of Continental origin and having some experience of such places elsewhere, had attempted to do so during the early eighteenth century. Hogarth, who did not want to imitate foreign institutions, nevertheless wanted an academy. It was an essential adjunct to – or rather, the definitive manifestation of – a flourishing school of painters and sculptors. Without it, the disciplines required for the proficient practice of the arts could not be effectively instilled. With it, the national school had a lively guarantee of its virtue, and of its future.

When the Royal Academy was founded in London in 1768 it encoded the training requirements of the profession. From the beginning a Professorship of Painting was established, as were Professorships of Architecture, Anatomy and Perspective. Two years after the foundation Professors of Ancient History and Ancient Literature were appointed (these were Oliver Goldsmith and Samuel Johnson). Not until 1810 did a Professor of Sculpture make his appearance; the first was John Flaxman (1755–1826). From 1769 Reynolds, as President, undertook to bring together the various disciplines by delivering an annual general lecture, or Discourse, on art in theory and practice. In these he concentrated on broad issues, and particularly on those aspects of painting that he considered most worthy of the student's serious attention. Despite his own practice, and the evident importance of portraiture in English life, he deliberately played down its value, emphasising rather the intellectual and creative pre-eminence of historical painting. This was a received preference of the time; but Reynolds was perfectly well aware of the areas in which portraiture and history overlap, though he was conscious that they are separate disciplines – separate ways of seeing the world. For instance, he warned that if a portrait painter were to attempt history, he would be likely to bring too much specific character into his heads; for 'An History-painter paints man in general; a Portrait-painter, a particular man, and consequently a defective model' (Discourse IV, Wark, p.70). Among the notes that he made on a tour of Flanders we find him putting it the other way: 'imitating exactly what we see in nature, makes but a poor historical picture, but an admirable portrait' (Malone II, p.332).

Similar principles applied to clothes. The question of costume in portraiture was one that Richardson had tackled fifty years earlier. Reynolds echoes much of what Richardson had said. He acknowledges that some form of historical dress is the logical, indeed the natural, means to endow the sitter with dignity. He points out that the current habit of depicting great men in Roman dress is a consequence of the association between that costume and public distinction in surviving statues of Roman dignitaries. He argues that since only sculpture, and not painting, has survived from the ancient period, 'we could no more venture to paint a general officer in a Roman military habit, than we could make a statue in the present uniform' (Discourse VII, Wark, p.138). This awareness of precedent is a good indication of the rigour with which Reynolds pursued the implications of his historical knowledge. His conclusion is contradicted by works of the high Baroque period like De Wet's Marquis of Atholl (no.19); but Reynolds is enunciating rules for the present, not for a past and, on the whole, an aesthetically less sophisticated age. He notices, too, the fashion for clothing sitters in Van Dyck costume (he sometimes did so himself), which also endows them with a spurious and anachronistic dignity. He astutely points out that this dignity is associative – that is, it is only if we know the costume to be that worn by the subjects of many of Van Dyck's masterpieces that we infer both authority in the sitter and quality in the painting.

This is an important principle behind much portraiture that sets out to be grand. The use of easily understood signposts in the form of costume or setting tells us how to evaluate the sitter. The greatest masters – Titian, Velásquez, Van Dyck – can convey the dignified status of their sitters while concentrating with remarkably little distraction on their appearance alone; but the mastery they bring to this lends their work an authority that can be alluded to by lesser artists simply by copying the accessories that were incidental to the originals. Lawrence was to make ironic use of this semiotic technique in his large portrait of Queen Charlotte (no.50), which contains all the signals for the grandest of public statements, but presents a daringly intimate likeness that contradicts these. He had learned from Reynolds that a traditional formula can be used for purposes other than the imposition of a literal interpretation. In this instance, he applies them almost as a feint, to distract us from his real purpose.

As in real life, so in art, clothes have been of paramount importance in establishing the rank and standing of the person depicted. Reynolds was well aware of the function played by dress in the communication of his message, which was, of course, itself a subtle mixture of his own creative intentions and the wishes of the sitter. Ancient costume, Reynolds maintained, was useful to the painter on account of its simplicity of structure, 'without those whimsical capricious forms by which all other dresses are embarrassed':

> He therefore, who in his practice of portrait-painting wishes to dignify his subject, which we will suppose to be a lady, will not paint her in the modern dress, the familiarity of which alone is sufficient to destroy all dignity. He takes care that his work shall correspond to those ideas and that imagination which he knows will regulate the judgement of others; and therefore dresses his figure something with the general air of the antique for the sake of dignity, and preserves something of the modern for the sake of likeness. By this conduct his works correspond with those prejudices which we have in favour of what we continually see; and the relish of the antique simplicity corresponds with what we may call the more learned and scientific prejudice.
>
> (Discourse VII, Wark, p.140)

The conception of portraiture that Reynolds proposes here is far from being the universally accepted rule that he suggests. He delivered the seventh Discourse in 1776, and we can point to the 1770s as the very period when the fashion for 'classical' drapery in portraiture was at its height. By the early 1780s it had all but disappeared. Some artists favoured it more than others; Cotes and Romney used it extensively, Ramsay and Gainsborough hardly at all. From this we might deduce that Reynolds had hit the nail on the head; for both Ramsay and Gainsborough are inclined to favour the direct and literal rather than the elevated and metaphorical in portraiture. What Reynolds intended by his recommendation was, of course, not to prescribe details of design but to encourage the kind of generalisation that he believed characterised all great painting, including portraiture. The classical overtones of antique costume were less important than their freedom from fussiness and commonplace associations. Clothes that could be arranged in large simple masses conduced to a broad, imposing design. He was critical of artists who subordinated this breadth to variety of detail. In praising Gainsborough for 'forming all the parts of his picture together; the whole going on at the same time, in the same manner as nature creates her works', he found fault with Batoni who 'in his portraits completely finished one feature before he proceeded to another. The consequence was, as might be expected; the countenance was never well expressed; and, as the painters say, the whole was not well put together' (Discourse XIV, Wark, p.251).

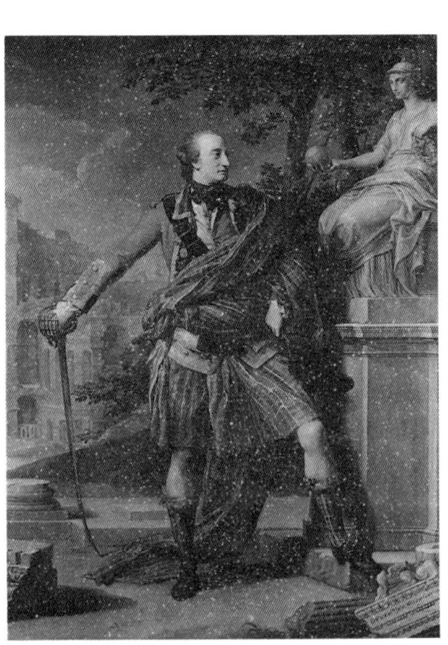

fig.10 Pompeo Batoni **Colonel the Hon. William Gordon** 1766 Oil on canvas *National Trust for Scotland, Fyvie Castle, Aberdeenshire*

Needless to say, Batoni was not one of those portrait painters who favoured classical costume, though he did occasionally dress his male sitters in a vaguely Van Dyck fashion (no.29), and his extraordinary portrait of Colonel the Hon. William Gordon (fig.10; National Trust for Scotland, Fyvie Castle) treats the Scottish plaid and kilt exactly as though they were 'Roman' military apparel, as in de Wet's Marquis of Atholl (no.19). It is ironic that England should be contrasted with Italy in this way: Reynolds wanted very much to paint in a manner redolent of the Italian Renaissance, and his advocacy of 'breadth' was largely aimed at achieving this; contemporary Italian artists, however, were practising an almost Dutch refinement of detail at the expense of the greater whole. This may explain why Reynolds was impressed by developments in Paris, for there a more 'elevated' style still prevailed, and artists were prepared to present their sitters in allegorical disguises, accompanied by suitably grand accessories and backgrounds.

Generalisation as conceived by Reynolds did not entail elaborate drawing techniques. These were required for the more mundane tasks of recording the details of perceived reality, and hardly entered into the process of imaginative creation as he understood it. It was by the brush that the artist 'must hope to attain eminence' (Discourse II, Wark, p.34). But the use of the brush was not specifically taught, either at the Academy or anywhere else. This omission had the important consequence of liberating the English painters from many of the inhibitions of over-formalised practice and enabling them to develop individual systems and techniques, which made possible the revolution in expression that developed into Romanticism. In all this Reynolds played a key role. His own technical experiments are famous, and because they quickly led to the deterioration of his pictures have been regarded as short-sighted and even unprofessional. But it is not possible to separate Reynolds's technical adventurousness from his inventiveness as a designer of portraits: the two are twin aspects of his creative personality. By his example, many other works of unorthodox manufacture but great significance for the development of Romanticism came into being in the late eighteenth century.

But Reynolds of course prescribed assiduity in drawing as an essential part of an artist's training; and the very existence of the Academy ensured that in the long run the discipline of draughtsmanship would become more refined and acquire greater importance. During the late eighteenth century and beyond, standards steadily rose. The drawing skills of Thomas Lawrence and David Wilkie are superlative. Indeed, it was possible for J.C. Horsley to summarise

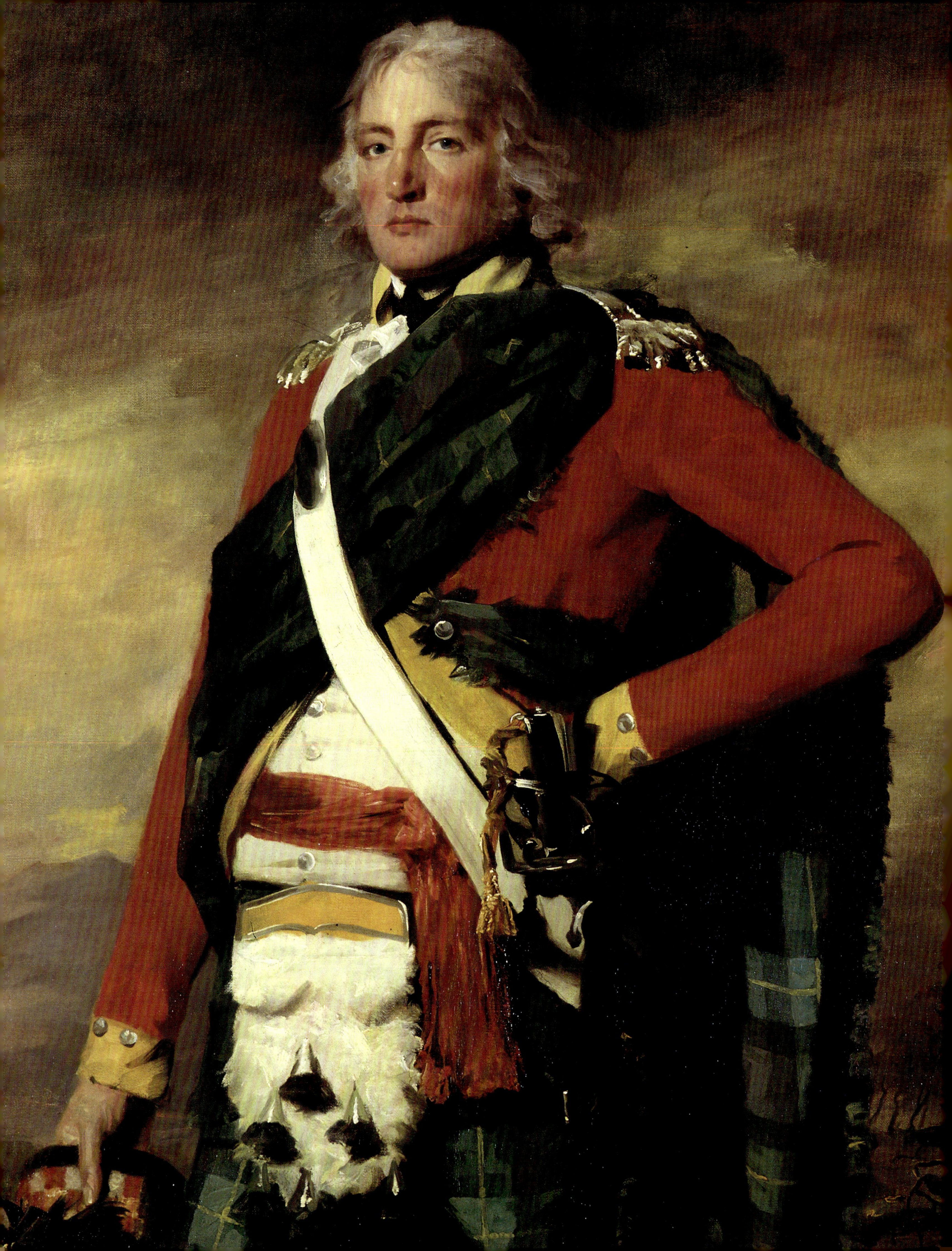

Lawrence's whole system of producing a portrait as 'totally opposed' to that of Reynolds. Horsley quotes Lady Callcott as describing Lawrence's procedure as follows: 'He began by a very careful chalk drawing of the head on the canvas, and then painted in detail the various features. He painted very elaborately, perhaps an eye only at one sitting, and so on' (Horsley, p.63). This development does not precisely coincide with the decline of the grand portrait, but it is certain that as the nineteenth century progressed, and as refined drawing became more a matter of course among all professional artists, portraiture became more intimate, more dependent on the detailed articulation of character and costume, less on the sweeping gesture and rhetorical effect. This was of course largely a function of changing tastes; but it can also be seen as a by-product of the Academic system in England.

The Grand Manner

There was an obvious theoretical objection to placing the two genres of history and portrait on an equal footing, in so far as history concerned archetypes, declining to describe any specific person, while portraiture was concerned precisely with doing that. History painting, indeed, was art for the intellectual few; the Earl of Shaftesbury even went so far as to say that women as a class could not appreciate it – 'Ladies hate the great manner'. Because they have no grasp of general ideas, or 'the grand outline of human nature', they must be 'satisfied with common nature' (*Second Characters*, p.131, quoted in Barrell, p.68) – the kind of nature offered by the portrait. It is a sign of Reynolds's broader humanity that in giving the formal portrait many of the characteristics of history painting, he used his formidable invention to present women in a very wide range of roles and activities, thereby tacitly endowing them with a social and intellectual status that had, perhaps, been denied them previously. The perception of portraiture as specific and therefore limited, as opposed to the grand generalisation of history, was one that he was determined to break down.

In claiming high moral importance for the art-form that he practised, Richardson has been accused of deliberate self-aggrandisement (e.g. West, p.227). But it was inevitable that in a country where religious painting was all but unknown other genres should have attracted the didactic connotations of that form. It was as necessary as ever to assert that painting could uplift the mind, and that its contemplation tended to improve the character. As the eighteenth century proceeded, the notion of the 'history picture' was developed to satisfy this need for intellectual and moral respectability. But however much history painting was advocated as the highest branch of art, the portrait remained the staple fare of most English patrons. So portrait painters developed Richardson's hints in the direction of a new style that amalgamated the two. History painters for their part took to incorporating portraits of the famous in

Sir Henry Raeburn **Sir John Sinclair Bt** (detail, no.46)

reconstructions of important contemporary events, which became in effect large and dramatic group portraits. Conversely, it was possible to paint the portrait of an individual in such a way that, however undistinguished, the sitter took on the aspect of a hero or heroine of modern or ancient history. The long tradition of emblematical painting, beginning in the Middle Ages and appropriated by portrait painters in the Renaissance, had by this time been transmuted into a purely decorative formula, so that historical allusion could be implied without specific reference. In eighteenth-century France, this was done to splendidly decorative effect: countless duchesses and royal mistresses were portrayed in the guise of Venus or Hebe or even the Magdalen, but always with a result that is purely visual: we are not expected to attach actual moral values to the emblems represented. For the painter who most prominently championed the *rapprochement* between history and portrait, Joshua Reynolds, the state of affairs in France presented a particular and direct challenge. He could appreciate the pictorial assets of purely decorative historical allusion, but, armed with Richardson's definition of the moral role of the portrait painter, needed to re-establish the full value of such symbolism. How he did this constitutes a classic case of English compromise which created a wholly new form of portraiture.

In the light of what has been said about the relationship between the personality of the portrait painter and his social role it is worth noting that Reynolds, according to Lawrence, was 'of a Cold Temperament – a Philosopher from absence of the Passions'. He compensated for this in practice by his social adroitness and by his gifts as an intelligent conversationalist. With Reynolds one frequently has the feeling that a satisfactory composition has been arrived at by the careful manipulation of a social situation. Gestures and expressions occurring casually in conversation have been caught and rendered permanent as an expression of the sitter's temperament. Reynolds's skill in this respect is one of his distinguishing marks, and illustrates how the dimension of social interaction may play a crucial part in the evolution of any portrait. Unlike the history or landscape painter, the portraitist must, as Richardson said, be a social animal, and cannot function if he is not.

Of all the great eighteenth-century portrait painters, Reynolds was most equipped by temperament to address the literary implications of his chosen genre. His biographer Malone succinctly points up the difference between Reynolds's style and that of his predecessors: 'For several years . . . the painters of portraits contented themselves with exhibiting as correct a resemblance as they could; but seem not to have thought, or had not the power, of enlivening the canvas by giving a kind of historick air to their pictures' (Malone I, pp.xxiii–xxiv). Crudely though this is expressed, it reiterates precisely what Richardson had suggested in his *Essay*. Richardson asked for something of the 'historical genius' in the make-up of the portrait painter but did not stipulate how in mechanical terms this was to be achieved; Malone's phrase too is extremely vague. Reynolds actually created a process by which these ideas could be attained in the physical terms of a picture. His first attempts to do so were prompted by his visit to Italy in 1752, and perhaps even more by the stay he made in Paris on the way back. Two pictures painted in London in that year reflect the impact of Continental ideas. One is a portrait of Commodore Keppel (fig.11; National Maritime Museum), who is presented in all the urgency of his profesional avocations,

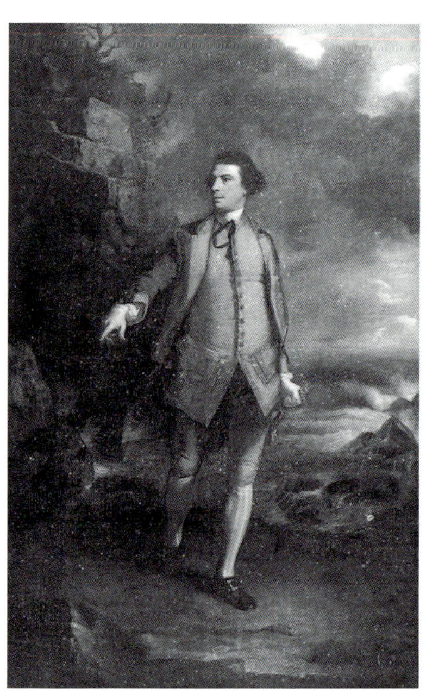

fig.11 Sir Joshua Reynolds **Commodore Augustus Keppel** *c.*1753–4 Oil on canvas *National Maritime Museum, Greenwich*

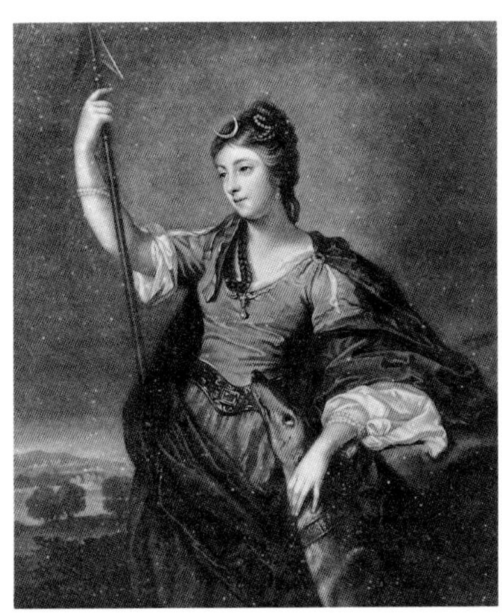

fig.12 James McArdell after Sir Joshua Reynolds **Lady Anne Dawson as Diana** *c.*1755 Mezzotint *Fitzwilliam Museum, Cambridge*

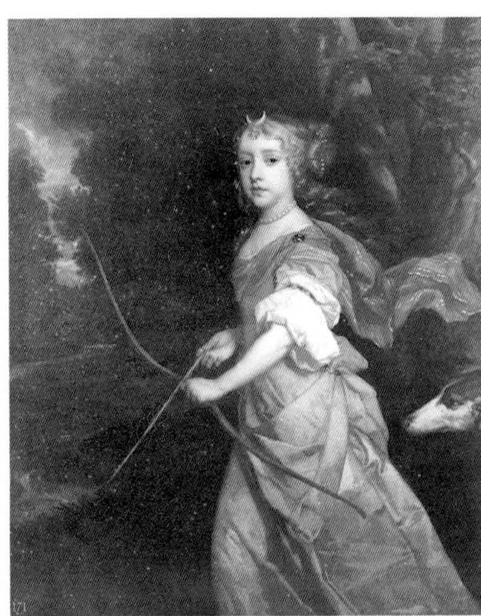

fig.13 Sir Peter Lely **The Princess Mary as Diana** *c.*1672 Oil on canvas *Her Majesty The Queen*

striding along a turbulent seashore. The rhetorical gesture of the figure has always been associated with the pose of the Apollo Belvedere, and has therefore been celebrated as an imaginative 'borrowing' from the antique. But the attitude is only vaguely reminiscent of the famous statue, and it seems that in fact Reynolds had a more recent model in mind: a modern and not an ancient Apollo, a figure by Pierre Legros (1629–1714), which he may well have encountered in Paris.

But the question whether Reynolds was inspired by a recent or an ancient source is of less significance than his relationship to the future: a more important point to be made about this image is that it is a romantic portrait – one that anticipates the theatricality of Géricault or Lawrence by fifty or sixty years. In that respect Reynolds is an extraordinary figure. We should not lose sight of Walpole's comment that through the medium of mezzotint engravings his work was distributed widely in Europe and much admired: his influence on Continental Romanticism was considerable. Already in the Keppel portrait he has transformed a tradition and fitted it for use by two or three generations to come. As Malone put it, 'the only question was, whether the new painter, or Vandyck, were the more excellent' (Malone I, p.xxiii).

About the same time as the Keppel, Reynolds produced his first female portrait embodying a classical allusion, of Lady Anne Dawson as Diana (fig.12; collection Her Majesty The Queen), which is presumably a reference to Lely's portrait of the Princess Mary as Diana (fig.13; collection Her Majesty The Queen). It has also been seen as making more up-to-date comment on the current French fashion for allegorical portraits (Rosenblum, in *Reynolds*, 1986, p.50). If he imported that taste into mid-eighteenth-century London Reynolds grafted it on to a longstanding indigenous tradition and in doing so transformed it into a new commodity, altogether more in tune with the ethos of the place. He was, first of all, driven by the powerful motive of bringing English painting up to a new level of importance in international terms, and his assumptions about serious art were formed in Rome, not Paris. If the French had anything to offer, it was to be 'translated' into English, but English that was liable to have a strong Italian accent.

That accent needs analysing. It was not the accent of Batoni, the most obvious of models. Reynolds was too strongly wedded to Rembrandtian chiaroscuro, and to technical experiment, to cultivate the suave enamelled finish that gives Batoni's pictures their character. His male portraits rarely use the cross-legged pose of Batoni, which Gainsborough, on the other hand, employed frequently, to his own indiosyncratic ends. It is not Gainsborough's accent, certainly: no two contemporary portrait painters could be further apart. But there is spontaneity in Reynolds as well as in Gainsborough. Reynolds's Englishness shows in his pragmatic interest in the accidents of appearance and personality, which, as we have seen, provide the driving force for many of his finest conceptions. That directness of approach is often so well-judged and effective that it carries with it the authority of a highly evolved invention. But intellectual as much of Reynolds's work is we should not assume that he is always self-conscious, let alone 'learned'. Reynolds could be instinctive on occasion, and his response to many of his sitters, especially children, is disarmingly simple. The success of the Kenwood portrait of Catherine Moore, for instance, with its delicious play of light and shade across the face, and the glow of reflections from flesh and blue silk (fig.14), is the creation of an innate visual sense, and not the product of some masterly manipulation of ideas. We should perhaps give Reynolds more credit than we do for being a 'natural' painter. This assessment is given support by the character sketch given of him by James Northcote, who as his pupil might have been expected to emphasise the public qualities of Reynolds's work: 'Sir Joshua . . . was not without his faults: he had not grandeur, but he was a man of a mild, bland, amiable character; and this predominant feeling appears so strongly in his works, that you cannot mistake it; and this is what makes them so delightful to look at, and constitutes their charm for others, even without their being conscious of it' (Hazlitt, p.108).

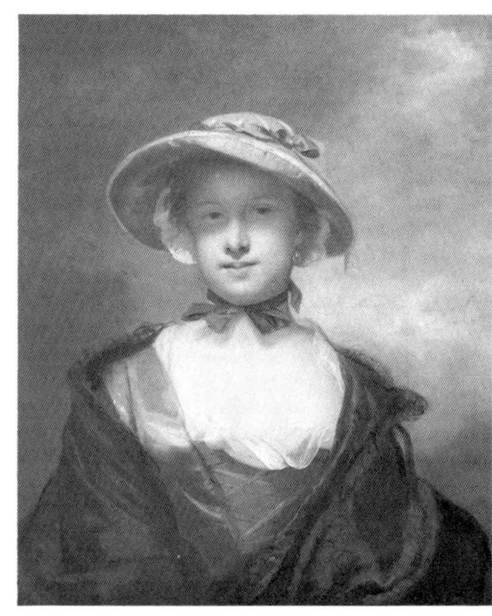

fig.14 Sir Joshua Reynolds **Catherine Moore** 1752 Oil on canvas *Iveagh Bequest, Kenwood*

Having drawn attention to the professional facility, the spontaneity, that manifests itself at all stages of Reynolds's career, we can go on to isolate those pictures, or types of pictures, in which he can be seen deliberately engaging his (and our) intellect. These are often works, like the 'Three Ladies Adorning a Term of Hymen' (no.35), involving groups of figures, which have to be disposed in relation to one another in a relatively tight space. He only gradually came to realise that this was one of the most taxing challenges of his art. His acknowledged failure to appreciate Raphael on first visiting the Vatican is perhaps connected with the point: he says that he found himself 'in the midst of works executed upon principles with which I was unacquainted'; but he came to see that Raphael's supreme achievement lay in 'the judicious arrangement of his materials', and 'the grace, the dignity, and the expression of his characters' (Malone I, p.xv); that is, his ability to compose groups, relating figures to each other in a poetic and expressive manner so as to expound narrative, moral and spiritual ideas. Once understood, this subtlety of thought operated as a challenge to Reynolds's ambitious and experimental temperament, and he was able to fuse it with his more instinctive grasp of character and pose to produce portraits that combine intellectual sophistication and spontaneity with extraordinary skill.

The consequence of this marriage of tendencies is that the mood of Reynolds's work is one of judicious poise, of counteractive forces kept in delicate balance. The learning is worn lightly, the playfulness dignified, the intimacy restrained, the formality shot through with a wit based on allusion to the antique, to Raphael and to other great masters. Reynolds is able to present his subject matter complete with its own critical commentary, so that whatever is said is not said, what is not said is implied. The potential for undermining the formulas of conventional portraiture is immense, and Reynolds does it consistently, though of course always with the decorum that preserves respectability – and marketability.

Given the ambiguity of Reynolds's work, it is significant that he attained the position and reputation that he did. The most accomplished of his contemporaries – Ramsay and Gainsborough – never approached him in the deployment of nuance, nor attempted to load their portraits with so many contradictory signals. Yet such is the refinement with which he keeps the elements in balance, there can be no objection, no cry of 'Shocking!' The frivolity of contemporary French art is transmuted into a witty sobriety, and hints of sensuality conveyed with poker-faced dryness. Intellectual respectability is conferred on pretty young women when they are shown to us as the cup-bearer of the gods, as a vestal, or as Grecian damsels decorating a term, and yet their charm is enhanced by the fiction.

Reynolds's programme meant little to Thomas Gainsborough (1727–88). In his view, 'the principal beauty and intention' of portraiture was 'likenesses'. This echoes Reynolds's comment that 'imitating exactly what we see in nature, makes an admirable portrait'. But whereas Reynolds saw the portrait painter's role as involving much more than that, including perhaps the invention of a new 'reality' in which the sitter might acquire a fictitious identity, Gainsborough preferred to impose an interpretation on his subject matter by the use of the brush alone. His compositions are rarely complex, and he does not take a pride, as Reynolds does, in making every portrait different, as if it were the outcome of an elaborate calculation as to the optimum means of conveying the uniqueness of the sitter. For Gainsborough, the individuality of each of his subjects was a fact that could be relied on to provoke the portrait that was required. The simplicity of his purpose is what makes him stand out from his contemporaries. He responded most readily to the physical presence of individual human beings, not as the wearers of splendid or outlandish costume, or the protagonists of some imagined drama. His work succeeds best when it is most direct, and thrives on familiarity. As Roger Fry suggested, 'Gainsborough never tries to be impressive or noble or dramatic; unlike Reynolds, he has no repertory of artistic devices for making a portrait interesting . . . he poses the model in a good light and paints him as he sees him' (Fry, p.57). On this account, he constantly undermines the notion of grandeur in portraiture, and insists that the surface appearance of his subjects is in itself attractive: their facial characteristics, their clothes, their gestures are all subjected not to the flattery of an unctuous manner of painting but to that of an assumption of ease and elegance, taken for granted in his rapid, cheerful handling. The theatrical rhetoric of Reynolds is discarded: in his whole-lengths, Gainsborough presents his sitters conversationally, at eye level, rather than as though seen from below by a humble admirer; the romantic wind that blows hair and horses' manes about Reynolds's pictures is stilled to a calm in Gainsborough's, the fitful stage candles replaced by an even, gentle daylight.

Gainsborough began his career in Suffolk as a painter of small, intimate portraits and conversation pieces. In this latter genre he was a master; its intimacy suited him perfectly, and his later, larger single portraits often present the sitter as though in a conversation-piece. The conversation-piece is perhaps the quintessential eighteenth-century genre; it had been pioneered by Hogarth, and by the 1770s it was in the capable hands of Johan Zoffany (1733–1810), a German from the Rhineland who, like many other foreigners (Van Dyck included), had been able to judge the market perfectly and, thanks to a Continental training, outshine the native practitioners. His refined finish was well suited to the almost miniature medium of small-scale group portraits, though he also applied it on occasion to whole-lengths (no.33). Gainsborough, by contrast, as he moved on from conversation-pieces to full-lengths, broadened his handling until it became impressionistically free, so much so that its character determines the character and mood of his portraits. The literary connotations of Reynolds are replaced in Gainsborough by a poetic sentiment inherent in the very texture of the paint, the 'kind of magick' that, as Reynolds observed (Discourse XIV, Wark, p.258), ensures that the 'chaos' of his brushwork 'at a certain distance, assumes form'. He had worked as a young man in the studio of a Frenchman, Hubert Gravelot (1699–1773), and had there imbibed the spirit of the rococo which remained with him all his life. This was not the academic Parisian art that Reynolds looked at, but the decorative work of book illustrators and ornamental engravers. The light, fresh colouring and gentle rhythms of the rococo give Gainsborough's work its grace and charm; his free and vigorous brushwork its strength and permanence. His great achievement was to combine the evanescent with the permanent, to create monumental images out of flicks of pale paint which remain palpably delicate and indeed transparent on the canvas. The result, in his finest work, is an indefinable poetic quality; the figure seems to be gently enthralled by some highly civilised entertainment, some Vauxhall Gardens of the imagination. As Roger Fry put it, it is 'as though music were going on somewhere' (Fry, p.62).

This potent technical presentation is what enables Gainsborough to dispense with extraneous properties to aid him in the creation of a powerful image. Even Romney, a remarkably unpretentious portrait painter who rarely ventured into rhetoric, was capable of dressing up his subjects as something other than they really were. Gainsborough virtually never does this. He does not seem to wish to infringe Reynolds's prerogative of allegory and personification. Even when he uses the formula of crossed legs for his male portraits, he does not, like Batoni, invoke a pagan god or an ideal of beauty, but simply conveys easy confidence and informality. This is consistent with the English assumption that portraiture should flatter only within the bounds suggested by common sense.

But if he eschewed deliberate 'meaning' in his portraits, Gainsborough's painterly indifference to content may itself be seen as significant in a way that the twentieth century especially can understand. The emancipation of the image from its accustomed framework of allusion and association, the pure aesthetic pleasure of paint applied with virtuoso abandon, imbues the portraits – certainly the later ones – with what has been seen as the quality of abstractions. The portrait of Mr and Mrs Hallett (no.43) is known as 'The Morning Walk' not because Gainsborough called it that, but because it irresistibly projects the mood of its sitters in such a way as to transform it from a mere portrait into an atmospheric landscape with figures. It is a portrait that functions as a 'fancy picture', evoking the pleasures of rustic love and companionship as much for their sentimental charm as for any psychological value they may have in describing the depicted characters. Similarly the portrait of Lady Bate Dudley (fig.15; collection Lord Burton, on loan to the Tate Gallery) hardly goes so far as to present its subject as a melancholy nymph in a woodland glade: it announces no deliberately contrived programme to that effect. The paint itself seems simply to allow a pensive, sylvan atmosphere to permeate the image and imbue it with qualities from a branch of painting quite other than portraiture. In this Gainsborough perhaps reveals his ultimate indifference to portrait painting itself: as he himself admitted, he preferred painting landscapes. But they are not those statements of 'ideas' that recent commentators have looked for. They are purely painterly meditations in which the pigment itself is the principal component.

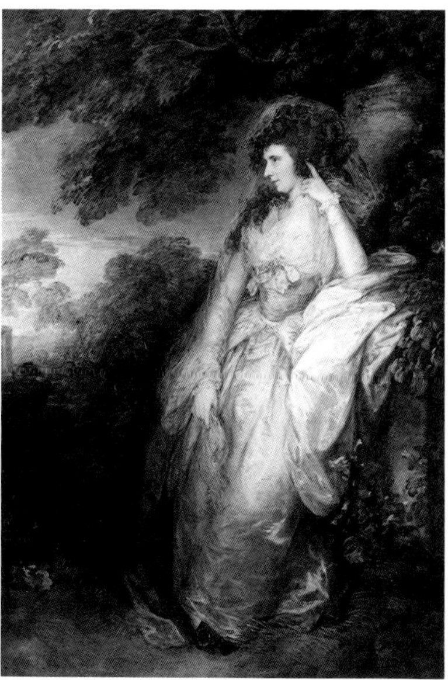

fig.15 Thomas Gainsborough **Lady Bate Dudley** *c.*1787 Oil on canvas *Lord Burton*

In this, Gainsborough is easily related to the Van Dyck tradition of portraiture, in which virtuoso brushwork plays a key role. But whereas Van Dyck, Lawrence or Sargent used brushwork to endorse the status of their sitters by implying glamour and richness, Gainsborough uses it for much more exclusively aesthetic ends. His sitters become ingredients in the mysterious concoctions of his imagination, endowed with glamour not as important personages, but as the subjects of his alchemical creativity.

The generation of British portrait painters that included Ramsay, Reynolds and Gainsborough would be accounted hard to follow at almost any time, but Lawrence effectively outdid them all. He could, if he chose, be more serious than Reynolds, more meltingly seductive than Ramsay, more technically brilliant than Gainsborough. His technical virtuosity also ensured that when he tackled a historical subject he succeeded more decisively than Reynolds had done. Almost his sole, and certainly his most important, exercise in that genre was 'Satan Summoning his Legions', which is couched in the form of a huge dramatic portrait, of the type that he made of the actor John Philip Kemble in the years around 1800 and called 'half-histories'. Kemble was the brother of Mrs Siddons, and in the series of pictures depicting him in different tragic roles (no.52), Lawrence consciously took up the ideas that Reynolds had developed in his portrait of her as the Tragic Muse (no.37).

Psychological power was a principal aim in these theatrical portraits, but it was not only in that context that Lawrence's admirers found this quality. Even though he might be accused of flattery in his likenesses, his purpose was deeper: 'he was always the more intent in shewing "the mind's construction in the face" '(Knowles, I, 333n.). A less indulgent view was taken by Hazlitt, who 'thought L—'s pictures might do very well as mirrors for personal vanity to contemplate itself in (as you looked in the glass to see how you were dressed), but that it was a mistake to suppose they would interest any one else or were addressed to the world at large'. This leads Hazlitt to the somewhat surprising conclusion that Lawrence's portraits 'were private, not public property. They never caught the eye in a shop-window; but were . . . a kind of lithographic painting, or thin, meagre outlines without the depth and richness of the art.' (Hazlitt, p.116).

The charge of superficiality has ofen been raised against Lawrence, but it has usually been admitted that that superficiality served the purpose of making a striking public statement. Hazlitt's criticism seems to go beyond this to the point of denying any merit in his work except to the prejudiced eye of the egregiously flattered sitter. The judgement gives some inkling of the distance that existed between the accepted techniques of portraiture in England and Lawrence's bravura style. Hazlitt is protesting against a showiness that must by its nature be meretricious. This is a good illustration of the innate suspicion of swagger that subsists in England.

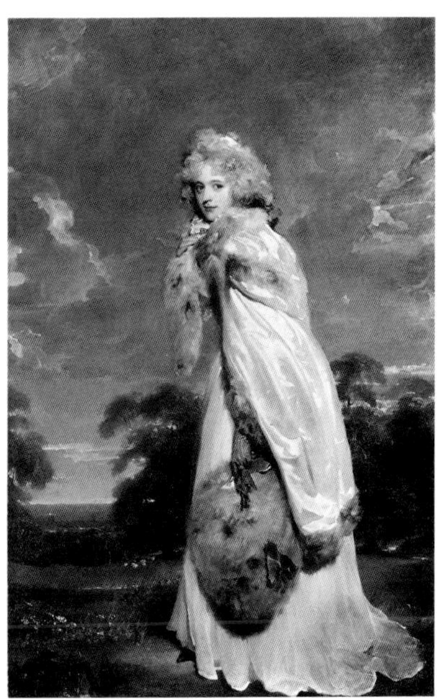
fig.16 Sir Thomas Lawrence **Elizabeth Farren** 1790 Oil on canvas *Metropolitan Museum of Art, Bequest of Edward S. Harkness, 1940*

But Lawrence himself often, and even when working on a large scale, instinctively undercuts or subverts the potential for grandeur in his portraits, offering instead a group of romping parents and children, or an introspective, intimate and ultimately truly private likeness. The large portrait of Queen Charlotte (no.50) illustrates this point supremely well, but so does the equally unexpected portrait of Miss Farren (fig.16; Metropolitan Museum of Art), where a well-known actress and beauty, caught, it seems, entirely unaware as she strolls out-of-doors, turns coyly away from us, pretending to prefer like Greta Garbo not to be noticed. The effect is, of course, to increase the allure of the lady. It can be argued that Lawrence deliberately avoids making a public statement, but a private statement can be used for public purposes, and it is a typically English ploy to do so.

On the large scale, though, Lawrence can be claimed as the sole native portrait painter to have succeeded in producing an equivalent to the Continental grand manner in both style and execution, and that claim is borne out by the acknowledgment he received in Europe. He was, of course, particularly lucky in being on hand to paint the victors of Waterloo, which brought him into contact with a range of important foreign sitters; but it is also true that he was eminently suited to the task of portraying them. He was immediately rewarded with acclaim not only in Europe but in America. He was the first British portrait painter to reach a wide international audience; significantly, perhaps, he was also the first British artist ever to paint a portrait of the Pope (fig.17).

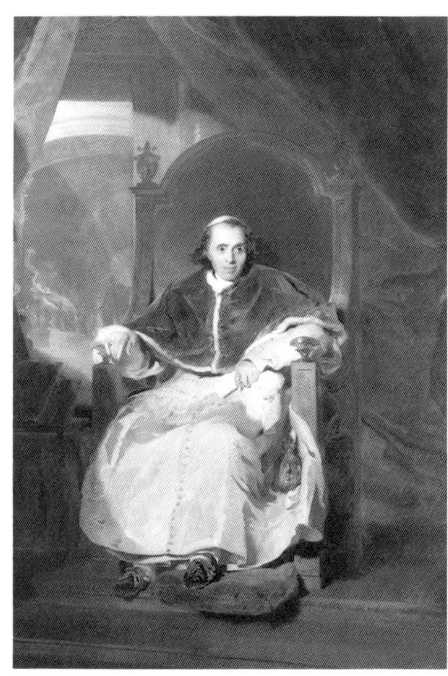

fig.17 Sir Thomas Lawrence **Pope Pius VII** 1819 Oil on canvas *Her Majesty The Queen*

If there was something European about Lawrence's technical accomplishment, he worked nonetheless in a very English way. His use of paint is founded on a strong sense of its tactile qualities – a sense that goes back through Reynolds and Hogarth to Dobson. This Englishness of touch is combined with a more Continental crispness and clarity of definition to act as an almost physical presentation of the object depicted rather than as an irrelevant film through which that object is perceived. The brilliancy of Lawrence's white highlights has always been admired, though it is precisely such details that provoke the judgement of superficiality. Anything that tends to vivid glamour is condemned as vulgar. Because he was specially adept at recreating on canvas the charms of young women, this dangerous power was questioned and denigrated. Even today Lawrence's position as possibly the most remarkable of all English portrait painters remains controversial.

These technical qualities take the place of the complexity of thought that Reynolds brought to portraiture. Lawrence approaches his subject matter more directly than Reynolds, but he does so nonetheless with great inventive ingenuity. His compositions are frequently original and unexpected, and even the simplest of his designs is enhanced by a sensitive use of tone. He was a member of the first generation of portait painters who were compelled by fashion to devote a large part of their output to gentlemen in plain black coats – the onset of nineteenth-century imperial responsibility went together with sobriety of dress. (One might compare Dutch seventeenth-century costume at the time of the mercantile supremacy of Holland.) In the hands of many painters the black coat was an insuperable problem, a sure recipe for monotony. Lawrence delighted in it. He revelled in the deep unmodulated blacks and the sharp white or cream of well-laundered collars and cravats. The sartorial austerities of dandyism were a source of inspiration, and some of his most memorable images are those in which his sense of composition has been stimulated by cleanly pressed lines and strongly starched contrasts of tone.

Not that he was indifferent to colour. In his historical subjects – including the theatrical 'half-histories' – Lawrence favoured the rich dark chiaroscuro, the 'historical colour', that Reynolds advocated for the most serious kinds of subject matter. In most of the portraits, however, and especially in the full-lengths, colour is often vivid, almost garish. The contrast indicates very accurately the perceived difference in function between portraiture and historical painting at the time. It has been said that Lawrence's sense of colour was unsubtle; that he relied too heavily on saturated reds and greens, on tawdry blues and golds. If so, that is partly what makes him so effective as a public painter. The bright trappings of public ceremonial create their own palette, entirely appropriate to the state portrait. The same dignity can be captured for lesser sitters by transference of colour from these grand contexts. But if the colours are brilliant, their deployment is not crude. Lawrence was not afraid of opulence, but he often allows his figures, in their black coats and white dresses, to provide a cool foil for backgrounds of reverberant primary colour.

Some of the backgrounds take the form of landscape, and these too are emotive. At first glance they are much like the landscapes that figure in nearly all late eighteenth-century portraiture, and no doubt they were sometimes put in by assistants; but Lawrence was interested in scenery as a subject for painting in its own right, and his preoccupations frequently appear in the glimpses of nature that we find in his best portraits. Two romantic woodland scenes by him (private collection) convey a highly charged emotion that we might expect from Constable. The flickering paint, the sharp white lights, the rich green foliage and glimpses of bright blue sky have an almost Expressionist force. Introduced into the background of a portrait, such as that of Lady Manners (no.51), a landscape of this sort introduces a dimension of feeling that raises the work as a whole to an intenser level of Romantic expression. It is used to even more dramatic purpose in portraits of soldiers, where Lawrence takes up the imagery of battle and storm bequeathed by Reynolds and infuses it with a new passion.

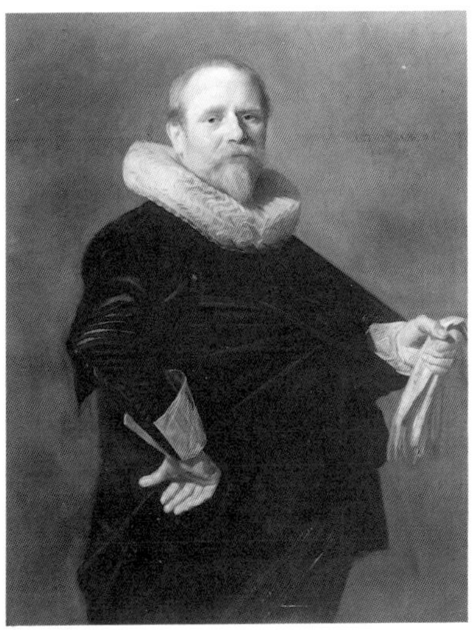

fig.18 Frans Hals **Portrait of a Man** 1630 Oil on canvas *Her Majesty The Queen*

Some of the same Romantic preoccupations distinguish the work of Sir Henry Raeburn (1756–1823), who was also painter to a generation of black-coated administrators, and the possessor of a broad, incisive technique. It is usual to class Raeburn with George Romney (1734–1802) and John Hoppner (1758–1810) among the followers of Reynolds, and to think of him as bringing eighteenth-century portraiture to a kind of plateau from which Lawrence, with his virtuoso artistry, took off into the Romantic empyrean. He has recently been presented as the exemplar of a pragmatic Scots approach to painting which makes him the perfect illustrator of the down-to-earth society that flourished in the 'Athens of the North'. If he has been compared with Frans Hals (1584–1666), he is, as much as Hals, the painter of a decidedly Protestant community, and his bravura is always subordinate to a strict sense of the seriousness of life. Like Hals (fig.18) – or, for that matter, Rembrandt – he preferred to concentrate on the inner qualities of human personality, rather than on outer forms. He rarely presents his female sitters as 'beauties' in the sense that Reynolds, Gainsborough and Romney had done. He is the archetype of the reliable bourgeois portrait painter, whose work can always be recognised for its solidity of construction and sobriety of presentation.

Yet this view of him does not give proper emphasis to the astonishing breadth and sheer daring of his handling of paint which is what prompts the comparison with Hals. And when we consider Raeburn's technique, we have to recognise that his vision was of an order rather less mundane than at first sight appears. The man who could evolve so telling and so vivid a shorthand with which to register the visible world was capable of imaginative leaps of an impressive kind – leaps not simply from reality to representation, but from the complexity of perceived form to a finely judged and essentially abstract deployment of exciting pigment. The contradiction between the sobriety of the image and the sensuousness of the materials is a characteristically Scottish achievement (paralleled perhaps in some Spanish painting). The portrait of Spencer, Marquess of Northampton (no.48) illustrates this. It is, on one level, exceptionally plain and understated, using a simple pose and subdued colour. But its very simplicity seems to infuse it with an electric charge, and the assurance of both sitter and artist endows the image with a smouldering glamour. This is not, of course, the ebullient swagger of the Flemish or French tradition, though there are perhaps parallels to be drawn with the brooding portraits of Pierre-Paul Prudhon (1760–1823).

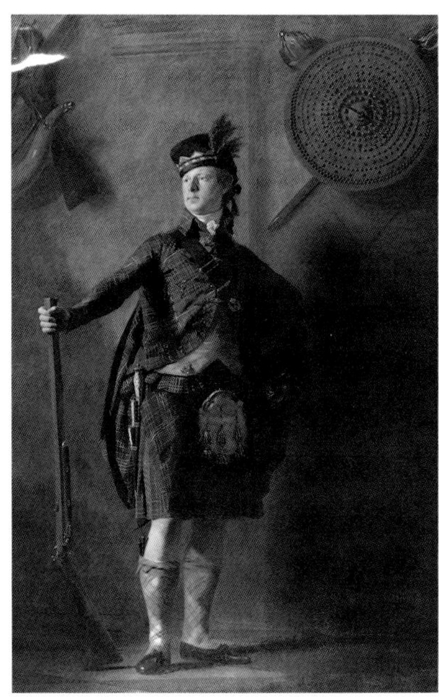

fig.19 Sir Henry Raeburn **Colonel Macdonell of Glengarry** 1812 Oil on canvas *National Gallery of Scotland*

If such a comparison seems far-fetched, it is not inconsistent with the tone of much of Raeburn's work. His range as an artist was put to the test when he painted portraits of Highland chiefs, like that of Sir John Sinclair (no.46). Many of these were men of confirmed eccentricity, lords of remote clans with a long tradition of independence and determination. They often had strongly Jacobite and Roman Catholic leanings, and were very different in temperament from the dwellers in the Protestant Lowlands. Since the seventeenth century they had often chosen to be painted wearing plaids, and Raeburn responded with gusto to the challenge that this set him. His enormous picture of Colonel Alastair Macdonell of Glengarry (fig.19; National Gallery of Scotland) characteristically takes a very low viewpoint in order to present the figure as dramatically as possible – a device conspicuous in Lawrence's theatrical portraits.

Indeed, the coincidence of Lawrence's unavoidable presence as a rival portrait painter may have been partly responsible for putting Raeburn so much on his mettle. If Lawrence was uniquely disposed by temperament to paint swagger portraits, Raeburn's capacity to handle paint led him, too, naturally towards bold and striking effects. The key to his use of paint is his use of light, which tends always to simplify the image by increasing contrasts between highlights and shadows, allowing him to choose very precisely which areas of the image are to be given prominence. These are scattered as touches often of pure white pigment across a dark background which then becomes the space in which the sitter is placed, the shadows that envelop form and imply gesture and expression. In all this he is unlike Lawrence, whose white highlights illuminate the whole canvas rather than shining out from a mass of shadow.

Raeburn was also unlike Lawrence in the matter of landscape backgrounds. When told by Sir Walter Scott that Lawrence employed a painter to add these (though he certainly often executed them himself), Raeburn responded: 'Of that I do not approve. Landscape in the background of a portrait ought to be nothing more than the shadow of a landscape; effect is all that is wanted. Nothing ought to divert the eye from the principal object – the face' (Pinnington, pp.137–8).

This singleness of purpose, this focusing only on essentials, is what gives Raeburn's portraits their exceptional concentration, and explains his repeated use of elliptical and heavily cropped compositions. This is well illustrated in another portrait with a low viewpoint, that of Sir William Maxwell of Calderwood (no.47), which has an unusually narrow format, squeezing man and horse into a towering vertical structure that looms over us with the maximum grandeur. The design is neo-classical in its simplicity and power. This is no flamboyant Highlander, but a military man portrayed as responsible and serious, if kindly. In works of this kind Raeburn makes a claim for the inherent grandeur of rational man, arguing, or rather seeking to demonstrate by optical means, that the glories of human achievement require no gaudy trappings to persuade us of their importance. It is a supreme statement of the rationalist Protestant ethic, and should perhaps be regarded as the focal point of this survey: a moment, not when a British artist succeeds in emulating the Europeans, but when true northern pragmatism and avoidance of show find their natural expression in a dignified and self-sufficient image of real rhetorical force and contained energy.

The Final Phase

The achievements of Lawrence and Raeburn were then in a sense opposite: Lawrence summarised the tradition that stretched back to Van Dyck from Gainsborough and Reynolds and brought it to a triumphant culmination; Raeburn, building on the same foundations but with a stronger admixture of the Dutch style, produced an art that was in essence far more radical. He was, as it were, the Sir John Soane of the portrait painters, an innovator who was prepared to discard much of the superfluous vocabulary of contemporary portraiture in favour a new, more purposeful austerity and directness of utterance. In doing so, he created a language that might have remained current for the rest of the century. Lawrence's legacy was a formula for grand manner portraits that was taken up by several generations of official painters – Sir Martin Archer Shee, Sir George Hayter and Sir Francis Grant all relied heavily on his example, and throughout the 1830s, 40s and 50s we watch the brio that was Lawrence's distinguishing characteristic gradually fade out of portraiture, much as Van Dyck's quality was slowly lost in the later seventeenth century. With all these artists, energetic execution is not supported by a technique sure enough to carry off the most splendid effects. The enthusiam for display that had been fostered by George IV's narcissism dwindled in the reign of William IV and when an interest in the arts revived after Prince Albert's arrival in 1840 the transformation into a bourgeois culture heralded by the Reform Act of 1832 had already, with remarkable rapidity, come about. Portraiture was either a matter of tired state convention, or it passed into the hands of a very earnest middle class.

Here it might quite meaningfully have taken up the precedent supplied by Raeburn, who had almost reinvented the portrait as a bourgeois object. The sober-suited gentlemen of High Victorian administration, and their busy, charitable wives needed just such a medium to relay their particular dignity to the world. G.F. Watts addressed himself to this class of portraiture, among many other activities, but he was ambitious. Painting for him was defined by the achievements of the Venetian and Florentine Renaissance, and his models in portraiture were Titian and Tintoretto, not Reynolds and Raeburn. The High Renaissance was thought a fitting analogue of the glories of modern Britain, and much of the official art of the period alludes to it. This was a taste that ran

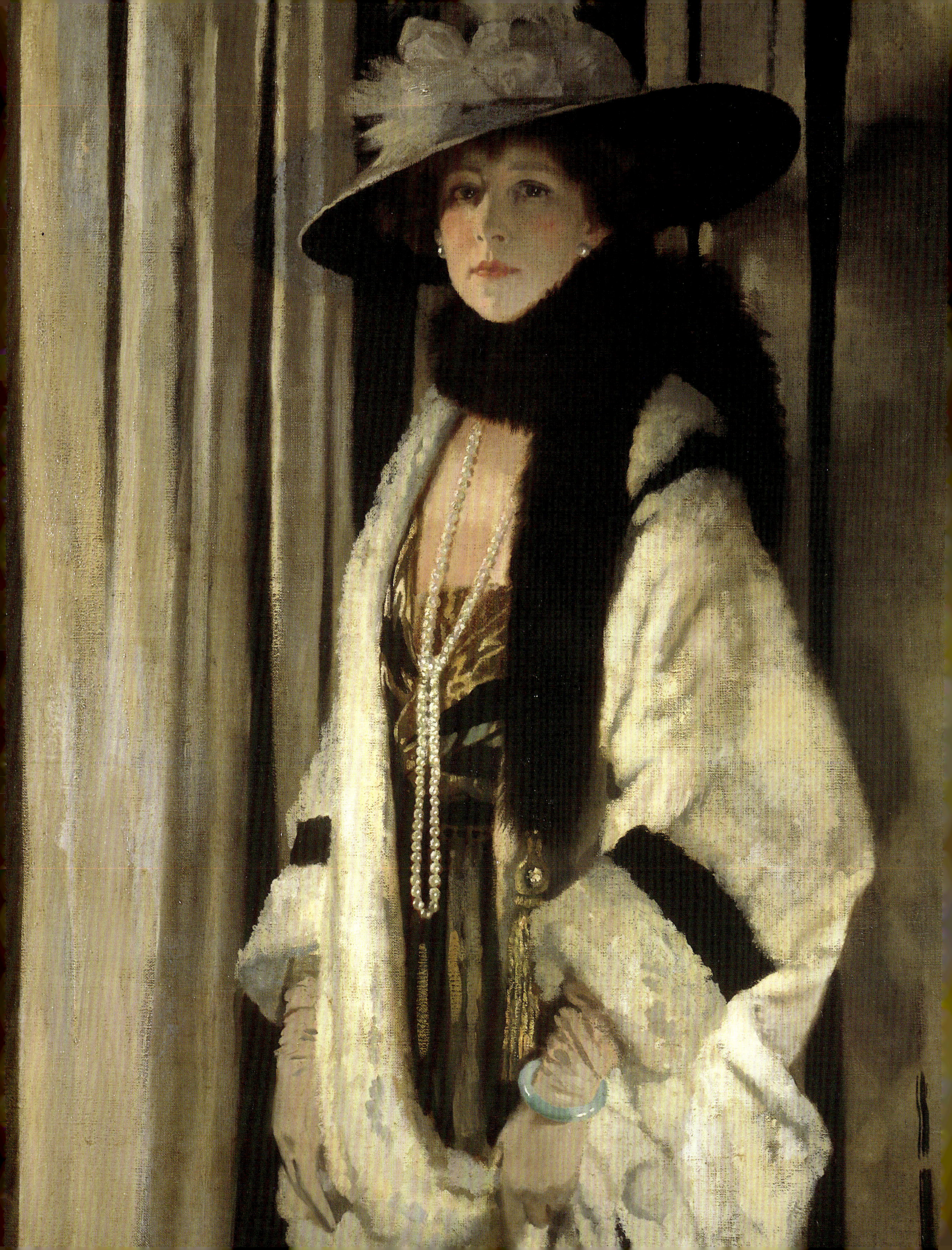

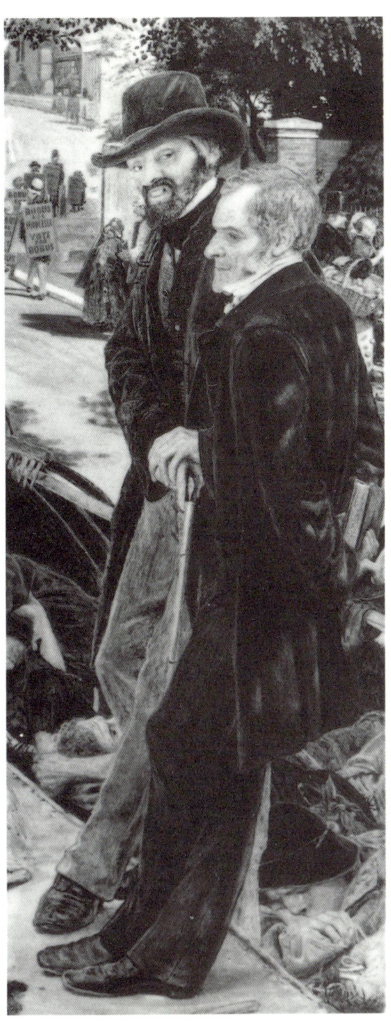

fig.20 Ford Madox Brown **Work** 1863 (detail) Oil on canvas *Birmingham Museums and Art Gallery*

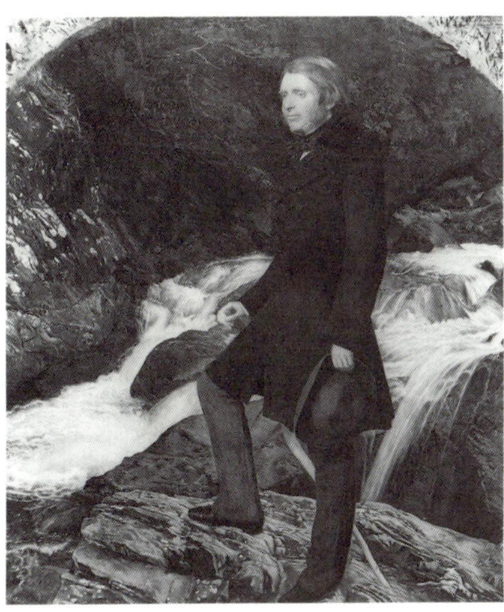

fig.21 Sir John Everett Millais **John Ruskin** 1853–4 Oil on canvas *Private Collection*

Sir William Orpen **Mrs St George** (detail, no.73)

counter to current fashion, which had for some years been strongly influenced by the medievalising art of contemporary Germany. The Queen was in love with Prince Albert, and the royal favour fell for a time under the spell of German Romanticism. Victoria plumped for Franz Xaver Winterhalter, trained in Munich and in the early 1840s a fashionable portrait painter in several European courts. He was producing a type of portrait that was in its way the antithesis of Raeburn's. For all the Germanic seriousness that settled on Windsor, Winterhalter was not an overwhelmingly serious artist, but he was adept at suggesting the glamour of his subjects and so proclaims once more the advantages of a Catholic-dominated training. Technically, he displayed all the refinement and polish of a Batoni, and it was this – though not any echo of Batoni's actual portrait types – that appealed to the finish-loving Victoria. Winterhalter was the equivalent in portraiture to Edwin Landseer (1803–73) in the portrayal of animals. But whereas Landseer appealed to a wide Victorian audience, Winterhalter aroused the innate English suspicion of glamour in human beings and was not extensively admired outside the court. His 'sensual and fleshy visions' as the *Athenaeum* revealingly put it, could not but disturb the prevailing sense of propriety. Yet ironically, Winterhalter's work was ultimately Biedermeier in its terms of reference: neat, precise, glossy, with a bourgeois fear of generalisation and a love of flashy detail, especially in the matter of clothes. He could instinctively endow even the most businesslike of pictures with an impressive panache, as his portrait of Prince Albert shows (no.59). A taste for minuteness of finish was disseminated throughout the country, partly by means of Albert's Great Exhibition of 1851, and partly through an enthusiasm, in which the Consort was a pioneer, for Italian and German primitive art which set new standards of miniature precision and delicacy, both of technique and content. It was from this soil that Pre-Raphaelitism grew.

Millais, one of the founders of the Pre-Raphaelite Brotherhood in 1848, was never meant to paint the splendours of the aristocratic way of life. As a Pre-Raphaelite he was committed from his youth to a truly Germanic earnestness of approach to subject matter which took for its predominant concern the visual and emotional experience of ordinary people. The portrait paintings of the Pre-Raphaelites are generally of friends, and usually executed on a small scale, however much detail is crammed in. There is often a lot, for the purpose of most of these portraits was to record as much as possible about their subjects: their appearance, tastes, affections and family attachments. This idea was extended so that the portrait ceased to be the dominant motif of the work. Ideally, portraiture was simply a part of the process of making a record of the world. Ford Madox Brown (1821–93), in his great document of modern London, 'Work' (fig.20; Birmingham City Museums and Art Gallery), incorporated portraits of John Stuart Mill and Thomas Carlyle for which he called in the aid of the camera (Maas, p.198). When Millais painted Ruskin (fig.21; private collection), he showed him on a rock beside the river at Glenfinlas, surrounded by the geology and flora that Ruskin loved to study, exemplifying in his very execution of these details the minute and scrupulous investigation that Ruskin himself advocated. The portraiture of the evangelising and prophetic mid-nineteenth century is steeped in ideas, ideals and enthusiasms, and every part of each picture reflects the buzzing exploratory activity of the epoch.

Millais severed his ties with Pre-Raphaelitism in the 1860s, and it was into just such a serious, responsible portraiture that his earlier work naturally transformed itself. His intense searching concern for detail melted into a broad interest in texture and effect; he remained among the most technically accomplished painters of his time, but translated that accomplishment into an idiom much closer to the traditional English portrait style: impasted, vigorous and much preoccupied with the rendering of flesh, hair and the differing textures of fabrics. Immediately historical influences begin to be felt: Titian, Van Dyck, Hals and, especially, Velásquez, who had been rediscovered by David Wilkie (1785–1841) and others visiting Spain in the early part of the century, and who was to exert a vital influence on the tradition of grand portraiture until its effective demise in the 1920s. (Though influences of this kind cannot be said to cease; they continue in other forms. Velásquez is still a model for portrait painters today.) The British portrait painters of the late eighteenth century enjoyed a revival, both on the market and as an influence on a new generation of artists. The dormant spirit of Raeburn in particular could now effectively return to British portraiture, and for the next six decades his work was to enjoy unparalleled popularity among collectors, and be a significant stimulus to many painters.

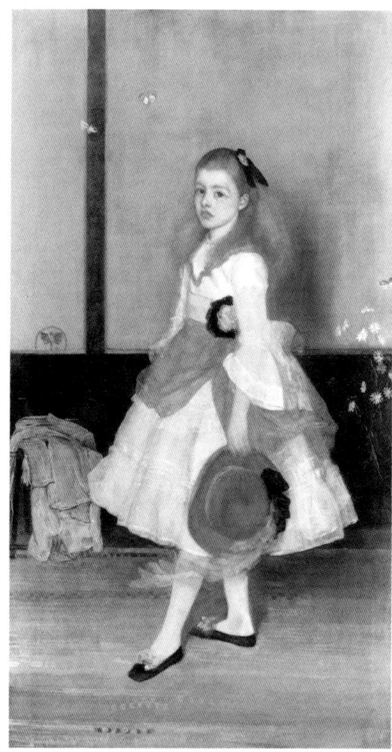

fig.22 James Abbott McNeill Whistler **Miss Cecily Alexander: Harmony in Grey and Green** 1872 Oil on canvas *Tate Gallery*

If the full impact of Raeburn's art was deflected by the tastes of Prince Albert's generation, he should perhaps nevertheless be included among the influences on James Abbott McNeill Whistler (1834–1903), an American of Scottish ancestry whose work is also spare and restrained, and who was to make his mark in England with two particularly dour portraits, of his mother (Paris, Musée d'Orsay) and of that earnest Scot, Thomas Carlyle (Glasgow, City Art Galleries). Whistler had spent much of his early career in France, and his reverence for Velásquez has to be traced through the more recent influence of Edouard Manet (1832–83), whose 'Lola de Valencia' (Paris, Musée d'Orsay) provided the pose for Whistler's 'Miss Cicely Alexander: Harmony in Grey and Green' (fig.22; Tate Gallery). Like Whistler, Manet was much impressed by Japanese woodcuts and it is impossible to understand the next phase in the history of the swagger portrait if this unlikely source of ideas is not borne in mind. The bold simplifications of structure and outline, the subtle orchestration of colour, which Japanese woodcuts were revealing to the Western world for the first time, could be used to great effect in the evolution of grand portrait compositions (fig.23). The Orient seemed to supply the hint that was needed to make new sense of tired art-forms. Whistler himself was highly sophisticated in his manipulation of these hints, but many other artists made some use of them in one way or another. The vision of several early twentieth-century painters was radically affected by his example; Orpen's 'Mrs St George' (no.73) and Lavery's 'Hazel in Black and Gold' (no.75) are unimaginable without him.

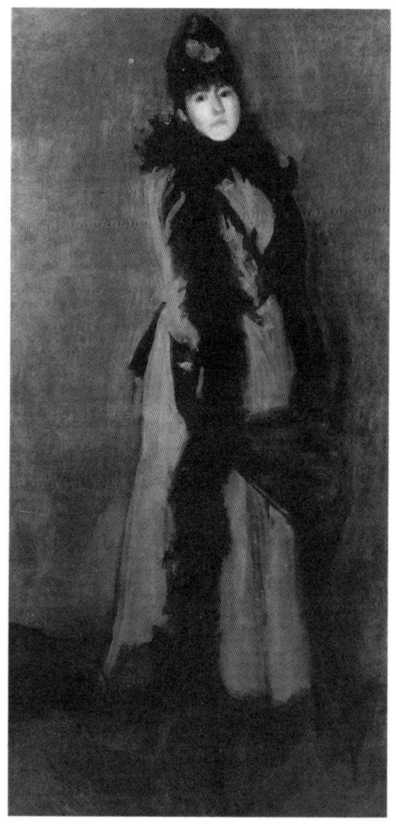

fig.23 James Abbott McNeill Whistler **Red and Black: The Fan** *c.*1890 Oil on canvas *Hunterian Art Gallery, University of Glasgow*

These pictures are essays in a self-conscious aestheticism which had already been modified by compromise with the mainstream of traditional portrait painting. Their hold on the grand tradition is partly owing to the survival of the economic patterns that had always facilitated the portraiture of display. The rich still lived in houses large enough to require big pictures, and portraits were, as ever, the most satisfactory way of impressing oneself and the world with one's status. It is also partly owing to the relative independence of the twentieth-century artist. The students at the Slade School in Bloomsbury – among whom were William Orpen (1878–1931) and Augustus John (1878–1961) – were a more bohemian generation than their Victorian predecessors, and were as likely to make a portrait an excuse for fantasy as to respond in a businesslike way to a bona fide commission. Lavery's portraits of his wife are Whistlerian studies before they are likenesses; John's 'William Nicholson' (no.76) takes its cue directly from Whistler.

If Whistler's message was heeded by more than a few of the later nineteenth-century portraitists it was because the style was easily applicable to the austerities of traditional English (and especially Scottish) portrait painting. Most artists continued to paint men in sober suits and women in pretty dresses, often accompanied by arrangements of flowers which recreated colour schemes that are at least nominally 'aesthetic'; but their sense of design is by no means the stringent and taut affair that Whistler would have had it, and their intention is nearly always palpably to produce a charming likeness and not an original work of art. One man, at least, knew how to graft Whistler's lessons on to the European tradition and he did so smoothly and effectively. Like Whistler, John Singer Sargent was an American; but he had been born in Florence and trained in Paris, and so had the classic cultural background for a society portrait painter.

Many people still wished for a portraiture that proclaimed itself a part of the Van Dyck tradition. Sargent's achievement was to paint pictures that managed to evoke the atmosphere of Van Dyck, but did so without in any way copying him. As was almost inevitable in the late nineteenth century the great influences on his virtuoso technique were Velásquez and Manet, a lineage beautifully illustrated by the picture he painted (at his own suggestion) of W. Graham Robertson (no.66). His style, which involved presenting sitters as haughty and self-consciously grand, linked him to a sentimental idea of the royal portrait as Van Dyck had painted it. But if his appeal to Van Dyck was in a sense spurious, so his appeal to the English was qualified. His work was greeted with suspicion in some quarters, and a large proportion of his most appreciative sitters were not British but Americans and middle-European immigrants. They were not the middle-class and very private English men, women and children who had been painted by the Pre-Raphaelites. All were rich and Sargent made a point of emphasising the fact.

In this he betrays a fundamental difference in the social structures of his day from those of Lawrence's or Van Dyck's. His patrons' wealth is, as it were, built into the aesthetic of the picture. Yet it is all done with the greatest decorum. There are few properties in these pictures to tell us about the interests or possessions of their subjects. This is a subtle new development of the time-honoured systems of indicating status. Dobson's piles of accessories would be considered vulgar; Reynolds's elaborate role-playing embarrassing and unnecessary. There is simply the figure, or group of figures, staring solemnly out of a flickering interior, a small, almost claustrophobic space which is only large by implication – like the aristocracy of the sitters themselves – in which precious things are vaguely sensed glimmering. Clothes are usually expensive and immaculate; but as the tightly draped overcoat in the Robertson portrait goes to show, Sargent could make something out of almost any garment, and did not need high fashion to aid him. He had an infallible sense of style.

At the height of his career, in the 1880s and 1890s, his British manner is inescapable, stamping itself on one splendid portrait after another with an assured, elegant handwriting entirely his own. The effortless aristocracy of the resulting likeness is in a sense a caricature of Van Dyck: his sleek pale hands are elongated still further and still more pallid; the calm, superior faces acquire still more patrician expressions, and the slender bodies are stretched to an almost Mannerist extent. All these features would be unusual in the work of English-trained artists of the period. The Italian Giovanni Boldini (1842–1931) shows the same tendency; but his extreme distortions go to show how subtly, by contrast, Sargent balanced exaggeration with credibility (no.72).

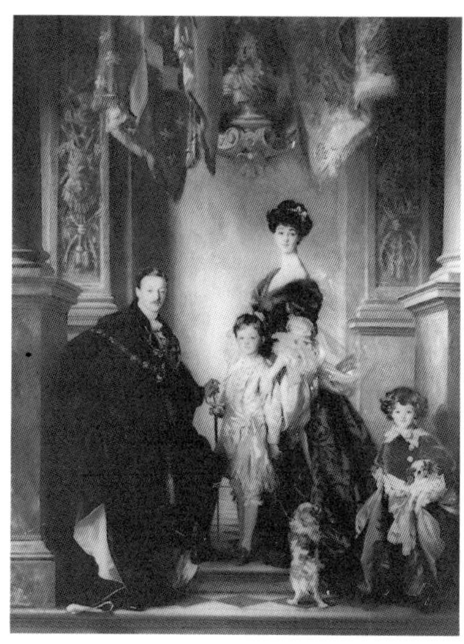

fig.24 John Singer Sargent **The Marlborough Family** 1905 Oil on canvas *Duke of Marlborough, Blenheim Palace*

Sargent's effortlessness was, almost inevitably, facile, and this quality irritated many people, and especially, in the later part of his career, the avant garde – Roger Fry, who admired Lawrence, found Sargent's brilliant handling difficult to take; but it was precisely what was required by the slightly less than aristocratic patrons who made up much of his sitters' list. Osbert Sitwell may have muttered resentful comments about 'the sly hordes from the Orient' who figure in so many Sargents; but Asher Wertheimer, about whom Sitwell was gratuitously rude, was a dealer in Old Masters who understandably wished to have himself and his family immortalised as Van Dyck or Gainsborough might have done it. His consistent patronage was a connoisseur's recognition of the skill with which Sargent adapted the tradition. There is something completely apropos about Sargent's portraits of the *nouveaux riches*. If they were anxious to seem grander than they were, he was practising an art that seemed grander than it was. It was brilliant and stylish but too dependent on surface. The clever characterisations are fashionable masks, the confections of wealth and success. For all their spontaneous verve, these pictures have no room for unselfconscious humour. This limitation has been well summed up in a comparison between Sargent's enormous canvas of the family of the Duke of Marlborough and its prototype by Reynolds (figs.24–5; both at Blenheim): 'in the Reynolds portrait, one daughter is shown frightening another with a mask, while two of the older children gaze at their eldest sister with expressions of rapt attention. Sargent's figures are stiffly and self-evidently posed . . . One false gesture, and the whole illusion would collapse' (Ormond 1970, p.65). The artist feels and records, unconsciously, the impending annihilation of the tradition of painting to which he belongs and the civilisation it had depended upon.

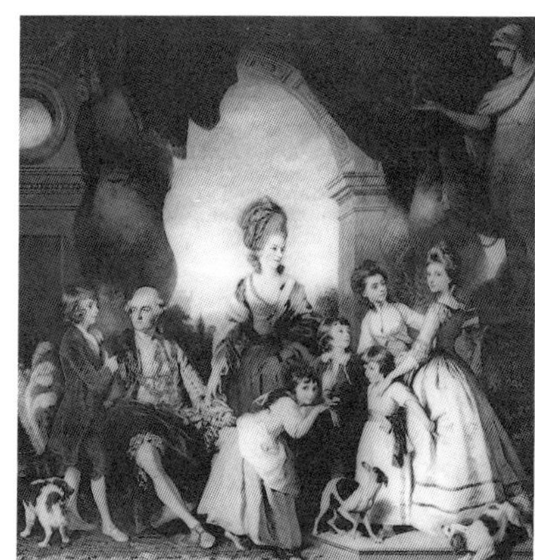

fig.25 Sir Joshua Reynolds **The Family of the 4th Duke of Marlborough** 1777–8 Oil on canvas *Duke of Marlborough, Blenheim Palace*

There were those, like Sickert, who perceived the weakness and judged accordingly. 'Tintoretto created jewels of painting from the most ordinary subjects: Sargent ordinary paintings from the most jewelled subjects' (Emmons, p.173). But although his procedures were often regarded as suspect, and despite the facts of his birth and training, Sargent was long before his death adopted as an Englishman. 'British art can hold its own *contra mundum*', *The Year's Art* said when the Wertheimer portraits were given to the nation in 1922. In that too Sargent willy-nilly followed the example of Van Dyck. And like Van Dyck he was succeeded by a line of imitators in whom the flame burned ever more feebly; but one more foreigner was to achieve success in precisely the same way as Sargent before the tradition finally burnt itself out. This was the Hungarian-born Philip de Laszló, (1869–1937) who after wide experience in many European capitals painted a portrait of Queen Victoria in 1900 and settled in England in 1908.

De Laszló's fluency of handling and easy command of the rhetoric of grand portraiture announced him as heir to the great European tradition. In keeping with that broad historical view, his own statements about portrait painting have a classic ring to them:

> confidence and sympathy between the artist and his sitter are essential, because the truly great portrait is the one in which this contact has been so close that it has spurred the artist to his highest achievement . . . The artist, it is true, can only record what he sees, but when the opportunity is afforded him to look into the mind and soul of his subject he can, if he is equal to his task, produce a portrait in which everyone will be able not only to recognise the physical features of the sitter, but to perceive also the deeper-lying qualities by which he is distinguished.'
>
> (de Laszló, p.44)

This seems to echo Reynolds's comments on 'exact imitation' and Gainsborough's concern for 'likenesses'. Like those remarks, it belies the appeal to a long tradition of grand portraiture that is inherent in the artist's style. The details of presentation that were so important for earlier painters – the cherubs of Van Dyck or Huysmans, the clouds and eagles of Reynolds or Lawrence – are irrelevant: the painter's task is to express character – 'the mind's construction in the face' as Fuseli recognised, but no more: there is no room for grand painting as Reynolds understood it. When we examine the methods used by de Laszló in constructing his portraits we see that this inference is borne out. The gradual elimination of context, of background, that can be traced from Raeburn onwards is carried still further in his work. The swirl of sombre, shadowy paint takes the place of battle-smoke or Parnassian clouds: the portrait, however grand in conception, is a study in character and expression and there it ends. Its ancillary function, to create miniature worlds in which the sitters can live out lives of imaginary perfection, has lost its validity. As a result, the undeniable superiority that de Laszló gives to his sitters seems to have been achieved by sleight of hand: by a cunning distortion of likeness, and by the application of paint alone, which often flirts with the idea of the unfinished sketch or study – a token of the influence of Impressionism on even the most conservative taste.

To judge the conservatism of de Laszló's style it is not necessary to compare him with the contemporary avant-garde; that would be inappropriate. Augustus John, his junior by nine years, was almost as prolific and innately perhaps more accomplished, but he was by temperament a non-conformist whose style reflects an undisciplined love of experiment and a refusal to be bound by social requirements. His portraits, as a result, are unpredictable, but tend to the impromptu, the intimate. His sense of the spirit of his own times was more acute than de Laszló's and he never became the painter of swagger portraits that he would almost certainly have been in an earlier age. His instinct was all for bravura and theatricality, and he was capable of the boldest effects: witness his splendid essay on the theme provided by Madame Suggia (no.77) – an essentially Whistlerian exercise in painting for painting's sake, in which the element of portraiture is merely a starting-point for a sumptuous invention. But the exigencies of twentieth-century life ensured that this ebullience was confined for the most part to small-scale portraits that employ a free technique much as Gainsborough did, to reinforce a sense of informality rather than to evoke grandeur. When working to order on large-scale public commissions he again recalls Gainsborough in being, on the whole, dutiful rather than inspired. The artist's attitude to authority reveals itself in awkwardness and embarrassment.

It took the conformism of de Laszló to produce a large-scale portrait of public import that could hold its own as a work of art in the old-fashioned way. The culminating irony of this survey is that it should end with the portrait of an Anglican Archbishop, the only ecclesiastical portrait to be included here. This is de Laszló's large picture of Archbishop Randall Davidson enthroned (no.79), which is, even by this artist's standards, an exceptionally grand work. Given the observations we have already made about the Protestant mentality we should not expect to find anything like it. Even Van Dyck could not make a truly swagger portrait out of Archbishop Laud (fig.26; Fitzwilliam Museum) although Laud was of all post-Reformation Archbishops of Canterbury the closest to Rome. As John Ingamells has observed, 'There is no Protestant equivalent to those splendid Papal portraits of Titian, Bernini, and Velásquez,' and he goes on to point out that the great exception to this generalisation is Lawrence's portrait of Pope Pius VII (collection Her Majesty The Queen) – which is exactly what we should expect, given that Lawrence was the most instinctively swagger of English painters, and that his subject was not a Protestant. Ingamells suggests that 'the dependent and introverted role of the English Bishops' has been largely to blame for the lack. He notes that 'when our greatest exponents emerged, Reynolds and Gainsborough painted only ten Bishops amongst some fifteen hundred sitters' (Ingamells, p.1). In the 1920s, however, the Church of England commissioned several portraits from de Laszló, and one of Davidson's successor, Cosmo Gordon Lang, in 1932. De Laszló had gone further in breaking down the distinctions of type that so many artists like him had tended to conform to. This is not to say that his manner of painting was more 'democratic'; on the contrary, he maintained the 'grand manner' to the end – it was Augustus John who translated the genre into a more demotic language. De Laszló marks the final adoption of the aristocratic style as a univerally acceptable language of portraiture – kings and clergymen, duchesses and departmental secretaries all get the same highly effective treatment, are all endowed with that suave glistening sophistication of pose and surface that is so characteristic of de Lazsló. The longstanding distinction between civic merit and social glamour which had obtained in formal portraiture since Van Dyck is now abolished – at the precise moment when the genre falls into desuetude, to be replaced by the various informal portraitures of modern times.

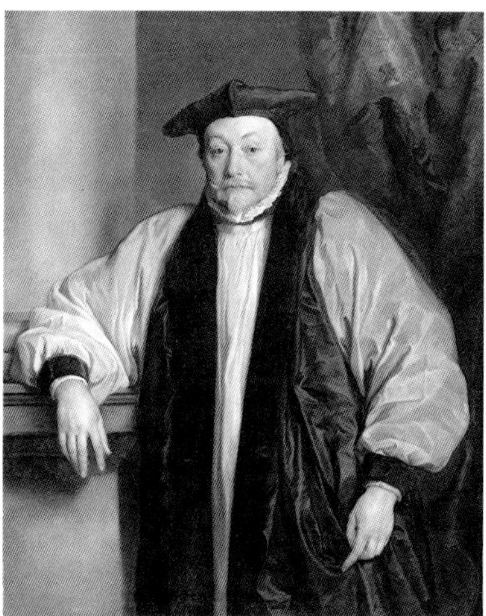

fig.26 Sir Anthony Van Dyck
Archbishop Laud *c.*1633 Oil on canvas
Fitzwilliam Museum, Cambridge

Catalogue

Works are catalogued in chronological order under artists, who are listed approximately chronologically.

Measurements are given in centimetres, followed by inches in brackets; height before width.

Exhibition history (when appropriate) is confined to the first occasion on which the picture was shown at the Royal Academy, with catalogue number. Other early exhibitions are mentioned if significant.

For books to which abbreviated reference is made in the text, see the Bibliography.

1 Queen Henrietta Maria and her Dwarf Sir Jeffrey Hudson *c.*1633

Oil on canvas 228.6 × 129 (90 × 51)
Inscr. lower left (not by the artist): *Henriette Mary Queen of England Wife to King Charles the First*
The Trustees of the Rt Hon. Olive, Countess Fitzwilliam's Chattels Settlement, by permission of Lady Juliet de Chair

A version of the picture now in the National Gallery of Art, Washington D.C., this was formerly considered to be the original; it was painted for Charles I who paid £40 for it and presented it to the Earl of Strafford (see no.3) in 1633. As a work executed for the King the canvas is a notably fine studio replica, probably largely touched by Van Dyck himself. With its rich colour and sumptuous accessories it approaches more closely than most English Van Dycks to the spirit of his Genoese work, while the presence of the dwarf inevitably suggests comparisons with Velásquez, although there is no likelihood of Van Dyck's having had Velásquez in mind. The dwarf was a particular favourite of the Queen's. When fully grown he measured three feet nine inches, and he had first been introduced to her when he was served up in a pie at a banquet given by the Duke of Buckingham, who then employed him. He was himself a Roman Catholic, and Henrietta Maria found him highly congenial company. She took him with her wherever she went, commissioning several portraits of herself with him. It has been suggested that this was because she considered him a suitable and flattering foil, since she herself was short of stature. Certainly the combination of the two is piquant, and is enhanced by exotic details like the orange tree and the monkey. These, however, have a more direct bearing on the subject matter of the picture. The Queen was 'a great wit and beauty', according to a contemporary, and, following the example of her brother-in-law Prince Henry and his mother Anne of Denmark, she encouraged an enthusiasm for Italian gardens in England. The oranges do duty for the many Mediterranean plants she imported, and also compliment her on her chastity and constancy, which virtues they symbolise. The monkey, on the other hand, carries a symbolism reminiscent of the moral allegory of 'Venetia Stanley, Lady Digby, as Prudence' (no.2): it stands for lust, and, chained and gently restrained by the Queen as it is here, represents passion tamed and controlled. As in many other portraits of the period, woman is presented as virtuous and chaste, though in a pictorial context that is deliberately orchestrated to suggest sensuality as much as regal dignity.

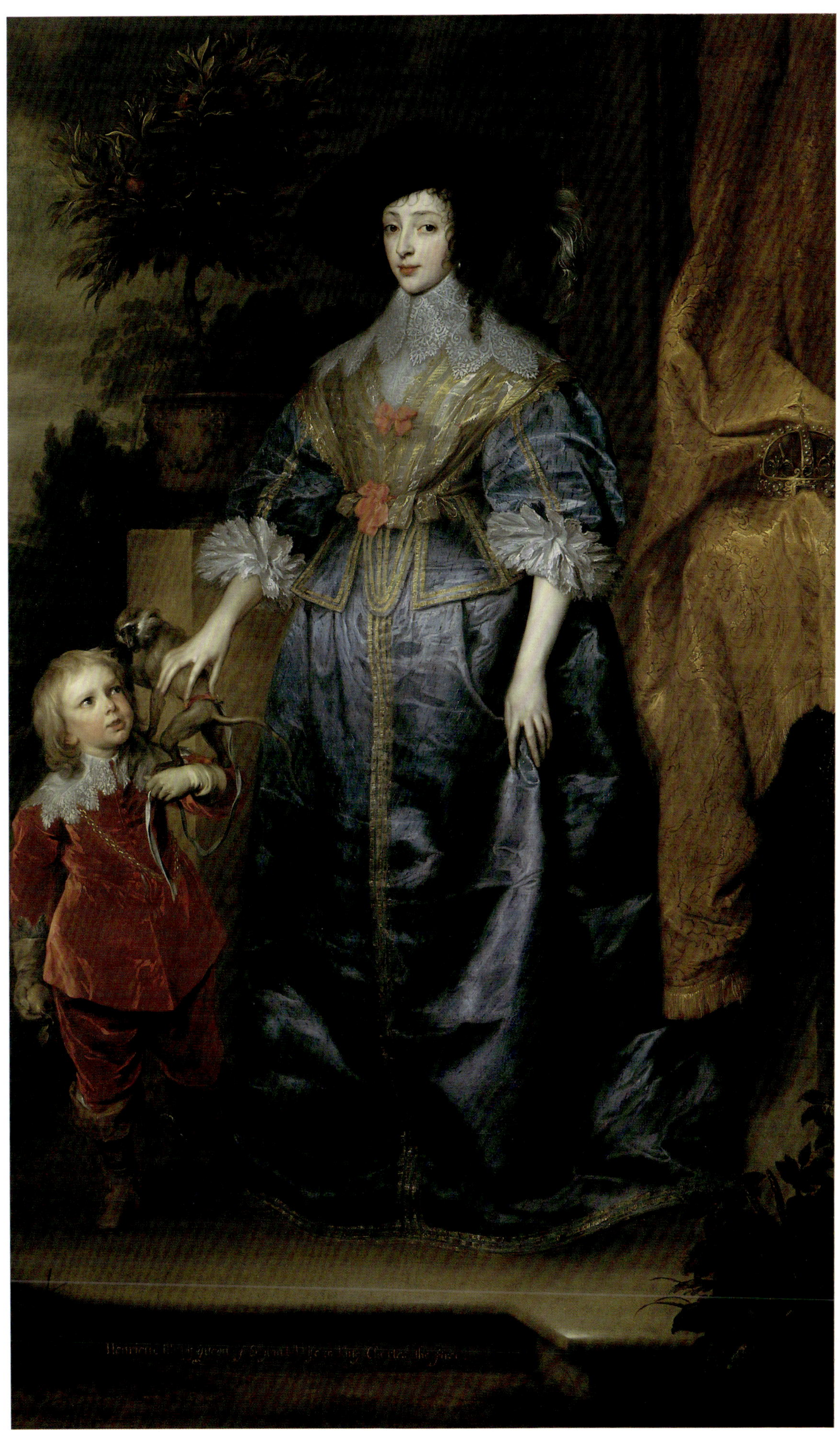

2 **Venetia Stanley, Lady Digby, as Prudence** 1633

Oil on canvas 101.1 × 80.2 ($39\frac{3}{4}$ × $31\frac{1}{2}$)
National Portrait Gallery

Venetia Digby was the daughter of Sir Edward Stanley and Lady Lucy Percy, daughter of Thomas Percy, 7th Earl of Northumberland. She was born in 1600 and married Sir Kenelm Digby, three years her junior, when she was twenty-five. He was a staunch Catholic and close associate of the Queen, as well as being a friend of Van Dyck's, to whom he was a regular and imaginative patron. In the year of Venetia's death, 1633, he commissioned a full-size portrait of her, known in several versions including one in the Royal Gallery, Turin, and another at Windsor. Whether the picture was intended as a memorial to her, or was begun before she died, is not certain. (Van Dyck also produced a little canvas of Lady Digby on her deathbed; now at Dulwich.) This small version of the large portrait, which is different in several important respects, is said have been executed simply because Van Dyck was pleased with his work, though the fact that it also belonged to Digby himself suggests that he was responsible for requesting it. He was apparently anxious to exonerate his wife from charges of promiscuity, occasioned, as such charges often are, by her beauty, and by an alleged earlier liaison with the 3rd Earl of Dorset. According to John Aubrey, her 'strict living' after her marriage to Digby was such that 'she redeemed her honour' (Sackville-West, pp.68–9).

In response to this commission Van Dyck has produced a work which exemplifies an important portrait type. He has recourse to a complex system of allegory which is carefully constructed to convey a delicate and very specific message. That system stems directly from contemporary and earlier religious morality painting: the picture is populated by a cast of symbolical characters – the doves of Chastity, the serpent of Wisdom, the two-faced figure of Deceit, and the naked child Cupid, with his torch of flaming desire, who is crushed beneath Venetia's heel. The three airborne putti who bestow on her the laurel wreath of victory are equally familiar from Renaissance painting. Like so much of Van Dyck's work, the whole image is redolent of Titian. He paid Titian lifelong homage, a touching testimony of admiration that reverberates in almost everything he painted.

The specific approach to allegory employed here is, nonetheless, very much a part of the English court culture that gave rise to the portrait. It is closely linked with the allegorical masques that were mounted at Charles I's court, and would have been readily interpreted by those accustomed to witnessing such spectacles.

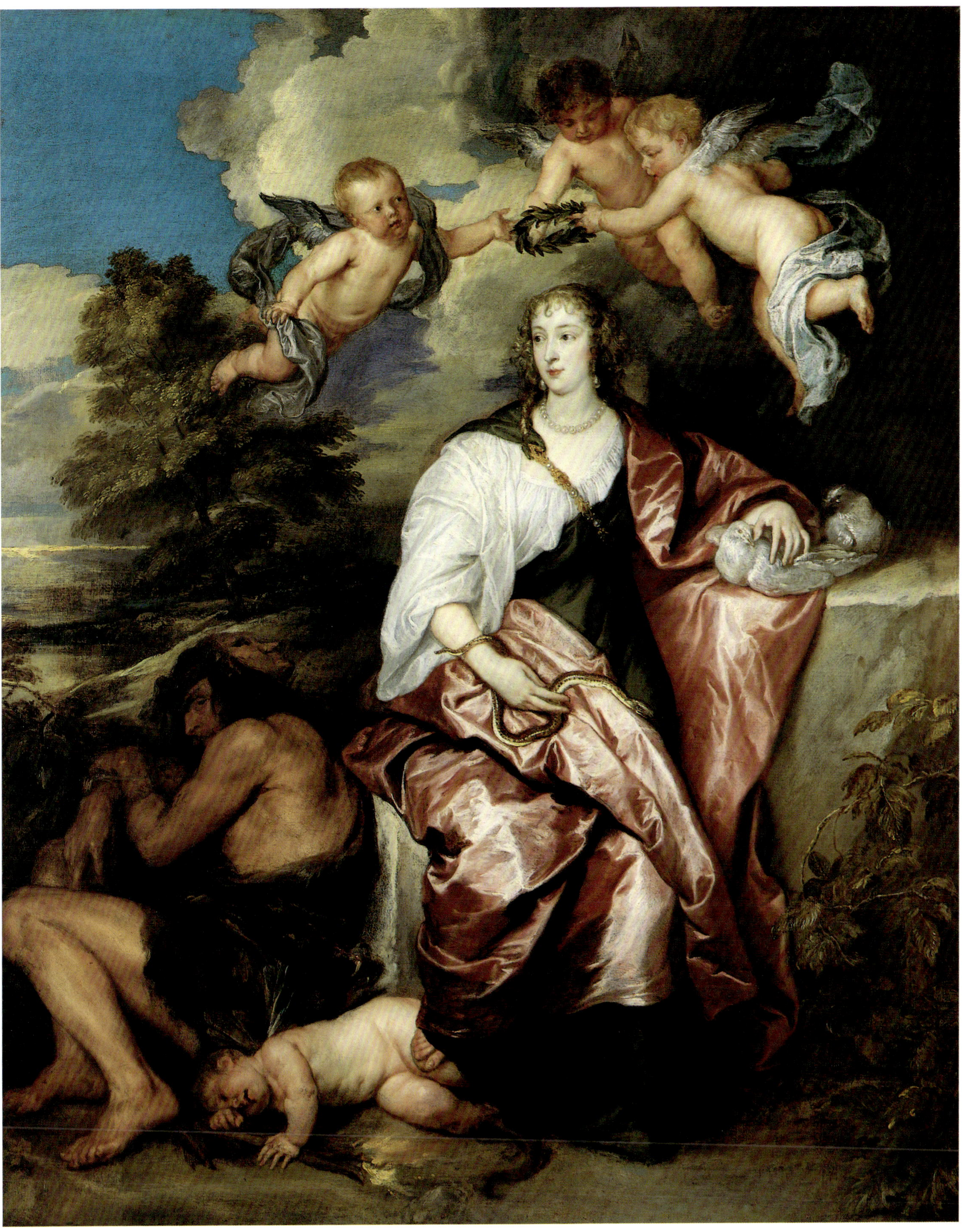

3 **Thomas Wentworth, 1st Earl of Strafford** 1633–6

Oil on canvas 229.9 × 142.9 ($90\frac{1}{2} \times 56\frac{1}{4}$)
The Trustees of the Rt Hon. Olive, Countess Fitzwilliam's Chattels Settlement, by permission of Lady Juliet de Chair

Strafford (1593–1641), was one of the chief architects of Charles I's autocracy and was painted by Van Dyck on several occasions. One, a half-length, shows him in an informal group with his secretary, Sir Philip Mainwaring (private collection). Two others present him full-length in armour; one of these has descended in the family of the Dukes of Portland; the other is shown here. Both seem to have been painted as a form of political propaganda. Van Dyck's predilection for allusions to Titian serves a useful purpose in this context, for the composition echoes Titian's full-length portrait of 'The Emperor Charles V with a Hound' (Prado), which was in London at the time. In both, the Irish wolfhound gazes affectionately up at its master, who holds its head or collar with a gesture that creates an almost tender interrelationship between man and beast. This detail reinforces the telling likeness by means of which both artists present the individual beneath the formal exterior without allowing the sitter's private personality to affect the composition in any other way. But the dog is also a symbol of nobility, of social power. In essence, this is a very public portrait. It speaks in serious terms of the probity and competence of the sitter, and thus functions as the channel through which the dignified state portraiture of Titian was adapted in the later seventeenth century to the spirit of English civic pragmatism. It anticipates in its sober mood the portrayals of soldiers and statesmen that dominate so much of British portraiture. In this capacity, it illustrates especially tellingly the subtleties of design and handling whereby Van Dyck endows such a subject with his characteristic elegance.

Strafford was a politician and administrator, not a soldier; the armour may therefore not even be symbolic, but simply a distant echo of the courtly and chivalric armour of the late Middle Ages and Renaissance. To that extent the portrait acknowledges the demands of pure glamour. But the armour also seems to carry overtones of civil authority (wielded by means of the army), and probably refers specifically to the Lord Deputyship of Ireland, which Strafford took up in 1633, though this portrait of him 'at large' was not taken to Wentworth Woodhouse, Strafford's Yorkshire seat, until 1636 or later. Ironically, his military activity, which largely belongs to the period after his return to London, was concentrated in a disastrous campaign in Scotland that led directly to the events that ended with his execution.

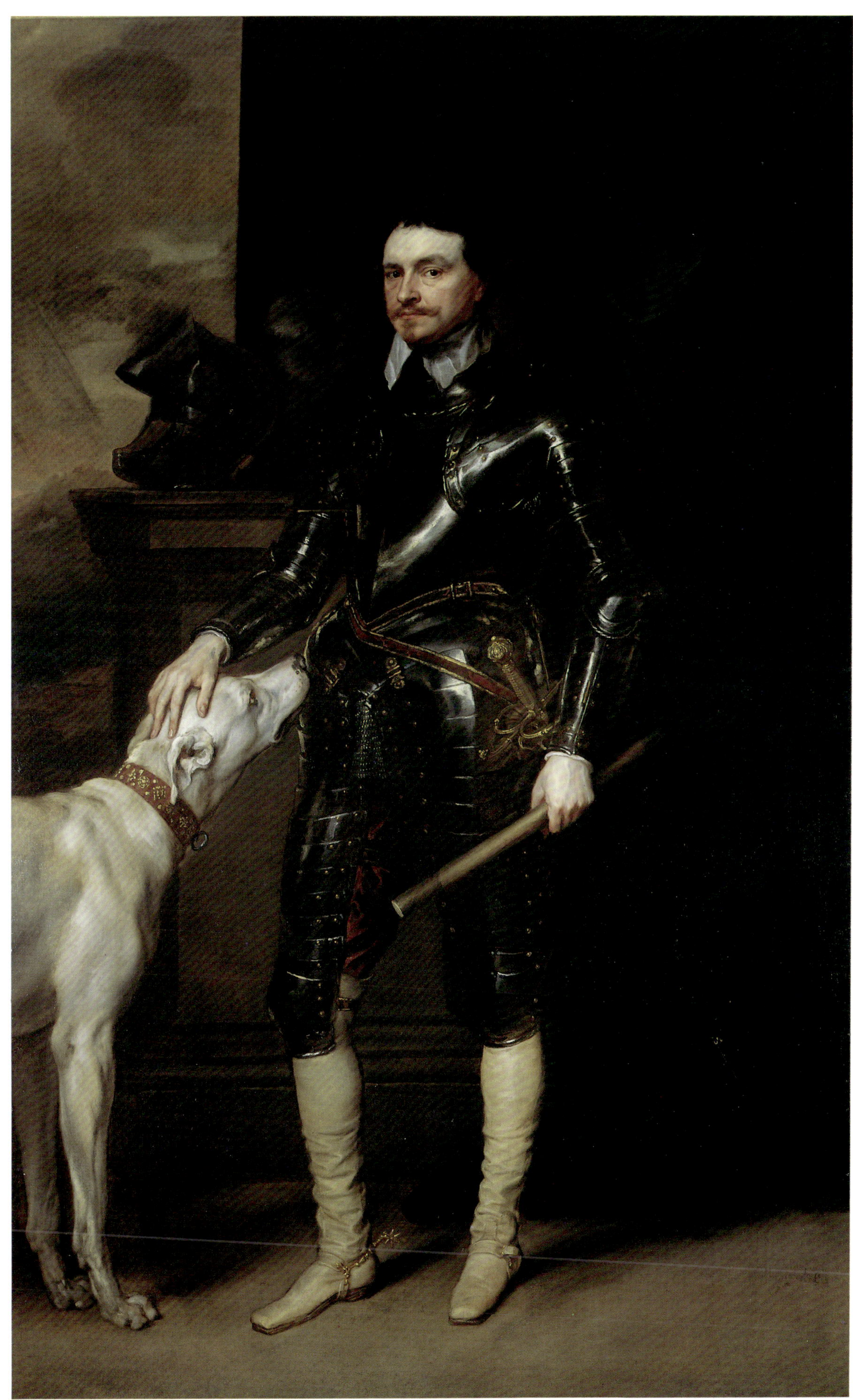

4 **Lucy Percy, Countess of Carlisle** *c.*1637

Oil on canvas 218.4 × 127 (86 × 50)
The Trustees of the Rt Hon. Olive, Countess Fitzwilliam's Settlement, by permission of Lady Juliet de Chair

Lucy Percy was the youngest of the four surviving children of Henry, 9th Earl of Northumberland, and so was second cousin to Venetia Digby (see no.2). She married the 1st Earl of Carlisle in 1617 and died on Guy Fawkes' Day 1660, the same day on which her father had died twenty-eight years earlier. Her portrait was included by Honthorst among the heads that throng the cloud occupied by Charles I and Henrietta Maria as Apollo and Diana in his great canvas for Whitehall (fig.1 on p.21). Van Dyck's treatment of this dangerously attractive woman illustrates his lightness of touch when dealing with the English aristocracy. He responds to the 'active and tempestuous' character of the sitter with an animated and almost playful design, in which the requisite dignity is conveyed entirely by means of elegant rhythms and breathtakingly applied paint. These are qualities that Gainsborough sought to introduce into his portraits; but although he was very successful, he did not, as an exceptionally free and easy Englishman, attempt to imbue the resulting composition with the kind of public panache that Van Dyck achieves so effortlessly. Here, the impression of grandeur is in no way undermined by the joke of having the lady seem to lead us on into a dark and covert place, accompanying her gesture of invitation with a knowing smile. This may be a form of erotic playfulness, but it also suggests the sitter's penchant for political intrigue. The device of twisting the head towards the spectator while the body remains not only in profile but in motion towards to the interior space beyond the left edge of the picture, creates a particularly effective combination of public and private gesture. In a parallel arrangement, the lateral impetus of the diagonals of the figure is stabilised by the vertical of column and plinth beyond. The general pose had been used by Van Dyck in an earlier portrait of Beatrice de Cusance, Princesse de Cantecroix (collections Her Majesty The Queen), and recurs in the portrait of Maria Villiers (Cracow). A drawing of the head and shoulders of Lucy Percy is in the British Museum.

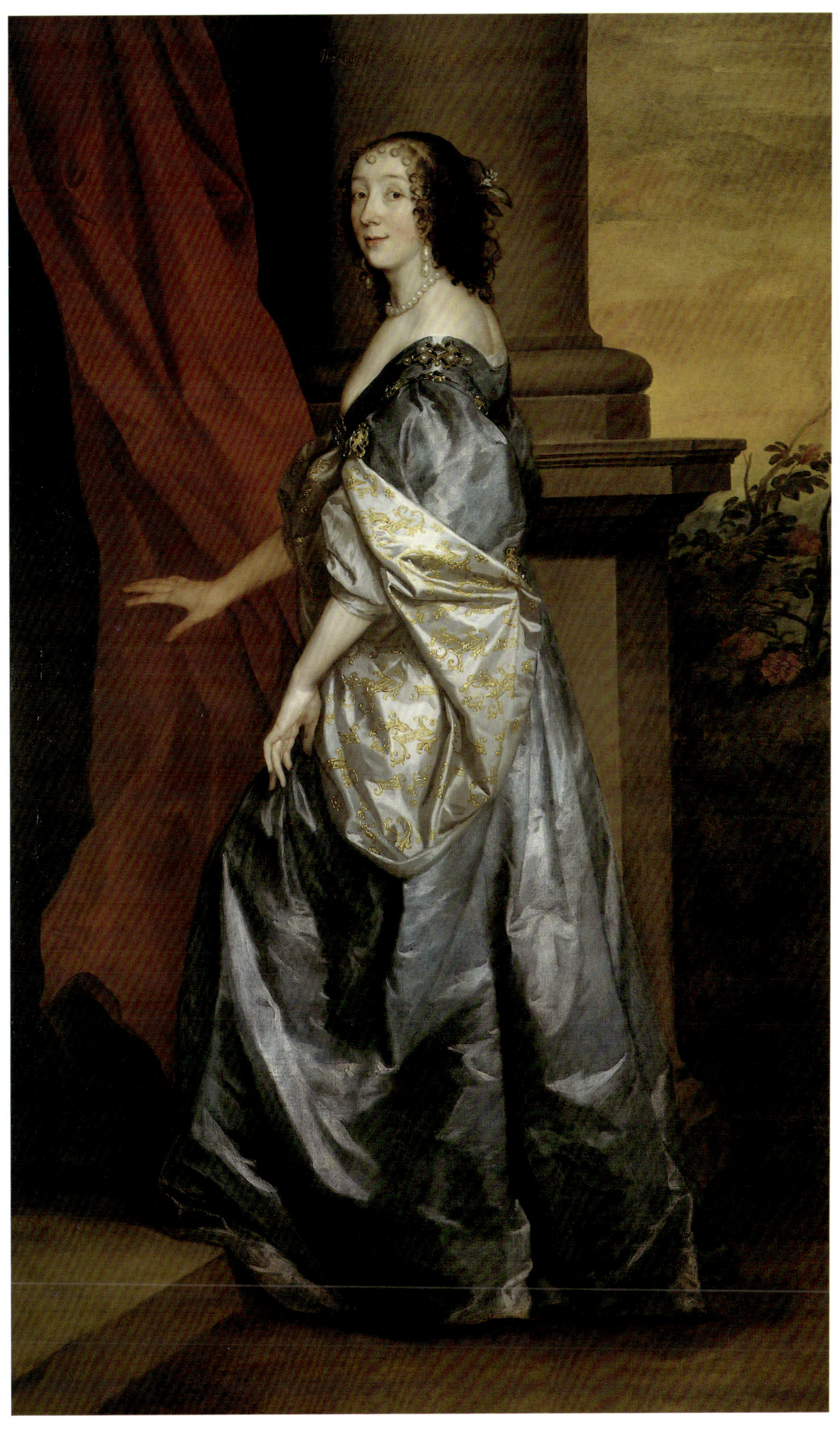

5 Olivia, Wife of Endymion Porter *c.*1637

Oil on canvas 135.9 × 106.7 (53½ × 42)
His Grace The Duke of Northumberland

The sitter was born Olivia Boteler, her mother a Villiers, half-sister of the Duke of Buckingham. She married Endymion Porter (no.8) in 1619, and became a close associate of the Queen, so close, indeed, that in 1637 she became a convert to Rome. Van Dyck seems to have responded to the lady's lively personality with a portrait that is, in some respects, a *jeu d'esprit*: there is an abandonment in the pose and a freedom in the whole design that anticipates more closely than usual the atmosphere of Lely's Restoration portraits. These often use the motif of a vertical rock which Van Dyck employs here, apparently quoting from Titian's famous picture of Mary Magdalen. In this context, however, the rock has a more direct (and likely) connection with the scenery of court masques (fig.27): it is a stage-set wing, evocative of something that is not really there. Indeed, although the picture has been described as arcadian it is only so in the sense that it evokes a masque, and seems to present the sitter as a character in a masque. 'Mistress Porter' is known to have taken part in Ben Jonson's masque *Chloridia* in 1631, for which Inigo Jones designed a number of loose flowing costumes for allegorical characters such as Disdain and Dissimulation. Her animated gesture, like her costume, belongs to a stage role and not to real life. The windblown drapery, whose form is echoed by the irregular outline of the jutting rock, creates an unstable counterpoint that sets the figure in vigorous motion. It is very similar in general character to the drapery worn by the Countess of Southampton in her clearly 'theatrical' portrait, no.7. Similar rocky backdrops occur in portraits of actors by, say, Lely's pupil John Greenhill (*c.*1640–1676). When Lely himself adopts the same feature for a military portrait he implicitly accepts its value as 'scenery' for creating a general mood, while stripping it of its theatrical associations. Mrs Porter is the prototype also of those windblown girls of Reynolds – the society beauties, such as Lady Jane Halliday (see fig.34 on p.134), who chose to be portrayed like Crazy Kate on a stormy heath (Waddesdon). The pose of Mrs Musters (no.36), indeed, may be a direct reference to that of Olivia Porter, which it imitates in reverse.

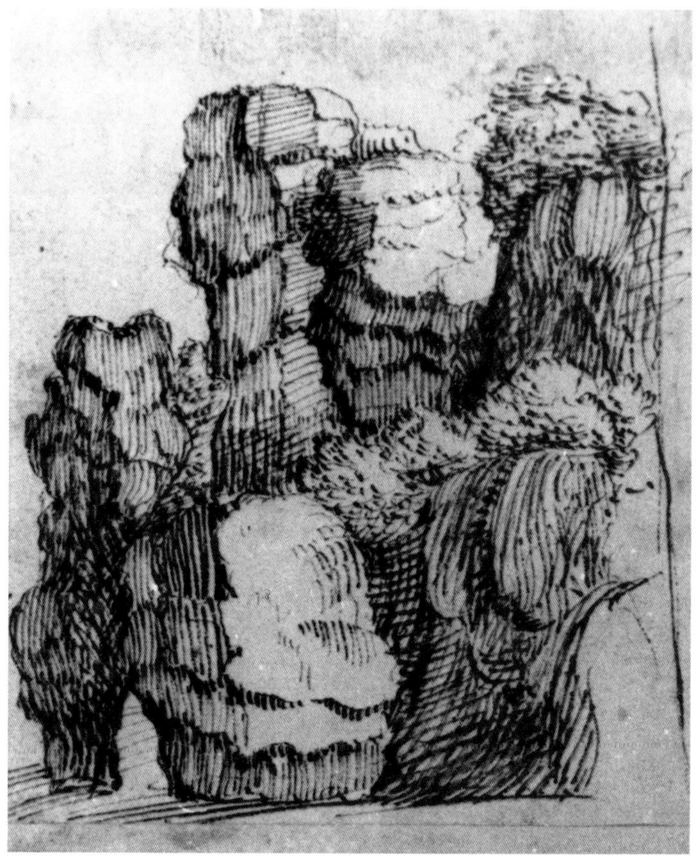

fig.27 Inigo Jones **Design for a Scene: Mountains** *c.*1630–40 (detail)
Pen and brown ink *Duke of Devonshire, Chatsworth*

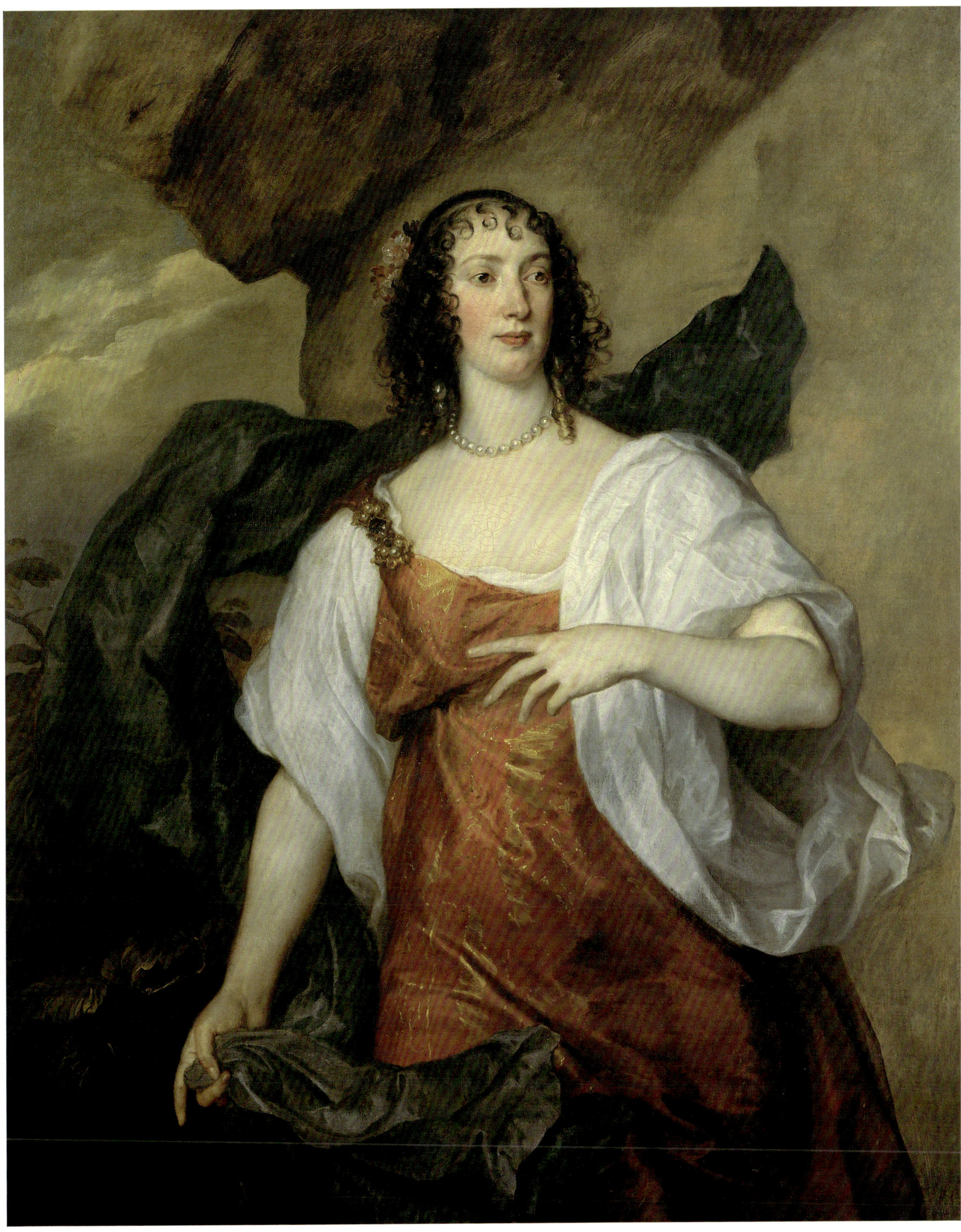

SIR ANTHONY VAN DYCK

6 A Lady as Erminia, Attended by Cupid *c.*1638

Oil on canvas 109.2 × 129.5 (43 × 51)
His Grace The Duke of Marlborough

The sitter for this portrait has not been identified; like so many images of women in this period (including those of Queen Henrietta Maria and Venetia Digby, nos.1 and 2), the picture seems to present her as an embodiment both of sensuality and its conquest: she is accompanied by the god of love, yet armoured against his arrows. One suggestion has been that she is shown as Pallas Athene, and the tradition at Blenheim, where the picture usually hangs, is that the subject is Van Dyck's English wife Margaret Lemon in the character of Psyche (with an unsuitably youthful Eros at her side). But it is generally accepted that the portrait is cast in the form of an illustration to Tasso's *Gerusalemme Liberata*, book VI, in which Erminia, in search of her lover Tancredi, dons armour to enter Jerusalem in disguise. The poem had been translated into English in 1600 by Edward Fairfax and was immensely influential, not least on the whole atmosphere of the court masques. The homely landscape background of this picture, with its rustic cottage among English-looking trees, does not at first sight appear to support this interpretation; but Van Dyck's other illustration to Tasso, the great 'Rinaldo and Armida', now in the Baltimore Museum of Art, makes use of an arcadian woodland setting equally implausible. And in the Blenheim picture the formal division of the background by a firm vertical line suggests an artificial setting such as the scenery of a masque. The rocks on which the lady rests her helmet are reminiscent of the distinctly stagey rock that Van Dyck used as backdrop to his portrait of Olivia Porter (no.7). Cupid stands on this rocky foreground shelf and directs the lady to her object with a lively gesture, touching her shoulder as he does so, in the character of a genius or spirit of Love who inspires and animates her. Her right hand plucks at her sleeve, to roll it up for action, with a movement that is timid as well as determined, suggesting subtleties of characterisation which may be appropriate for the sitter as well as for her assumed role. Van Dyck blurs the boundaries between portraiture and history painting in a way that was to be adopted for quite different purposes in the eighteenth century by Reynolds and his generation.

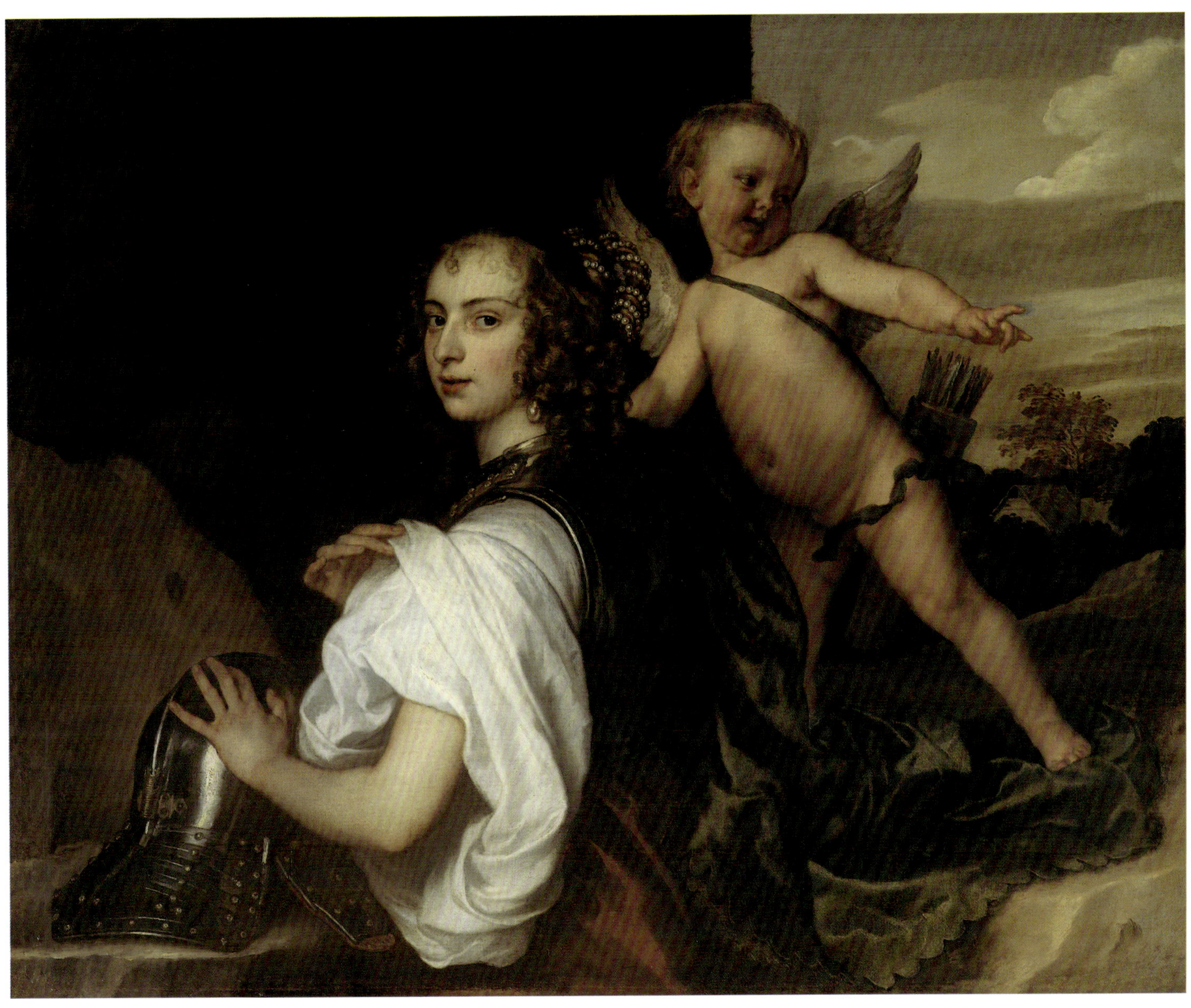

7 Rachel de Ruvigny, Countess of Southampton, as Fortuna *c.*1638

Oil on canvas 219.5 × 133 (86⅜ × 52⅜)
Inscr. lower right (not by the artist): *Rachel, 1st Countess of/Southampton*
The Syndics of the Fitzwillam Museum, Cambridge

The sitter (1603–40) was French, the daughter of Daniel de Massue, Seigneur de Ruvigny, and widow of Elysée de Beaujeu, Seigneur de la Maisonfort. It was in France, at Charenton near Paris, that she married, at the age of thirty-one, Thomas Wriothesley, Earl of Southampton, who was to be a faithful supporter of the King throughout the Civil War. She died in childbed early in 1640.

There is a version of this spectacular picture, equally large, in the National Gallery of Victoria, Melbourne, which is also attributable to Van Dyck or his immediate workshop. Some half-length variants also exist. The composition must rank as one of the artist's most extravagant conceptions, and seems to stand halfway between portrait and altarpiece. Whereas the portrait of Venetia Digby (no.2) assembles symbolic attributes round the sitter in order to build up a statement of her qualities, this presents the sitter as the complete embodiment of an idea which has little to do with her identity as an individual. While Sir Kenelm Digby wished his wife to be perceived as prudent and virtuous, the association of Lady Southampton with Fortune is in some sense arbitrary, with all the abstract grandeur of the Madonna in an immaculate conception. Van Dyck was not in the habit of enthroning his sitters in clouds, although Reynolds was to adopt the idea for some of his most splendid portraits (see nos.36–7). Catholic art is full of such figures, which had been used for centuries to personify abstractions, and it was not unusual for artists to depict illustrious sitters as the embodiments of virtue, either public or private.

But it is possible that in choosing the character of Fortune for his sitter Van Dyck was not acting on a whim, but had a specific reason for it. An immediate stimulus for the picture must have been the court masques that were so conspicuous a part of life in the royal entourage in the 1630s. These frequently involved deities descending (fig.28) in elaborate machinery from the flies onto the stage, and it is possible that Lady Southampton was cast in such a role: for instance, she is named among the masquers in Sir William Davenant's *Luminalia*, which took place early in 1638 – about the time this portrait was probably painted. It was full of effects reminiscent of Van Dyck's picture: 'The morning star appears sitting on a bright cloud ... On the other side of the heaven came forth Aurora in a chariot touched with gold, borne up by a rosy-coloured cloud, her garment white trimmed with gold'. *Luminalia* ended with a particularly spectacular transformation: 'the upper part of the heaven opened, and a bright transparent cloud came forth far into the scene, upon which were many *zephyri* and gentle breaths with rich but light garments tucked about their waists and falling down about their knees, and on their heads garlands of flowers ... Which apparition for the newness of the invention, greatness of the machine, and difficulty of engineering was much admired, being a thing not before attempted in the air' (Orgel and Strong, II, p.709).

The principal attribute of Fortune as she is presented by Van Dyck is her all-conquering power over the lives of men. She rules the world, holding the sceptre of royal authority. A sphere was often used to designate Opportunity or Chance, yet the vast sphere the Countess holds is less terrestrial globe than crystal ball, in which the fates of mankind are to be divined. Fortune is usually portrayed standing on a globe, symbol of instability or inconstancy, and as Van Dyck shows it, under her hand, that aspect of its meaning is emphasised, since it is also a bubble, fragile and transitory. All these points are reinforced and given point by the introduction of a skull at her feet. Thus Lady Southampton triumphs over mankind (or simply man?) just as Venetia Digby conquers lust. The symbolism of the parts is however less than the authority of the whole image, which borrows its conviction from Van Dyck's familiarity with the ideas of religious painting. The picture is set off by a particularly splendid example of a 'Sunderland' frame.

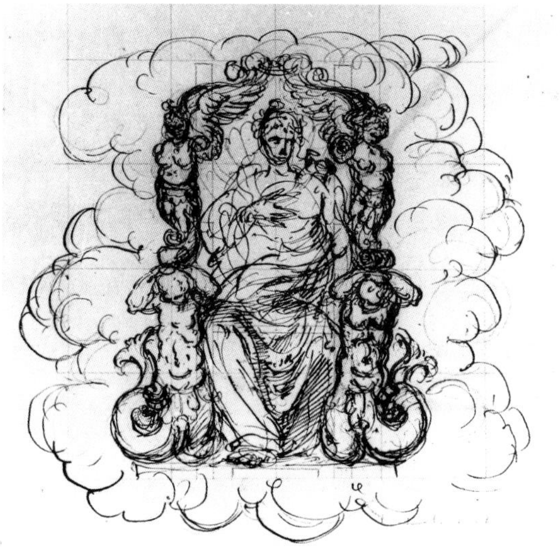

fig.28 Inigo Jones **Masque Design: Venus** *c.*1631 (detail) Pen and brown ink, squared for enlargement with black lead *Duke of Devonshire, Chatsworth*

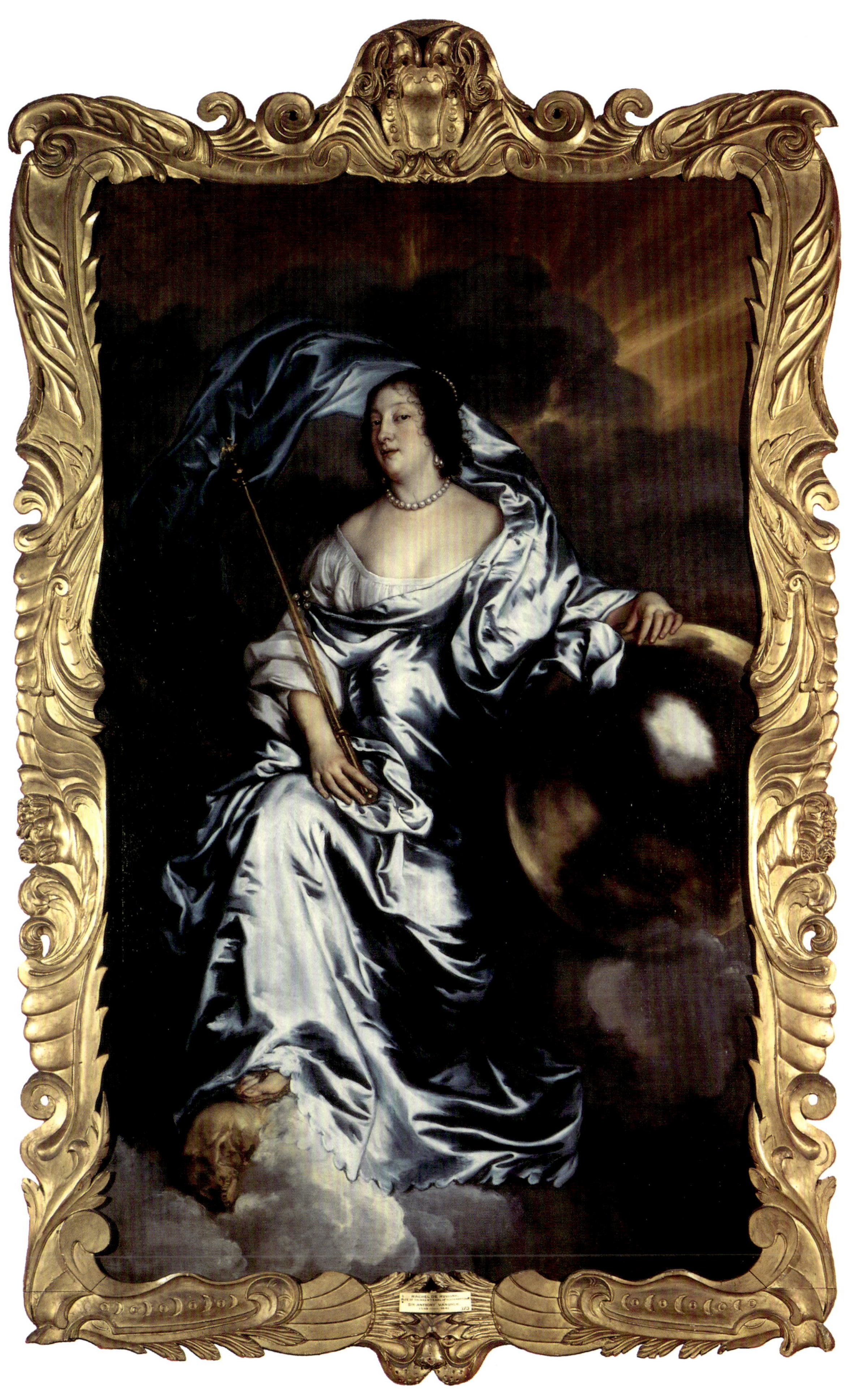

WILLIAM DOBSON 1610/11–1646

8 **Endymion Porter** *c.*1640–3

Oil on canvas 149.9 × 127 (59 × 50)
Tate Gallery. Purchased 1888

Porter (1587–1649) was one of the most colourful figures of the court of Charles I, which he joined when Charles was still Prince of Wales whose Groom of the Bedchamber he became. The King favoured him on account of his 'general learning, brave stile, sweet temper, great experience, travels and modern languages'. He had Spanish blood on his mother's side, was born in Madrid, and had spent much of his youth in Spain, so that it was natural that he should be involved in a series of diplomatic negotiations with the Hapsburgs there. The most notable of these missions was that of 1623, when he accompanied Charles and the Duke of Buckingham, to whom he was at first attached, in their attempt to create an Anglo-Spanish alliance by marriage.

He was an imaginative, though not always a successful, speculator in mercantile and maritime projects, and in such useful schemes as draining the Lincolnshire fens. Perhaps more significant historically was his liberal enthusiasm for the arts: he was a poet and friend of poets, friend and patron too of important painters like Mytens, Gentileschi, Rubens and Van Dyck, whose self-portrait with Porter is in the Prado. There are at least three other portraits of Porter by Van Dyck. He advised both the King and the Earl of Arundel in the formation of their famous collections. His wife was a Catholic and a member of the Queen's entourage (see no.5). In all respects, therefore, he is a personality whom one would expect to see portrayed in swagger terms, as Dobson does here.

It has been pointed out that the wealth of symbolic and allusive accessories in this picture contrasts with the much plainer and more direct approach to his sitters that was Van Dyck's usual practice. The bust of Apollo, god of poetry and the arts, on the Corinthian capital beside him seems to dedicate the whole composition to those activities, despite the gun which signals another, heartier, side of Porter's personality: he was a keen rider to hounds and followed the outdoor pursuits of a country gentleman. The relief on which he leans shows the personifications of the arts of sculpture, painting and poetry contemplating a statue of Minerva, another deity with a special portfolio for the arts. Although Van Dyck is as always Dobson's primary inspiration, the design of the portrait as a whole looks back beyond Van Dyck to the great progenitor of Italian portraiture, Titian: the pose and disposition of the figure on the canvas are based on Titian's portrait of the Emperor Vespasian, one of a series depicting the Twelve Caesars which hung at that time at St James's Palace. The assemblage of classical allusions here is formidable, and contributes to a dense texture of ideas which help to build up a complete picture of the sitter. Their symbolism is more direct than that of the allegorical language employed by Van Dyck in his portrait of Venetia Digby (no.2). The picture thus bears witness the transformation of full-blown allegorical portraiture during the seventeenth century into a more immediate expression of abstract ideas which was to lead to the rapid banishment of all but the most literal of allusions in the portraiture of later generations.

The picture is traditionally dated to the mid 1640s – a time when the Civil War was closing round Charles's court. A recent suggestion that it belongs to a slightly earlier period – say about 1640 – seems convincing, and is borne out by Porter's clothes which should surely be in high fashion and not a year or two out of date. In 1645 he went into exile in France and the Low Countries, and did not return to England until shortly before his death in 1649.

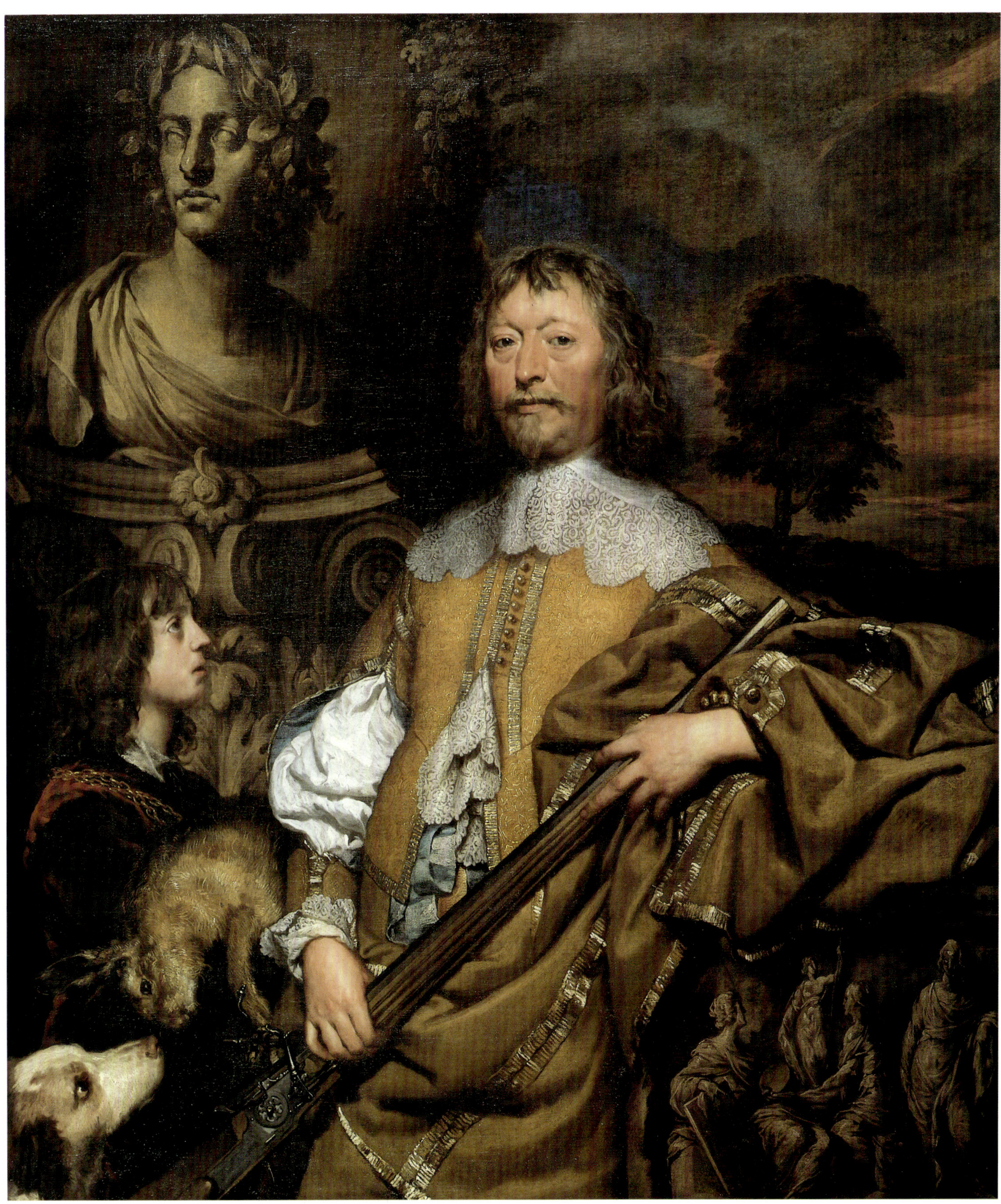

9 **John, 1st Baron Byron** *c.*1643

Oil on canvas 142 × 120 ($55\frac{7}{8}$ × 47)
University of Manchester, Tabley House Collection

Byron, an ancestor of the poet, was one of seven royalist brothers, and among the most impetuously devoted of Charles I's supporters. He fought his way through the Civil War with more enthusiasm – the *Dictionary of National Biography* calls it 'pathetic dogged loyalty' – than judgement, and was created Baron Byron of Rochdale by the King after the Battle of Newbury in 1643. He held the city of Chester until February 1646; after its surrender he marched under safe-conduct to Caernarvon which was given up on orders from the King in May that year. He followed the Queen into exile, and held the office of Superintendant-General to the Duke of York's household. This did not prevent him from taking part in the royalist uprising in Scotland in 1648, and Parliament duly proscribed him. He died in exile in 1652.

In its extreme theatricality, this portrait is perhaps the most swagger to have been produced by an English artist in the seventeenth century, and contrasts interestingly with the more introverted bombast of Dobson's 'Endymion Porter' (no.8). Dobson has presumably gauged the tone of his picture carefully to suit the bravado of a soldier who, we are told, was wont to 'engage the enemy when he needed not'. Byron was perhaps proud of the scar on his cheek, acquired in a skirmish at Burford in January 1642/3, and Dobson allows it, with its long black patch, to play a conspicuous part in defining his sitter's character. The haughty look and theatrical gesture enhance this image, as do the black page and ornate Salomonic columns crowded into the tight composition along with a white horse. These trappings serve a much less precise descriptive function than the various accessories that figure in the picture of Endymion Porter, though it has been suggested that the twisted columns, associated as they are with the temple built by the wise and just Jewish king, have strong connotations of wisdom and justice in conjunction with royalty. They would therefore assert the royalist cause in the defence of which Byron received his wound. This point is already made by the bulky red sash with which Byron announces his affiliation, and which is used to focus the rich Venetian colour scheme of the whole picture.

Dobson may have taken the idea for Byron's pose from either of two Van Dyck prototypes, both now at Petworth. One, 'Mountjoy Blount, Earl of Newport, and Lord George Goring, with a Page' is a three-quarter-length double portrait in which the gaze of Blount, on the left, almost matches the directness of Byron's, while his arm, with stick in hand, crosses his body in a diagonal similar to that in Dobson's picture. The other is the three-quarter-length version of the portrait of Strafford of which there are whole-lengths elsewhere (not the same composition as no.3 here). In this design, Van Dyck has Strafford walking gently across the picture from left to right, grasping a baton in his left (farther) hand, while he holds out his right hand in a gesture of explanation, so that the arm, again, cuts across in front of the figure. Dobson's Byron is more forceful, facing us more fully and pointing quite deliberately out of the picture to the right, so that, if Strafford seems to be in conversation, Byron appears to be distracted momentarily in the middle of urgent action. Indeed, riders are galloping across a battlefield in the direction he points towards, so we are left in no doubt as to his pressing business. The horse is taken, and it has to be said, somewhat perfunctorily adapted, from the horse in Van Dyck's great portrait of 'Charles I with M. de St Antoine' (collection Her Majesty The Queen).

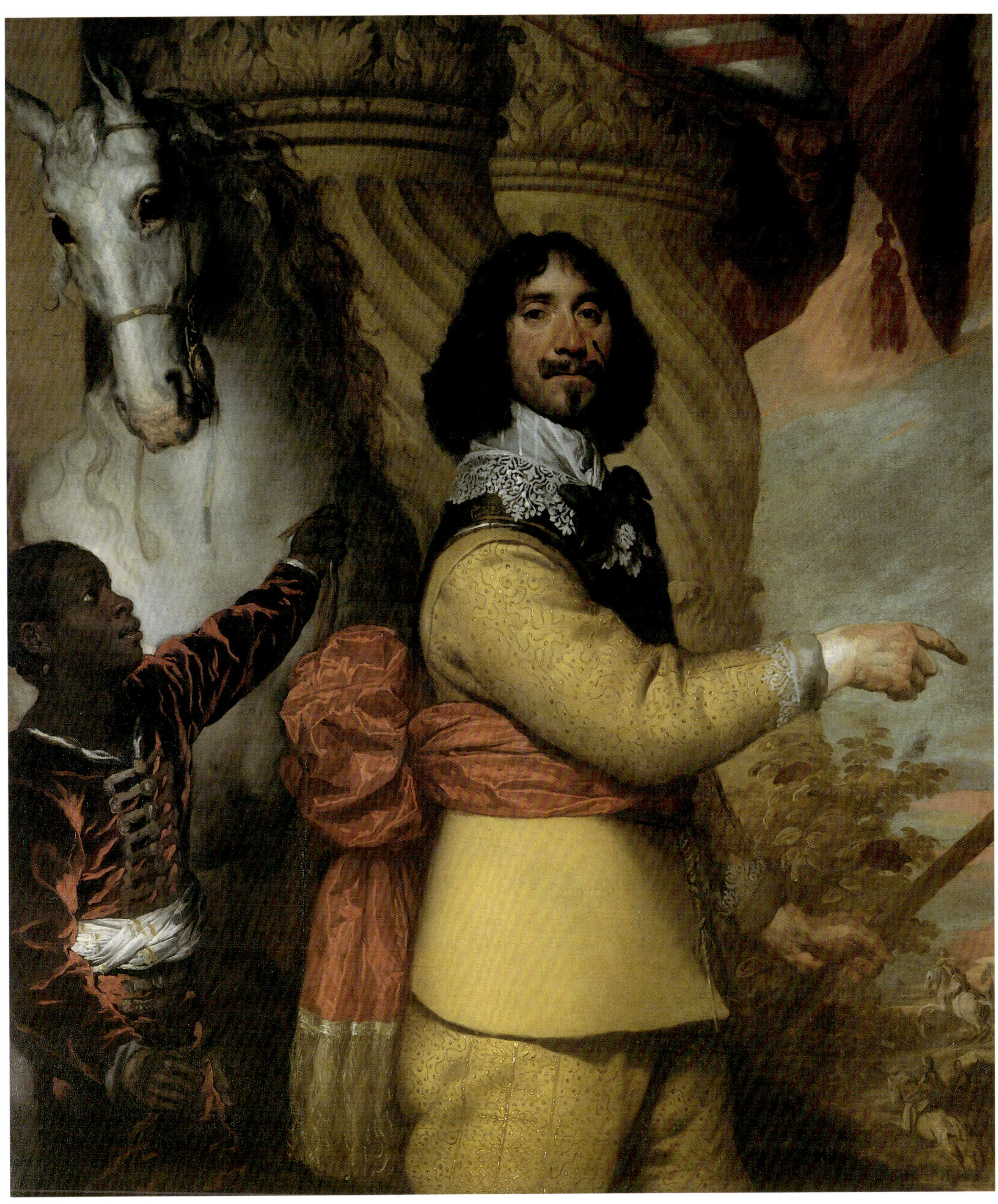

SIR PETER LELY 1618–1680

10 Henry Hyde, Viscount Cornbury, and his Wife, Theodosia Capel 1661–2

Oil on canvas 142.2 × 180.5 (56 × 71½)
Signed lower centre: *PL* (monogram)
The Earl of Clarendon, on loan to Plymouth City Museum and Art Gallery

An old inscription, on the plinth of the statue, reading 'LORD CORNBVRY AND HIS LADY' has recently been removed. The half-length double portrait is a format that was popular in the Low Countries and much used by Van Dyck, who adapted it with creative enthusiasm, and developed it into perhaps the most 'English' of his formulas. Reynolds was to adopt it and pass it on as a staple device to Lawrence, with whom the line ends. The intimacy that is implied by the close-up view of two people linked by marriage or some other friendly bond militates against many of these works being considered truly 'swagger'; but the panache that Lely injects into this example earns it a place here.

Some of Lely's double portraits are crowded into the picture-space and allow little latitude for expansiveness of mood; an example is the 'Earl and Countess of Southampton' (private collection) of about the same date as this work. The roomier design here allows for the development of each figure both individually and in relation to the other. Husband and wife seem to be engaged in separate dialogues with the spectator, and either half of the composition would be self-sufficient in elegance and rhythm. But Lely increases the rhetorical force of the picture by making the two engage in a purely visual relationship of their own, primarily by means of gesture and the sweep of drapery. Viscount Cornbury's gesture of pointing towards his new young bride is the sole explicit indication of their relationship, but the picture reinforces the idea in implied harmony and subtle counterpoint, and a statue of Cupid stands between them, alluding symbolically to their love.

Henry Hyde was the son of the great Edward Hyde, 1st Earl of Clarendon, minister to Charles II, and was born in 1638. His younger brother was Earl of Rochester. He spent much of his youth abroad during the Commonwealth, but in 1660 returned to England and, as Lord Cornbury, married Theodosia Capel, daughter of Lord Capel. She died in March 1661/2 and this portrait of them both, which must have been conceived as a wedding-picture, was probably hardly finished when it became a commemorative portrait. We know the details of Theodosia's death because of a curious incident recounted by Clarendon to Samuel Pepys forty years later. Cornbury and his new wife were dining with the Earl of Newborough and an unnamed Scotsman who kept staring 'steadfastly' at Theodosia. Lord Newborough asked him,

> What is the matter, that thou hast had thine eyes fixed upon my lady Cornbury ever since she came into the room? Is she not a fine woman? Why dost thou not speak? – 'She's a handsome Lady, indeed,' said the gentleman, 'but I see her in blood.' Whereupon my Lord Newborough laughed at him, and all the company going out of the room, we parted; and I believe not one of us though more of the matter; I am sure I did not. My wife was at that time perfectly well in health, and looked as well as ever she did in her life. In the beginning of the next month she fell ill of the small-pox; she was always very apprehensive of that disease, and used to say , if she ever had it, she would dye of it. Upon the ninth day after the small-pox appeared, in the morning, she bled at the nose, which quickly stopt; but in the afternoon the blood burst out again with great violence at her nose and mouth, and about eleven of the clock that night she dyed, almost weltering in her blood.
>
> (Braybrooke IV, pp.281–2)

Cornbury was at that time Member of Parliament for Wiltshire, and a loyal adherent of his father's cause, becoming strongly anti-court after Clarendon's dismissal in 1667. When Clarendon died in 1674 he succeeded to his title. He formed close ties with the King's brother and heir, James, Duke of York, who had indeed married his sister Ann, a clandestine Catholic. Hyde's own religion and politics were, in the words of the *Dictionary of National Biography*, 'Church of England tory of a narrow type'; though he managed to temper family loyalty with common sense at the time of the Revolution, he was soon disgruntled with the new regime and formed an attachment to the exiled court at St Germain, for which he was imprisoned for some months. He was something of an antiquarian and collector, with a particular interest in medals. He died in 1709.

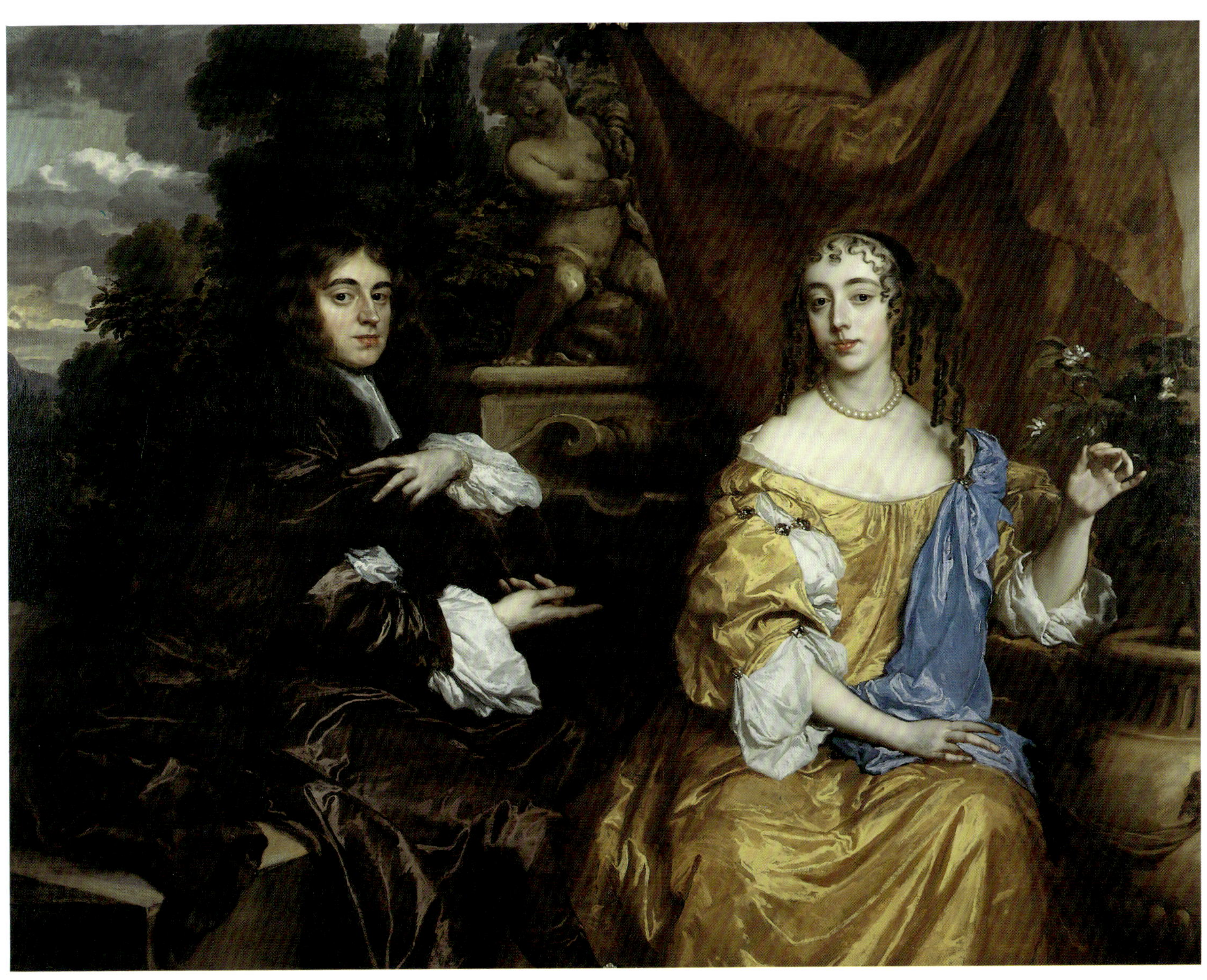

SIR PETER LELY

11 **Horatio, 1st Viscount Townshend** 1662

Oil on canvas 221 × 129.9 (87 × 51⅛)
National Museum of Wales, Cardiff

Townshend (?1630–87), of Raynham in north-west Norfolk, was one of the pillars of the royalist cause in East Anglia. In 1648, when his elder brother died childless, he inherited the family estate and baronetcy and in 1658–9 was Member of Parliament for Norfolk, 'one ready', it was said, 'to attempt anything for the King'. He was a conspicuous supporter of the Restoration and, in 1660, one of the deputation to The Hague which invited Charles to return to London. That year he was appointed Governor of King's Lynn, a town he had attempted to take towards the end of the Commonwealth, and in 1661 his loyalty was rewarded with a barony. He became Lord Lieutenant, then Vice-Admiral of Norfolk, and became involved in schemes for draining the fens. These services, together with further patriotic action in the Dutch war of 1667, earned him a viscountcy, which was conferred on him in 1682. This portrait shows Townshend at about the age of thirty, in the first flush of success as his loyalty to the royal cause was rewarded at Charles's restoration. His newly won baron's coronet is proudly displayed beside him. Townshend's son, the 2nd Viscount, married Elizabeth Pelham, whose portrait by Kneller is no.18 here.

Townshend's pose, with one foot turned at right angles to the other, is a standard one for the period, and was used regularly by Lely with various modifications. It allows the sitter's robes to exert their maximum effect in the design, their long folds continuing the lines of the equally voluminous wig to reinforce the sitter's self-conscious and somewhat arrogant gaze. The picture epitomises Lely's ability to emulate the easy dignity of Van Dyck's portraits, with great ecomony of means. Walpole, who judged that 'if in nothing but simplicity, he fell short of his model, as Statius or Claudian did of Virgil', and that 'In the portraits of men, which he seldom painted, Lely scarce came up to Sir Antony', yet conceded that 'there is a whole-length of Horatio, Lord Townshend, by the former, at Rainham, which yields to few of the latter' (Walpole II, pp.92–3). The work remained with the Townshend family until after the Second World War. The artist's extension of the canvas, bringing it to 94 × 58½ inches, has at some time been folded back at top and sides to fit into a smaller space. Lely's full-length portraits are to be found in both larger and smaller formats, and it is not always clear what his own intention was. Portraits were required for many different settings and adapted as necessary.

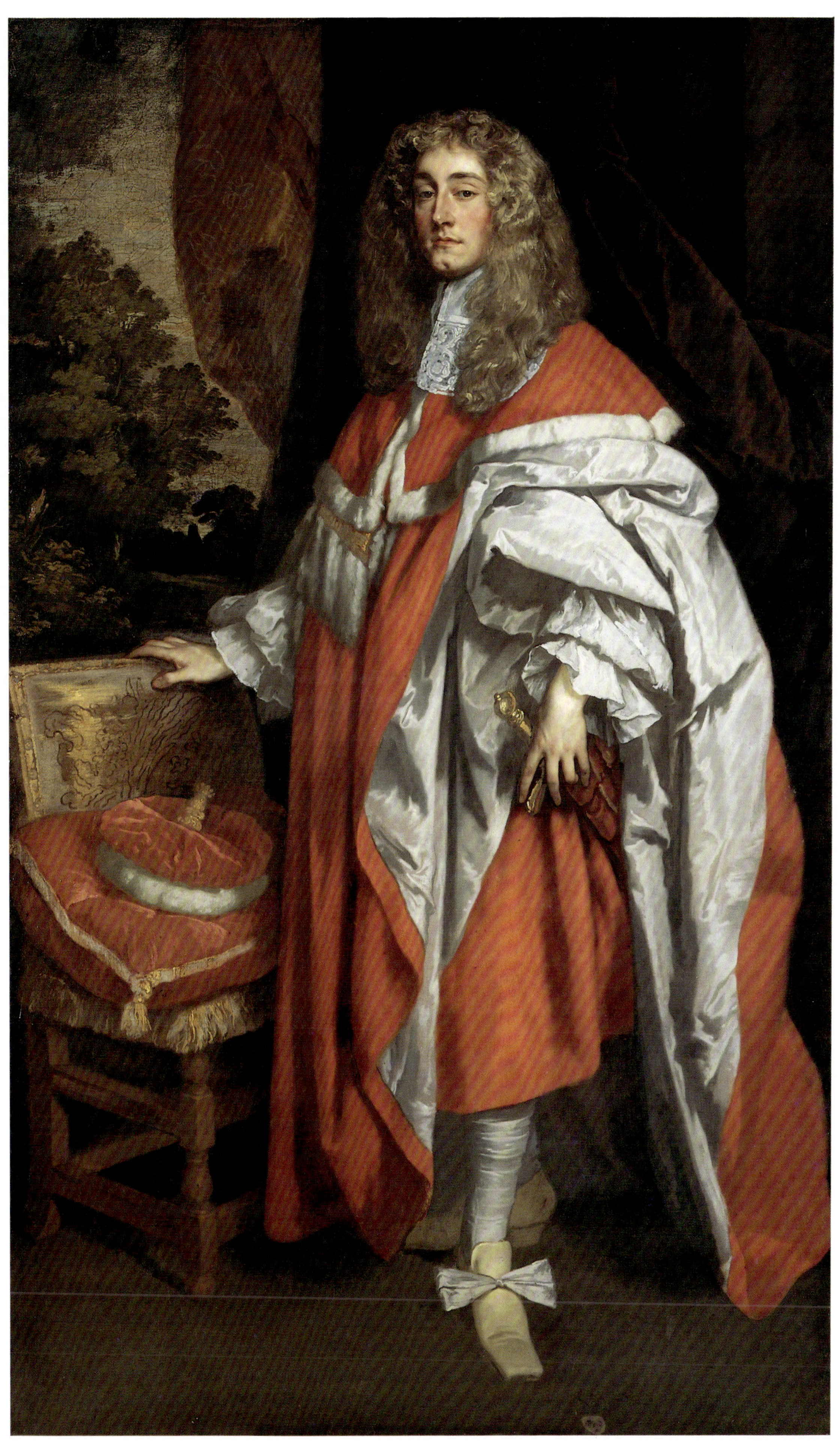

12 **Barbara Villiers, Duchess of Cleveland** *c.*1665–70

Oil on canvas 125.7 × 100.6 ($49\frac{1}{2} \times 39\frac{1}{2}$)
The Earl Bathurst

Barbara Villiers was the most important of Charles II's many beauties – important for her looks, her promiscuity and her enormous influence on the art of Lely, who painted her often. He was so impressed by her that 'he used to say, that it was beyond the compass of art to give this lady her due, as to her sweetness and exquisite beauty'. If the court ladies looked languishing, it was because Villiers taught them to do so; if Lely endowed all his female sitters with the same appearance, it was because he could conceive of no more perfect countenance. Barbara Villiers was born around 1641, the granddaughter of Lord Grandison, and married Roger Palmer, later Earl of Castlemaine, in 1659, having before this conducted a passionate liaison with Philip Stanhope, Earl of Chesterfield. That did not prevent her from moving rapidly into the King's intimate circle; she was given the title of Lady of the Bedchamber to the Queen, but it was to the bed of the King that she more materially ministered. She remained his mistress for many years, bearing him six children or more and being created Duchess of Cleveland in 1670. During her period of favour she had to endure several rivals for the King's affections, including Nell Gwynne. Her position was eventually, in 1673, usurped by Louise de Kerouaille, Duchess of Portsmouth. She died in 1709.

She was to Lely something of the inspiration that Emma Hamilton would be for George Romney a century later. Romney followed the fashion of his time, tending to cast Emma as the model for historical figures, rather than as the sitter for true portraits; Lely sometimes did the same, painting Cleveland as the Magdalen or the Virgin or Minerva (collection Her Majesty The Queen), or St Catherine of Alexandria, as here: behind her to the left can just be glimpsed the wheel on which St Catherine was martyred. The sword and palm branch are also attributes of the saint. Such a role is patently inappropriate and invites us only to enjoy a wry joke which tends suggestively to enhance the allure of the sitter. In such works the serious allegorising of the earlier part of the century is deliberately rendered meaningless for the sake of an immediate effect. Despite these strange accessories, Lely contrives to present his sitter very directly, relying on her charms, and a glorious gold dress, to carry the whole design. In this example, very little supervenes between us and the woman he depicts, and there is a strong sense of intimacy; but there is also a vivid sophistication that gives the image the sharp relevance of a fashion-plate. In looking at the picture we experience something of what Pepys experienced when, as he wrote in July 1661: 'I sat before Mrs Palmer, the King's mistress, and filled my eyes with her, which much pleased me.' (Braybrooke I, p.371)

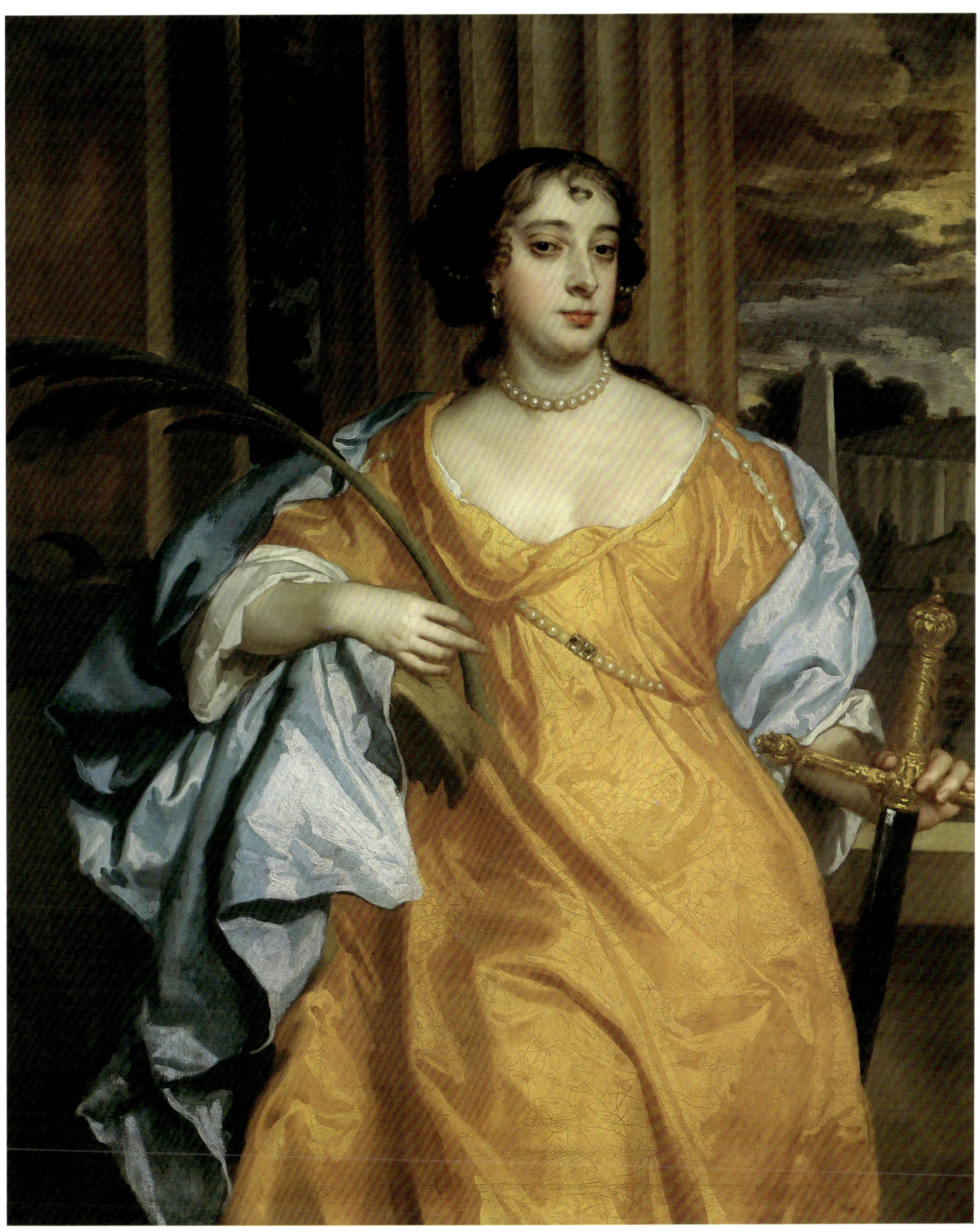

13 Jane Bickerton, Duchess of Norfolk *c.*1677

Oil on canvas 230 × 139.7 ($90\frac{1}{2}$ × 55)
Signed: *P Lely fet. A 167*[7?]
His Grace the Duke of Norfolk

Jane Bickerton (*c.*1644–93) was an archetypal product of her epoch: her father was a gentleman of the royal Wine Cellar; by 1670 she was mistress to Henry Howard, Baron Howard of Castle Rising, and had borne him a son. His first wife, Lady Anne Somerset, had died in 1662, leaving him overcome by a longstanding depression from which he tried to escape by bouts of dissipation – 'base, & vicious Courses', as John Evelyn described it. He succeeded his brother as 6th Duke of Norfolk in 1677, and about the same time made public the fact that he had married Jane Bickerton. Evelyn disliked her, and recorded that the Duke had referred to her as an 'idle Creature & common' whom he did not intend to make his wife. The King too seems to have disapproved of her, and tried to dissuade Norfolk from the liaison. But the Duke commissioned this and a portrait of himself (Arundel Castle) from Lely to celebrate their formal union. The picture duly registers the blend of refinement and blowsiness that characterises the type and the time. It is on one level a formal portrait in the tradition of Van Dyck, both dignified and relaxed; yet Lely infuses it with a raffish quality of which Van Dyck would have been incapable. The gesture, the languishing expression and the standard accessories – urn, drapery and column – contribute to no serious statement concerning the character and qualities of the sitter: one cannot 'read' the flowers (carefully painted by an assistant) as bearing any symbolic message, and the movement of the arms is one of lazy self-admiration, hardly conveying any rhetorical sense. The elements of the design simply combine to create an image of elegant and expensive sexuality. The formula was to be a commonplace of grand female portraiture for the rest of the century, though in the hands of most of Lely's followers – Wissing and Riley, for instance – it lost its sensuous force and became altogether more prosaic. But in combining the accessories of grand official portraiture with a splendidly casual 'undress', Lely brings together two quite separate strands of Van Dyck's practice and creates an important link with the work of Reynolds and his contemporaries a century later.

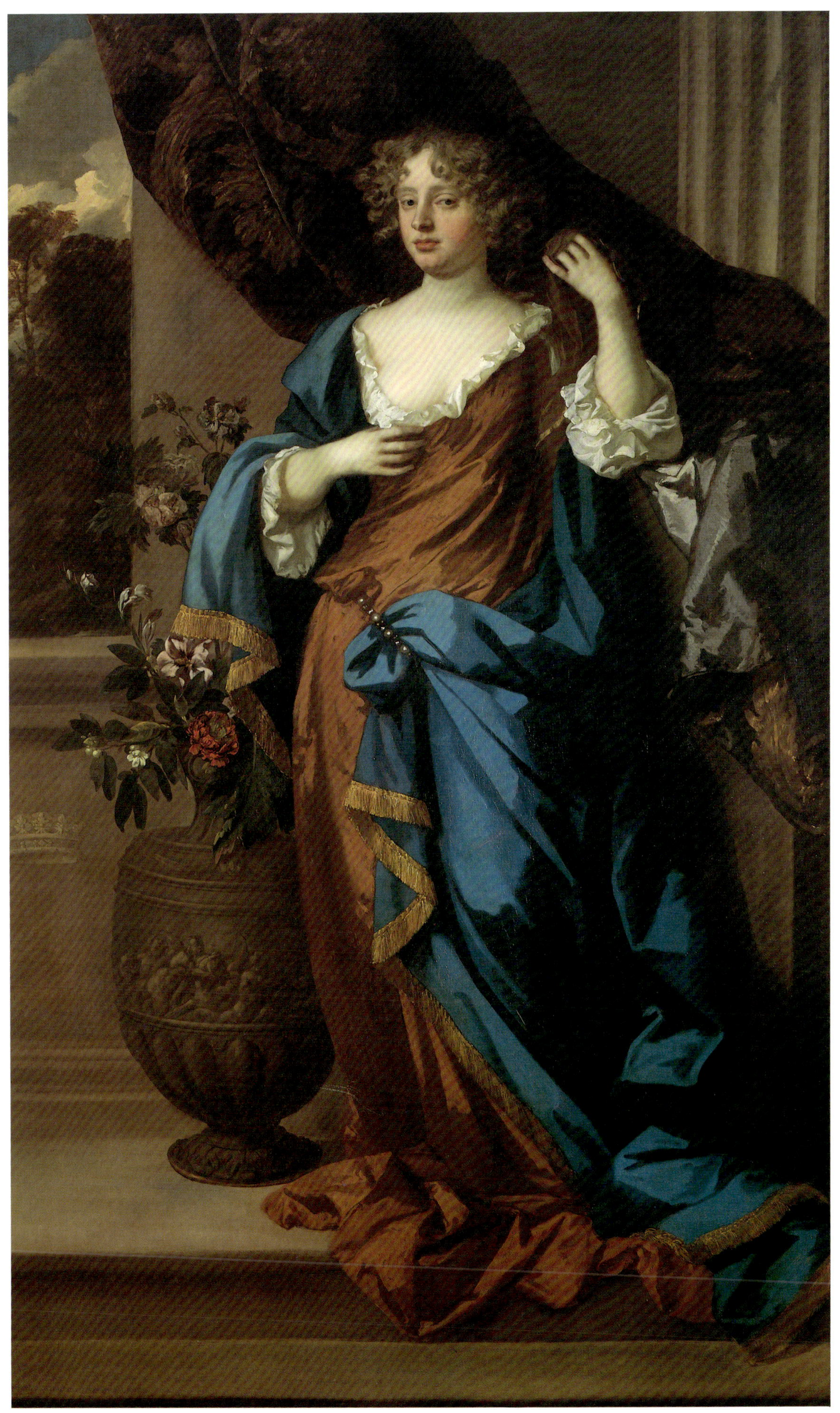

JACOB HUYSMANS *c.*1633–*c.*1696

14 **Elizabeth Somerset, 1st Marchioness of Powis** *c.*1665–70

Oil on canvas 238 × 147.3 ($93\frac{3}{4}$ × 58)
The Powis Estate Trustees, Powis Castle, on loan to the National Trust

Huysmans came to London in 1662 from Antwerp, where he trained around 1650, and where he presumably absorbed a Baroque taste for effects of swirling drapery and glossy fabrics which makes his work distinctively busier and often lusher than that of Lely, whose chief rival he became. He was patronised extensively by the Queen, Catherine of Braganza – whom he painted in an opulent compositon as St Catherine and in another, rather similar to this work, as a shepherdess (both collection Her Majesty The Queen) – and by English Catholic families, among whom was that of the Earl of Powis. Elizabeth Somerset was daughter of another prominent Catholic and royalist, the Marquess of Worcester. In 1654 she married William Herbert, created Earl of Powis by Charles II in 1674. He became 1st Marquess in 1687. Both were closely attached to the court of James II, to whose children Elizabeth was Governess. After the Revolution of 1688, they accompanied the royal family into exile at St Germain and were created titular Duke and Duchess of Powis in 1689. The Duchess died there in March 1690/1, and her husband in 1696.

Huysmans's Flemish, Catholic background brings his work closer to the tradition of grandiose portraiture that was maintained in Italy and France than Lely ever approaches. The full panoply of the Baroque whole-length is deployed here, with brocaded curtains, tassels, columns and, instead of a mortal attendant, a well-grown and elaborately draped putto holding a bowl of equally well-grown fruit. The sportive dog at his feet ensures that the eye finds no rest in this energetic and crowded design.

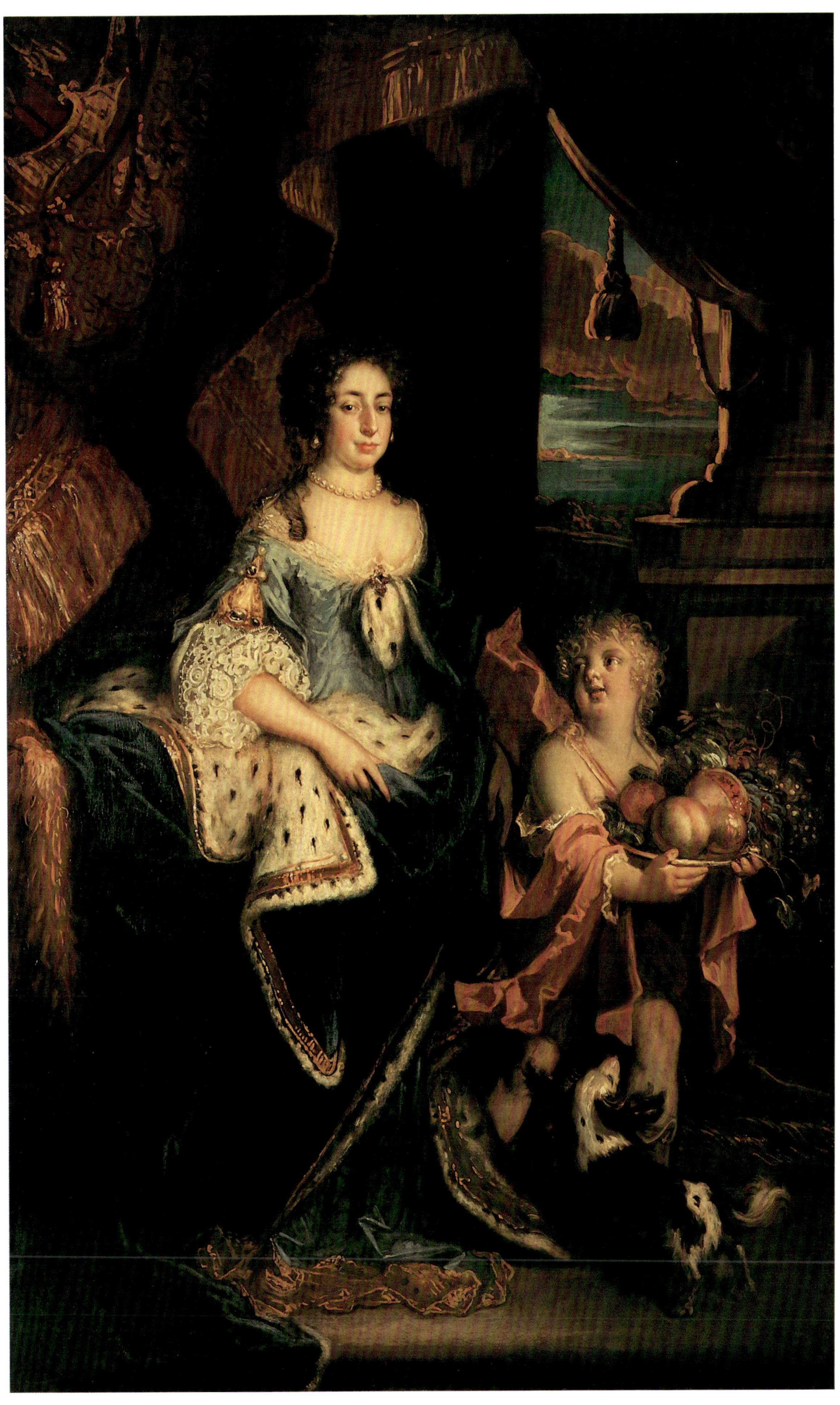

JOHN MICHAEL WRIGHT 1617–1694

15 A Lady in Masquerade Costume *c.*1679

Oil on canvas 212.1 × 148.6 ($83\frac{1}{2} \times 58\frac{1}{2}$)
Private Collection

The tradition of what we may term the theatrical portrait had been begun by Van Dyck in those of his works that place the sitter in a costume and setting appropriate to the court masque; as in, for instance, the 'Countess of Southampton', no.7. This picture of an unknown woman has recently been known as 'Portrait of a Lady with a Riding Crop', and interpreted as though she were literally dressed for the hunt. But it has long been recognised that her costume is not exactly standard hunting wear. When the picture was sold from Hatfield Peverel Priory (Robinson, Fisher & Co., 1 February 1912, lot 101), it was ascribed to Nicolaes Maes (although ironically its owner at Hatfield Peverel was a John Wright, Esq.) and called 'A Lady as Diana', implying a general allegorising intention. But it is clear from the presentation of the figure that there is a more precise explanation for her attire. She is dressed neither literally for the hunt nor in some vague allegorical character, but for the stage, and her elaborately plumed headdress is precisely what we should expect to be worn by a personage in a masquerade (fig.29) or a theatrical performance. (Though it is worth noting that similar feathered caps are to be found in Dutch pictures of the period; and an almost identical headdress is shown by Wright in another picture, worn by the two-year-old boy in his double portrait of Lady Catherine Cecil and James Cecil, Lord Cranborne, later 4th Earl of Salisbury, as children; collection The Marquess of Salisbury). If the unknown lady were Diana she would probably have been depicted with a crescent moon on her head, bow and arrows or a spear in hand, and perhaps an attendant stag. The lady in Wright's picture has none of these accessories. Her riding-crop, and the distant glimpse of a groom leading away a horse, suggest that she has just dismounted, perhaps to escape the storm that is presaged by the threatening sky. These details make one think of Dido, in the passage from Virgil's *Aeneid* (Book IV) in which the Queen of Carthage and Aeneas hunt together and are overtaken by a storm. The lowering landscape background takes on a very specific meaning in the context of this reading, though it should be said that atmospheric backdrops of trees and sky are often to be found in Wright's work.

Despite the theatrical connotations of the subject, there is little likelihood that the sitter is an actress. Her costume is altogether too splendid, and so much in the tradition of masque designs by Inigo Jones that we should be safer in assuming that she is a lady of the court of Charles II. There is similar uncertainty as to why she is depicted in this role. Perhaps the sitter took the part in a masquerade; but she was presumably not intended to be associated in private with Dido's qualities. This suggests a radical change of emphasis in the way such portraits were conceived, and leads on to the more elaborate games that Reynolds was to play with theatricality.

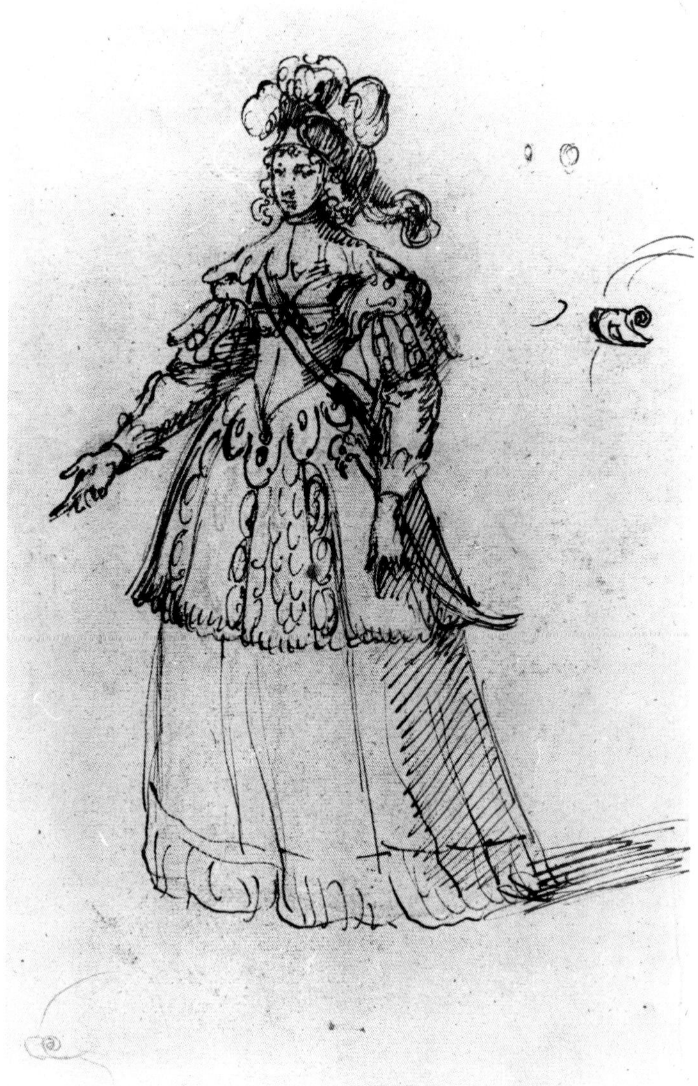

fig.29 Inigo Jones **Masque Design, a Lady in Amazonian Habit** *c.*1641
Pen and brown ink *Duke of Devonshire, Chatsworth*

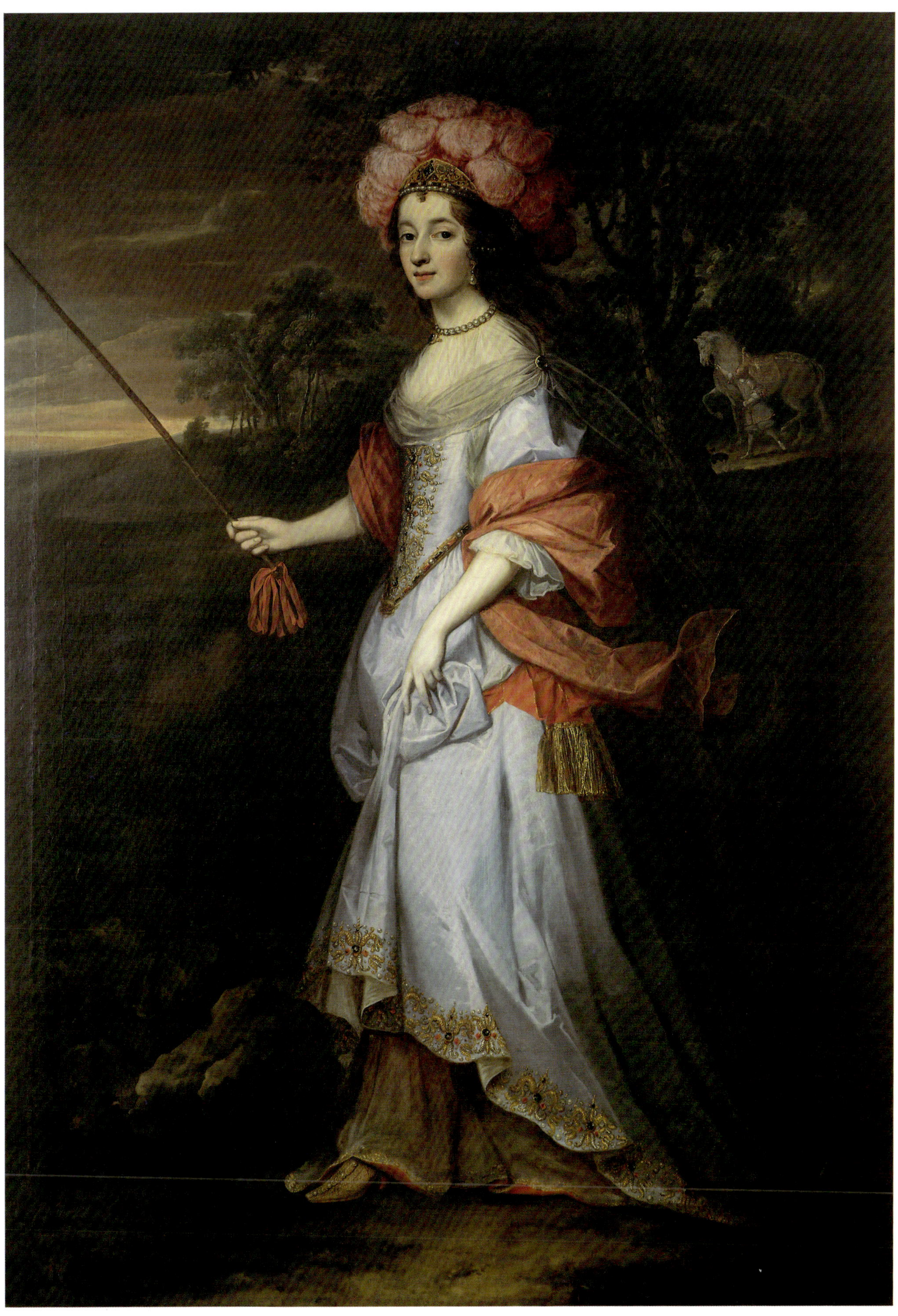

JOHN MICHAEL WRIGHT

16 **Lord Mungo Murray** *c.*1688

Oil on canvas 224.8 × 154.3 ($88\frac{1}{2} \times 60\frac{3}{4}$)
Scottish National Portrait Gallery

The tradition of painting clansmen in their ceremonial costume is a long one; there are several examples included here. They are all remarkable for the relative flamboyance with which they are treated. Whereas most Scottish portraiture is, as we should expect, dourly Protestant, the Highland chieftains, usually strongly Jacobite, were a rather different strain from their Lowland cousins, and often highly eccentric characters. This may explain why they elicited special treatment from their painters. Tartan patterns had been in use in Scotland only since the sixteenth century and this portrait is among the earliest to feature the splendours of Highland dress. So great is the emphasis on tartan finery, indeed, that the picture has been seen as a study of costume rather than as a portrait – the identity of the sitter has only recently been discovered. The picture was for many years treated as a pair to Wright's 'Sir Neil O'Neill, 2nd Baronet of Killeleagh' (Tate Gallery), and together they form a remarkable early record of ceremonial dress, as Bainbrigge Buckeridge noted in a paragraph on Wright in his *Essay towards an English School of Painters* (1706): 'He . . . drew a Highland laird in his proper habit, and an Irish Tory in his country dress; both which whole-lengths were in so great repute at the time when they were done, that many copies were made of them.' (p.437)

The sitter has now been fairly confidently identified as a member of the clan Murray, who became Dukes of Atholl in the early eighteenth century. He is apparently the fifth son of John Murray, 2nd Earl and 1st Marquis of Atholl (see no.19), and was born in 1668. His career was brief: in the late 1690s he set sail for the New World with the intention of founding a Scottish colony in the remote region of Panama. It was there that he died in 1700.

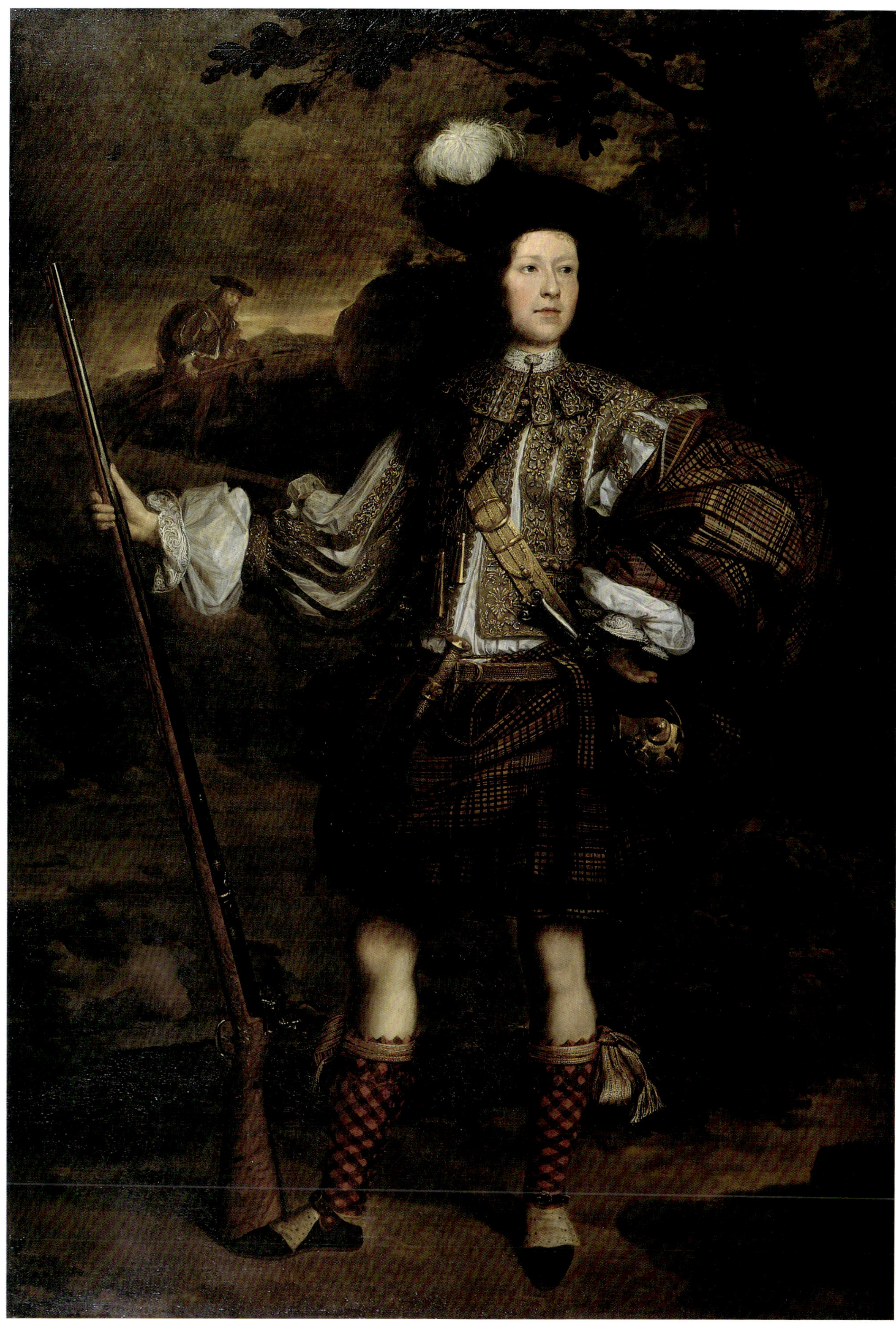

17 **Charles II** 1685

Oil on canvas 224.7 × 142.8 ($88\frac{1}{2} \times 56\frac{1}{4}$)
Signed: *Gotfred Kneller/Ad vivum fecit/Ao 1685*
The Trustees of the National Museums and Galleries on Merseyside, Walker Art Gallery

One of the standard representations of Charles II, frequently copied, and reproduced in mezzotint by Robert Williams, this dates from the last months of his life, and is itself a derivation from a type evolved by Lely in the mid-1670s (an example is in the collection of the Duke of Grafton; see Millar 1978, no.52). The relaxed pose and conversational air create an ambiguity: are we to respond to the presentation of the King or to the presence of the man? The Garter robes are those in which Charles was usually shown; as Millar points out Lely never painted him in full state robes, and Kneller only did so towards the close of his reign. This is, however, essentially an image of state: the orb and crown on the table at the King's side confirm that. At the same time, it is a picture that has been described as the 'most masterly' of Kneller's portraits of Charles (Stewart, p.27), because it is the only one that 'really lays bare the secret of why he "never went on his travels again" ', though this seems to give the artist the benefit of hindsight. The likeness of the King is apparently an 'official' one, and gives little indication that he was already suffering from the 'distemper' which, within a month of the portrait's being painted, would lead to a fit of apoplexy that was to be fatal.

Although his father, Charles I, was short of stature and refined of feature, Charles II was exceptionally tall and very dark haired with a coarse face and swarthy complexion. He placed his sharp intelligence at the service of a lively wit which was frequently criticised for being unsuitably racy for a monarch, and made use of it to maintain his ascendancy over a succession of ministers. He was a valetudinarian and a notorious and inveterate womaniser; the list of his mistresses is extensive and was the cause of much public embarrassment during his reign (see no.19). But if he was a 'merry monarch' he was also a proud one, and was determined to reassert the divine right that his father had so tenaciously believed in. By the time this picture was painted, his difficulties with Parliament were beginning to seem like a repeat of the prelude to the Civil War, and within months the country would be in the hands of a Catholic king. In portraying Charles as both affable and regal Kneller accurately registers the two facets of his personality as monarch.

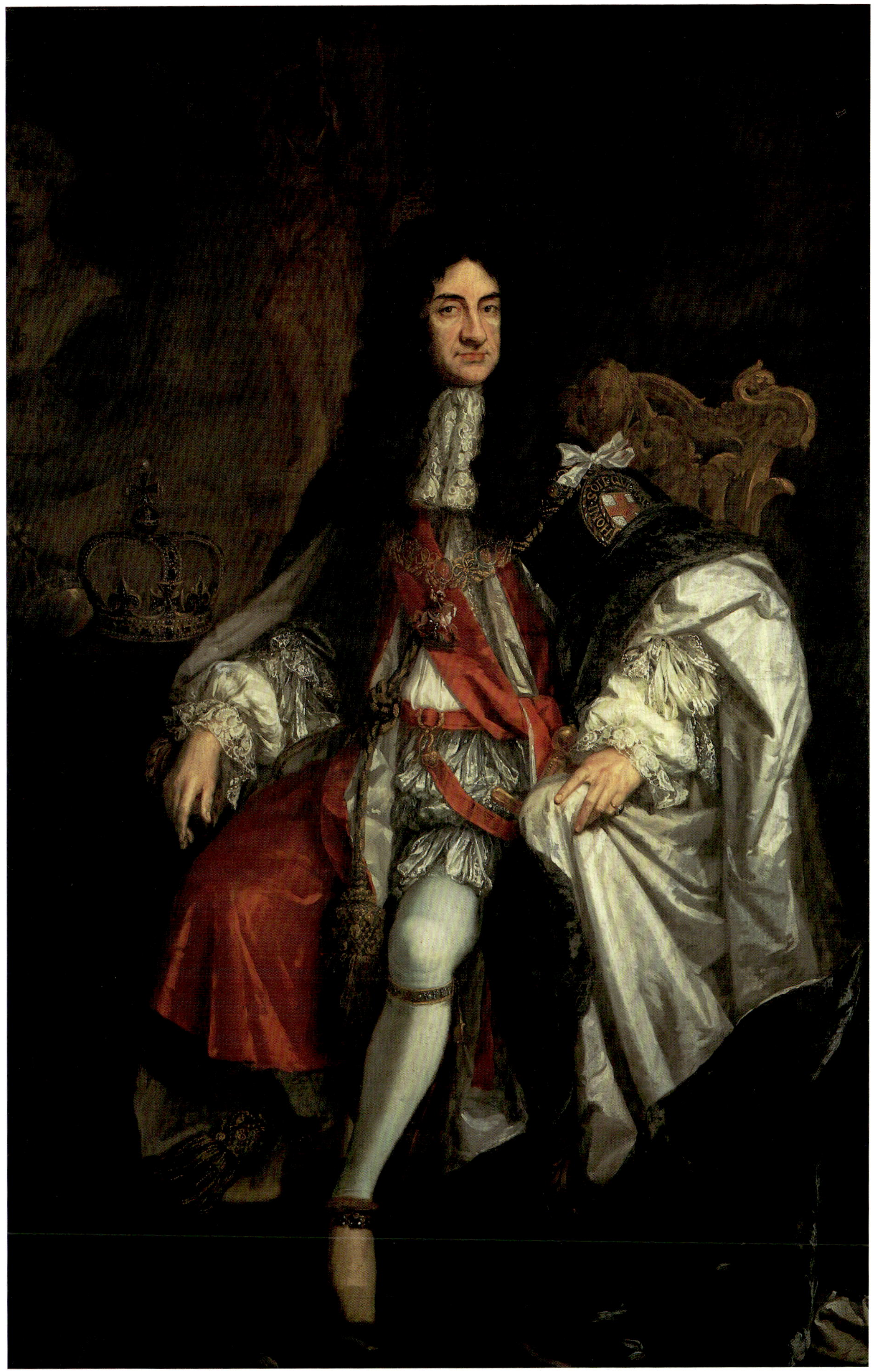

18 Elizabeth Pelham, First Wife of Charles, 2nd Viscount Townshend *c.*1698

Oil on canvas 241 × 148 ($94\frac{7}{8} \times 58\frac{1}{4}$)
Inscr. lower right (not by the artist): *Elizabeth Pelham.| 1st Wife to Charles Ld Townshend.*
Private Collection

Although not one of the famous set of 'Beauties' painted by Kneller for Queen Mary in the 1690s and now at Hampton Court (collection Her Majesty The Queen), this portrait follows the pattern he had established there for female whole-lengths. The format is modelled on Lely's treatment of similar subjects in the 1660s and 70s; compare the portrait of Jane Bickerton, Duchess of Norfolk (no.13). However, the mood of this later period is very different, being altogether more sober and restrained. The classical or religious overtones that Lely and his contemporaries had used to lend the *frisson* of deliberately irrelevant seriousness to the portrayal of attractive women are now invoked more sparingly. Their intention has become simply to confirm an essentially moralistic statement about womanly virtue and dignity. The sitter is presented here in more public terms than her forerunners. The lazy gestures of Lely's Duchess of Norfolk are replaced by a stiff pose that combines a rather precarious grace with a careful decorum. Indeed, such is the *gravitas* of the image, focused as it is on an entirely serious presentation of the face, that Lady Townshend seems to enjoy some of the status accorded to men in the same period.

This flattering presentation is probably more the consequence of the routine application of Kneller's formula than of any special qualities in the sitter. The classical relief against which she stands, the balustrade through which roses can be seen, and the house glimpsed beyond trees against a sunset sky, are all features that recur almost identically in other portraits by Kneller; for example, in the whole-length of Jane Leveson-Gower, Countess of Clarendon (collection Avon and Somerset Constabulary, King's Weston) engraved in mezzotint by John Faber as one of the 'Hampton Court Beauties', though the picture was apparently not intended as one of that set.

Lady Townshend was born in 1681, the only daughter of the 1st Lord Pelham by his first wife, and married Charles, 2nd Viscount Townshend in 1698. It may have been in recognition of that occasion that the picture was painted. She bore he husband several sons before her death in 1711.

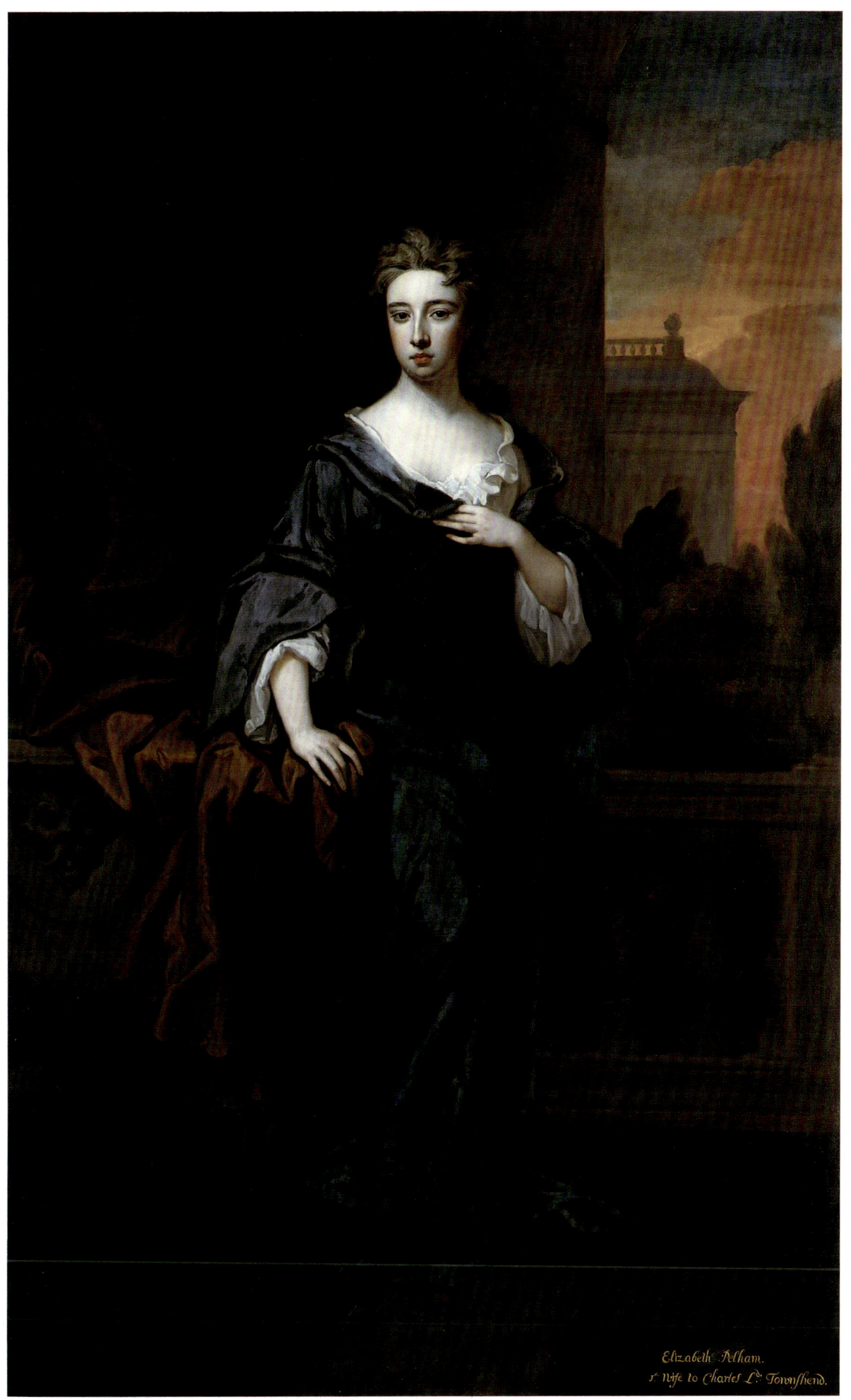
Elizabeth Pelham.
1st Wife to Charles Ld. Townshend.

JACOB DE WET 1640–1697

19 John, 1st Marquis of Atholl *c.*1680

Oil on canvas 240.4 × 167.5 (96 × 66)
Inscr. on a slip, lower left (not by the artist): *John Mar. of Atholl/died ye 72nd year of his age 1703.*; and with an epitome
His Grace the Duke of Atholl, Blair Castle, Perthshire

John Murray, 2nd Earl and 1st Marquis of Atholl (1631–1703), was a leading figure in Scottish seventeenth-century history, prominently involved in the disputes between the Convention and the Covenanters, whom he actively persecuted. It was in the course of one of these excursions, in 1679, when the Convention's 'Highland Host' conducted an extensive raid on the Scottish Shires, that Monmouth, leading an English army, bloodily defeated the Covenanters at Bothwell Brig. Although one of the victorious captains himself, Atholl was shocked by the barbarities he witnessed and joined a deputation to Charles II pleading leniency towards the nonconformists. This brought him recrimination and a temporary loss of position. In 1680 he was appointed Vice-Admiral of Scotland, and began the persecution of the Duke of Argyll, who was reduced to ruin. When the monarchy fell in 1688 he was unable to conceal his mixed feelings and acquired the reputation of a turncoat. After the Battle of Killiecrankie he was captured and interrogated in the Tower of London, but released. He was stigmatised by Macaulay as 'the falsest, the most fickle, the most pusillanimous of mankind'.

De Wet (whose name is also sometimes given as de Witt) was the most important painter working in Scotland in the middle years of the seventeenth century. He brought to the Protestant Scots a sophisticated and elaborate style from Holland which must have seemed highly unusual there at that date. This portrait seems to have been commissioned shortly after the adventure at Bothwell Brig; the inscription at the lower left corner was added as a commemoration after the sitter's death. Atholl is shown dressed in a fanciful adaptation of Roman armour and wearing a full-bottomed wig, his body twisted in a histrionic pose. This antique idiom, common enough at the time, is that of the Franco-Flemish late Baroque; a somewhat similar work is the portrait of James II as Duke of York by Henri Gascars in the National Maritime Museum, which is probably roughly contemporary with this picture; but in comparison with even that elaborate invention, de Wet's picture is extraordinarily tortuous and intricate. The contrapposto of the pose may be compared with the direct gesture of Dobson's 'Baron Byron' (no.9), and the subtle interplay of classical allusion and modern character in Dobson's 'Endymion Porter' (no.8) contrasts with de Wet's insistence on a somewhat crude superimposition of roles. No attempt is made to design the sitter's armour in such a way that it symbolises martial virtues, and the Roman relief in front of which he stands is not allegorically pointed, although it seems to show Cupid at the forge of Vulcan, blacksmith to the Gods, who made armour for Mars, god of war. Atholl's gesture is more theatrical than military, just as the background depiction of the Battle of Bothwell Brig can hardly be related to the sitter in any rational historical context but seems to belong to drama or myth. The one element of restraint is the colour. A cool palette of silvery greens and yellows replaces the more usual regal reds and blues, and invests the picture with a poetic dignity somewhat at odds with its rhetorical language.

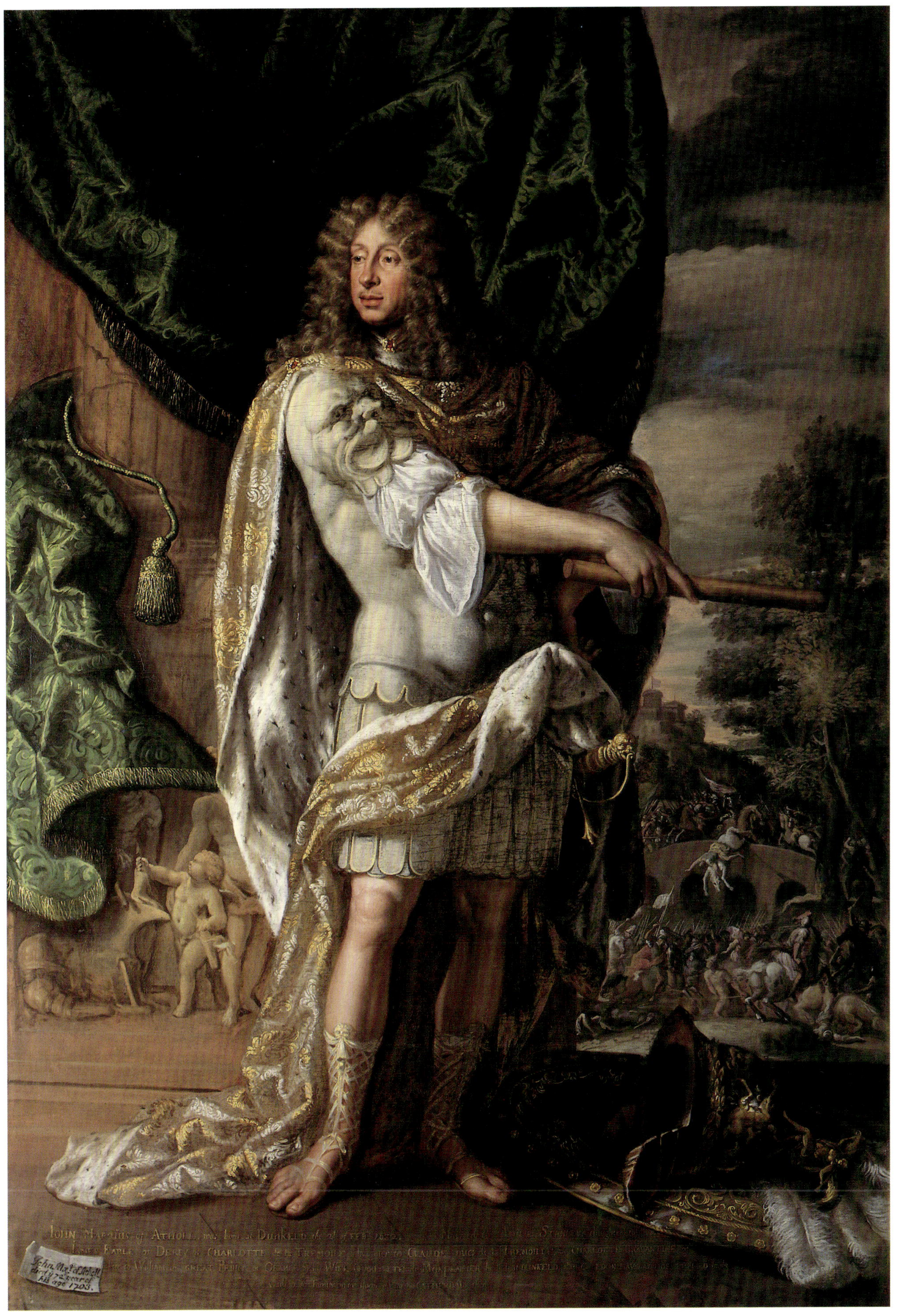

JONATHAN RICHARDSON *c.*1665–1745

20 Edward and Constantia Rolt *c.*1695

Oil on canvas 167.5 × 122 (66 × 48)
Mrs Kitty Lemos

Edward was the son and heir of Sir Thomas Rolt of Sacombe Park, Hertfordshire, who was President of the East India Company at Surat. He was born about 1680, admitted to Lincoln's Inn in 1702, and married Anne Bayntun, whose mother, Anne Wilmot, was sister to the celebrated Earl of Rochester and to Henry Hyde, 2nd Earl of Clarendon (see no.13). He died in 1722, leaving a son, also Edward, who took the name Bayntun and inherited his mother's property of Spye Park near Calne, Wiltshire. His sister Constantia remained single until after his death, marrying Timothy Caswell in 1726.

Richardson was a pupil of John Riley (1646–91), and inherited Riley's somewhat earnest approach to portraiture, though with an intellectual grasp of the philosophy behind his art that emerges clearly in his important writings on the subject. In this lively double portrait which belongs to a fairly early stage of his career, he reveals himself in a distinctly Baroque guise which goes considerably beyond what Riley usually achieved. It is not, however, very typical of Richardson's output as a whole, and although his portraits usually evince solid worth they rarely expand into such an atmosphere of freshness and charm as this. The figure of the boy leaning against a plinth and holding a spear seems to be a reminiscence of Lely's little picture of a youth holding a shepherd's *houlette* and pipe, traditionally identified as Abraham Cowley (Dulwich), which itself looks back to Van Dyck's pastoral portraits of the Seigneur d'Aubigny (National Portrait Gallery) and of Philip Lord Wharton (Washington, National Gallery of Art). All these have the rocky background evocative of the arcadia of Inigo Jones. But the poetic connotations of those pictures are transmuted here into something more authoritative: Edward Rolt takes up a decidedly rhetorical pose, silhouetted against the sky and looking out at the spectator, gesturing towards the landscape rather grandly, if vaguely. The *houlette* is changed for a spear. But an effective psychological link is established between him and his sister by the movement of his arm in her direction and the attentive gaze that she directs at him. The fact that his spear points towards the fruits that she has gathered suggests the symbolic intention of wishing on her an appropriate fecundity, just as he is envisaged as a future leader of men.

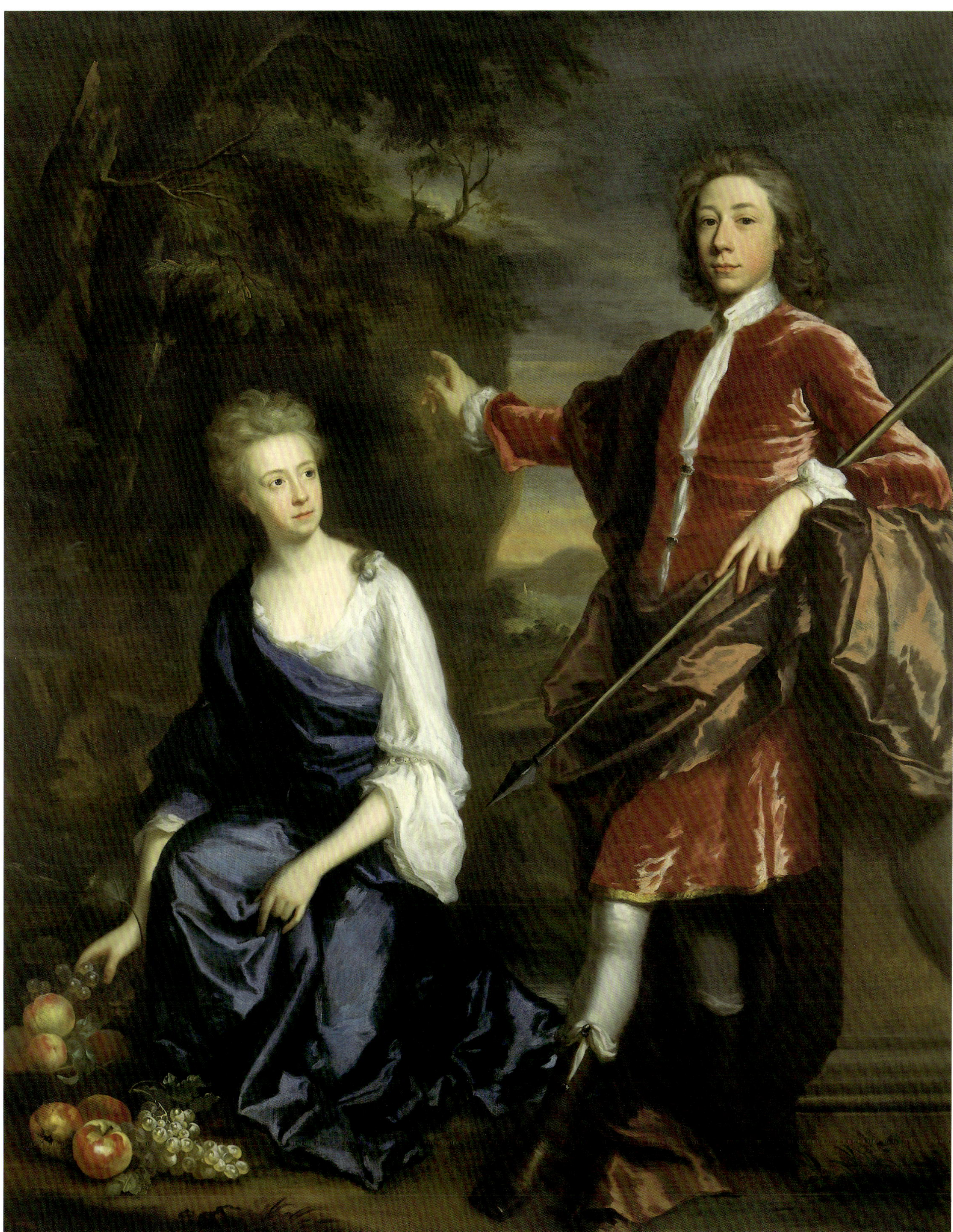

JOHN CLOSTERMAN 1660–1711

21 The Children of John Taylor of Bifrons Park, Kent *c.*1696

Oil on canvas 189.8 × 271 ($74\frac{3}{4}$ × 107)
National Portrait Gallery

Closterman is one of the most inventive of the northern European artists who flourished in England at the end of the seventeenth century. His German training (his father was an artist in Osnabrück, and Closterman was initially taught by him) was overlaid with close experience of French Baroque painting in the studio of François de Troy, where he spent some time in 1679, and he brought to London two years later an exceptionally luxuriant inventiveness which was responsible for some of the most remarkable portraits of the period. He spent a couple of years as drapery painter in partnership with the staid John Riley; this practice hardly prepared the English for the richness of his own work. By the middle of the decade he had set up independently, and was working for well-to-do and often distinguished professional people; but he quickly progressed to a more patrician clientele, including the Catholic Duke of Somerset. That relationship was soured by a quarrel over a picture that Closterman had acquired for his master: he did some business in buying and selling works of art, some of which he acquired in the course of two visits to Italy. He also went to Madrid in company with James Stanhope (later 1st Earl Stanhope) and the 3rd Earl of Shaftesbury, then Lord Ashley. While there he was asked to paint the King and Queen of Spain. In Rome his exuberant Baroque manner was somewhat modified when he came under the sobering influence of Maratta, whose almost neoclassical style is reflected in many of his later works. That visit to Rome, however, was in 1698, two years after the presumed date of this fine canvas.

In it, the children are treated as seriously as an adult group, though with a wit and charm that suits their status perfectly. One of the daughters, Mary (born 1690), is seated in the centre of the wide composition, holding a cornucopia from which she has taken a white rose that she hands to her brother Nathaniel (born 1687). The younger siblings are grouped at the right: an infant, Bridges (born 1695) offers another flower to the very new baby Upton (born 1696), on a plinth beside his brother John (born 1687), making a subsidiary composition that imitates a High Renaissance Holy Family. Complementing this incident, at the left, two of the sisters, Olive (born 1681) and Margaret (born 1683) hold trumpets signifying fame and crown the eldest son, Brook (born 1685) with a wreath. 'Fama candida rosa dulcior' runs the family motto – 'Fame is sweeter than the white rose' – and Closterman thus allegorises upon it. Brook was a clever boy who was to become a celebrated mathematician and theorist of perspective.

This way of subdividing the composition of large group portraits is not uncommon in the period. A large canvas of the Bathurst family by James Maubert (1666–1746), dating from about 1716 (fig.30, Weiss Gallery), has the husband in hunting gear, attended by a negro servant, as a separate, whole-length portrait at the right while his wife and latest baby, apparently portrayed posthumously, take on the roles of Madonna and Christ-child in a throne-like niche. The two groups are bound together by other figures and various visual links so that the composition remains coherent; and this is even more true of the Taylor children, whom Closterman unifies masterfully in a single chain of interlocking gestures across the wide canvas that anticipates Reynolds's 'Three Ladies Adorning a Term of Hymen' (no.35).

Another important patron was the Duke of Marlborough, who in about 1698 commissioned from Closterman a large family group (still at Blenheim) that derives its inspiration from Van Dyck's Pembroke group at Wilton, and takes its place in the grand line of such groups that includes both Reynolds's and Sargent's large pictures of the Marlborough family (Blenheim). See also no.44.

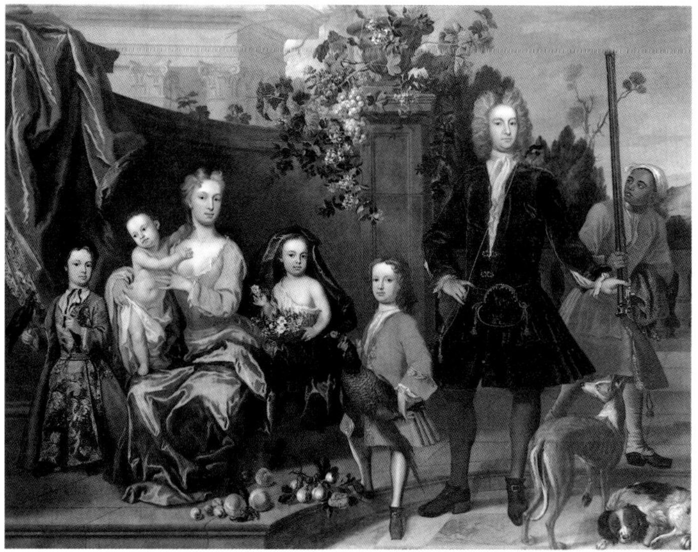

fig.30 James Maubert **Edward Bathurst and his Family** *c.*1716 Oil on canvas *Weiss Gallery*

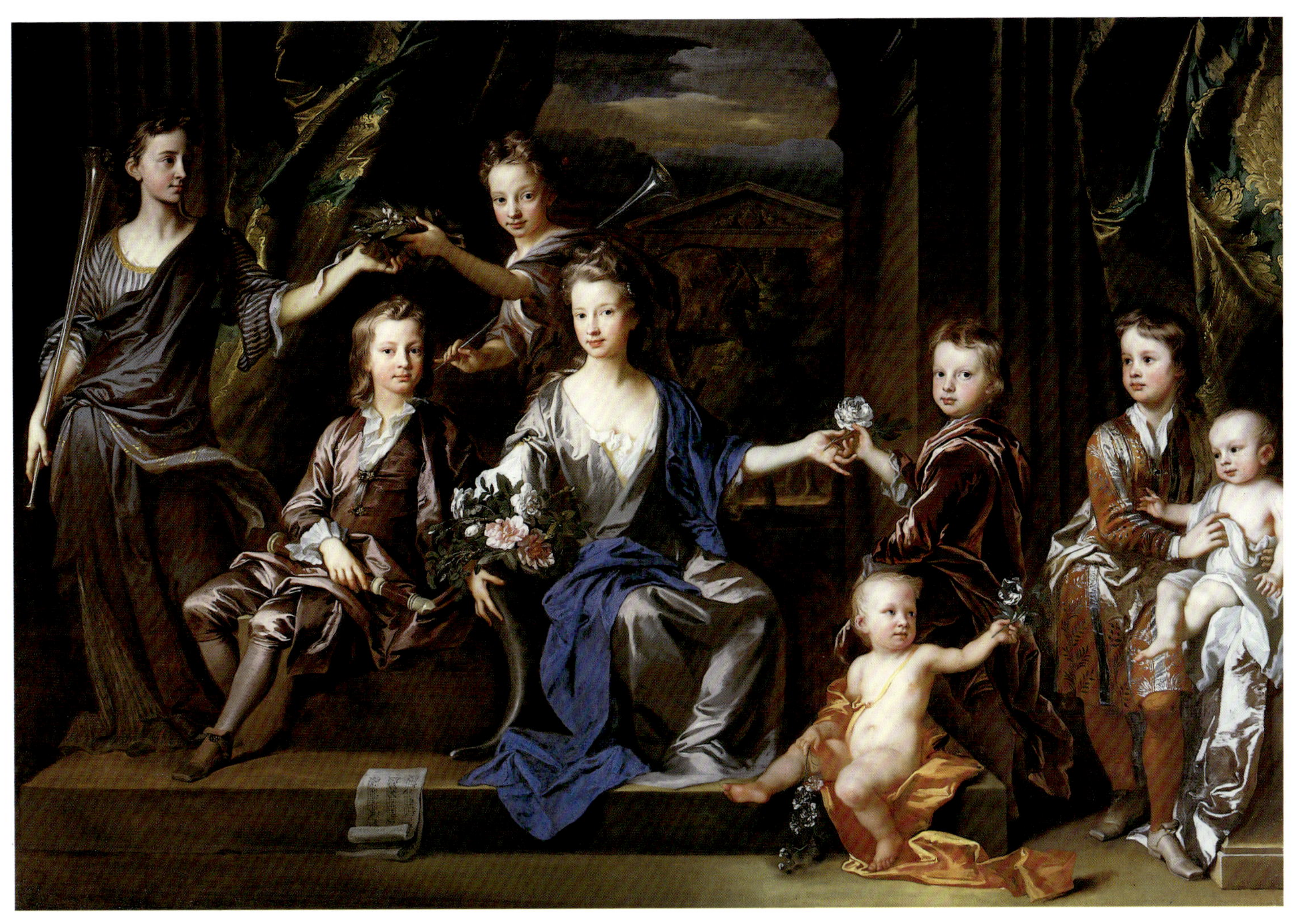

JOHN CLOSTERMAN

22 **Portrait of an Unidentified Man** *c.*1702–5

Oil on canvas 208.3 × 146 (82 × $57\frac{1}{2}$)
Inscr. lower left (not by the artist): *John D. of Marlborough/by Sir Godfrey Kneller.*
Private Collection

The subject of this picture has traditionally been known as the Duke of Marlborough, though there are no grounds for the identification. Closterman did produce a large and Rubensian equestrian portrait of Marlborough, now in Chelsea Hospital. The present work is inspired not so much by Rubens as by the Italians: it has been pointed out that the background landscape with its fitful, stormy light shows the direct influence of Salvator Rosa, and introduces a Romantic element into the portraiture of the time that anticipates late eighteenth-century developments. In this background it differs most markedly from another very similar portrait by Closterman, of about 1702, which shows the Hon. Maurice Ashley-Cooper (collection The Earl of Shaftesbury) in an altogether less dramatic woodland setting. It has been suggested that the portrait of Ashley-Cooper is a pendant for one of the sitter's brother, the 3rd Earl of Shaftesbury, and shows the active as opposed to the contemplative life. The Maratesque neo-classicism of the 'Earl of Shaftesbury' contrasts strikingly with the more Frenchified and convoluted Baroque of the hunting portrait, but neither has the intense atmosphere of this canvas. It is worth comparing the picture with John Michael Wright's 'A Lady in Masquerade Costume' (no.15), which also has a dramatic landscape setting. But the complexity of the sitter's pose is in total contrast to Wright's much more straightforward presentation; indeed, with its pronounced contrapposto it is more elaborate than almost anything produced in England at the time, and approaches the kind of rhetorical extravagance more commonly encountered in the work of French Baroque artists like Largillière. Despite the broad theatricality of its treatment, the picture is remarkable for the refinement of much of its detail, notably the graining of the butt of the gun, and the powder-pouch that the sitter carries at his waist. The attendant who holds his master's horse is apparently also a portrait.

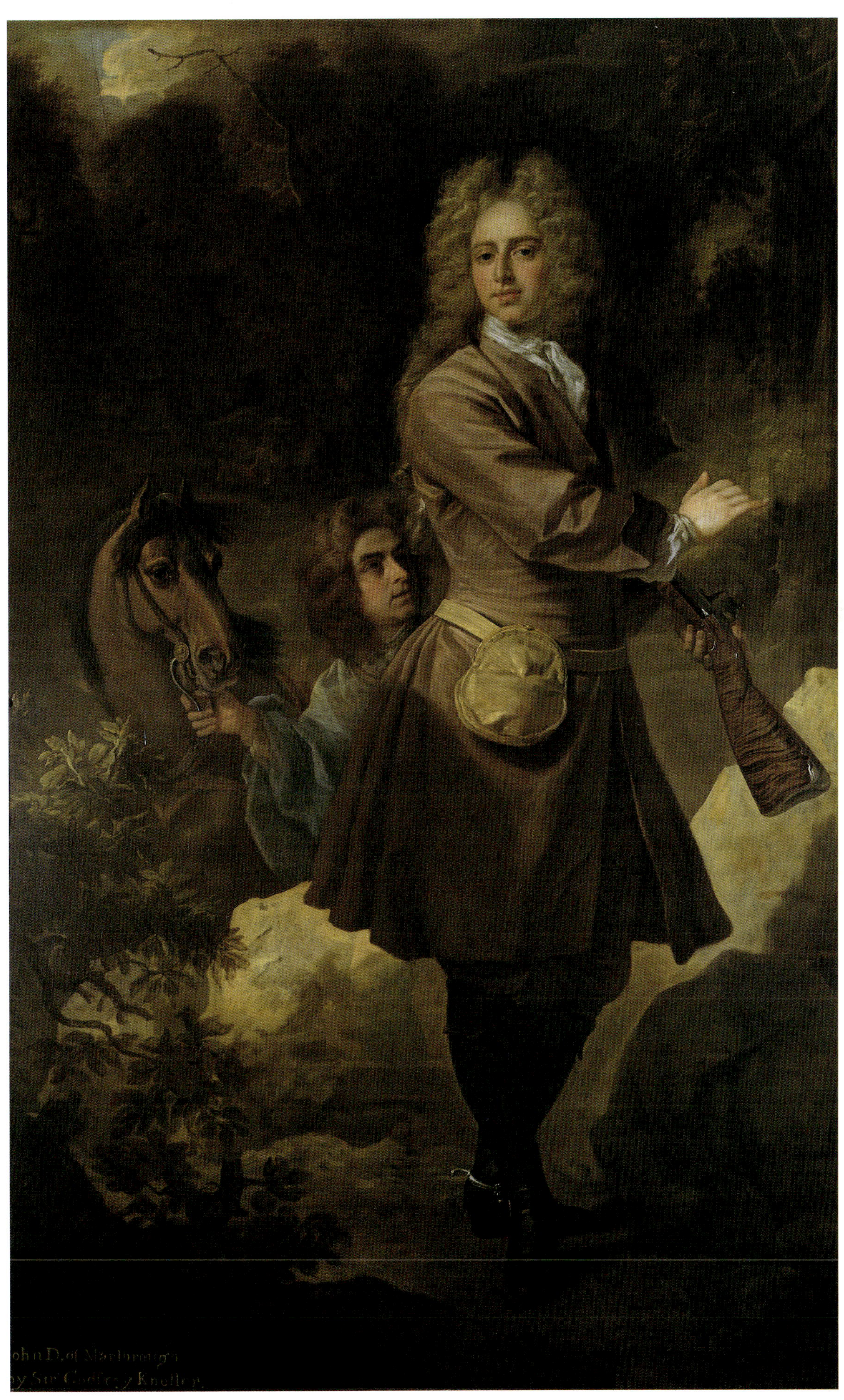
ohn D. of Marlbrough
by Sir Godfrey Kneller.

GIUSEPPE GRISONI 1699–1769

23 Colley Cibber as Lord Foppington ?*c.*1725

Oil on canvas 127 × 102 (50 × 40⅛)
Inscr. lower left (not by the artist): *Colley Cibber Esq:r/in the/ Character of L:d/Foppington*
Garrick Club

Pierre-Joseph Grison was born in the Flemish city of Mons, but Italianised his name when he went to Florence, where he trained. He came to London in 1720 with John Talman (d.1726) for whom he had worked in Rome, and remained in England for eight years painting pictures of all types and also executing book illustrations. In 1724 George Vertue thought him 'a good painter of History. especially midling sizd figures paints portraits very well & designs & invents very freely' (Vertue III, p.20). A tradition that the portrait was owned by Addison, who died in 1719, suggests that the portrait of Cibber was painted when the artist was still in his teens. His training in Rome and Venice reveals itself in the instinctive gusto of this work. It borrows some of its verve, of course, from the theatrical context, but in its rhythmic energy is typical of much Continental portraiture of this date and contrasts markedly with the staid productions of contemporary English painters, including Kneller and Michael Dahl (*c.*1659–1743).

Colley Cibber (1671–1757) was a playwright as well as an actor, and the son of a sculptor who is best remembered for the two reclining figures of lunatics (Museum of London) that he executed for the Bethlehem Hospital (Bedlam). Cibber's first name was given him after his mother's maiden name. Having failed to get in to Winchester College he found employment with his father in the entourage of William Cavendish, Earl of Devonshire. In 1690 he abandoned his prospects there and joined the Theatre Royal company, and eventually scored successes in plays by Otway and Congreve. His play *Love's Last Shift, or, The Fool in Fashion* was performed in 1696, Cibber taking the part of Sir Novelty Fashion. It was highly successful, and marked a shift away from the Restoration comedy of manners towards the sentimental comedy that was to dominate the eighteenth-century stage. Vanbrugh wrote a sequel, *The Relapse, or, Virtue in Danger*, in which Sir Novelty is elevated to the peerage as Lord Foppington. In this role, as Grisoni shows him here, Cibber achieved celebrity, and was from then on the leading comic actor, specialising in foppish characters. His ambition to play in tragedy was thwarted by his unsuitably light voice. He became a successful theatrical manager, providing an example for Garrick, and continued to write plays himself, sometimes collaborating with Vanbrugh. His adaptation of *Richard III* (1700) became a standard text. In 1730 he was made Poet Laureate. Arrogant and scheming, he was constantly entangled in the rivalries and jealousies of his profession, and after a quarrel with Pope acquired somewhat unfair notoriety as the protagonist of a revised version of the *Dunciad*, and was also the butt of satire by Fielding and Johnson. His *Apology for the Life of Mr Colley Cibber, Comedian* (1740) is an important source for the details of Restoration stage performance.

It has been suggested that the picture shows Cibber performing the Epilogue to Vanbrugh's play, at the point when he says the lines

> Did ever highway-man yet bid you stand
> With a sweet bawdy snuff-box in his hand?

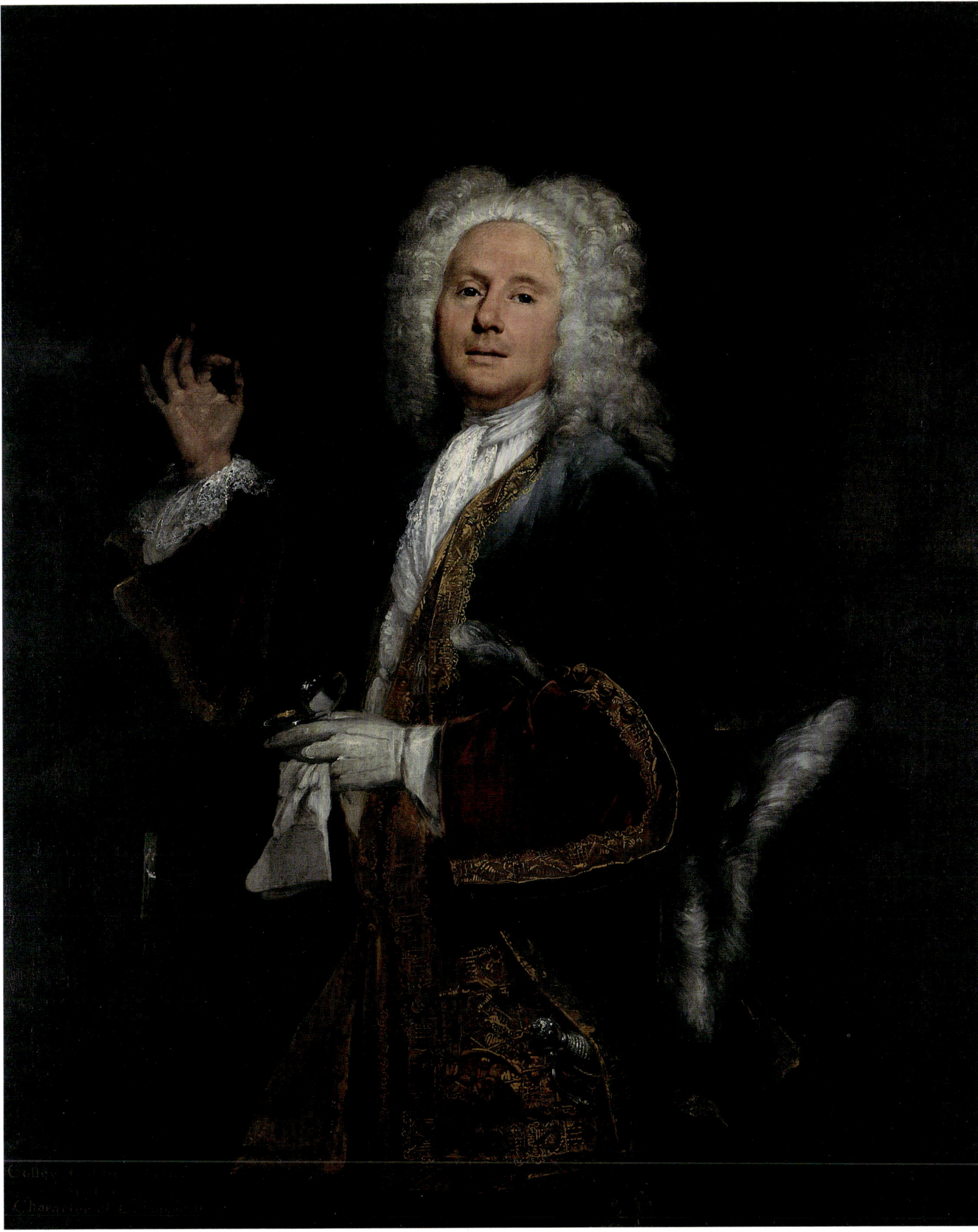

WILLIAM HOGARTH 1697–1764

24 Captain Coram 1740

Oil on canvas 239 × 147.5 (94 × 58)
Inscribed lower left *William Hogarth Pinx^t 1740*, and on step (not by the artist)
Painted and given by Wm Hogarth 1740
Thomas Coram Foundation for Children

In his portrait of Captain Thomas Coram, Hogarth celebrates the irruption into eighteenth-century public life of the industrious and liberal middle classes. Coram was a shipbuilder, and had operated in America as well as England. Like many men who have amassed a fortune in trade or business he went on to spend it in charitable works – a typically Protestant pattern. His most celebrated achievement was the endowment of an orphanage, the Foundling Hospital, which continues to dispense charity in London to this day. Through the good offices of his friend Hogarth, Coram was able to offer in his foundation not only the care of abandoned children but also a gallery of art featuring the best painters of the time, and open to the public on a regular basis: the first museum of modern art, and a powerful stimulus to those who wished, as Hogarth did, to promote the British School.

That aim is served unequivocally by this work. It deliberately bids for a place among the grand portraits of the French and Italian Baroque, with its seated figure raised on a dais, and column and curtain behind. It has been suggested that the model which Hogarth seems to have followed most closely is Hyacinth Rigaud's portrait of Samuel Bernard, as engraved by Pierre Drevet, where there is also a marine backdrop and a large globe. But the English work is monumentally solid beside that flickering French Baroque, and Hogarth was to use the same compositional plan in an even more sober form a year or two later for his full-length portrait of Bishop Hoadly (1742; San Marino, Huntington Library and Art Gallery).

The attributes of Coram's trade and attainments are grouped about him: in his hand he holds the seal of the Royal Charter incorporating the Foundling Hospital, and behind him on the wall is a representation of Charity succouring children. At his feet the globe shows the 'Western or Atlantick Ocean' in allusion to his activities as shipbuilder on both sides of that sea. The book and letter thrown down beside it complete a wonderfully painted still life which is, nevertheless, remarkably casual in its arrangement. That casualness permeates the composition. Coram's big red coat is nonchalantly unbuttoned, and his feet are planted without any attempt at elegance on their podium. The ruddy, evidently benevolent face looks out at us proudly, but without any superiority. This is decidedly the swagger of the bourgeois, not of the nobleman; the picture is an entirely suitable commemoration of the bourgeois virtues, and therefore emerges naturally from the more aristocratic civic sense of earlier, Augustan painters.

The lighting of the picture deserves note. The reflection of a four-light window in the shiny surface of the globe is consistent with the top-lighting of the figure and papers. No luminosity proceeds from the broad expanse of sea which again reminds us of the origin of Coram's wealth. It is not, of course, the real sea: the balustrade, column and curtain define the limits of the portrayed space, and the panorama is itself painted on the wall. It is like a photographer's backdrop, and Hogarth makes no bones about presenting it as scenery. The vividly illuminated reality of the man himself is placed in the immediate present, defined by a group of properties which, although they allude to the past, do not blur that immediacy. The seascape is simply that: an illusion/allusion to an aspect of the sitter's history which has been overlaid by the more insistent importance of his humanity – in all senses of that word.

Hogarth himself pointed to 'Captain Coram' to demonstrate the enduring value of his own achievement: 'is it not strange that one of the first portraits as big as the life of Captain Coram in the foundling hospital should stand the test of twenty years as the best Portrait in the place notwithstanding all the first portrait painters in the Kingdom had exerted their talents to vie with it[?]'(Burke, p.212).

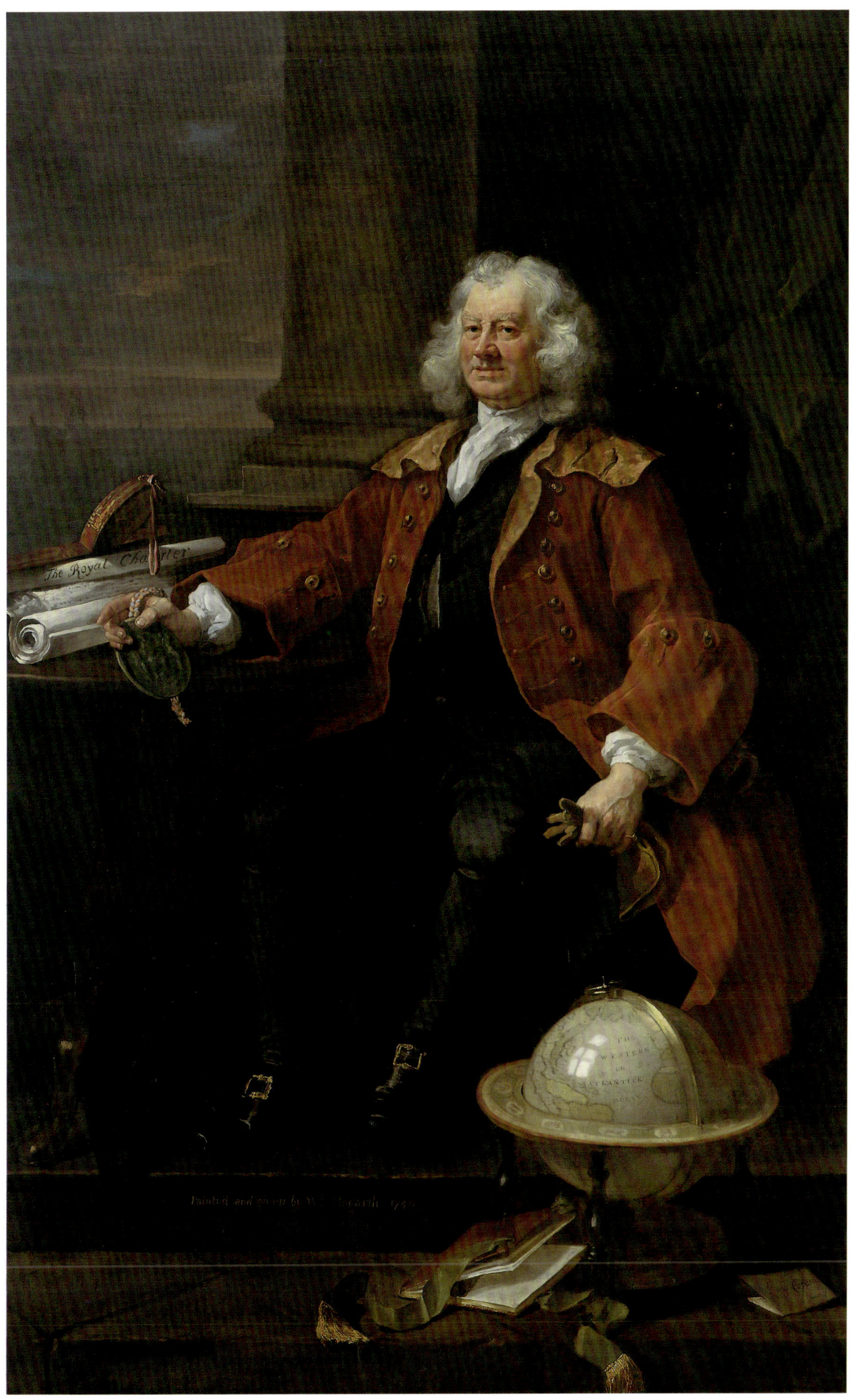
The Royal Charter

THOMAS HUDSON 1701–1779

25 Admiral Sir Chaloner Ogle *c.*1740

Oil on canvas 212.7 × 144.7 ($83\frac{3}{4}$ × 57)
Private Collection

Ogle was born in 1680 or 1681 and joined the navy in 1697. He was a promoted lieutenant in 1702 and given his first command the following year. He served in the war against the French, taking several prizes, and after defeating a notorious pirate, Bartholomew Roberts, in the Mediterranean was awarded a knighthood in 1723. In 1739 he became Rear-Admiral of the Blue and in 1740 sailed in Sir John Norris's fleet with reinforcements to Jamaica, where Admiral Vernon had recently captured Portobello. The Governor of Jamaica was Edward Trelawney, with whom Ogle quarrelled and fought; he was charged with assault and found guilty but Trelawney asked that no sentence should be passed. Left by Vernon in charge of the fleet, Ogle found himself in a position to exercise similar clemency when a lieutenant of marines, George Frye, was found guilty of disrespect. Nevertheless, Ogle sentenced him to fifteen years' imprisonment, in addition to being cashiered. Frye retaliated by claiming false imprisonment, and won £800 damages from Ogle, who however did not pay the money. Having been promoted Vice-Admiral of the Blue in 1744, he returned to England to sit on further courts-martial and, in due course, to be made Admiral of the White and, in 1749, Admiral and Commander-in-Chief. He died the next year. His son Chaloner (born 1727), and grandson Charles both became admirals.

Ogle's confident presence in this portrait is typical of the new realism that was seeping into English portraiture in the first half of the eighteenth century, and which finds its fullest expression in Hogarth's work (see no.24). The stolid dignity of the piece looks back to such works as Kneller's portrait of Prince George of Denmark (fig.31; National Maritime Museum), who leans on an anchor before a maritime backdrop with something of the same self-satisfaction as Admiral Ogle. But Kneller's prince, with his voluminous robes and his hauteur of expression, belongs to a world rather different from that of Hudson's Admiral. In fact, the most 'swagger' element in this picture, and indeed in many of Hudson's male portraits, is the embroidered waistcoat, and it may be assumed that this was the work of another hand – very likely the drapery painter Joseph Van Aken (see no.26), who seems to have been largely responsible for a portrait of the Admiral's wife which has been attributed both to Hudson and to Ramsay. Hudson is the more likely candidate; it was presumably painted about the same time as the Admiral himself and remains in the same collection. His maritime background was likewise added by another artist, the shipping painter Peter Monamy (1681–1749).

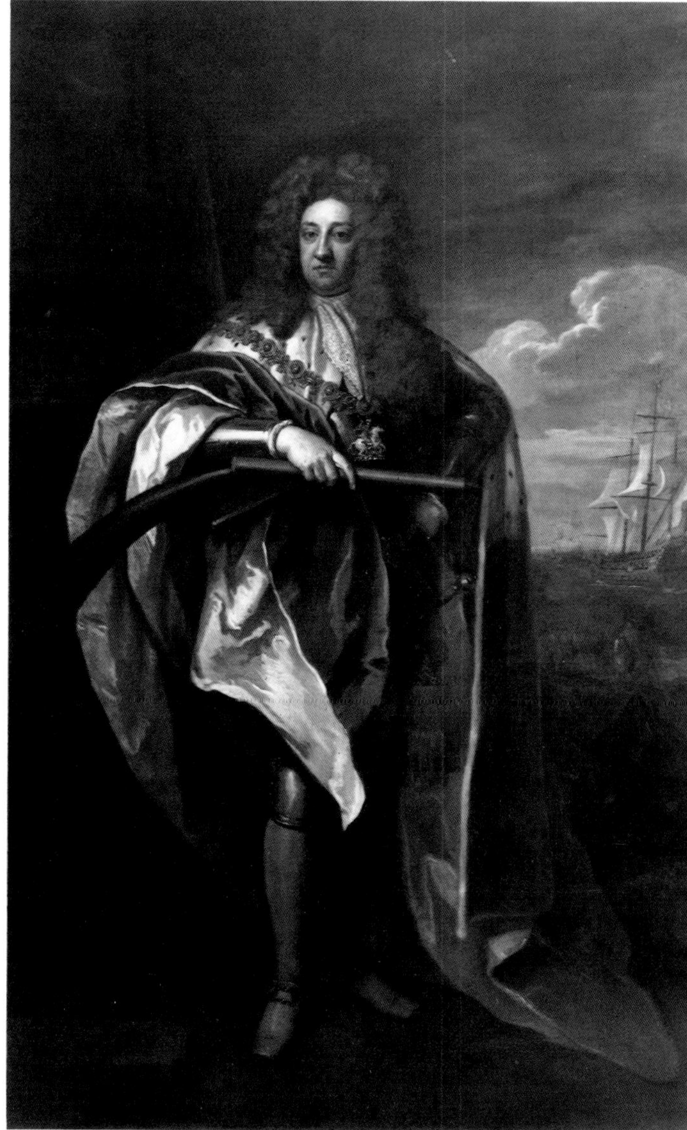

fig.31 Sir Godfrey Kneller **Prince George of Denmark** 1704 Oil on canvas
National Maritime Museum, Greenwich Hospital Collection

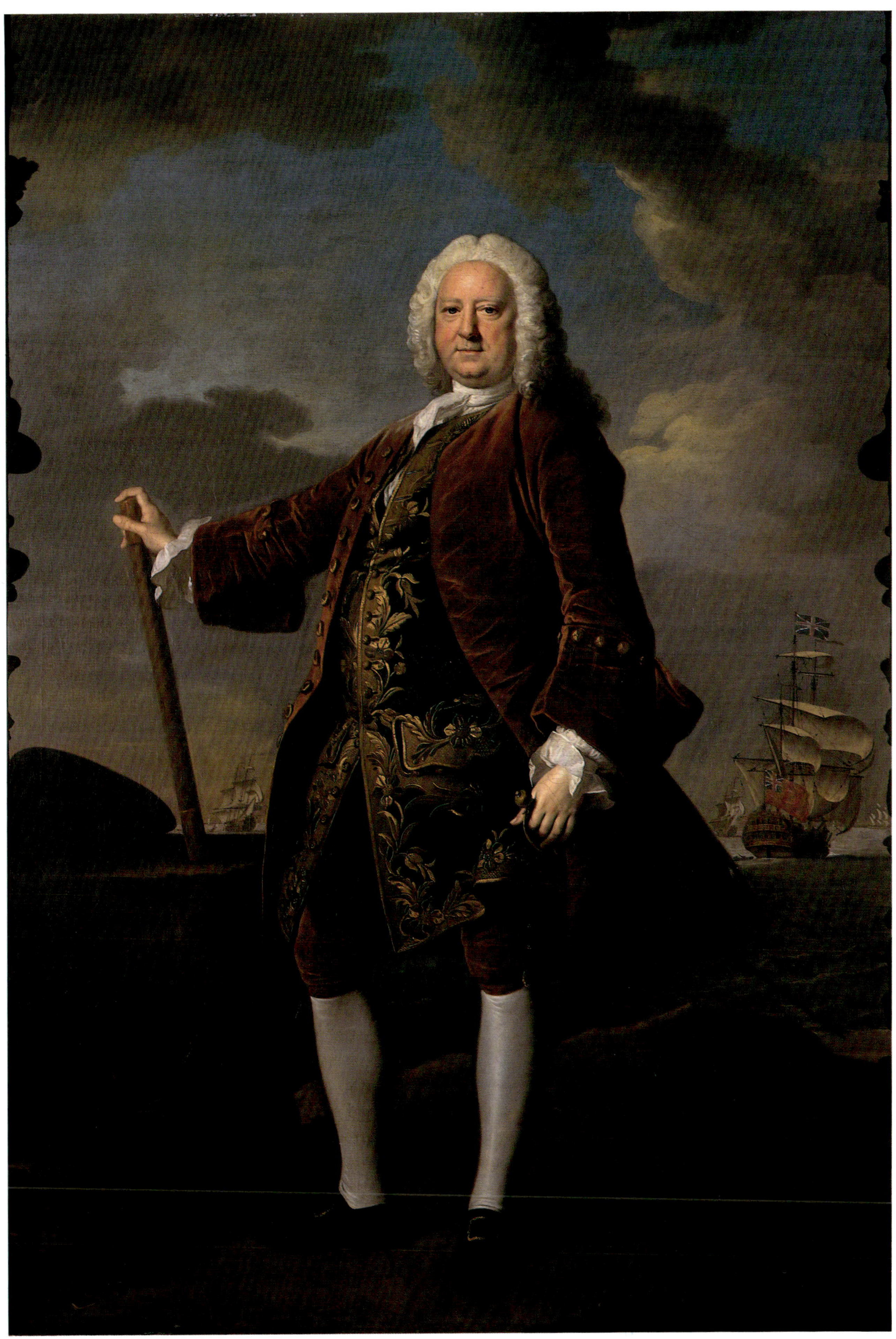

26 **Mary Panton, Duchess of Ancaster** 1757

Oil on canvas 239 × 137 (94 × 54)
Signed: *Hudson Pinxit 1757*
Grimsthorpe and Drummond Castle Trust

Mary Panton's career offers a later parallel to that of Jane Bickerton (see no.13). She too was the daughter of a royal servant, her father being Master of the King's running horses at Newmarket. She too became the second wife of a duke, marrying Peregrine Bertie, 3rd Duke of Ancaster, in 1750.

The genre of masque portraiture that Van Dyck developed in the 1630s enjoyed a revival in the mid-eighteenth century as part of the general resurgence of interest in Van Dyck as model for serious portrait painting. By this time, though, the amorphous masque costumes of Charles I's court were replaced by costumes in the style of Van Dyck himself. A popular model was the portrait of Susanne Fourment by Rubens (collection Fundaçao Gulbenkian, Lisbon) which was then in Sir Robert Walpole's collection, and thought to be the work of Van Dyck. Hudson sometimes deliberately imitated that picture more or less exactly; more usually, he settled for the kind of composite fancy-dress adopted here. The model seems to have been first resorted to as early as the 1720s, and continued to be used throughout the eighteenth century, though it was at the height of its popularity in the 1740s and 50s. An important disseminator was the portraitist and drapery man Joseph Van Aken, who was responsible for several variants on it, which he employed in pictures by Ramsay and Hudson. The lines of Mary Panton's costume are essentially those of the 1750s and not at all of Van Dyck's time, but the rocky backdrop is in the direct line of Van Dyck's masque-inspired compositions. However, it is unlikely that the use of such a costume here is intended to carry either literary or artistic connotations: the building in the background is the rotunda at Ranelagh gardens, and the presumption must be that the Duchess's lavish attire is a record of what she wore to a costume ball there. If so, it would follow that the portrait was the first, and not merely one among many, to be painted showing the 'Van Dyck' dress in this mid-century manifestation. It was mezzotinted by James McArdell (*c*.1729–65) and would therefore have been widely known; several artists copied the general arrangement of both dress and background, among them Joseph Wright of Derby (1734–97). Hudson himself borrowed it for a number of three-quarter-lengths and it became an ubiquitous portrait type in the years around 1760 – as Aileen Ribeiro has said, 'sitters would be dressed as the Duchess of Ancaster at a masquerade, rather than as Rubens's wife, though the distinction might be missed by those not familiar with the original portrait'.

According to William Hickey, Hudson was a 'remarkably good tempered' man, though when Hickey knew him, around 1760, 'His figure was rather grotesque, being uncommonly low in stature, with a prodigious belly, and constantly wearing a large white bushy periwig' (Hickey, p.15). His work sums up the characteristics of portraiture in London immediately before the changes introduced by his pupil and follow-Devonian, Reynolds. These were quickly to put him out of fashion and consign his far from negligible abilities not so much to oblivion as to a position of exemplary unimportance, from which they have never since risen. This picture and no.25 illustrate the real strength of his talents at their best.

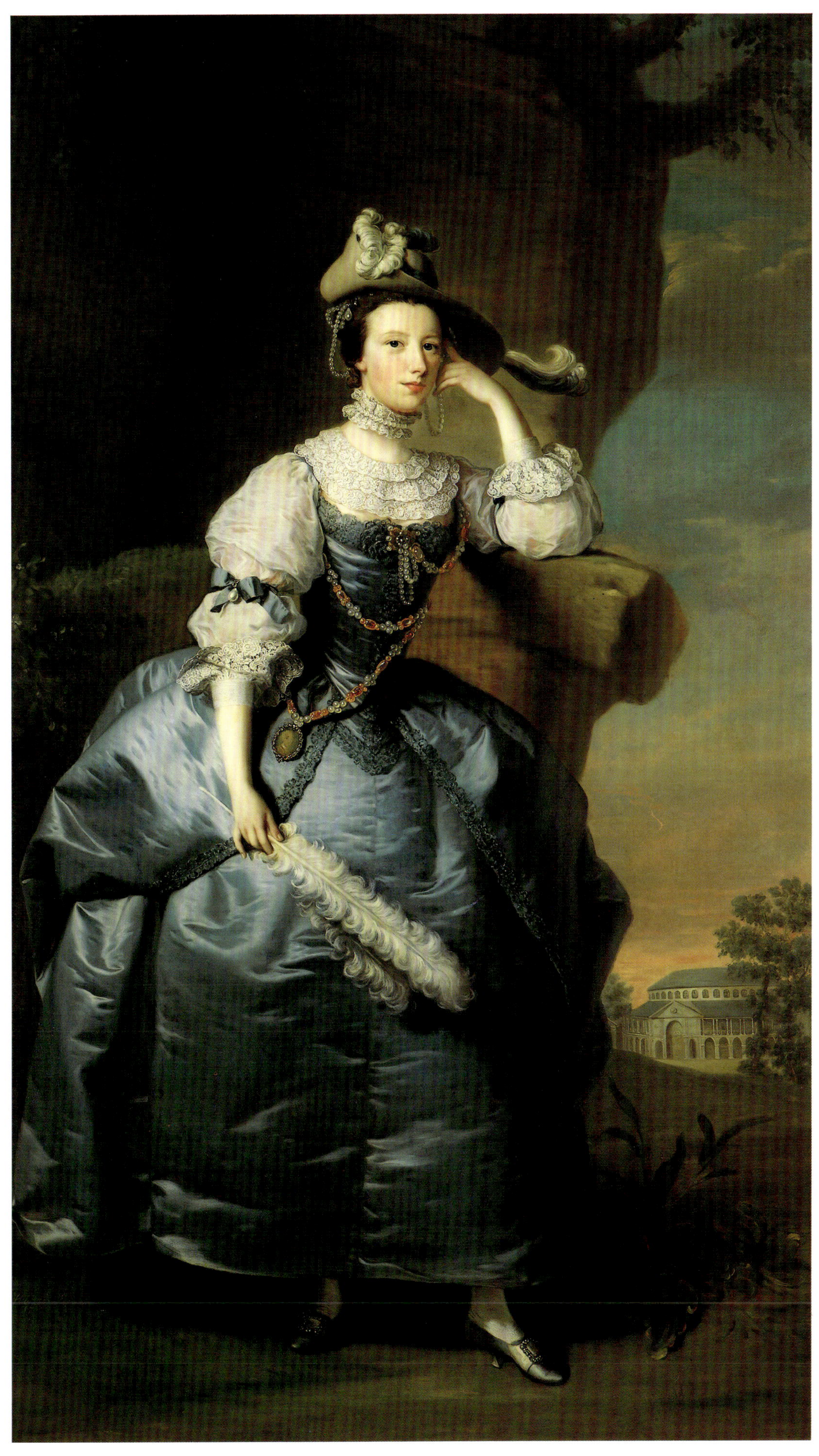

ALLAN RAMSAY 1713–1784

27 Norman, 'The Red Man', 22nd Chief of MacLeod 1748

Oil on canvas 223.5 × 137.2 (88 × 54)
Dunvegan Castle, Isle of Skye, by kind permission of John MacLeod of MacLeod the 29th Chief

Ramsay, one of the most sensitive af all British portraitists, did not often essay the grand rhetorical style. This is one of his most theatrical works. With it, he contributed decisively to the long line of portraits depicting Highland chieftains in their clan tartans, of which the most important are the astonishing Batoni of Colonel the Hon. William Gordon (fig.10 on p.43) and Raeburn's portraits of Alastair Macdonell of Glengarry (fig.19 on p.54) and of Sir John Sinclair (no.46). The picture should be compared with John Michael Wright's 'Lord Mungo Murray' (no.16) which epitomises the tradition as he found it. There is also a piquant contrast to be made with de Wet's portrait of the 1st Marquis of Atholl (no.19). Ramsay's MacLeod has long been associated with the famous statue of Apollo in the Belvedere of the Vatican, but it has been pointed out (Solkin 1986) that the quotation is actually from a common type of Roman sculpture depicting public officials such as magistrates. This is a use of classical precedent that is different in kind from de Wet's imaginary Roman armour. It is a more cerebral allusion, one that flatters the sitter in a more sophisticated way, suggesting the paramount importance of the qualities of civic virtue in the mid eighteenth century. The position of the sitter's right arm and hand conform to an identifiable rhetorical gesture – the *adlocutio*. As with Batoni's William Gordon the loose plaid of the Highland costume is treated so as deliberately to suggest the deep folds of the Roman toga. The linking of a remote Highland clan with ancient civilisation is however hardly more extraordinary than de Wet's conceit, and follows from it.

But it was not only the Highland portrait that Ramsay affected with this work. His compositon had an immediate influence on Reynolds, who used a similar scheme in his own picture of the Hon. Augustus Keppel of 1754 (fig.11 on p.46). As well as the pose of the figure, which has much in common with that of the MacLeod (though Reynolds seems to have had a rather different immediate source in mind), this takes over the general line of rocks and seashore that forms Ramsay's background – a detail that seems to confirm Reynolds's consciousness of the Ramsay. Since Reynolds's picture played a crucial part in his development, it can therefore be said that the MacLeod occupies a key place in the history of British portraiture.

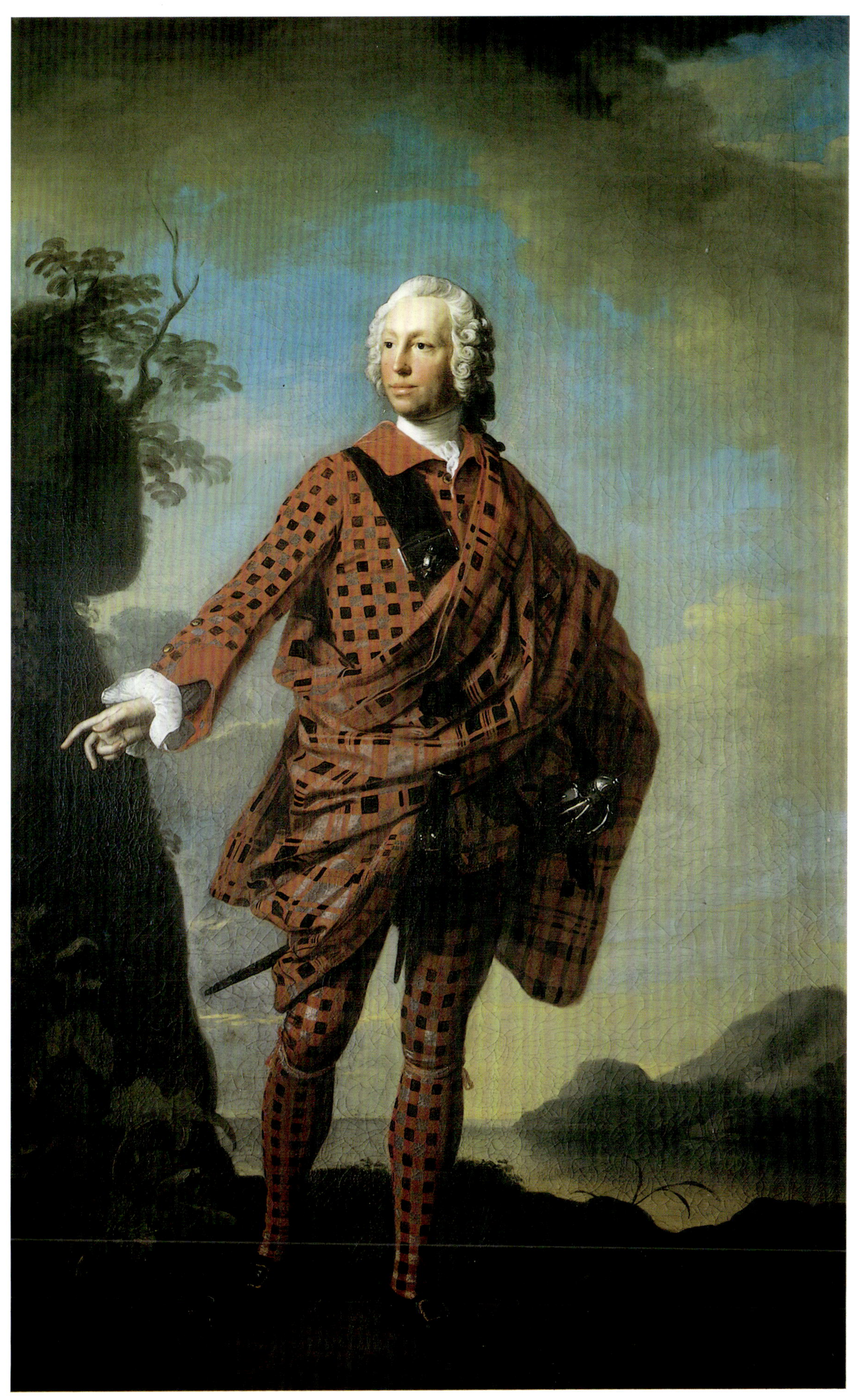

POMPEO BATONI 1708–1787

28 **George Lucy** 1758

Oil on canvas 132 × 97 (52 × $38\frac{1}{4}$)
Charlecote, The Lucy Collection (The National Trust)

Batoni was a native of Lucca in Italy, having been born there in 1708, and trained under his father who was a goldsmith. It was as a goldsmith that he first went to Rome in 1727; but he quickly decided to pursue the career of a painter. He settled in the city so emphatically that by 1769 he had married twice and had a family of eight daughters and four sons living; several of the children became artists. He was a fat, unpretentious, highly religious man who nevertheless acquired a reputation for meanness and hard dealing. His art found its origins in Roman religious painting, and much of his early work consists of subject pictures with biblical, mythical or allegorical themes. By the 1750s he had built up a formidable reputation, but was more and more taken up with painting portraits, and the British very soon dominated his sitters' list. He took over from Francesco Trevisani (1656–1746), Andrea Casali (1724–?70) and Marco Benefial (1684–1764) as the most fashionable face-painter of the period, sought out and recommended by every noble or celebrated visitor to Rome. He was to remain a prolific portraitist, especially to the grand tour trade, until the late 1770s; thereafter his health began to decline. He died in 1787.

This portrait belongs to the first period of his long success, and illustrates the formula that he took over from his predecessors and, although he made it thoroughly his own, hardly modified in its essentials for the rest of his career. The three-quarter format, the easy pose, the emphasis on fashionable clothes and personable appearance, the classical architectural background, all these elements became standard ingredients which over the years were gradually modified to accommodate changing fashions in dress. But within the simple formula Batoni displays remarkable inventiveness, creating over and over again a unique and fresh image that is genuinely the portrait of an individual, however conscious he may have been that so many of his young milords conformed to a recognisable type.

George Lucy no doubt did conform to that type, although he was no longer a youth when he sat to Batoni. He had been born in 1714, the second son of a Warwickshire landowner, Fulke Lucy, and inherited the estate from his elder brother at the age of thirty. Between 1756 and 1758 he travelled to Portugal, and then to Italy on a fairly standard grand tour. His collection of souvenirs was not particularly memorable, and his most significant contribution to the history of aesthetics was commissioning Capability Brown to redesign the grounds of Charlecote, in Warwickshire, in 1769. (An interest in plants may have occasioned the introduction of a pot of carnations behind the sitter, an unusual feature in Batoni's portraits of men.) He should also be given some credit for bringing this picture into existence. Batoni's particular brand of ego-massage did not come particularly cheap. 'These painters are great men, and must be flattered,' Lucy wrote, 'for 'tis the custom here, not to think themselves obliged to you for employing them, but that they oblige you by being employed.' The artist told Lucy the picture would take 'a month or five weeks, and that he would not undertake to do me in less time'. Lucy paid forty guineas for it.

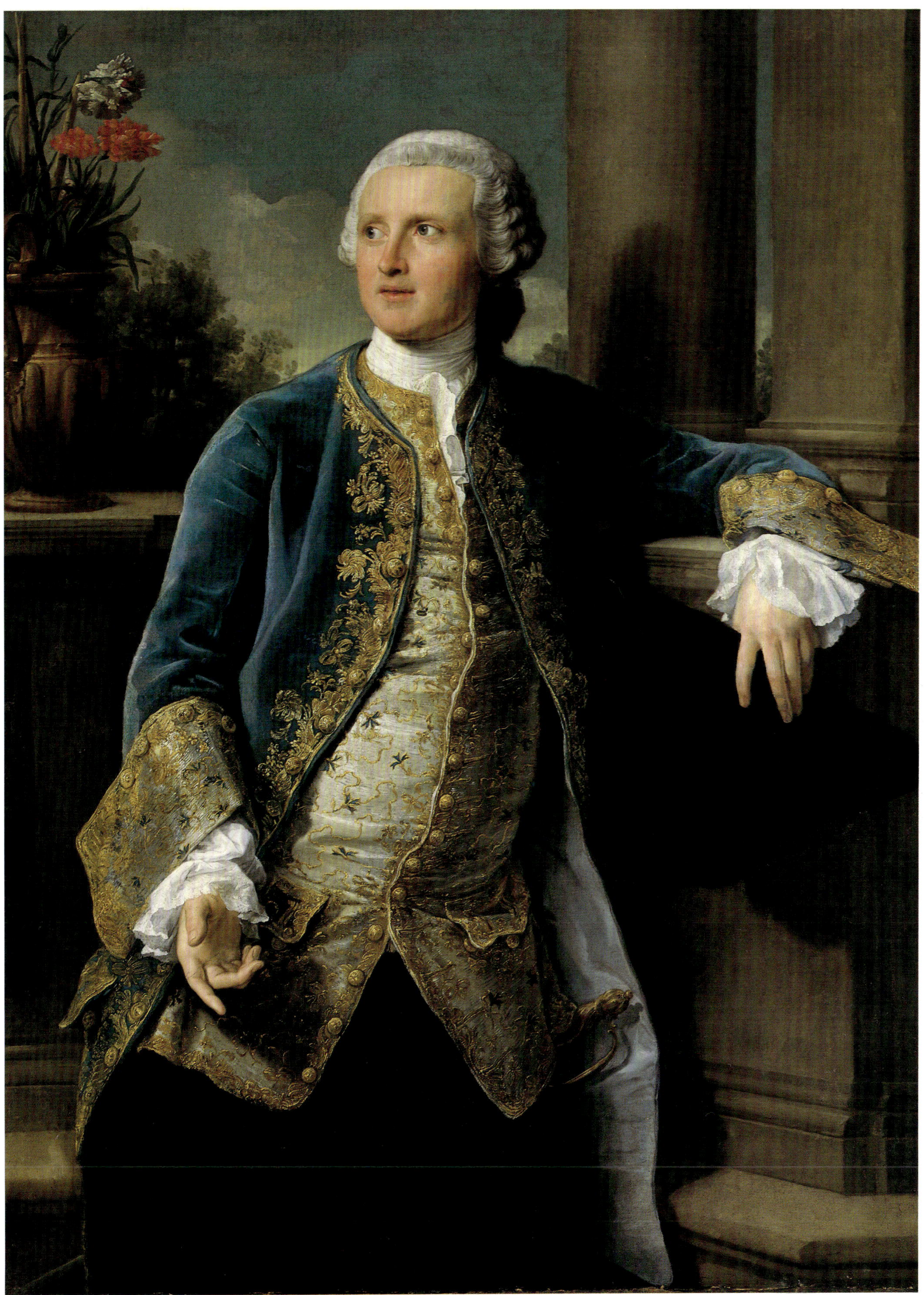

POMPEO BATONI

29 Thomas William Coke, later 1st Earl of Leicester 1774

Oil on canvas 241.9 × 167.5 ($96\frac{3}{4}$ × 67)
Signed lower right: P.BATONI PINXIT ROMAE AN. 1774, and inscr.: THIS PORTRAIT FOR/THE COUNTESS OF ALBANY, WIFE/OF PRINCE CHARLIE WAS/PRESENTED BY HER TO/MR T.W.COKE, AFTERWARDS/VISCOUNT COKE AND EARL/OF LEICESTER; and at left, on base of column: THOMAS WILL. COKE.
Viscount Coke and the Trustees of the Holkham Estate

Coke was the son of a Norfolk landowner, educated at Eton and, between 1751 and 1754, a traveller on the grand tour with an allowance of £500 a year from the Countess of Leicester. As heir to one of the largest estates in England he was much observed, especially since he was 'a very pretty Man', according to Lady Mary Coke, a verdict which seems to have been generally agreed with: another comment, from Joseph Wright in 1774, identifies Coke as 'the most beautiful' of all the fashionable participants in the Roman carnival that year: 'You know he is very handsome, and his dress, wch was chiefly white, made him appear charming indeed.' It may well be this very white costume that Batoni depicts him wearing here. It is a fine example of the Van Dyck style popular both for fancy dress and for portraits, and in its sumptuousness, emphasised by the ermine-lined cloak, perfectly complements the social and personal qualities of the sitter. Van Dyck may also have been a source for the pose, which occurs in a late portrait by him of an unknown gentleman wearing a cuirass (Ringling Museum of Art, Sarasota), though it is not clear whether Batoni could have known this work.

As so often in Batoni's portraits a piece of sculpture is the most prominent accessory. It is the reclining female figure in the Vatican collection known in the eighteenth century as the Cleopatra, now identified as Ariadne on Naxos. The face was thought at the time to bear a striking resemblance to that of the Countess of Albany, wife of the exiled Charles Edward Stuart (Bonny Prince Charlie), who was rumoured to be in love with Coke. In any case, Batoni has so placed the sculpture that the figure seems to lean round in admiration of the young man – a daring stroke, but perhaps one that was demanded by the commission, if as tradition states the picture was ordered by the Countess as a present for Coke. This is the story recorded in the inscription, which appears to have been added in Rome, perhaps by Batoni himself, and therefore carries with it some authority. It would seem more likely that Coke himself commissioned the portrait from Batoni as did dozens of his young contemporaries in Rome at the same time – and the Ariadne appears in several of them; but the more romantic interpretation is well-attested and, moreover, too interesting to be discarded.

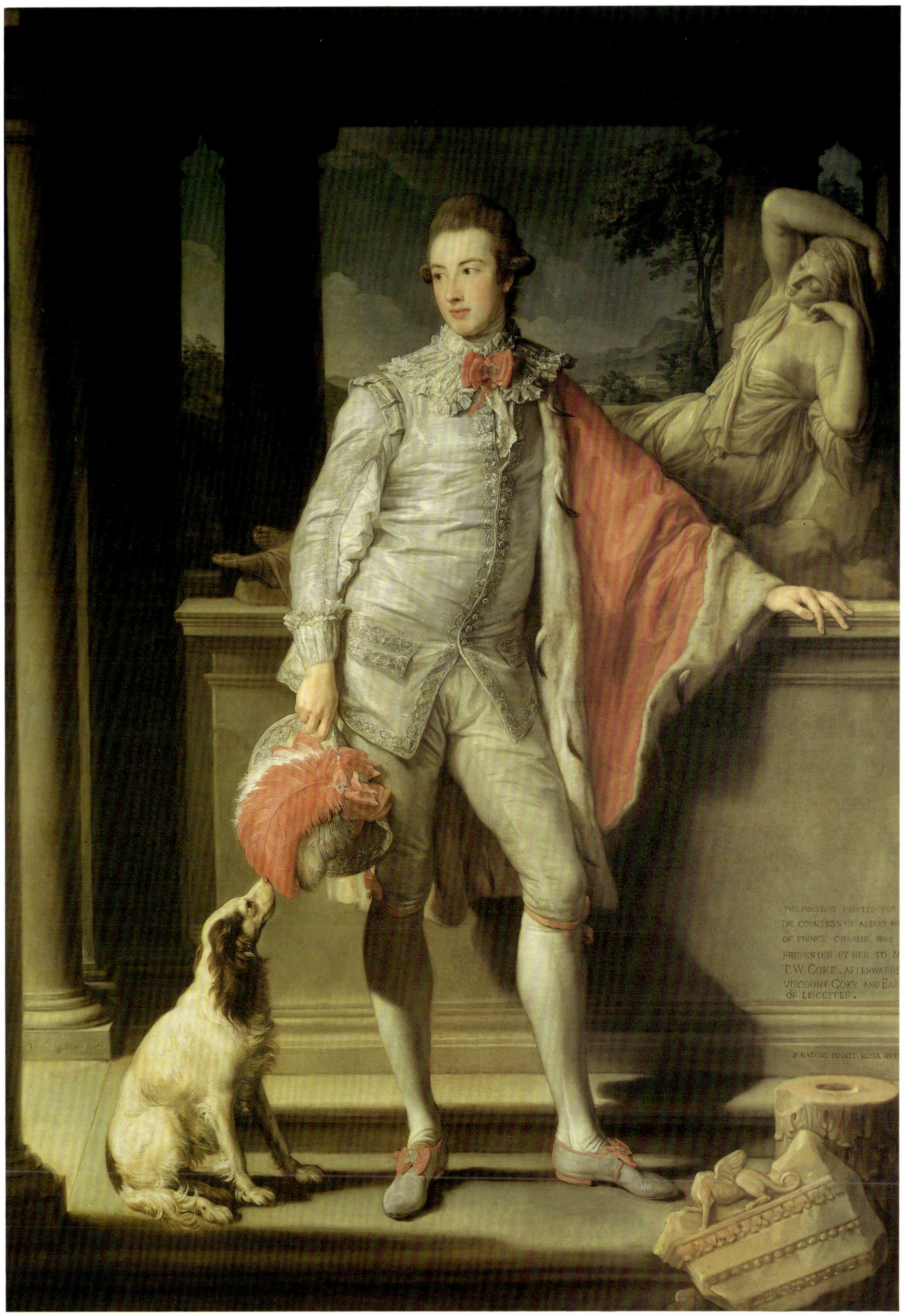
THIS PORTRAIT PAINTED FOR
THE COUNTESS OF ALBANY
OF PRINCE CHARLIE, WAS
PRESENTED BY HER TO
T.W. COKE, AFTERWARDS
VISCOUNT COKE AND
OF LEICESTER.
P. BATONI PINXIT ROMÆ

POMPEO BATONI

30 **George Gordon, Lord Haddo** 1775

Oil on canvas 259 × 170.2 (102 × 67)
Signed lower right: POM. BATONI. PIN. ROME.ANNO.1775
The National Trust for Scotland, Haddo House, Aberdeenshire

George Gordon, son of the 3rd Earl of Aberdeen, is known to have died from a fall from his horse in 1791. His date of birth is uncertain, though he was mentioned as 'a very agreeable young man' in a letter of 1777. By then he had evidently accomplished one of the principal exercises in any young nobleman's education – the grand tour, as the inscription on this portrait testifies. The picture also testifies to an interest in Roman antiquities which it was one of Batoni's main tasks to record. The distant view of buildings is intended to suggest the sitter's familiarity with the Campagna and its towns and villages, standing in for the view of a country seat which might occupy an analogous position in a portrait painted at home. (When Batoni painted Frederick Henry, Bishop of Derry and 4th Earl of Bristol, he included a view of the Bishop's new cathedral in his portrait.) The antiquities are equally items to which the sitter could lay no personal claim. The two most conspicuous ones, a statue of a priestess and a sarcophagus with a relief depicting the story of Prometheus, are both in the Capitoline Museum. They therefore represent a state of mind rather than any direct proprietorship. Whereas some collectors were anxious to be shown surrounded by their personal possessions, the fruits of their research or their connoisseurship (or those of a hired advisor), Haddo, like many of Batoni's other sitters, is seen with tokens of his interest, intellectual rather than material status symbols. Since they are not the usual works to figure in Batoni's portraits (the Ludovisi Mars, for instance, is a standard accessory), they may perhaps have been selected by the sitter himself as particular favourites – which would testify to some active concern on his part. The nonchalant yet elegant pose is absolutely typical. It derives, along with innumerable others like it, from an antique statue in the Uffizi, Florence, supposed to represent Mercury.

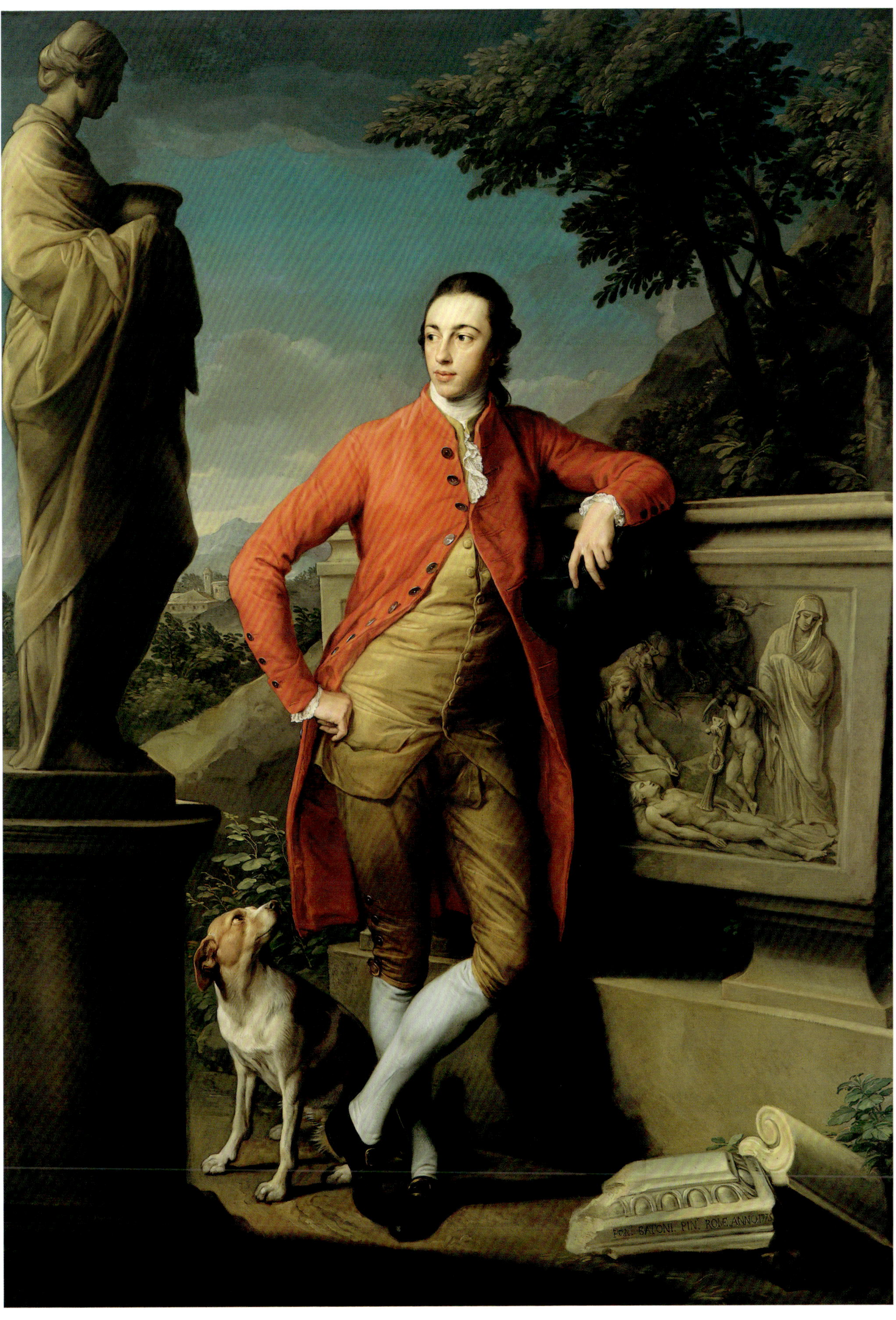
POM. BATONI. PIN. ROMÆ ANNO

TILLY KETTLE 1734/5–1786

31 Lady Frances Harpur and her Son Henry *c.*1766

Oil on canvas 242 × 153 ($95\frac{1}{4} \times 60\frac{1}{4}$)
Inscr., lower left: *Kettle Pinx.*
Calke Abbey, The Harpur-Crewe Collection (The National Trust)

Sir Henry Harpur, 6th Baronet, married the Lady Frances Greville, daughter of the 1st Earl of Warwick, in July 1762. Their eldest son and heir, also Henry, was born in 1763, and was still a small child when this picture of him with his mother was painted. It is a perfect example of the way in which English artists combined the grandiose with the intimate in their portraiture. The relaxed poses of the sitters are set against the monumental vastness of columns, parapet and urn to suggest, perhaps, natural ease in great surroundings, or even a studied indifference to the pomp of wealth and power. Mother and son are dressed handsomely but not grandly in the clothes of their time, with no allusion to the antique – a fashion that was being revived at the hands of Reynolds and others. The antique is however strongly evoked by the urn and the circular relief beneath it. The subject of the relief is the Judgement of Paris – we can make out the seated figure of Paris at the left, holding the apple which he is about to present to one of the three goddesses (two of them are visible) whose beauty he is adjudicating. The classical allusion is in itself a kind of compliment to the taste of the lady, although the Harpurs never went in for collecting such mementoes of their travels in Italy. But the circular shape of the relief is echoed by the round ball that her son Henry holds up to her, and this draws attention to the subject of the relief, suggesting very delicately that he is a modern Paris, doing homage to his mother. The idea is charming and entirely apt, though surely not intended to be taken too seriously. Henry succeeded to the baronetcy in 1789 and died in 1819, six years before his mother. The picture has remained on the walls of Calke Abbey, the house for which it was painted, to the present day.

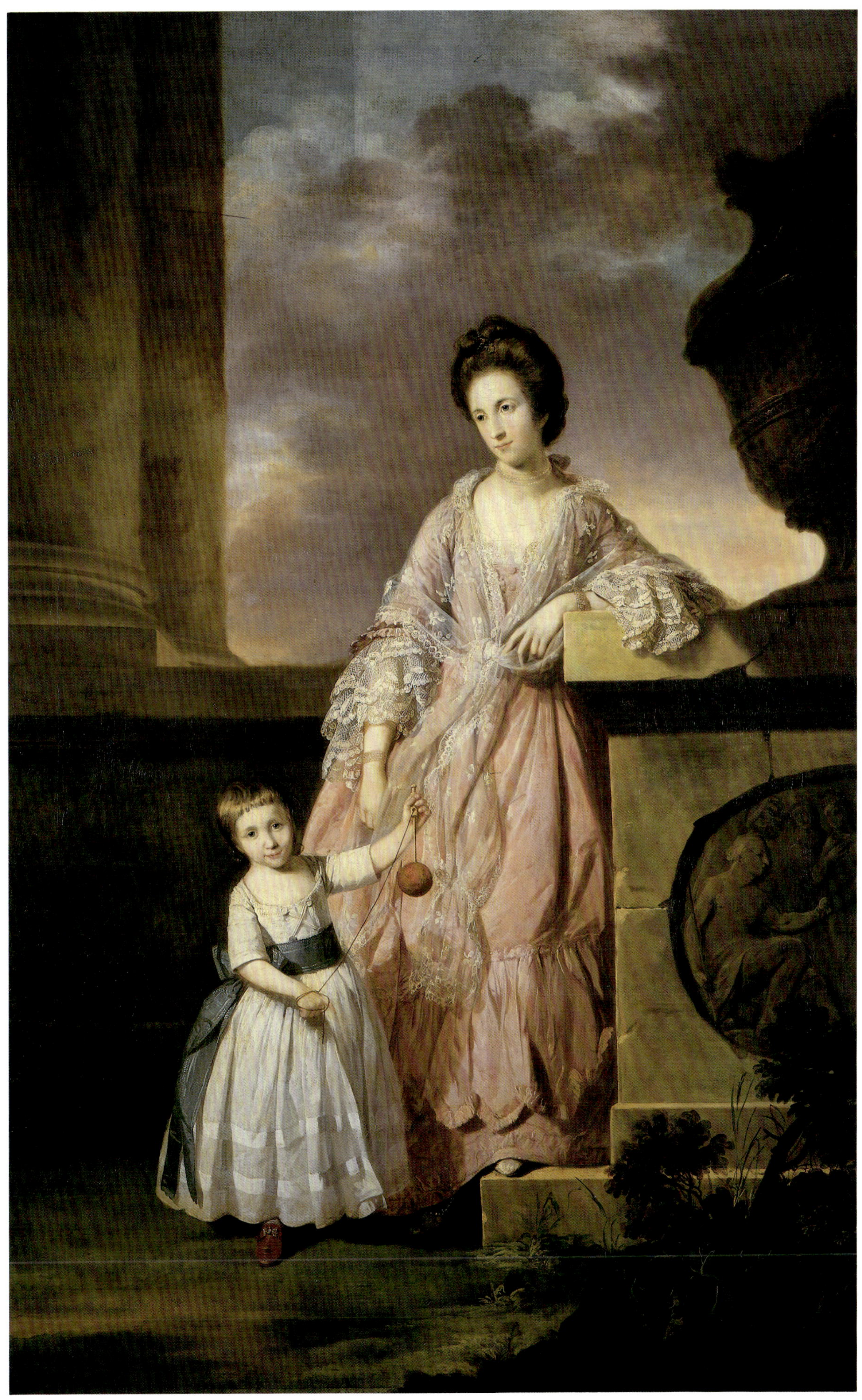

FRANCIS COTES 1726–1770

32 Lady Stanhope and Lady Effingham as Diana and her Companion *c.*1768

Oil on canvas 281 × 183 (110½ × 72)
Inscr. at right: *F Cotes* (initials in monogram) *pxt. 1765* and below, in another hand:
THE HON[able] LADY STANHOPE and KATH[a] COUNT[s] OF EFFINGHAM
York City Art Gallery

This grand picture belonged to one of its two subjects, Lady Stanhope, and came into the possession of the Earls of Mexborough when she bequeathed it to her sister Sarah, who married John Savile, 1st Earl of Mexborough, in 1760. The sisters were two of the eleven children of Francis Blake Delaval. Anne Hussey Delaval was born in 1736 and married Sir William Stanhope, younger brother of the 4th Earl of Chesterfield, as his third wife; he was to die in 1772, and she then married a Captain Morris, living until 1812. Cotes's other sitter was ten years younger than Lady Stanhope: she is Catherine Proctor, daughter of Metcalfe Proctor of Thorpe, near Leeds, who married Thomas Howard, 3rd Earl of Effingham in October of the year this picture was painted, 1765. She died at sea in 1791, and her husband died a month later.

The sitters were not related, but had been brought together socially. It is possible, as has been suggested, that they were involved in some amateur theatricals promoted by Lady Stanhope's brother, Sir Francis Blake Delaval, brother of Lady Stanhope. If this surmise is true, the picture, which is entirely typical of the classicising portraiture of the 1760s and 70s, suggests a connection once again between the grand manner and the stage. The flowing drapery, the rocky background, and the mythological characters all recall the atmosphere of Inigo Jones's masques and the portraits that Van Dyck painted under their influence. An interesting twentieth-century *reprise* of the idea, on almost the same scale, is de Laszló's 1919 full-length portrait, at Gorhambury, of 'Violet Brabazon, 4th Countess Verulam, and her Eldest Son as Venus and Cupid' (though she looks more like Diana), and once more the atmosphere of country-house theatricals is not very distant.

With this perhaps as his excuse, Cotes abandons his usual manner, with its fresh and rather informal qualities, in favour of the grand style practised at this date by Reynolds. The soft pinks and blues are familiar from his more characteristic work, but here they take on a classical resonance, echoing the palette of mythological subjects by, say, Guido Reni. The 'characters' are used to create a dialogue between the two figures, as the goddess instructs her attendant to unleash the hound that will pursue the distant stag – perhaps Actaeon. The interacting glances and gestures are reinforced by rocky and canine diagonals to give the composition its momentum. The picture has recently been called 'Cotes's unintellectual answer to Reynolds's "Lady Sarah Bunbury sacrificing to the Graces" (Lady Lever Art Gallery)' (Hayes 1991, p.100). Certainly the learned air of Reynolds is missing from this portrait; hence the aptness of the 'play-acting' suggestion. But it is also likely that there was a more practical reason for painting the two ladies together. The picture has a splendid frame which, while apparently inappropriate to the subject with its armillary sphere and martial emblems, is one of a set of similar frames commissioned for pictures in the Delaval family collection.

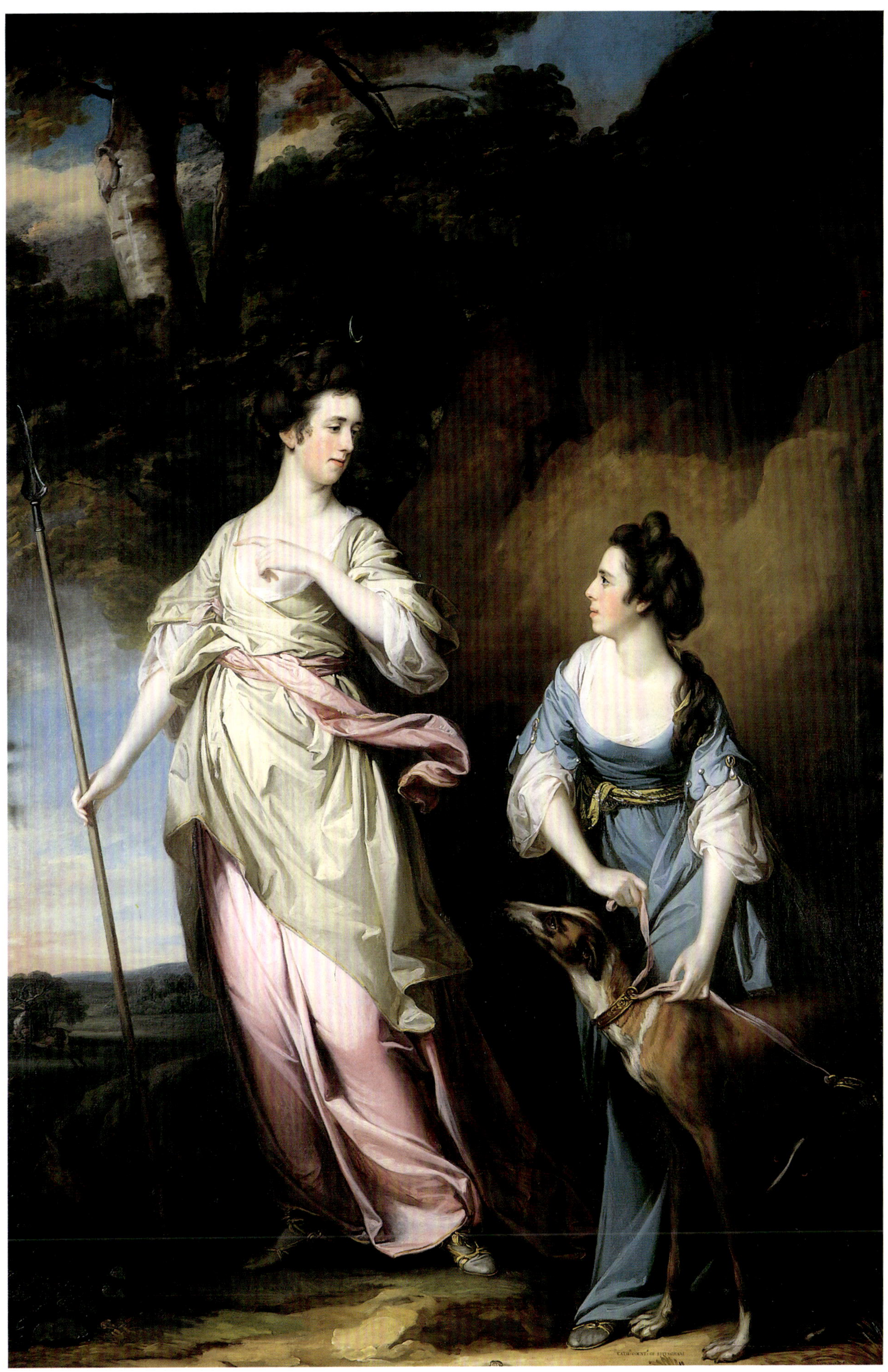

JOHAN ZOFFANY 1733–1810

33 **Mrs Woodhull** *c.*1770

Oil on canvas 243.8 × 165.1 (96 × 65)
Tate Gallery. Presented by D.M. McDonald 1977

Zoffany is better known for his small-scale portraits, often in groups or conversations; some are representations of theatrical scenes, recording famous actors in memorable roles. The task of painting a portrait on the scale of life, or larger, presents considerable problems to artists who habitually work on a smaller scale, but Zoffany handles it with panache. His training in Germany (he was born in Frankfurt-am-Rhein) and in Rome equipped him with a formidable technique, though not one adapted to the breadth of the grand manner. This portrait, commissioned in about 1770, was in fact conceived on the more modest scale of the half-length, and it was only when that was finished that Zoffany was asked to enlarge it. That he managed the alteration so successfully is a tribute to his powers of invention, for the larger design is highly successful and prompts surprise that he so rarely undertook work on this scale. It is, however, much less characteristic of him than the small-scale portraits that were his speciality, and bears a superficial resemblance in both composition and colouring to the work of Francis Cotes (see no.32), on whom perhaps he modelled this work.

Mrs Woodhull was born Catherine Milcah Ingram in 1744, one of the daughters of the Revd John Ingram of Wolford, Warwickshire. She died in 1808. Michael Woodhull, or Wodhull, who was twenty-one when she married him in 1761, was a Northamptonshire squire, a tall, handsome man, an antiquarian and an indefatigable book collector – the disposal of duplicates alone from his library occupied thirteen days of sales in 1801 and 1803. He also wrote poetry, and in 1782 was to bring out an important translation – the first in English – of the complete works of Euripedes. His politics were Whig, with a tinge of radicalism which already at school at Winchester earned him the nickname 'the long-legged Republican'. He was an enthusiast for the causes of religious and civil liberty and an admirer of Jean-Jacques Rousseau. It may be that the figure of Mrs Woodhull in her woodland setting had Rousseauesque overtones for her husband, recalling the atmosphere and ideas of *Julie, ou La Nouvelle Eloise* (1760). Her contemplative pose is appropriate for the philosopher who preaches the all-embracing power of nature. But the portrait is certainly not a Rousseauian tract like Wright of Derby's famous 'Sir Brooke Boothby' of 1781 (Tate Gallery). If it casts a token glance at the contemplative tradition of portraiture it does so through the medium of the classicising formal images of Reynolds, of which his picture of 'The Hon. Mrs Theresa Parker' (1773) at Saltram is a fair example. Women portrayed in the poetic pastoral vein sometimes have their legs crossed in a way that resembles the motif common in male portraits of the time, such as Batoni's 'Lord Haddo' (no.30). Actresses, as muses of drama, are also allowed this licence. Mrs Woodhull's legs are not strictly crossed, but they are shown in a somewhat similar informal position, which seems to imply a meditative and imaginative state of mind. Compare, for example, Reynolds's 'Mrs Abington as the Comic Muse' (fig.32; Waddesdon), and 'Mrs Lloyd' (private collection), Angelica Kauffmann's 'Mrs Hartley' (Garrick Club), and Gainsborough's meditative 'Lady Bate Dudley' (fig.15 on p.50).

The picture hung until Woodhull's death in 1816 at the Woodhull family seat of Thenford, near Banbury.

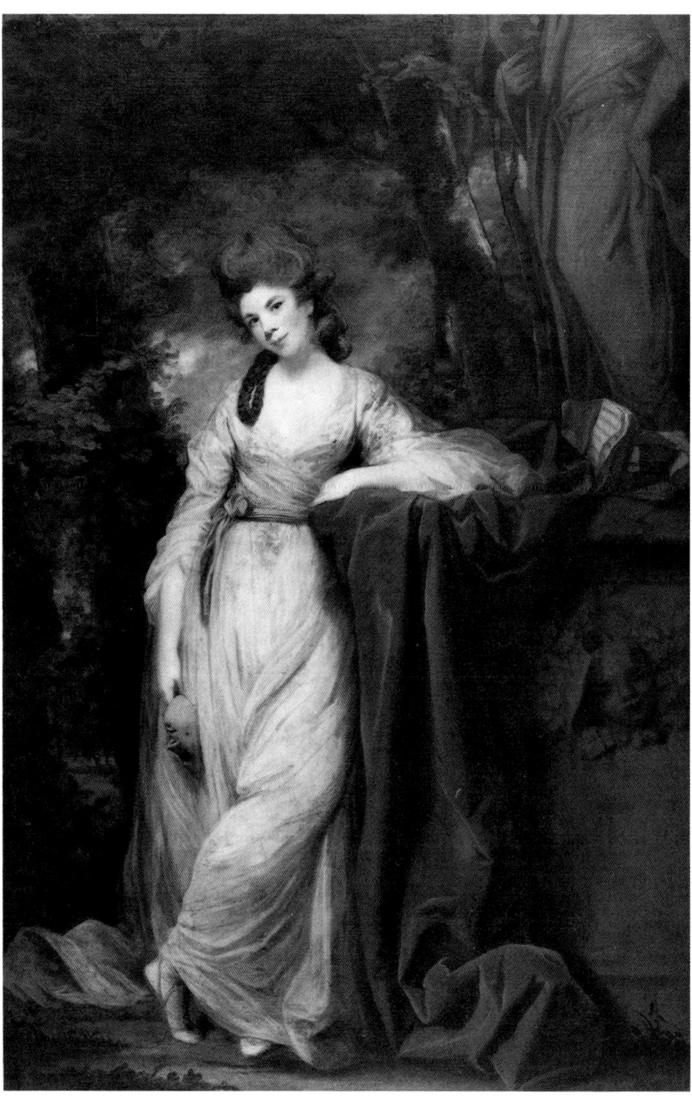

fig.32 Sir Joshua Reynolds **Mrs Abington as the Comic Muse** *c.*1768, revised 1773 Oil on canvas *National Trust, Waddesdon Manor*

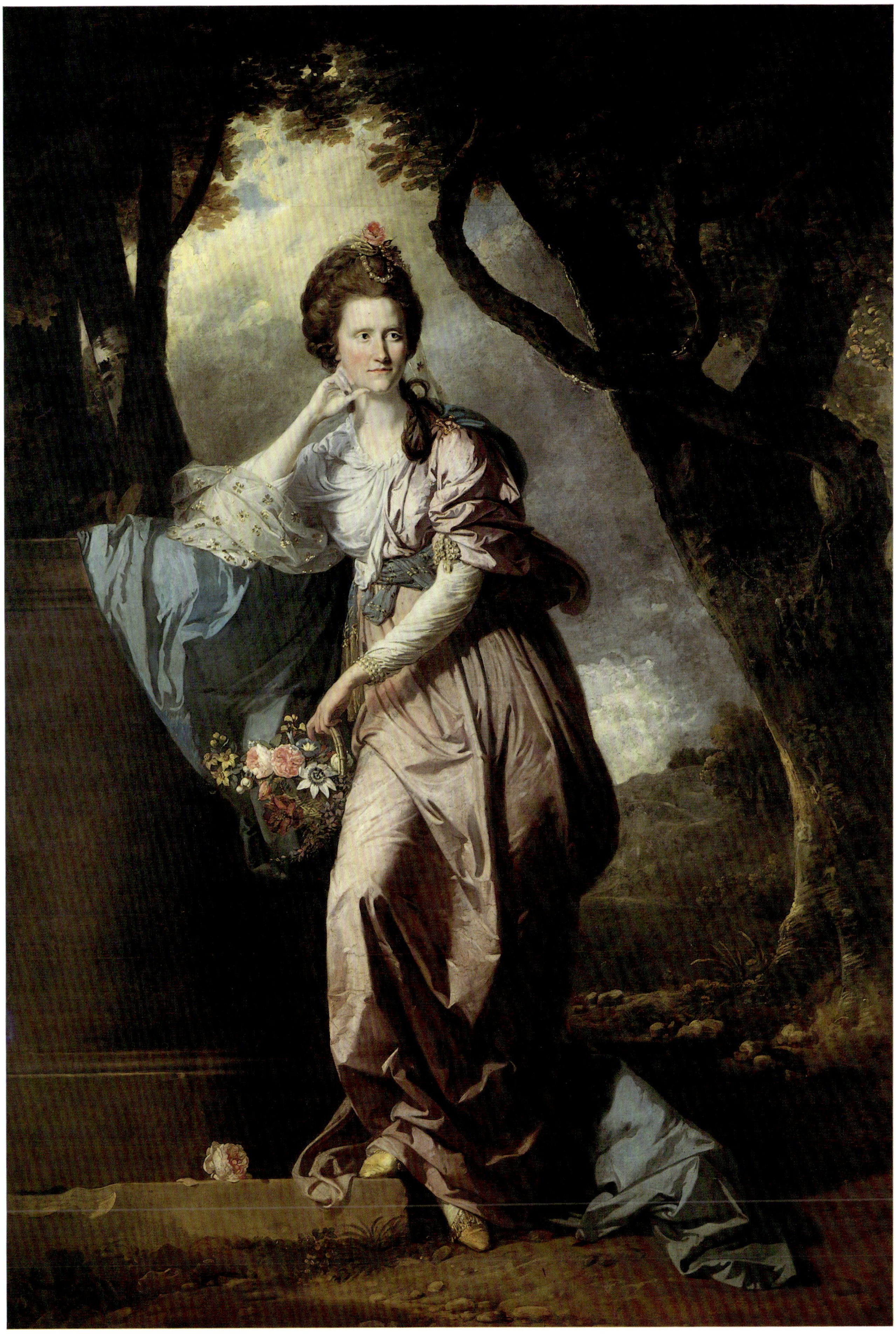

34 **William Augustus, Duke of Cumberland** *c.*1765

Oil on canvas 254 × 190 (100 × 74$\frac{3}{4}$)
The Duke of Devonshire and the Chatsworth Settlement Trustees

Cumberland was born in 1721, the third son of George II and his queen, Caroline of Anspach. According to Lord Waldegrave he had 'strong parts, great military abilities, undoubted courage', but was 'too much guided by his passions', which were 'often violent and ungovernable'; but 'his notions of honour and generosity are worthy of a prince'. The first important engagement of his military career was the Battle of Dettingen in 1743, where he 'behaved as bravely as a man could do', being wounded in the leg and ordering a French officer to be attended to before himself. In 1745, as Captain-General of the British land forces he fought the army of Maréchal Saxe at Fontenoy, where he was 'the whole day in the thickest of the fire'. The allied defeat in this action was blamed on the Dutch. The young Pretender, Charles James Stuart, saw the contretemps as a cue to launch his own attack on the English, and this time Cumberland was victorious, at Culloden in 1746, when he finally quenched Jacobite aspirations to the throne. He followed up with thoroughgoing purges of the Highlands, motivated at least in part by a failure to assess correctly the full extent of his success at Culloden: in July 1746 he wrote from Scotland: 'I tremble for fear that this vile spot may still be the ruin of this island and of our family'. These worries were unnecessary: he had dealt a death-blow to the clan system. For these achievements he was hailed as a hero, celebrated in song and story, and loaded with honours. But he was soon known widely (partly through the jealous machinations of his brother Frederick, Prince of Wales) as 'the Butcher', so that history has subsequently condemned him for his brutality – and also, perhaps, for his singularly unattractive appearance.

The year after Culloden, at Val (Laeffelt), Cumberland was again defeated by Saxe; Horace Walpole suggested that 'He behaved as bravely as usual, but his prowess is so well established that it grows time for him to exert other qualities of a general'. After the war ended in 1748 he took steps to improve the discipline of the army and the conditions of pensioners and invalids. His methods were regarded as too Prussian and increased his unpopularity. In 1757, during the Seven Years' War, he was again in Germany, in alliance with Prussia against the French, and defeated by them at Hastenbeck. He bore much of the blame for the Convention of Klosterzeven which provided for a brief interlude in the fighting but which was disliked by George II who told him when he returned to England: 'he had ruined his country and his army, and had spoiled everything, and had hurt, or lost, his own reputation'. Cumberland retired to Windsor, where as Ranger of Windsor Great Park he had greater success, planting trees and overseeing many improvements. He became grossly fat, lost the sight of one eye, and died of a stroke in October 1765.

Reynolds was no more disposed by temperament than any other English artist to shine in state portraiture but, as this example shows, his natural seriousness and instinct for composition enabled him to invent a design both authoritative and sympathetic, solid yet full of easy movement. The rhythms of brocaded drapery and costume harmonise in a single bold yet varied sweep, and the rich (though now somewhat faded) colour adds to the weight and grandeur of the scheme. Cumberland is arrayed in the robes of the Order of the Garter – in which he had been installed in 1730 – with the gold collar, blue velvet mantle and, on the table to the left, a tall-plumed hat. Reynolds's notes record that he saw Cumberland in the spring of 1758. It was then, presumably, that he made sketches from which he developed this and other portraits of him; many exist, in Garter robes and military uniform, half-, three-quarter- and whole-length. The high quality and splendour of this canvas suggest that it may be the prime version of them all. The 4th Duke of Devonshire was the Prime Minister who had acted as intermediary between Cumberland and the King after the controversial agreement of Klosterzeven; he may have ordered it before his death in 1764, and it is recorded in a ledger of 1765 as having been 'paid [for] in full', to the amount of £787.

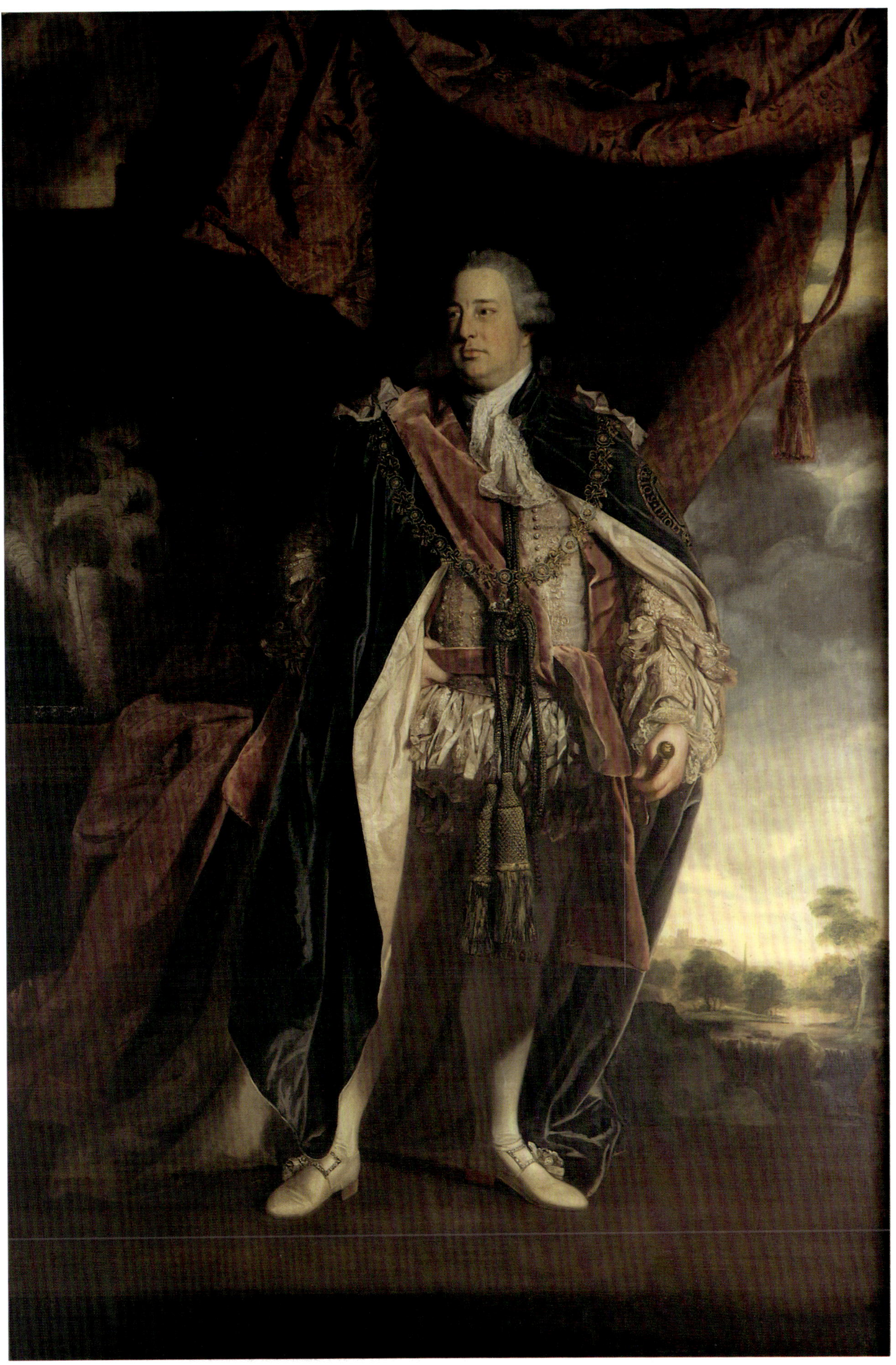

35 **Three Ladies Adorning a Term of Hymen** 1773–4

Oil on canvas 233.7 × 290.8 (92 × 114½)
Exh: Royal Academy 1774 (216)
Tate Gallery. Bequeathed by the Earl of Blessington 1837

This gorgeous fancy picture is in fact one of Reynolds's most ambitious portraits: it shows the three daughters of Sir William Montgomery Bt, of Magbie Hill, Peebles: Barbara, Elizabeth and Anne, at the ages, respectively, of seventeen, twenty-three and twenty-two. They are all about marriageable age and their attentions to the image of Hymen, god of marriage, are therefore precisely appropriate. Anne, indeed, was married on 19 May 1773 just before the picture was commissioned; it may have been intended to celebrate the event. Her husband was the forty-nine-year-old George, 1st Marquess Townshend, who had already been married once before. Her status may explain why she stands closest to Hymen, and separated by him from her sisters. Elizabeth, who kneels on a stool beneath it, but with such energy that she seems almost to run towards it, was engaged to the Rt Hon. Luke Gardiner, whom she married in July that year.

Thus Reynolds celebrates the preoccupation (which is both natural and socially induced) of these young ladies with love and marriage by making an elaborate and good-humoured joke of it. The picture is on one level entirely serious, relating the sitters to their stage and station in life, portraying them as elegant and charming and offering a composition in the grand manner that honours the Italian Baroque masters. But the symbolism of the term of Hymen, and the eagerness with which the sisters pay homage to it, should surely not be taken too seriously. A parallel has been pointed out in a composition by Reynolds's French contemporary Joseph-Marie Vien, 'Offrande à Cérès'; and Reynolds's awareness of what was currently happening in Paris will have reinforced his own strong sense of the decorative purpose of the picture. There is, then, a rococo echo here which, faint though it is, suggests how Reynolds was prepared to manipulate hints and styles from many sources, and in particular to adapt a French notion of glamour to an English purpose.

Reynolds had already made a single portrait out of the idea of the central figure here: his 'Lady Elizabeth Keppel' of 1761 (Woburn Abbey). Lady Elizabeth also decorates a term of Hymen with garlands, in recognition of her role as bridesmaid at the wedding of George III and the Princess Charlotte in that year (see no.50). Though clad in the fashion of the moment (classicism in costume had yet to become the rule), she takes up much the same pose as Elizabeth Montgomery in the later picture, and similarly turns back to address a companion, though not in this case a sister, but a Negro servant. The upright composition of 'Lady Elizabeth Keppel' prevents Reynolds from making such compositional capital out of the long swags of flowers that the three ladies toss across their picture, and which provide the design with its dominant rhythm – a rhythm that seems to stem from the chains of dancing figures in the Bacchanals of Poussin. That Reynolds had Poussin in mind can hardly be doubted: he derived the wooded background and single sculpture very closely from the corresponding parts of Poussin's 'Bacchaal before a Herm', now in the National Gallery, London. This picture was not in England in the eighteenth century, but Reynolds may well have had access to its composition through the medium of an engraving.

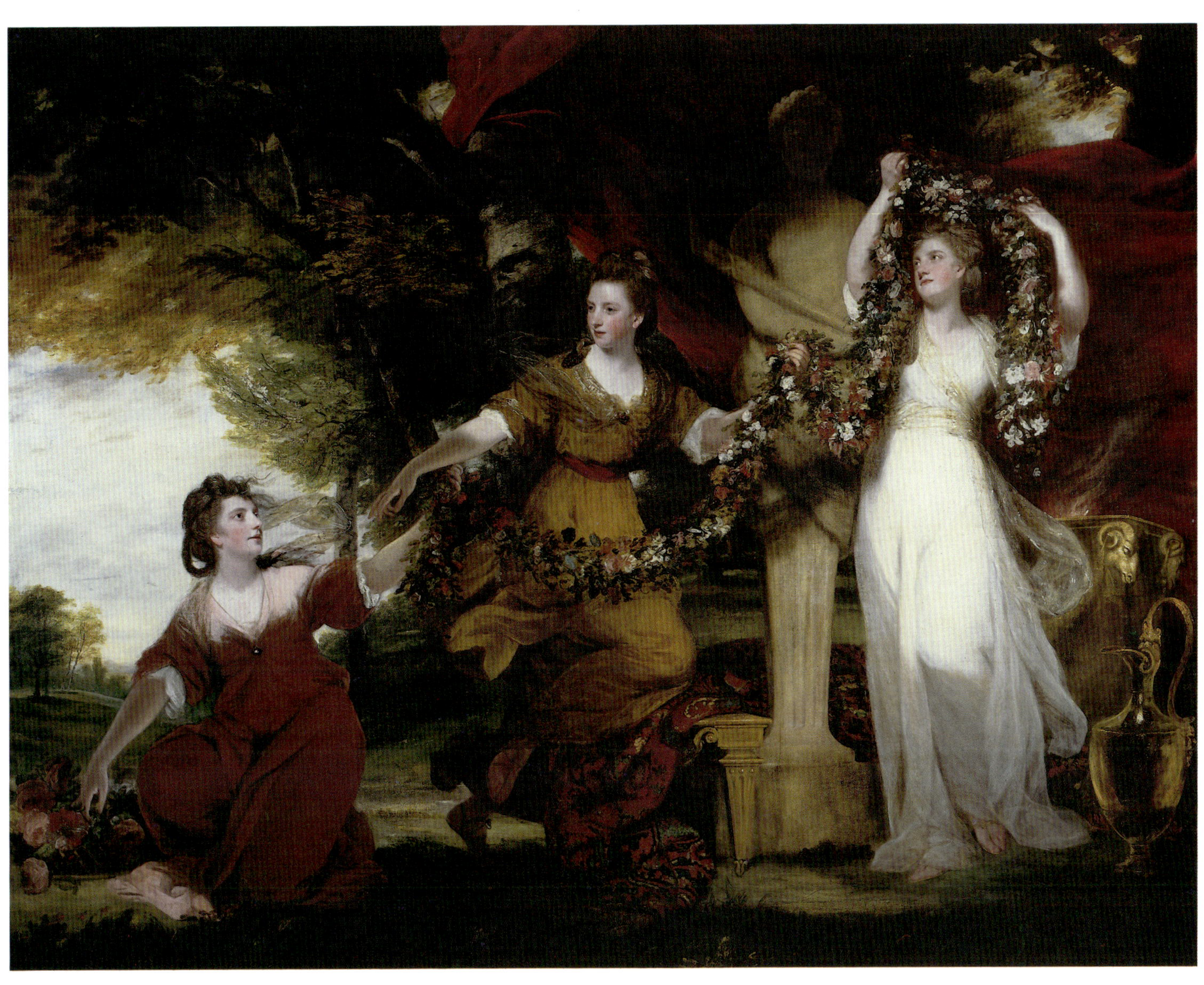

36 **Mrs Musters as Hebe** 1785

Oil on canvas 238.8 × 147.8 (94 × 58¼)
Exh: Royal Academy 1785 (18)
The Iveagh Bequest, Kenwood (English Heritage)

Reynolds often had recourse to a pattern for depicting pretty English girls in grand surroundings, their hair blown by the wind of divine inspiration, like 'Emily Pott' (fig.33; Waddesdon), whom he likened to Thaïs burning down Alexander's palace at Persepolis. In the picture of Jane Halliday (fig.34; also at Waddesdon) Reynolds has his heroine walking in stormy weather, buffeted into one half of the available space, the cloudy void beside her occupied only by her streaming tresses and ribbons. The ultimate prototype for such ideas may be to be found in Van Dyck's portrait of Olivia Porter (no.5), where a court lady is transported to a rocky (and evidently breezy) wilderness.

Whereas for Van Dyck the imaginary backdrop is closely related to the scenery of the court masque, with Reynolds the placing of the sitter in such settings instantly transforms them into beings on a higher plane than the real world. In this picture, that higher plane is made explicit: it is Olympus. Mrs Musters, whose husband (National Gallery, Washington) Reynolds showed as a blunt, very down-to-earth squire (making rather Gainsborough-like use of the crossed-legs motif), is literally up in the clouds, goddess of youth and handmaiden to the assembly on Olympus. It is possible that Reynolds had Olivia Porter in mind when he devised Mrs Musters's pose, which echoes hers in reverse, though Mrs Musters's has been likened to that of Galatea in Raphael's decoration for the Farnesina, Rome. However, the swirling design with its undefined spaces is far removed from the linear clarity of Raphael's world. The more compelling overtones are of a Madonna Immaculata borne heavenward in a Bolognese altarpiece by one of the Carracci. The precedent of Van Dyck's 'Countess of Southampton' (no.7) will not have been lost on Reynolds. Thus does he have his cake and eat it too: the young woman is both pure and pagan, her charms flattered and cunningly enhanced by this double and contradictory reference. The characteristic fitful lighting adds to the fascination, and the windblown dress and hair, suggestively unkempt, make this most formal of subjects into a wonderful exercise in informality. Mrs Musters is after all a fitting companion for her unpretentious husband: it was all a joke, as we should have noticed by observing the eagle, Jupiter, who is eating out of her hand.

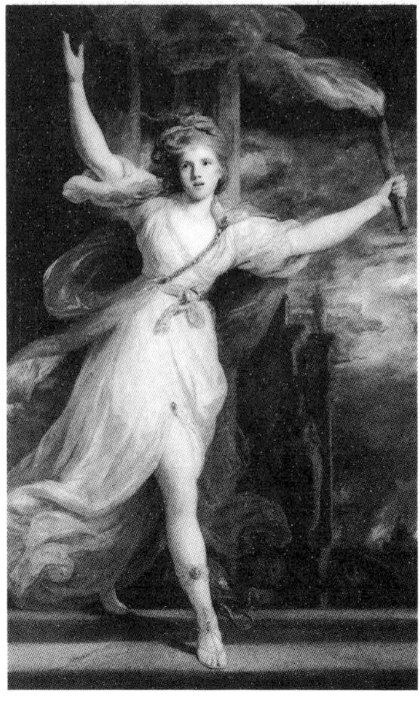

fig.33 Sir Joshua Reynolds **Miss Emily Pott, as Thais** 1781 Oil on canvas *National Trust, Waddesdon Manor*

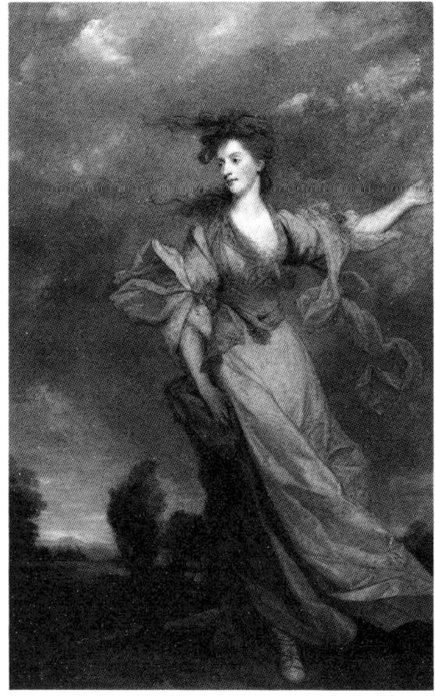

fig.34 Sir Joshua Reynolds **Lady Jane Halliday** 1779 Oil on canvas *National Trust, Waddesdon Manor*

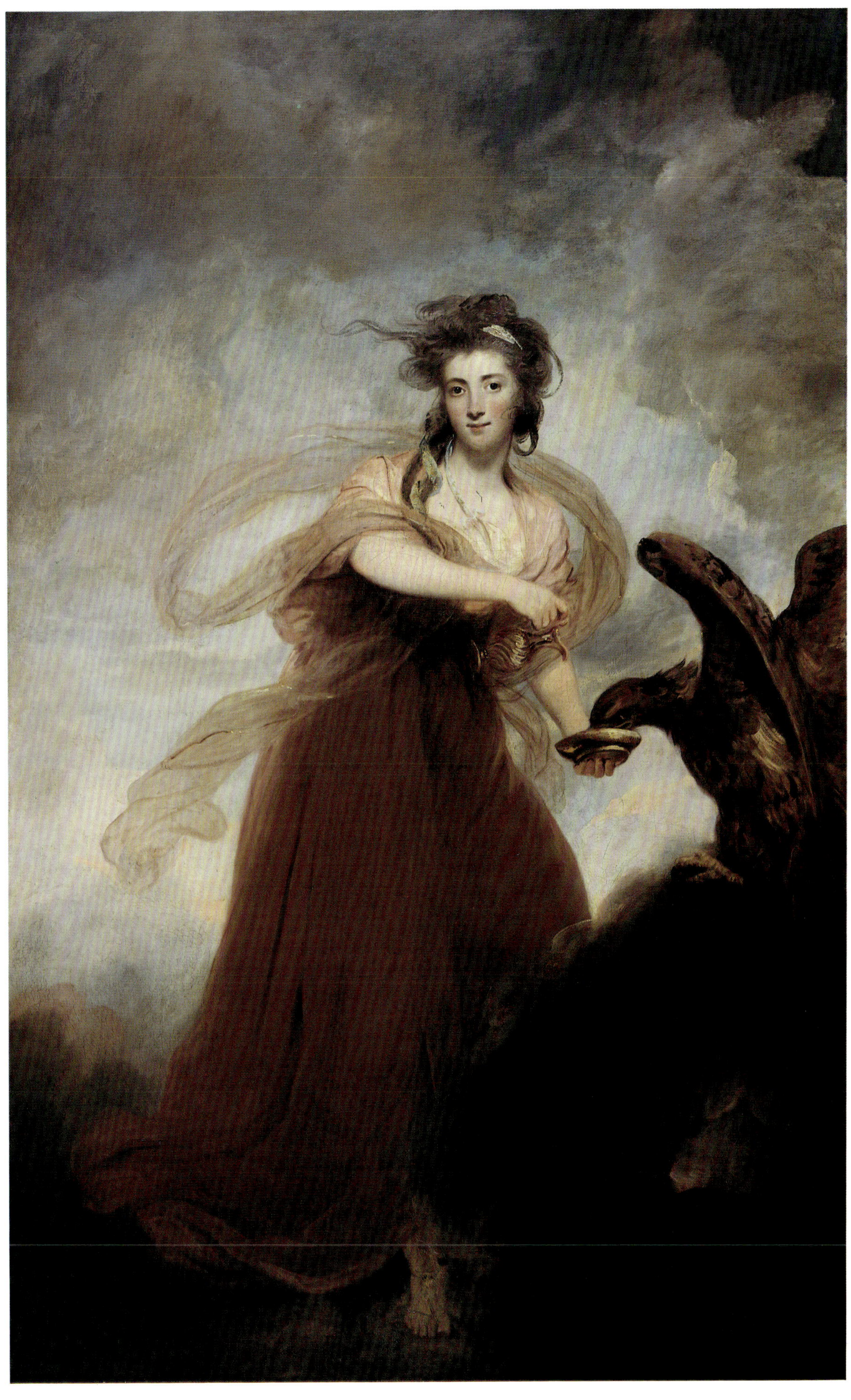

37 **Mrs Siddons as the Tragic Muse** 1789

Oil on canvas 239.7 × 147.6 ($94\frac{3}{8} \times 58\frac{1}{8}$)
Inscr. on hem of skirt: JOSHUA REYNOLDS PINXIT 1789.
The Governors of Dulwich Picture Gallery

Sarah Siddons (1755–1831) was the most celebrated tragic actress of the late eighteenth century. She was born in 1755, the daughter of an actor and the sister of the equally famous John Philip Kemble (see no.52). By the age of twenty she was already performing for Garrick at Drury Lane, one of her earliest successes being in the part of Bedivera in Otway's *Venice Preserved* in 1782. A drawing of her in performance in another famous role, Euphrasia in *The Grecian Daughter*, is in the British Museum. Reynolds first exhibited this subject at the Royal Academy in 1784 (190); the original is in the Huntington Art Gallery, San Marino. This is a replica painted in his studio four years later, and fully signed by him although it may well be largely by an assistant. By the 1780s it was common for actors to be depicted in paintings, but these usually took the form either of straightforward portraits or of small-scale scenes from plays showing them in performance. The master of that genre was Zoffany (see no.33). The idea of representing famous actors on the scale of the full-length and in character had been initiated in the late seventeenth century by John Michael Wright with his triple portait of John Lacy, and taken to an early climax by Hogarth in his remarkable picture of Garrick as Richard III (Walker Art Gallery, Liverpool). This shows him in Act v scene 3, when Richard wakes from his spirit-haunted sleep before the Battle of Bosworth. It is, as has been noted, as much a kind of history picture as a portrait, though its directness and typically Hogarthian lack of glamour combine to make it less than swagger. Reynolds himself had already in the 1760s essayed a portrait of Mrs Abington as the Comic Muse (fig.32 on p.128), which makes use of the whole-length format and 'classical' drapery and statuary to achieve a monumental effect, although the mood of the picture is relaxed if not light-hearted. Equally pertinent, perhaps, is the picture of another actress which George Romney exhibited at the Society of Artists in 1771 (139) under the title 'A whole length portrait of Mrs Yates, in the character of the Tragic Muse'.

But in his portrait of Mrs Siddons Reynolds took the notion on to a completely new plane. He deliberately quotes from a most exalted source: Mrs Siddon's pose, especially her raised left arm, is reminiscent of that of the prophet Isaiah in Michelangelo's Sistine Chapel ceiling, and the flanking figures echo the putti which support the returns of the niche in which the prophet sits. But whereas his feet rest on a stone slab, the throne on which the actress sits is poised on a vast and shadowy cloud. The atmosphere of the picture is Romantic in the manner of Reynolds's most heroic military portraits (see no.34), but suffused with the Olympian grandeur appropriate to a goddess. The monumental scale far outdoes that of Hogarth's large 'Garrick'.

Other modifications of Michelangelo's prototype are also illuminating. The position of the right arm and angle of the head are radically different: Isaiah's right arm is drawn across his body to grasp a book held vertically under his left elbow; Siddons's wrist is flung over the arm of the chair in a gesture both grand and spontaneous. The prophet looks to his right, to catch the whisperings of a spirit hovering at his ear; the actress raises her head heavenward in search of tragic inspiration. So effective is the whole pose that it has prompted considerable discussion. The sitter asserted that Reynolds simply asked her 'Ascend your undisputed throne and graciously bestow upon me some grand Idea of the Tragick Muse', a request she instantly and spontaneously gratified. Samuel Rogers, on the other hand, who claimed to have been an eye-witness, recalled that 'Mrs Siddons came in, having walked rapidly to be in time for her appointment. She threw herself, out of breath, into an armchair, having taken off her bonnet and dropped her head uypon her left hand – the other hand drooping over the arm of the chair. Suddenly lifting her head she said, "How shall I sit?" "Just as you are," said Sir Joshua, and so she is painted.' This is similar to a further version, which has Siddons suddenly breaking the pose by turning her head to look at a picture on the wall, and Reynolds adopting the chance effect. It would be quite in character for him thus to seize a telling gesture which was both grandly expressive and yet typical of the woman. His portraits often amalgamate the personal and the general in this way. The similarities with Michelangelo belie the story, but there may be an element of inspired coincidence in it.

The debt owed to this picture by Lawrence has been recognised: it is impossible to imagine Lawrence's theatrical 'half-history' portraits without this precedent, and his presentation of Siddons as Tragedy (no.53) is clearly inspired by Reynolds's example. It has recently been said that the picture 'handed on a limited legacy to the nineteenth century'; but there are surprising echoes from the 1890s and even later: Solomon Joseph Solomon's 'Mrs Patrick Campbell as Paula Tanqueray' (no.71) seems to allude to this work, and understandably, as Mrs Patrick Campbell was regarded as the Siddons of the day. In a less likely context, de Laszló referred impressively to Reynolds's picture when he painted the Archbishop of Canterbury, Randall Davidson, in 1926 (no.79).

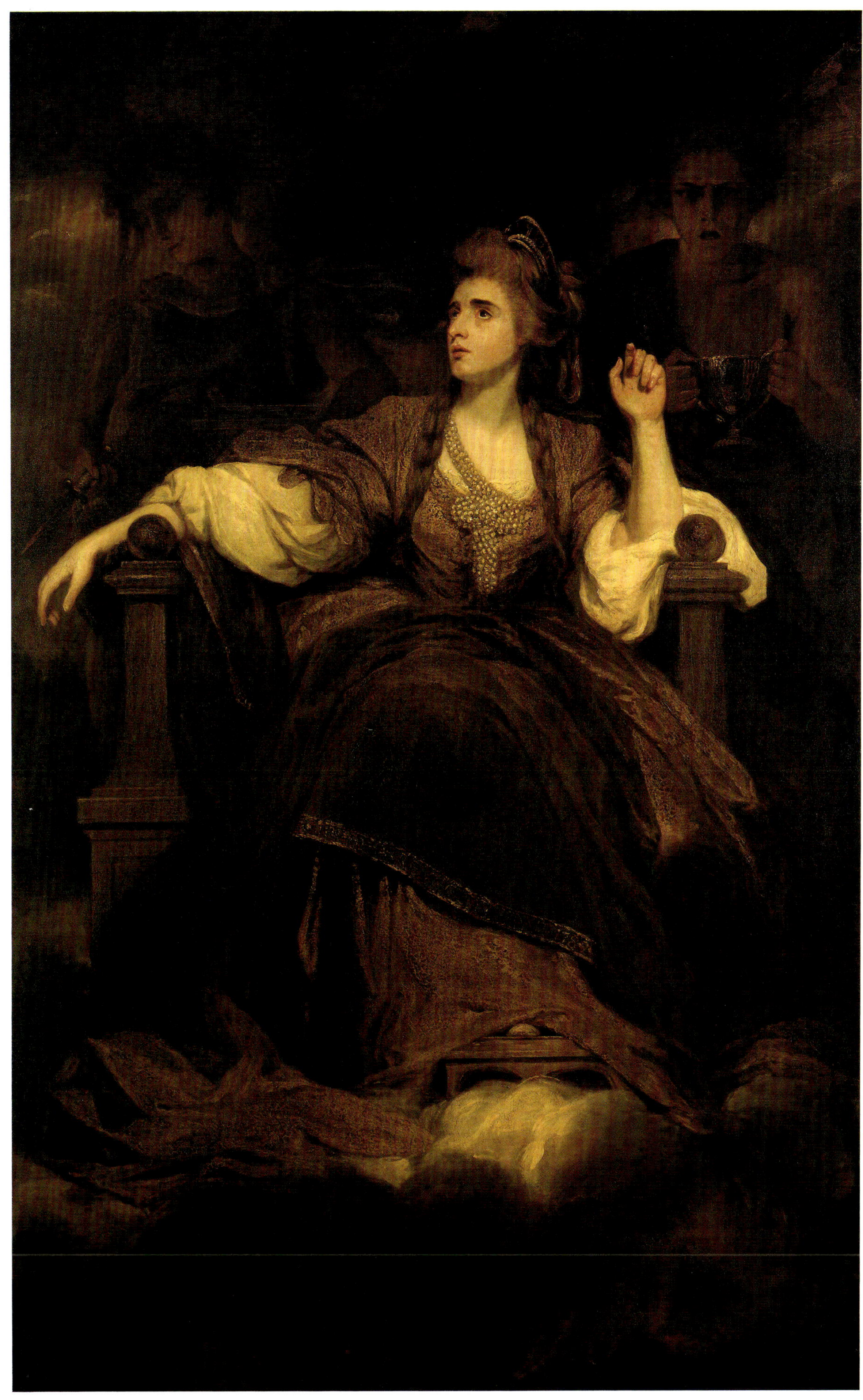

38 **George Augustus Eliott, Lord Heathfield** 1788

Oil on canvas 142.2 × 113.7 (56 × 44¾)
Exh: Royal Academy 1788 (115)
The Trustees of the National Gallery

George Augustus Eliott was born in Roxburghshire in 1718, and educated at Edinburgh and later at Leyden. He pursued a distinguished career in the army, being aide-de-camp to George II at the Battle of Dettingen, where he was wounded. In the course of the Seven Years' War he rose to the rank of Lieutenant-General, and in 1775 was appointed Governor of Gibraltar, which he defended in a famous action against the combined attacks of the French and Spanish. On retirement he was created a peer. He died in 1790 at Aix-la-Chapelle, where he had gone to take the waters. His portrait by Reynolds was commissioned by Alderman John Boydell, promulgator of the Shakspeare Gallery; this, according to James Northcote, was a specially significant concatenation: 'that truest and greatest encourager of English Art ... employed Sir Joshua's pencil, as the greatest painter, to portray for him the greatest hero of his day' (Northcote 1818, II, pp.234–5).

Reynolds rather unexpectedly took up the late Baroque fashion for portraying military celebrities amid swirling drapery and billowing battlesmoke (see for example the portrait of the 1st Marquis of Atholl, no.19) and turned it ingeniously to his own ends. In doing so, he created a new and essentially Romantic genre of portrait, which looks forward to the military subjects of Jacques-Louis David (1748–1825), Baron Antoine Jean Gros (1771–1835) and Théodore Géricault (1791–1824). It was also an essential precursor of the great military portraits of Lawrence. Here the format is relatively modest, being only three-quarter length; but the dignity of the sitter, enacted in a comparatively restrained pose, is combined with a rhetoric provided by the setting: the cannon on the battlements of Gibraltar, and the thick black smoke against which the fine head is lit in sharp contrast, evoke a stirring mood. His expression is one of intense thought as he grasps the key of the fortress and broods on military glory.

Lawrence singled out this picture when expatiating on Reynolds's affinities with Michelangelo: the 'sublimity of thought that marks the first-rate genius ... belongs only to that finer sagacity, which sees the essence of the beautiful or grand, divested of incongruous detail, and whose influence on the works of the great president is equally apparent in the calm, firm Defender of the National Rock, as in the Dying Queen of Virgil, or the grandeur of the Tragic Muse' (Cunningham V, p.207). In deliberately associating Lord Heathfield with those two works Lawrence makes an important point about the portrait; like the 'Death of Dido' and 'Mrs Siddons', it is cast in a consciously historical mould – even if, unlike the other two, no myth or allegory is involved. Reynolds is effectively creating a myth: Heathfield is presented as national hero, his action as a godlike feat. But it remains to be stressed that Reynolds achieves all this with remarkably little fuss. As Lawrence says, there is no 'incongruous detail'; indeed, there is only the powerful likeness of a man, tellingly posed and assisted by minimal properties. This is the kind of minimalism that Reynolds sometimes sought in his portraits, and which depends entirely on penetrating psychology and on perfect control of the atmosphere of the picture.

Artists and critics alike have consistently admired it. James Barry (1741–1806) praised its 'great animation and spirit, happily adapted to the indications of the tremendous scene around him' (Northcote, p.235). Constable (1776–1837), as a landscape painter, was particularly interested in the way Reynolds establishes the setting, though he perceptively relates this closely to the presentation of the figure itself: 'the distant sea, with a glimpse of the opposite coast, expresses the locality, and the cannon pointed downward the height of the rock on which the hero stands, with the chain of the massive key of the fortress twice passed round his hand, as to secure it in his grasp. He seems to say, "I have you, and will keep you!"' (Leslie and Taylor, II, p.517). In the early twentieth century, Roger Fry thought the picture 'a rhetorical portrait which does nothing to shock us. As usual he [Reynolds] sees his sitters in their role on the stage of life – they are not so much individuals with all their contradictions and complexities as actors who come on in their own roles. Here no doubt we get some kind of likeness of Lord Heathfield, but much more Lord Heathfield as the type of the man of action.' (Fry, p.55)

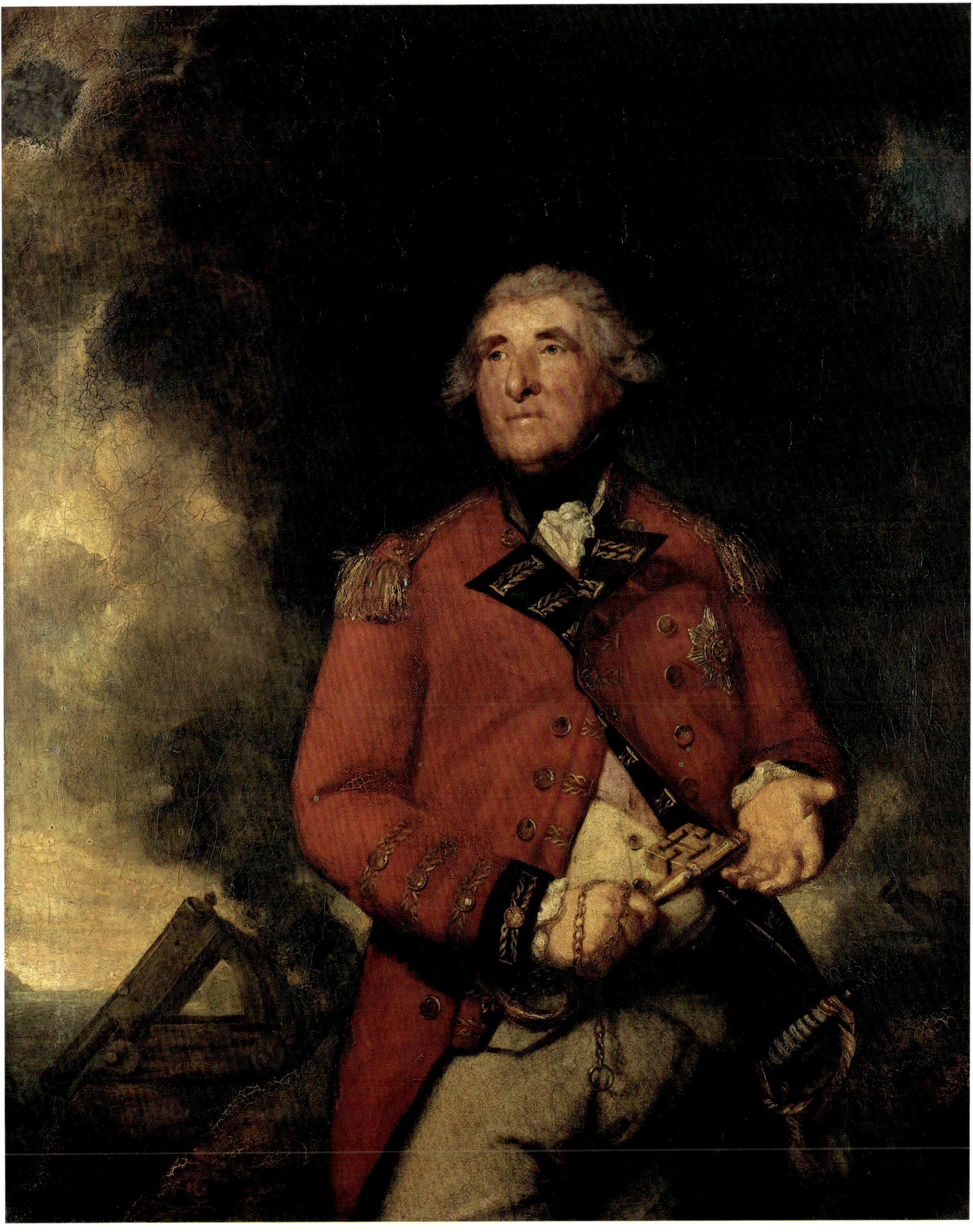

THOMAS GAINSBOROUGH 1727–1788

39 John Campbell, 4th Duke of Argyll 1767

Oil on canvas 231 × 153.7 (91 × 60½)
Exh: Society of Artists 1767 (59)
Scottish National Portrait Gallery

Gainsborough was not in his true element with state portraiture; his instinct to be on close friendly terms with his sitters – or to suggest that relationship in his pictures – militates against the creation of hierarchical distinctions. The variety of textures occasioned by ducal robes and ermine, however, gave plenty of congenial exercise for his brush, and these he exploits to the full here. He presents an ageing nobleman foursquare, feet firmly planted, asserting his rank by the unhesitating way he lays his hand on his coronet and grasps the ceremonial staff that he carried as Hereditary Master of the Royal Household. Argyll is dressed in full ceremonial ermine, and proudly displays the collar and badge of the order of the Thistle across his breast. Gainsborough's solution to the problems raised by this kind of formal image-making can be interesingly compared with those adopted by Reynolds in a work like his portrait of the Duke of Cumberland, executed at much the same time (no.34).

John Campbell was a venerable figure by the time this portrait was painted; he was born in about 1693, and so would have been about seventy-four when he sat to Gainsborough. He had served as a colonel of infantry, and as Colonel of the North British Dragoons (later the famous Scots Greys); like the Duke of Cumberland (no.34) he had been present at the Battle of Dettingen in 1741. He represented the Whig interest for various Scottish constituencies in Parliament, and during the 1760s was Governor of Limerick. He succeeded his cousin Archibald Campbell to the dukedom in 1761, and was made a Knight Templar in 1765. He died in 1770.

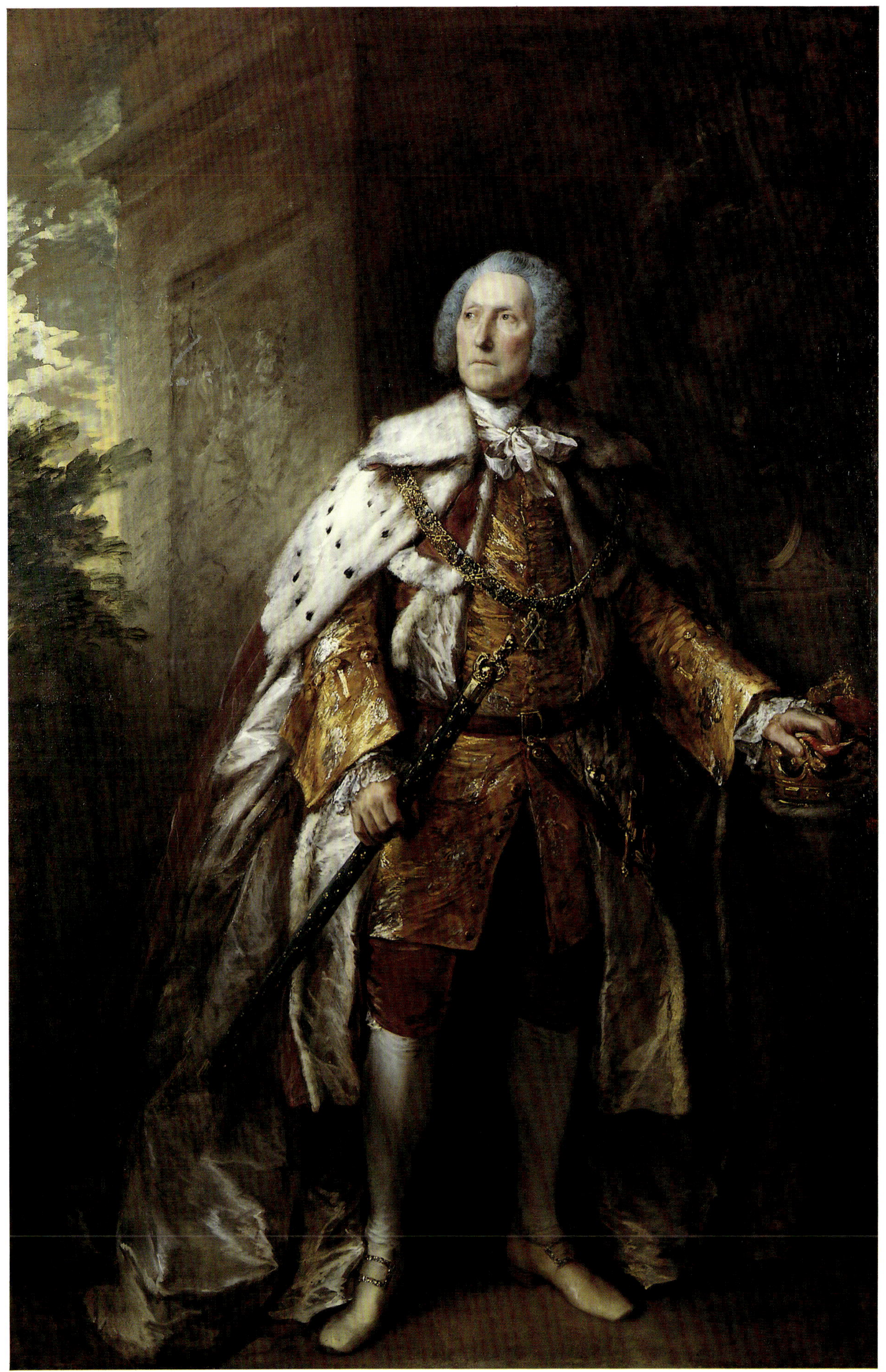

40 **Augustus John, 3rd Earl of Bristol** 1768

Oil on canvas 232.5 × 152.5 ($91\frac{1}{2}$ × 60)
Ickworth, The Bristol Collection (The National Trust)

This picture was exhibited at the Society of Artists in 1768 (60) as 'A sea officer; whole length'. The sitter was Augustus John Hervey, brother of George, 2nd Earl of Bristol, who died unmarried in 1775. The 3rd Earl had been born in 1724, and married in 1744, though he too was to leave no children and was also succeeded by a brother when he died in 1779. He pursued a naval career, rising to the rank of Vice-Admiral of the Blue. He was a Captain when Gainsborough painted this portrait, which well illustrates the artist's temperamental preference for informality: it is a grand conception, with the conventional trappings of the most formal naval portraiture, going back to Van Dyck's 'Algernon Percy, Earl of Northumberland' (fig.35; Alnwick Castle) – the anchor and marine backdrop can be seen in Hudson's 'Admiral Sir Chaloner Ogle' (no.25), for instance. But the easy stance, instead of lending the figure an air of assured and elegant dignity, as with Batoni (*cf.* no.28) tends to undermine such ideas and reinforce a sense of casualness that is ultimately confirmed by Gainsborough's rapid, free handling of paint, and by the slightly truculent look which he so frankly captures on Hervey's face. This too may be seen as part of a tradition: Admiral Ogle, in a less refined way, looks truculent too, and we should probably interpret the expression as indicative of those manly qualities appropriate to a naval officer.

The Herveys were a family with a talent for surprising behaviour, and a tendency to become involved in scandal. 'When God created the human race,' ran a *mot* attributed to various wits, 'he made men, women, and Herveys.'. The 3rd Earl's wife was the cause of one of the more sensational social events of the period. She was Elizabeth Chudleigh, a granddaughter of Sir George Chudleigh Bt, of Ashton, and Hervey had married her clandestinely. The year after this picture of him was exhibited, she married the Duke of Kingston in the full glare of publicity and without a formal separation from Hervey who seems to have condoned it and so put himself in a position in which it was impossible to obtain a divorce. She was duly arraigned by the House of Lords who declared the marriage illegal. She left England for the Continent where she died in the same year as Gainsborough, 1788.

Hervey's even more unpredictable brother, the Bishop of Derry, succeeded him to the title and towards the end of his life built the great house at Ickworth (which he was never to see) where this picture now hangs. The Earl-Bishop's daughter Elizabeth, later Duchess of Devonshire, was painted by Lawrence (no.54).

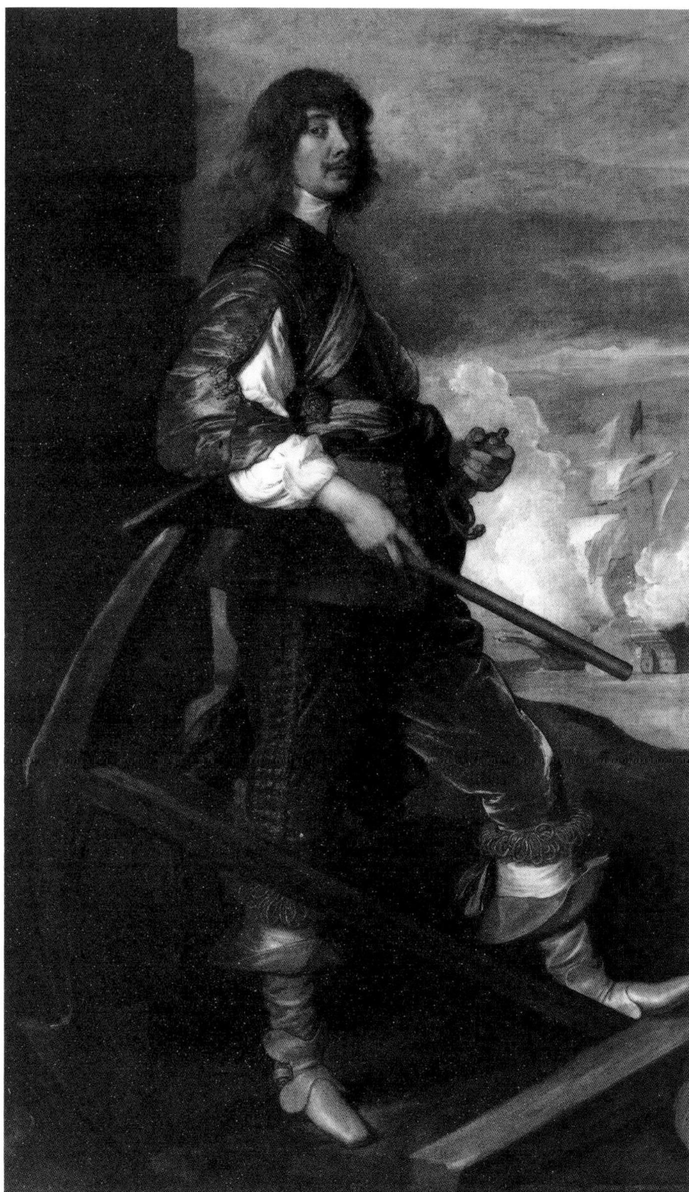

fig.35 Sir Anthony Van Dyck **Algernon Percy, 10th Earl of Northumberland** *c.*1636 Oil on canvas *Duke of Northumberland, Alnwick Castle*

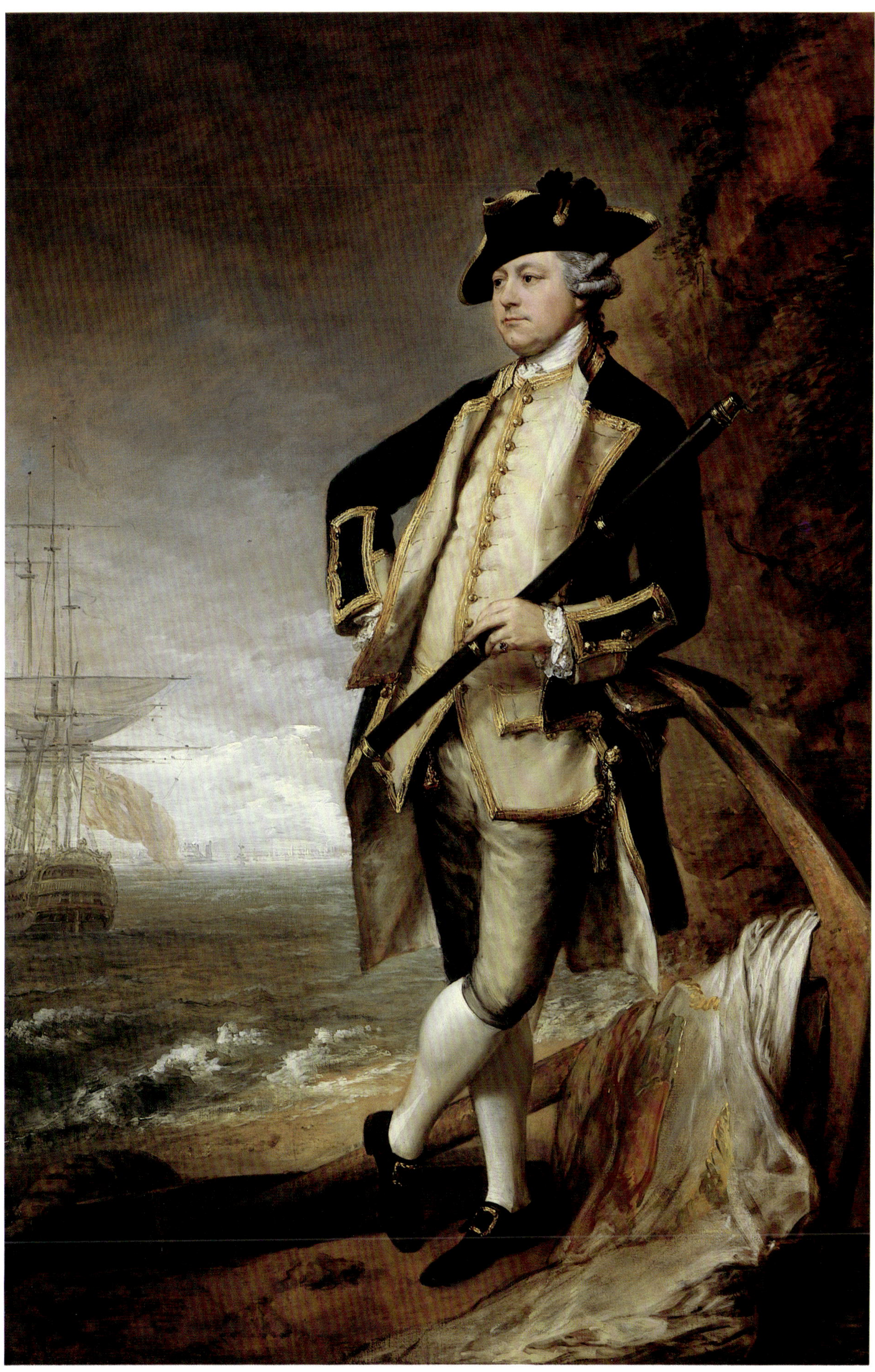

41 George, Prince of Wales *c.*1782

Oil on canvas 246.5 × 177.7 (97 × 70)
The Marquess of Zetland

Gainsborough made several portraits of the Prince of Wales; most are busts. This much grander composition is a version, painted for Sir Thomas Dundas, of the picture shown at the Royal Academy in 1782 (77) and now at Waddesdon. In the following year the subject was engraved in mezzotint by J.R. Smith. It is one of the most glamorous of all representations of the Prince, with none of the swirling romance of Reynolds's picture of him, either with a Negro servant (1787, Arundel Castle) or again with a horse (1784, Brocket Hall).

The Prince was about twenty when this picture was painted (he was born in 1762), and at the beginning of his public career. He had followed the traditional pattern of heirs to the throne in being obstinately independent and disrespectful to his father. His Whig affiliations and his morals were alike an embarrassment to the Crown. He was well known to have taken as a mistress the actress Mary Darby, Mrs Robinson, famous for her role as Perdita in *The Winter's Tale*, in which part she was painted by Gainsborough (London, Wallace Collection). He lived extravagantly the life of a dilettante, *bon vivant* and sportsman, and rebuilt Carlton House in lavish style. In 1782 he first visited Brighton, and two years later started work on the oriental fantasy of Brighton Pavilion – a 'costly absurdity' in the words of J.A. Hamilton. He accumulated enormous debts. Profligacy and sensuality remained distinguishing marks of his character throughout his reign as George IV (1820–30), which was in many repects a golden age of the arts in England.

Gainsborough's purpose in this portrait is to establish a note of well-bred assurance, perhaps deliberately countering the Prince's unfortunate public image, while affirming his qualities as a convivial and civilised man. Although this is a royal portrait, there is a nonchalance, typical of the artist, that seems to bring the sitter close to us for all his hauteur. The artist is indebted to Van Dyck above all for the achievement of this balance between royal dignity and gentlemanly ease.

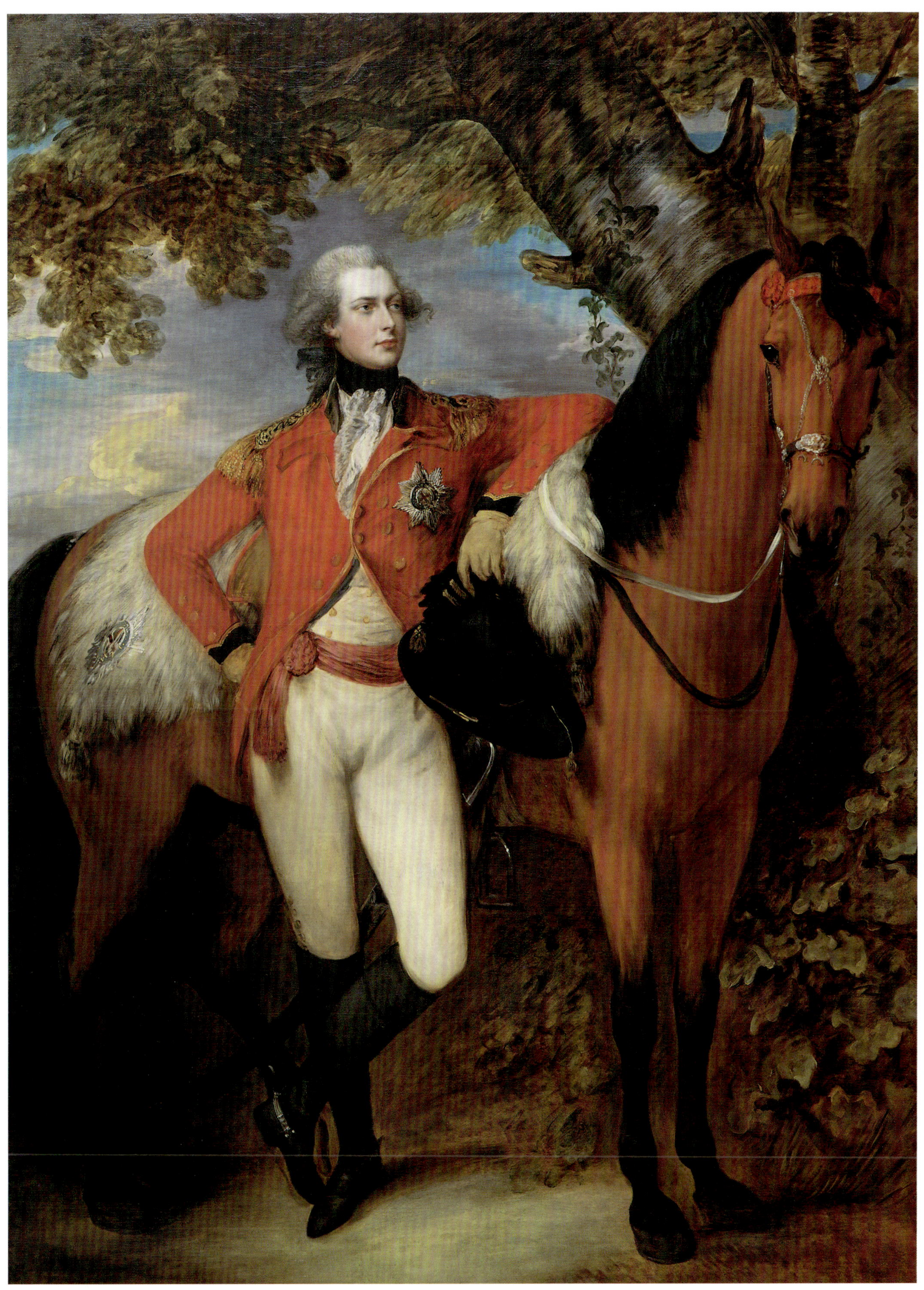

42 **Giovanna Baccelli** 1782

Oil on canvas 226.7 × 148.6 ($89\frac{1}{4} \times 58\frac{1}{2}$)
Exh: Royal Academy 1782 (230)
Tate Gallery. Purchased 1975

La Baccelli was the stage name of a Venice-born entertainer, Giovanna Francesca Antonia Giuseppe Zanerini (died 1801). She was by profession a dancer and soubrette, and made her first recorded appearance in London, at the King's Theatre, Haymarket in 1774. She was both charming and genuinely popular, noted for 'the grace and elegant symmetry of her person'; her obituary in the *Morning Chronicle*, May 1801, called her 'the most fascinating dancer that ever appeared on the Opera stage'. By 1779 she had become mistress to John Frederick Sackville, 3rd Duke of Dorset, with whom she remained for a decade, and who probably commissioned this portrait from Gainsborough. The Baccelli represents the theatre at its opposite pole from that of Siddons as the Tragic Muse (see no.37). Dorset asked Reynolds, too, to paint his mistress, and received from him an interpretation of her as a bacchante (Lord Sackville, Knole). At Knole also are a recumbent nude figure of Baccelli in plaster, by an unidentified sculptor, and a later (probably mid-nineteenth century) preparatory study for a genre painting showing the dancer posing to Gainsborough with her Chinese page Wang-y-Tong at hand.

Gainsborough's portraiture is the antithesis of Reynolds's: he presents the sitter not in generalised allegorical persona as a bacchante, or even as Terpsichore, but as herself in a popular entertainment, the French ballet *Les Amans surpris*. Her costume and attitude are recorded accurately as they were observed on the stage, and Gainsborough makes no effort to give added dignity or grandeur to his sitter: she speaks for herself as herself, in all her agility and elegant charm. Because she is a theatrical personality, however, she is larger than life, and the portrait is a public statement by virtue of being a likeness of a public figure. It is perhaps relevant, though, to compare Gainsborough's treatment of this subject with Reynolds's much earlier full-length of 'Mrs Hale as Euphrosyne' (Earl of Harewood), which also shows a woman, if not dancing, about to do so, with a strongly rhythmic movement forward across the design from left to right. Reynolds's sitter is presented as one of the Three Graces, or as the mirthful nymph in Milton's *L'Allegro*; the design has been linked (rather tenuously) with Raphael's 'St Margaret' (Louvre) and more convincingly with the engraving in reverse of Kneller's 'Countess of Ranelagh' (fig.9 on p.35). The fresh, pastel colours recall Guido Reni, who seems to be the prime inspiration behind Reynolds's picture. Although, significantly, no learned allusions of this kind can be said to apply to Baccelli's portrait, it may be that Gainsborough had 'Mrs Hale' in mind as exemplifying the light-hearted tone that he intended here.

A small oil modello for the subject has recently been recovered after its theft from the Beit Collection, County Wicklow.

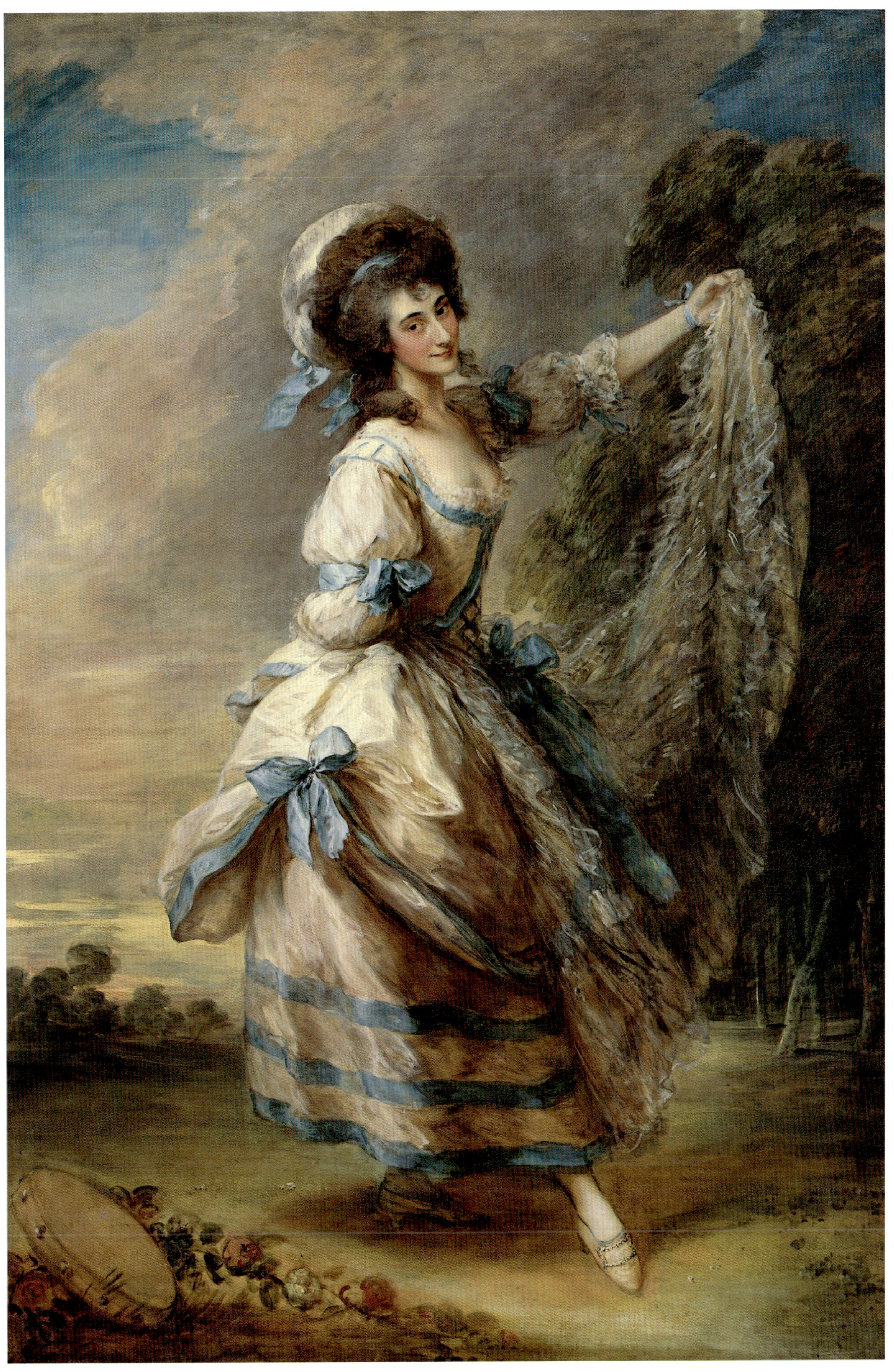

43 **Mr and Mrs Hallett ('The Morning Walk')** 1785

Oil on canvas 236.2 × 179.1 (93 × $70\frac{1}{2}$)
The Trustees of the National Gallery. Purchased with a contribution from the National Art Collections Fund

This celebrated picture is often seen as the epitome of Gainsborough's art and, one might say, in consequence the epitome of English portraiture. William Hallett married Elizabeth Stephen in the summer of 1785; he was twenty-one and she a few months older. Their marriage was destined to endure: she died aged sixty in 1833; he lived until 1842. The double portrait celebrates the happy union of two young people who make no claims on public attention; yet it is also a universal statement about wedded bliss, to which the summer weather and the devoted dog contribute important addenda. The fresh colouring and free handling of the paint are characteristic of the portraits that Gainsborough produced in the last years of his life, yet here they seem particularly well adapted to the theme of the work. It taps a long tradition of pastoral, making use of the connotations of Watteau that Gainsborough was exploring in several compositions of this time. His canvas of 'The Mall' (Frick Collection, New York) had been painted two years before: it shows groups of fashionable ladies (and one or two gentlemen) promenading under tall trees; despite the obvious evocation of Watteau there is little to suggest Watteau's characteristic melancholy although it has been suggested, rather oddly, that Gainsborough is trying in 'The Mall' to paint a 'modern moral subject' in the manner of Francis Wheatley (1747–1801), the English Greuze (Waterhouse 1958, p.33). If there is any 'moral' content in the picture it is more to do with the informal elegance of English fashions in the mid-1780s, and with the generalised effects of dappled light and shade that Gainsborough so often presented in his landscapes. That quality of generalisation is what, in much grander format, Gainsborough successfully brings to his portrait of the Halletts. He preserves the intimacy and charm of his subject while giving it the scale and presence of a full-blown society portrait: a piquant combination.

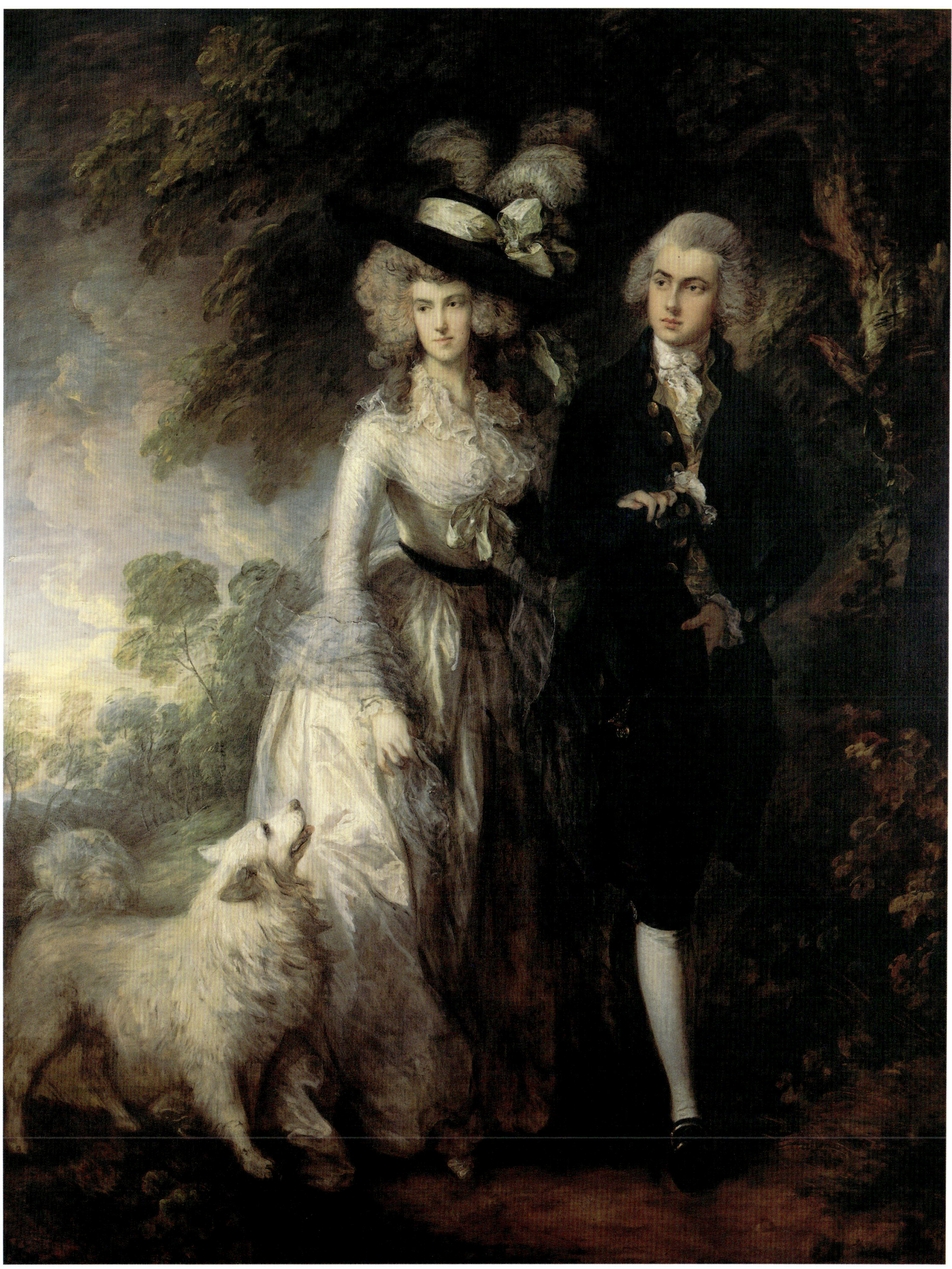

JOHN SINGLETON COPLEY 1738–1815

44 The Three Youngest Daughters of George III 1785

Oil on canvas 265.5 × 186.0 ($104\frac{1}{2} \times 73\frac{1}{4}$)
Inscr. *J.S. Copley 1785*; and on the cart: *PA* (monogram)
Her Majesty The Queen

The three girls are the nine-year-old Princess Mary (1776–1857), who stands at the left and shakes a tambourine for the amusement of her baby sister, the two-year-old Princess Amelia (1783–1810), sitting in a little carriage with the middle sister, Princess Sophia (1777–1848). All three children, it was reported, were fatigued by Copley's numerous and lengthy sittings, so much so that complaints were made to the King. George III in turn referred to Benjamin West who, as Historical Painter to the King and a fellow American, had procured Copley the commission. West duly explained that 'Mr Copley must be allowed to proceed in his own way, and that any attempt to hurry him might be injurious to the picture, which would be a very fine one when done'. The care that Copley expended in working out his design is recorded in a number of preparatory drawings.

His sense of the importance of the commission is reflected not only in the sheer size of the picture, but in the wealth of accessories that he has invented for it; in both respects it recalls Closterman's 'Children of John Taylor' (no.21) and seems to pick up the threads of a Baroque tradition of the group portraiture of children. At the same time, as a truly monumental composition that takes as its subject the light-hearted play of young people, it anticipates some of the more daring designs of Lawrence. With its crisply and finely painted details of flowers, birds, and dogs it introduces decorative elements that are greatly at variance with the generalisations of Reynolds's work at the same period: something of the love of precise detail that pervaded Copley's early colonial work in Boston seems to have survived into this very different milieu.

The buildings glimpsed in the distance place the cheerful scene at Windsor: we can see the Round Tower and the Queen's Lodge. At Windsor, too, there are echoes of this picture: the vine and parrots against a summer sky might have inspired the decorative panels painted by the girls' elder sister, the Princess Elizabeth, in the Cross Gallery at Frogmore House a few years later; and there are other, similarly swagged garlands in the decorations executed at Frogmore by Mary Moser (1744–1819); these also date from the 1790s.

When this picture was exhibited at the Royal Academy it struck most viewers as extraordinary, precisely because it insisted on an unfashionable profusion of detail. John Hoppner, who might have been expected to see it with an artist's eye for freshness and invention, was scathing: 'What delightful disorder! Why, you have plucked up harmony by the roots, and planted confusion in its stead! Princesses, parrots, dogs, grapes, flowers, leaves, are each striving for preeminence, and opposing, with hostile force, all attempts of our wearied eye to find repose' (*Morning Post*, 5 May 1785). Nevertheless, the picture is an icon of one of the most important developments of late eighteenth-century England: the recognition of children as individuals with habits and needs different from those of adults. It was a by-product of the Enlightenment, allied to the 'sensibility' of the period, and Copley's work is significant in recording that even royal children enjoyed the benefits of this liberalised state of affairs.

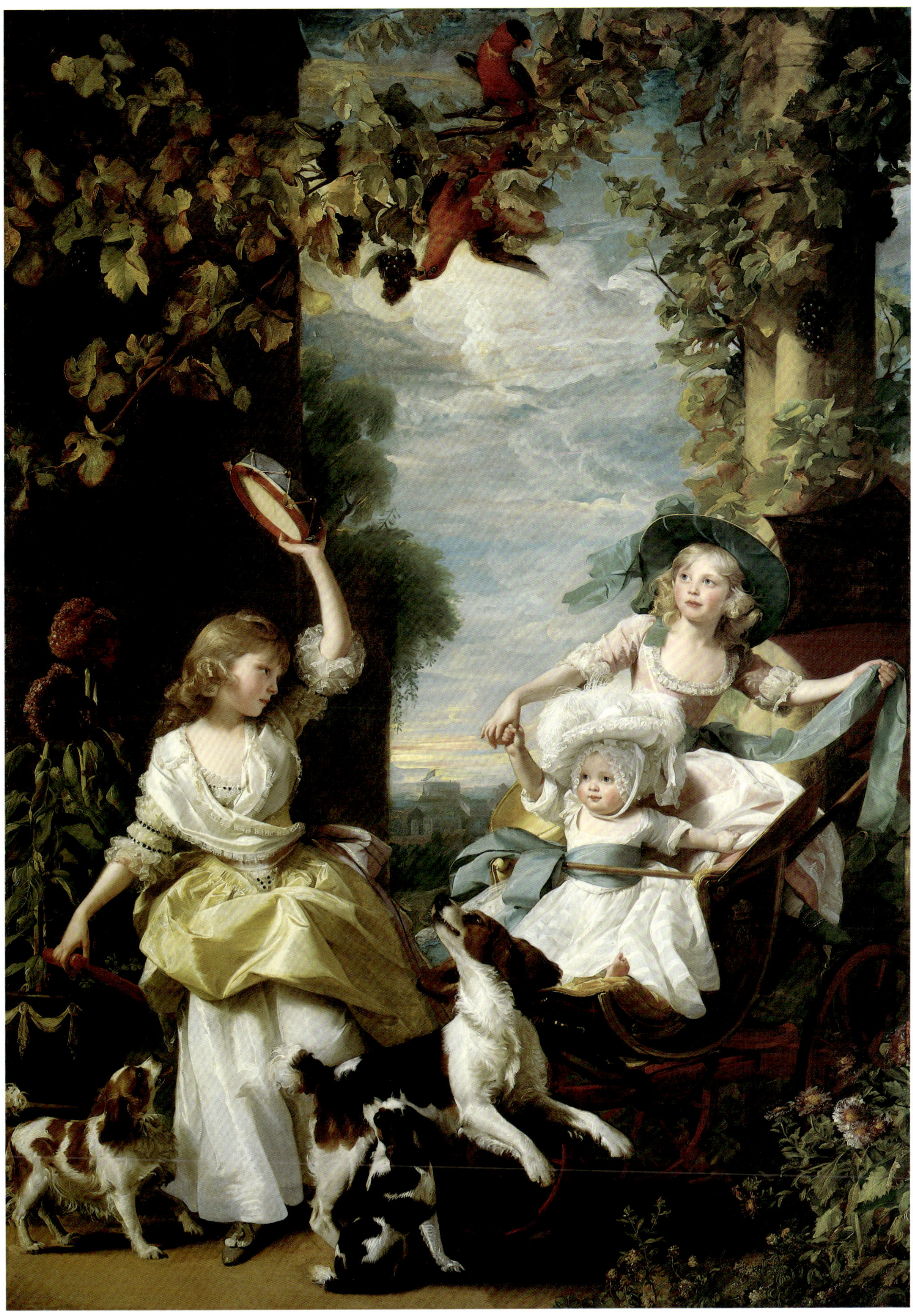

SIR WILLIAM BEECHEY 1753–1839

45 George IV when Prince of Wales *c.*1798

Oil on canvas 139.7 × 116 (55 × 45½)
Royal Academy of Arts, London

Beechey presented this portrait to the Royal Academy as his Diploma work when he was elected Academician in 1798. In that year he also received a knighthood from the King for his picture, shown in the Academy's spring exhibition, of 'His Majesty reviewing the Third or Prince of Wales's Regiment of Dragoon Guards and the Tenth or Prince of Wales's Regiment of Light Dragoons, attended by the Prince of Wales, the Duke of York, Sir W. Fawcett, Lieut.-General Dundas, Major-General Goldsworthy, etc.' (collection Her Majesty The Queen). (It is hard to know to whom the 'etc.' in this title refers, as only four men are shown apart from the King and the Prince.) Beechey had exhibited a portrait of the Prince of Wales alone in the previous year, and it may be that this was the picture under consideration here. At any rate, the Prince is here shown in the uniform of the Dragoons, and holds the sword that he is brandishing in the larger work, just as he can there be seen wearing the casquet that he here carries in his left hand.

There are obvious comparisons to be made between this military portrait and that of Lord Heathfield by Reynolds (no.38). Both are three-quarter-length male portraits with a highly charged martial atmosphere. But whereas Reynolds's picture is a self-sufficient design, deftly deployed in its allotted space, Beechey's composition has the air of being cut down from a full-length. The Prince of Wales's pose is less individual than Heathfield's; it is one commonly encountered in portraits of the time; in Romney's 'Major-General Sir John Burgoyne' (Holburne Museum, Bath) for instance. Indeed, the picture does not celebrate any particular achievement but makes a more general statement about the Prince's status as Commander-in-Chief of the Dragoon Guards. Similarly, the billowing clouds are less easily identifiable as battle-smoke, and we are certainly not expected to associate the sitter with a particular engagement.

Nevertheless the simple, static pose is authoritative and graceful. Appropriately, the forceful portrait of the Prince takes an equal place in the design with the silver frogging, sashes and decorations of his military jacket. Yet in the end it is his mild yet firm gaze out of the picture to the left which gives the whole structure its assurance as a public statement.

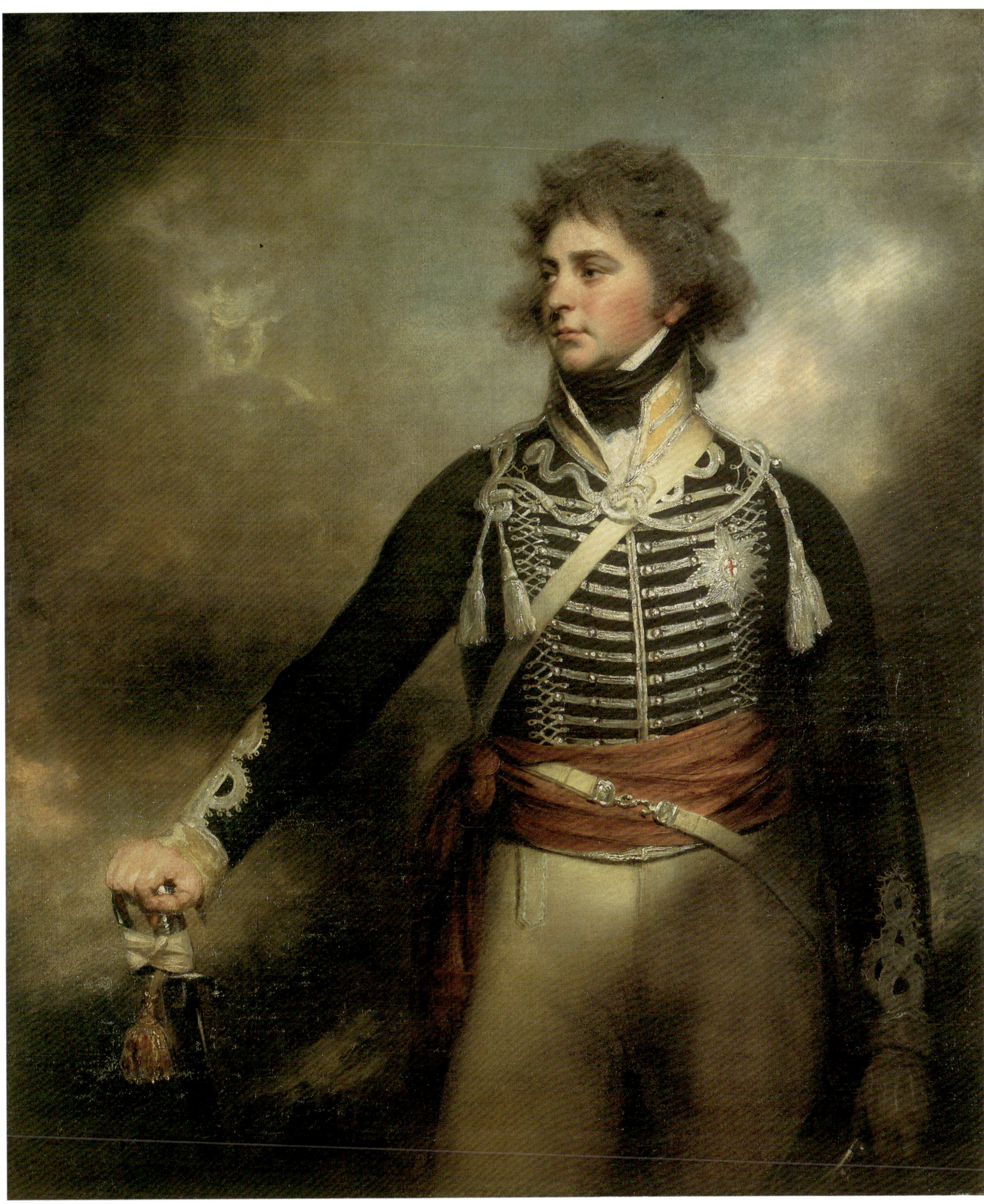

SIR HENRY RAEBURN 1756–1823

46 **Sir John Sinclair Bt** 1794

Oil on canvas 238 × 154 ($93\frac{1}{2} \times 60\frac{1}{2}$)
Inscr. lower right (not by the artist): RT HONBLE. SIR JOHN SINCLAIR BART/AS COLONEL of ROTHSAY & CAITHNESS FENCIBLES/BY RAEBURN.
National Gallery of Scotland

The Rt Hon. Sir John Sinclair of Ulbster, Caithness, was born in 1754. He trained in Edinburgh and London as a lawyer and became a politician, taking his seat as independent Member of Parliament for Caithness in 1780. In 1786 Pitt awarded him a baronetcy, but the two men later clashed over several issues, Sinclair being a leading member of the clique known as the Armed Neutrality Party. At home in Scotland he was enthusiastic experimenter in farming methods, and particularly interested in sheep-breeding: he founded the British Wool Society in 1791. He was an advocate of enclosure, and initiated wide-ranging improvements on his Caithness estates. In 1793, at the start of the war with France, on Sinclair's insistence, Pitt set up a Board of Agriculture and Sinclair was appointed its first president. As a pioneer statistician – and indeed the inventor of the terms 'statistics' and 'statistical' – he conceived a grand *Statistical Survey* of the whole of England on the lines of the Domesday Book, parish by parish, but the ambitious project was violently attacked and he was replaced. He earned further criticism when he published his opinions concerning bullion and a paper currency, and was finally, in 1811, given the sinecure post of Commissioner of Excise. This drew upon him the ridicule of Scott: 'Sir John Sinclair has gotten the Golden Fleece at last. Dogberry would not desire a richer reward for having been written down an ass.' He was, indeed, an easy butt for humour on account of his own humourlessness and self-important enthusiasm for misconceived philanthropic projects. As a youth of sixteen he had already revealed his lack of judgement and his instinct for ostentation by constructing a road across supposedly impassable mountains within a single day. The road, needless to say, did not last long. But his ideas on the study and recording of populations were of more permanent value, and were paid tribute to by more notable contemporaries, Jeremy Bentham and Thomas Malthus among others. His career was punctuated by literary effusions which he produced in large numbers throughout his life. One of the most curious is his *Dissertation on the Authenticity of the Poems of Ossian* (1807) which, in attempting to prove the credentials of Macpherson's famous hoax, only succeeded in confirming its spuriousness.

Raeburn painted Sinclair on at least three occasions, and in this portrait succeeds in capturing his 'harmless egotism'. It celebrates the founding of the Rothesay and Caithness Fencibles, a force he raised at Pitt's behest in 1794, and shows him in his uniform as its Colonel. The military connotation, and the romantic landscape background, give this picture a place beside Reynolds's evocative portraits of soldiers (see no.38 for instance), and anticipate the fitful light and slightly histrionic dignity of Lawrence's Waterloo series. The portrait is one of several that Raeburn painted showing Highlanders in ceremonial uniform, 'whose picturesque dress and martial bearing,' as Cunnningham observed, 'contrasted finely with the graver costume and sterner brows of the Lowlanders' – Sir William Maxwell of Calderwood, for example (no.47).

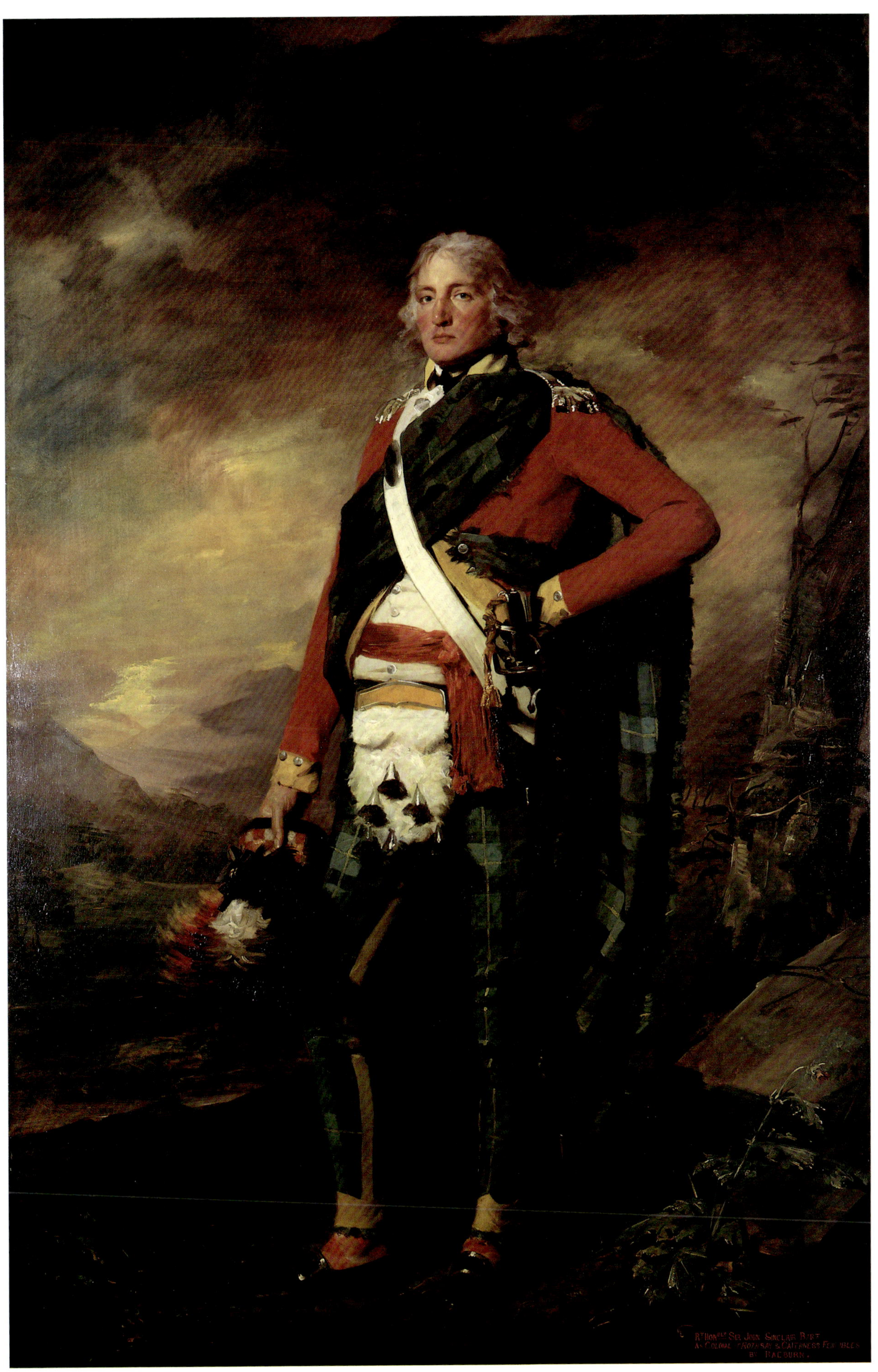
RT HONBLE SIR JOHN SINCLAIR BART
AS COLONAL OF ROTHSAY & CAITHNESS FENCIBLES
BY RAEBURN.

47 **General Sir William Maxwell of Calderwood Bt** *c.*1796

Oil on canvas 249 × 148 (98 × 58¼)
The National Trust for Scotland, Fyvie Castle, Aberdeenshire

There has long been uncertainty as to the identity of this sitter. The portrait has always been known as that of Sir William Maxwell of Calderwood, and assumed to be of the General of that name, the 7th Baronet, who was born in 1754, married in 1792 and died in 1837. He succeeded to the baronetcy in 1829, on the death his cousin the 6th Baronet, also Sir William Maxwell of Calderwood. Many of the details of the costume, carefully specified as they are, seem to fit better with the career of the 6th than the 7th Baronet, about whom less is known. He was born in 1748, and appears to have been a Captain in the 2nd Battalion, 1st Regiment of Foot during the later 1790s, and the badge on the shoulder belt shown here is consistent with that rank. There is a record of a Sir William Maxwell as major in the Lowland (West) Fencibles in 1794, and this may be the same person; the epaulettes are those of a major or lieutenant-colonel, though the uniform in the picture would not be correct for that regiment. The 6th Baronet had been created a Baronet of Nova Scotia, and that order hangs from the orange ribbon round the sitter's neck. The details of the costume are evidently of some importance for they are all carefully delineated and proudly displayed. Even the sword can be identified as of a type introduced about 1796. The magnifying glass that Sir William carries in his left hand presumably also has some personal significance. It is a detail that testifies to the care with which Raeburn has designed the portrait to give a full and graphic account of the man he is painting.

The date suggested by the costume and sword is borne out by the style of the picture, which displays the romantic interest in dramatic effects of light that preoccupied Raeburn in the 1790s, the decade when he first began to show his work in London. In 1795 he built himself a new studio in York Place, Edinburgh, with carefully considered lighting, and this stimulated him to experiment boldly. The viewpoint is very low, so that we are forced to look sharply up at the tall man and his fine horse, lit from behind by sharp flashes of sunlight bursting from among stormy clouds. The breadth of touch and simplification of form so characteristic of Raeburn's mature style are conspicuous.

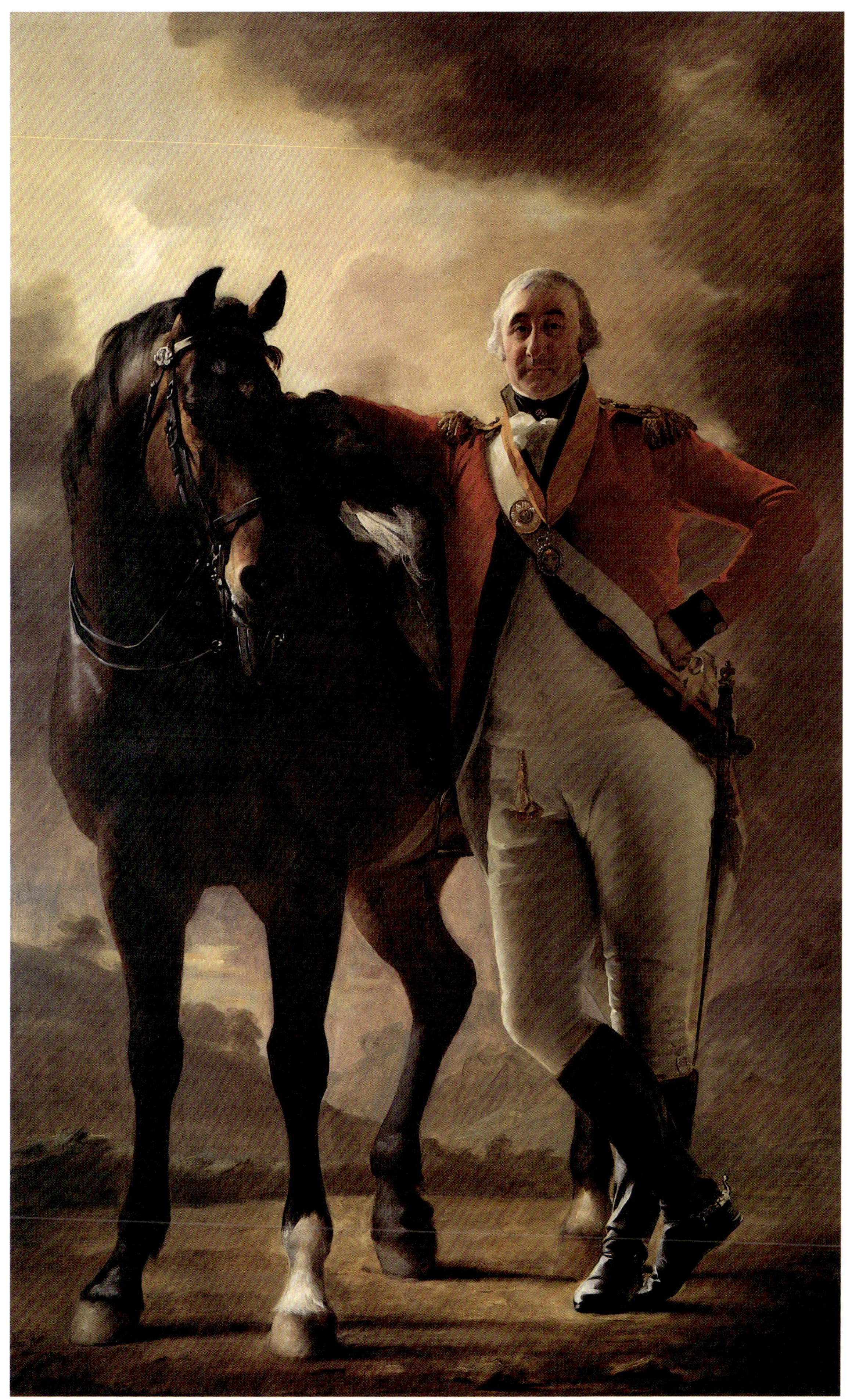

48 **Spencer, 2nd Marquess of Northampton** 1821

Oil on canvas 128 × 100.5 ($50\frac{1}{2}$ × $39\frac{1}{2}$)
Insc. lower left (not by the artist): *Spencer, 2nd Marquis of Northampton/by Raeburn*
Exh: Royal Academy 1821 (325)
The Marquess of Northampton

Spencer Joshua Alwyne Compton, 2nd Marquess of Northampton, was born in 1790, the second son of the 9th Earl and 1st Marquess whom he succeeded in 1828. His mother was Mary Smith, daughter of the Member of Parliament for Devizes. In 1812 he succeeded the recently assassinated Spencer Percival as member for Northampton, which he represented until 1820. Although he came from a high Tory family his own views were unpredictable and tended towards the liberal. He worked, for instance, with William Wilberforce for the abolition of the slave trade, and joined Sir James Mackintosh in campaigning for law reform. He married Margaret Maclean Clephane (see no.49) in 1815, and the couple spent the 1820s in Italy, where she died. Lord Northampton became a respected connoisseur of the arts and literature, taking a particular interest in disseminating the poetry of otherwise unknown authors, among them his wife, whose poems he had privately printed after her death. He was involved with several learned societies and became President of the Royal Society in 1838. He died in 1851.

The bold simplicity of Raeburn's approach to portraiture is exemplified in this work, which seems more remarkable for its understatement than for any rhetorical qualities. Despite that, it is a work of such concentration and intensity that it suggests a vividly romantic personality comparable with the brooding heroes of Prudhon and Géricault. The contained pose, with hands folded into the sitter's tightly wrapped cape, creates an enclosed silhouette that lends maximum dramatic effect to the brilliant highlights of red cloak lining and white of the collar and cravat.

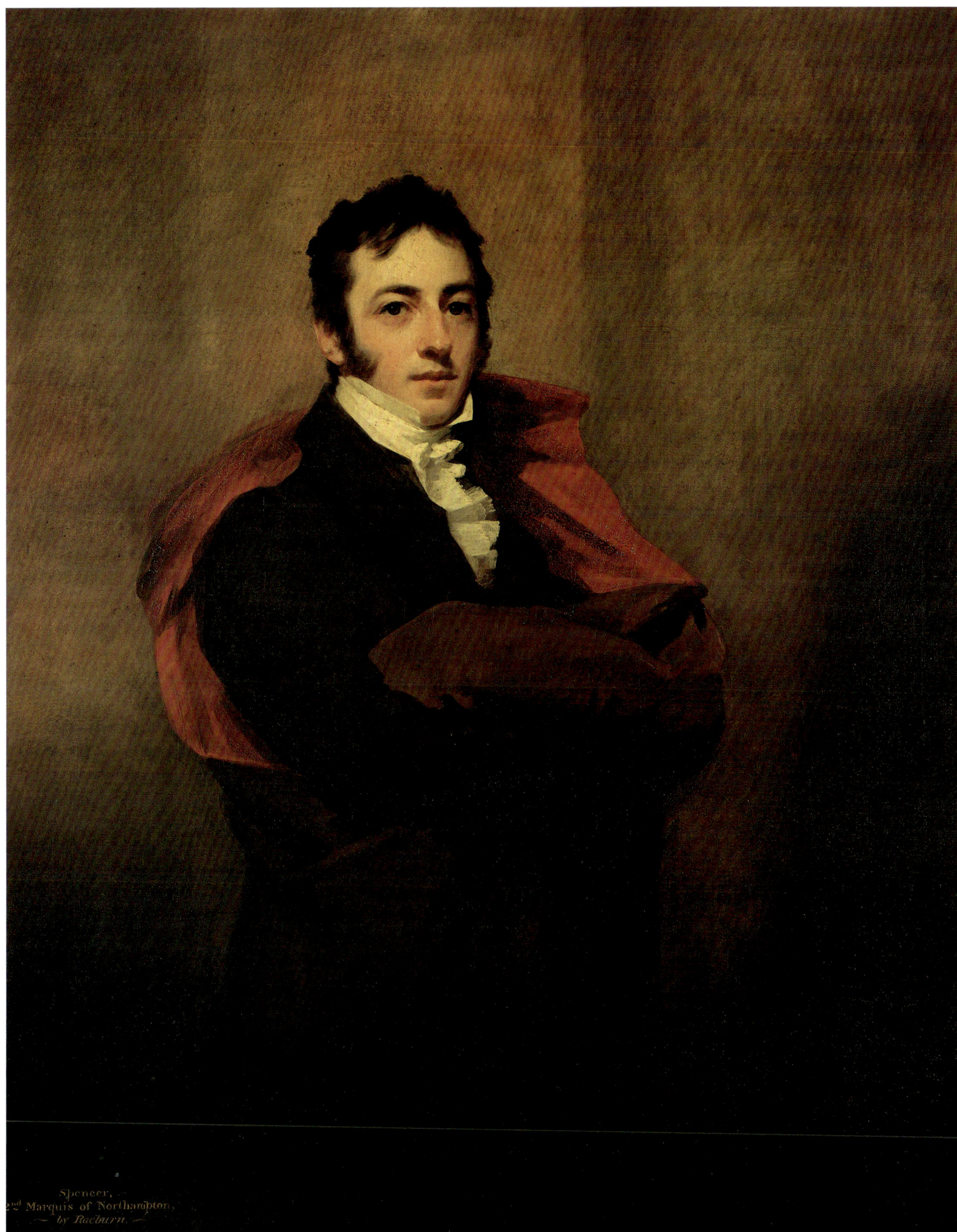
Spencer,
2nd Marquis of Northampton,
— by Raeburn. —

49 The Marchioness of Northampton, Playing a Harp *c.*1820

Oil on canvas 128 × 101.5 ($50\frac{1}{2}$ × 40)
Inscr. lower left (not by the artist): *Margaret,/2nd March^ss of Northampton/by Raeburn*
Exh: ?Royal Academy 1821 (420)
The Marquess of Northampton

Raeburn's breadth of handling often anticipates that of Sargent, and in this portrait of a beautiful young noblewoman he seems to adumbrate the school of early twentieth-century society painters that followed in Sargent's footsteps. The easy fluency of the paint, the melting intimacy established between sitter and viewer, are typical of artists of the later period, such as de Laszló; only Raeburn shows the taste of his own time in a touch that is unexpected at any rate from him: Lady Northampton is dressed as a bardic singer, in a rough pelt, apparently a wolfskin, with a heavy cross on a chain at her bosom. Although the harp is obviously a fine modern instrument, she is evidently singing some Gaelic ballad or a lay from Ossian or Scott. Such fantasies, commonplace with Reynolds and Hoppner, rarely occur in Raeburn's work, but it would be entirely appropriate in this instance, for Lady Northampton was well known as one of Scott's intimate friends. Margaret, daughter of Major-General Douglas Maclean Clephane of Torloisk married Spencer Compton, later Marquess of Northampton, in 1815 (see no.48), and it was Scott who presided over the arrangements for the wedding. Scott also knew her mother, Mrs Maclean of Clephane, with whom he agreed, according to J.G. Lockhart, 'on all subjects except the authenticity of Ossian' (Lockhart I, p.371).

Margaret inherited this interest in Gaelic poetry, of which she translated several examples into English verse. She also translated Goethe and Uhland and Petrarch, and composed a substantial work of her own, *Irene, A Poem in Six Cantos*, based on a story in the Comtesse de Murat's *Cabinet des Fées*. She was technically accomplished, and her work demonstrates mastery of several uncommon and demanding verse-forms. *Irene* is composed in Spencerian stanzas, with frequent touches of sly wit, in the manner of Byron's *Don Juan*. One of the Gaelic songs is convincingly like Scott:

> Now sinks the wild combat to silence and rest,
> And the field by the dead and the dying is prest,
> Where, mid the sad relics of slaughter I lie,
> And the corpse of my friend and companion is nigh.'

Raeburn has presumably shown her performing one of these songs, or perhaps the famous Hymn to the Sun from Ossian.

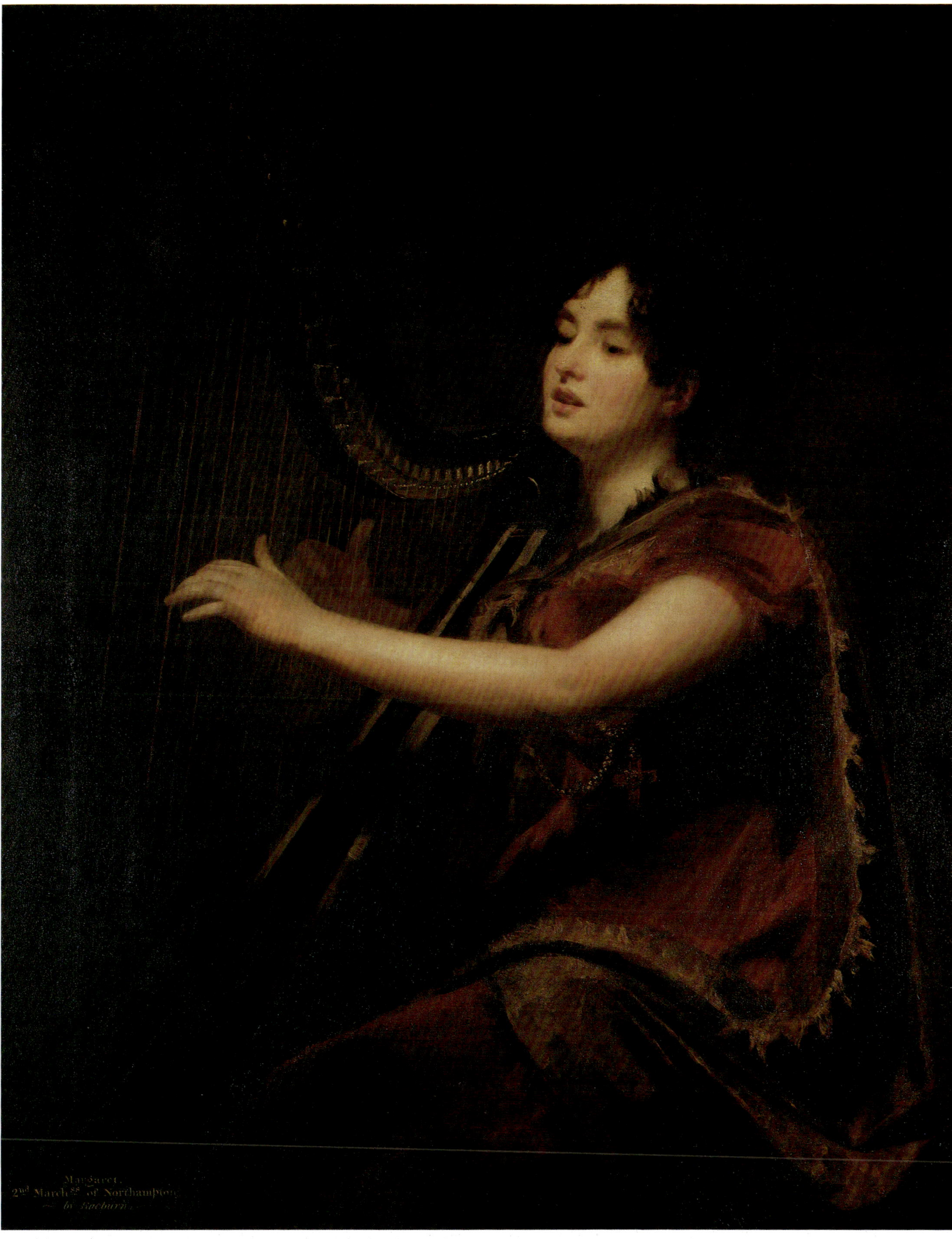
Margaret.
2nd Marchss of Northampton

SIR THOMAS LAWRENCE 1769–1830

50 **Queen Charlotte** 1789–90

Oil on canvas 238.4 × 147.3 ($93\frac{7}{8}$ × 58)
Exh: Royal Academy 1790 (100)
The Trustees of the National Gallery

Lawrence's ascent of the ladder of success was one of the most astonishing of any portrait painter's. In 1789 he painted his first important pictures, a pair of portraits of Viscount and Viscountess Cremorne (private collection and Tate Gallery), and the following year, thanks to the recommendation of Lady Cremorne, was commissioned to paint this portrait of the Queen. It is a *tour de force*, ambitious in scale and splendid in execution, exhibiting the silvery impasto for which Lawrence was to be famous in his early career. The *mis-en-scene* is that of a typical state portrait, with the subject seated on a dais beneath a canopy of fringed and tasseled drapery. There is a view of Eton College chapel in a landscape through the window to the left, so that we understand that the setting of the picture is Windsor Castle. But despite the grandeur of its layout, the picture is unexpectedly intimate: for so young a artist – he was only twenty-one – carrying out so important a commission, Lawrence evinces no awe, but presents the Queen simply and directly, with extraordinary honesty as a rather homely woman – which indeed she was. This is, then, hardly a state portrait, but it makes use of the conventions of state portraiture for its own novel ends. As an intimate insight into the character of royalty it may perhaps be compared with Goya's portraits of the Spanish royal family – though such a comparison can only point up Lawrence's tact and adroitness in combining frankness with sympathy and dignity.

Charlotte Sophia of Mecklenburg-Strelitz (1744–1818) had married George III in 1761, just after his accession to the throne; they were crowned King and Queen in September of that year. Horace Walpole, writing to Sir Horace Mann on the 10th, three days after her arrival, described her as 'not tall, nor a beauty; pale, and very thin, but looks sensible and is genteel.' Her accomplishments included singing and playing the harpsichord, which she was ready to do on all occasions. She fulfilled her role as Queen conscientiously, but as a mere cypher. Her devotion to her husband was complete. She bore him fifteen children, and declared that she never knew real sorrow from the day of their meeting till the time of his first attack of mental illness, which occurred in the second half of 1788 and lasted until early the following year – only a few months before this portrait was painted. During that time she took personal charge of the care of the King, a duty she resumed after the death of her youngest daughter Amelia (see no.44) in 1810, which precipitated the last and longest attack.

After painting this picture Lawrence was able to charge 100 guineas for his whole-lengths; by 1806 that sum had doubled, and by 1810 his price was 400 guineas.

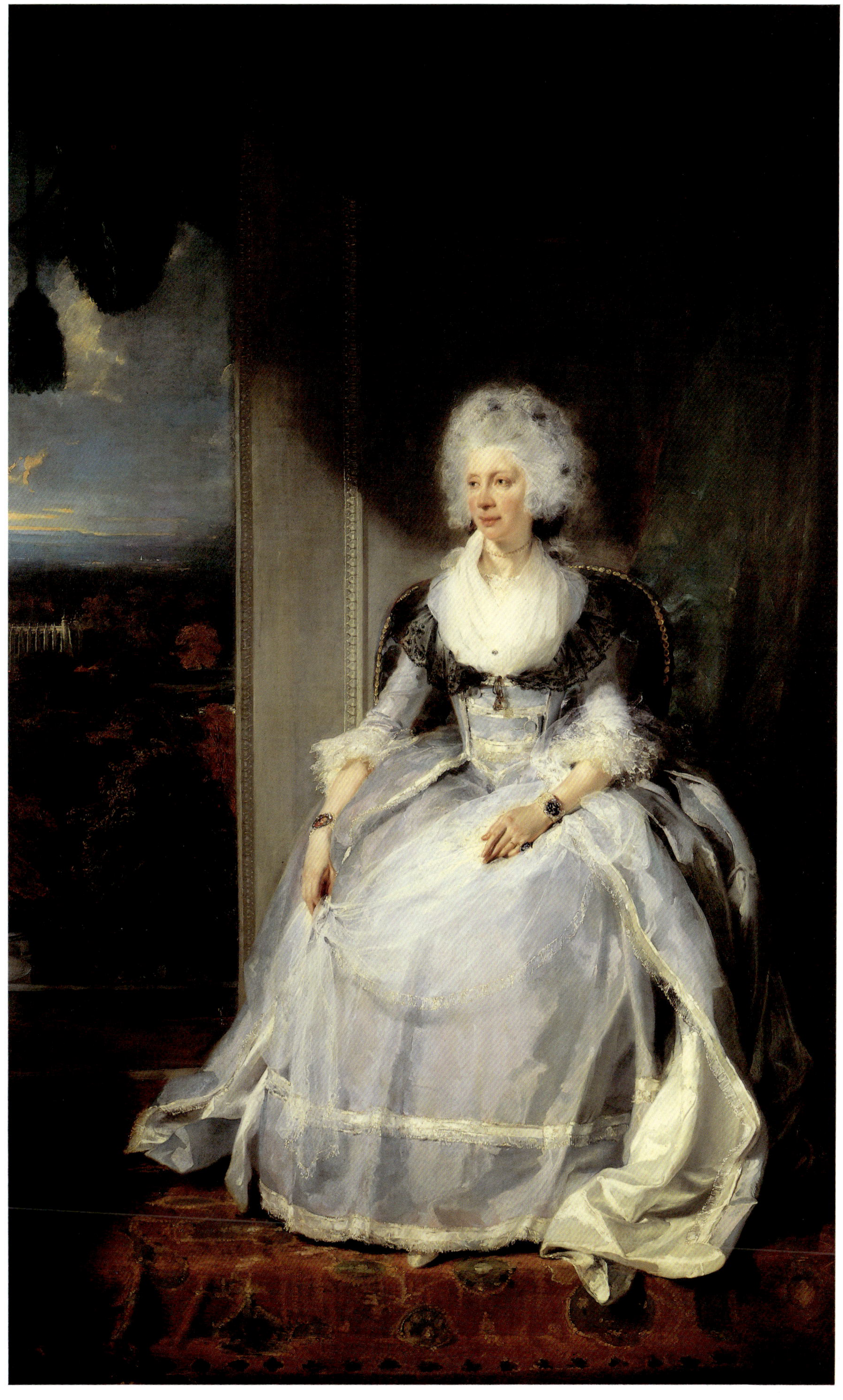

51 **Catherine Gray, Lady Manners** 1794

Oil on canvas 255.3 × 158 ($100\frac{1}{2} \times 62\frac{1}{4}$)
Exh: Royal Academy 1794 (160)
The Cleveland Museum of Art. Bequest of John D. Rockefeller, Jr

Joseph Farington, in a diary entry for 3 April 1794, mentions that when the Academy's exhibition for that year was being arranged, Lawrence was 'desirous to have the whole length of Lady Manners hung in the center at the head of the room'. The artist was evidently conscious of its exceptional grandeur and force, and it is odd that he should have painted so splendid a picture with no buyer in view: it was exhibited as 'To be disposed of'. The only other possibility is that it had been commissioned but rejected by some patron, and that is also curious, given its quality. It remained in his studio and probably appeared in the sale of his effects, Christie's 18 June 1831 (147), as 'A Lady, whole-length, in a Garden-Scene, and a distant landscape'. The identity of the sitter had already been lost, and until recently the work remained incorrectly described as a portrait of Lady Louisa Manners, Countess of Dysart. This was the daughter of the 4th Earl of Dysart, later Countess of Dysart in her own right; but she would have been forty-nine in 1794, and it is unlikely that so mature a woman would have been presented in virginal white, holding a pink rose and with other appurtenances of youthfulness and charm. On the other hand, she is accompanied by the peacock that goes with Juno, a decidedly matronly goddess. When the picture was sold by order of Viscount Oxenbridge at Christie's in 1888 (12 May, lot 21) it was called 'The Countess of Dysart'.

In fact the portrait shows the Countess's daughter-in-law, Catherine Rebecca Gray, daughter of Francis Gray of County Cork, who had married the Countess's son William in 1790. She became Lady Manners when he became a Baronet in 1793, which explains why she is so titled in Farington's note. It would be reasonable to suppose that the picture was commissioned as one of a pair celebrating their elevation, but there is no evidence for this. William died in 1833, and Catherine lived on until 1852, though neither she nor any member of her family ever owned the picture. The peacock may be introduced as the attribute of a married woman, though its connotations of pride may perhaps be admitted to refer lightheartedly to the superb bearing of the lady. Perhaps it is simply ornamental. The landscape looks somewhat Irish, though it is probably a romantic invention of Lawrence's.

The high tonality of the picture, with its brilliant whites, is typical of Lawrence's palette in painting women sitters (white was fashionable for women's dresses throughout the decades of the Napoleonic Wars); men are nearly always presented in organisations of darker colours, as was appropriate to the kinds of clothes they wore. An obvious source for the composition is Reynolds's whole-length of Georgina, Duchess of Devonshire (Huntington Art Gallery, San Marino). But if 'Lady Manners' is an early bid on Lawrence's part to continue the Reynoldsian tradition of high elegance in female portraiture, it nevertheless has qualities that suggest he was here benefiting too from the example of Gainsborough. The general tonality of the picture is blond, and the fresh outdoor setting recalls the airy atmosphere of such late Gainsborough canvases as 'Mr and Mrs Hallett' (no.43).

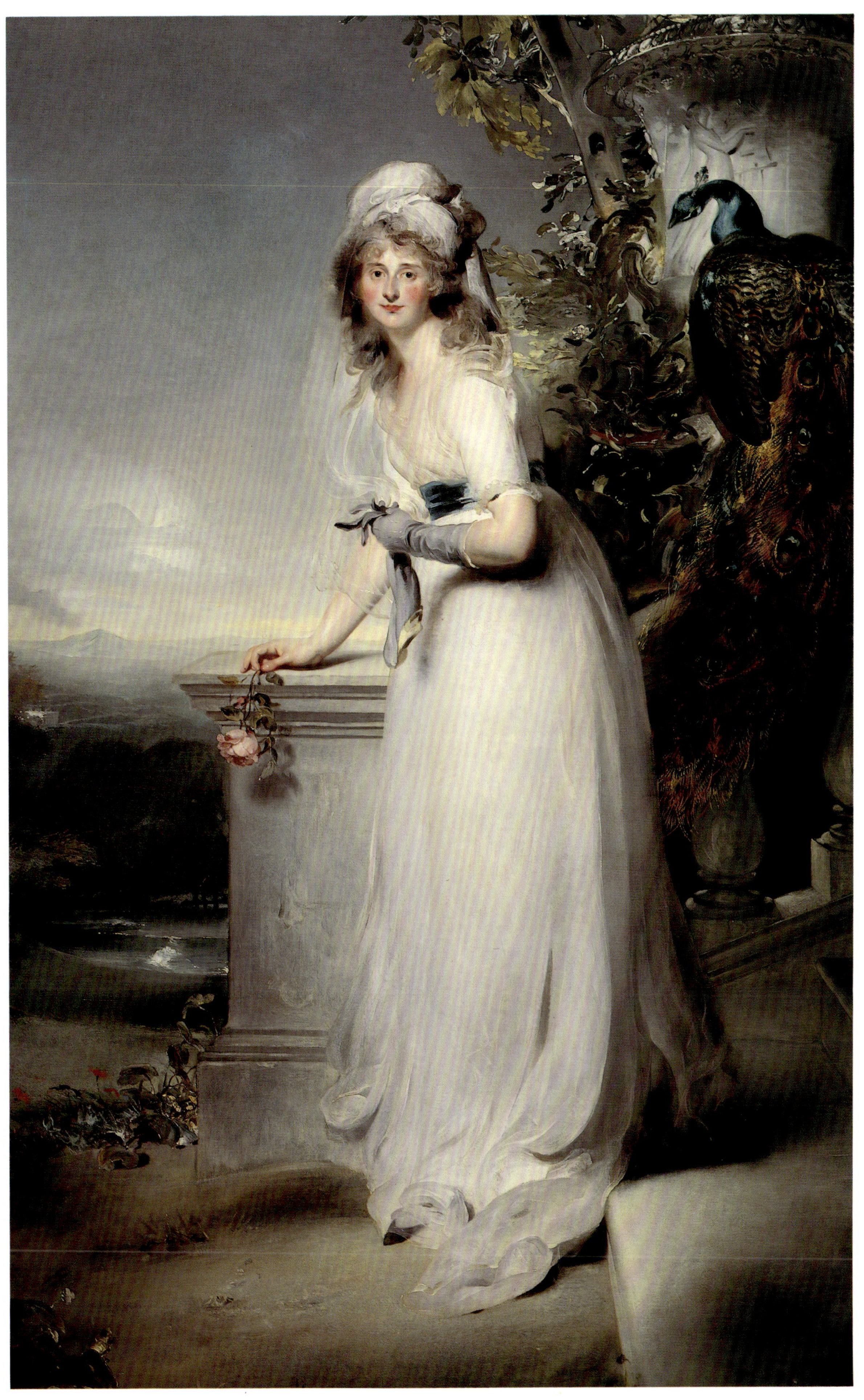

52 **John Philip Kemble as Hamlet** 1801

Oil on canvas 306.1 × 198.1 ($120\frac{1}{2}$ × 78)
Exh: Royal Academy 1801 (197); British Institution 1807 (97)
Tate Gallery. Presented by King William IV 1836

John Philip Kemble (1757–1823) was the eldest son of an actor, Roger Kemble, and one of a large and successful theatrical family. Lawrence himself was an enthusiastic amateur actor and keen follower of the London theatre who became a good friend of Kemble's in the 1790s. Kemble was distinguished first of all by his memorable stage presence; of him and George Frederick Cooke (famous for his portrayal of villains) the American artist Charles Leslie remembered: 'When they were on the stage it was impossible to look at or think of any body else. Each of them seemed to say "I am myself alone"' (Leslie II, p.33). That quality of Kemble's stage personality seems to dictate the atmosphere of this canvas. Hamlet was the role in which he made his London debut at Drury Lane in 1783. His interpretation of the part was innovative: 'the sweet, the graceful, the gentlemanly Hamlet', Hazlitt called it, distinguished as 'sensible' and 'lonely'. This new, romantic hero, as opposed to the more robust, ranting eighteenth-century Hamlets, is the subject of Lawrence's picture. The specific moment that is ostensibly recorded is Act V scene I where Hamlet comes upon the skull of his father's jester Yorick during the digging of Ophelia's grave, and muses on life and death. The towers of Elsinore castle can be seen dimly in the background. In practice, Lawrence generalises the subject so that his picture shows not so much a particular moment as an epitome of Kemble's interpretation of the role: brooding, heroic and monumental, a definitive romantic statement of the significance of Hamlet.

This is one of a series of theatrical portraits in which Lawrence aimed at a genre of 'half-history' which develops the notion of the historical portrait formulated by Reynolds, capitalising on the fact that the sitter was a well-known actor playing a well-known historical or literary character. 'Kemble as Coriolanus at the Hearth of Tullus Aufidius' (Guildhall Art Gallery, London) appeared at the Royal Academy in 1798 (225), and in 1800 'Kemble as Rolla in Sheridan's *Pizarro*' was shown there (193, Nelson-Atkins Art Museum, Kansas City). 'Hamlet' was exhibited in the following year (187), and a fourth showing Kemble as Cato, in Addison's *Cato* (private collection) was finished in 1812.

Kemble's sister Sarah became the great Mrs Siddons, and there can be no doubt that Reynolds's portrait of her as the Tragic Muse (no.37) – 'that divine work' as Lawrence called it – exerted a powerful influence on his conception of these works. The 'Cato', which shows Kemble seated and darkly contemplative, is particularly indebted to Reynolds's prototype, but the 'Hamlet', with its chiaroscuro and statuesque presentation, clearly belongs to the same world of what might be termed the 'theatrical sublime'. There is also a parallel with the composition of Lawrence's own full-length of Siddons (no.53).

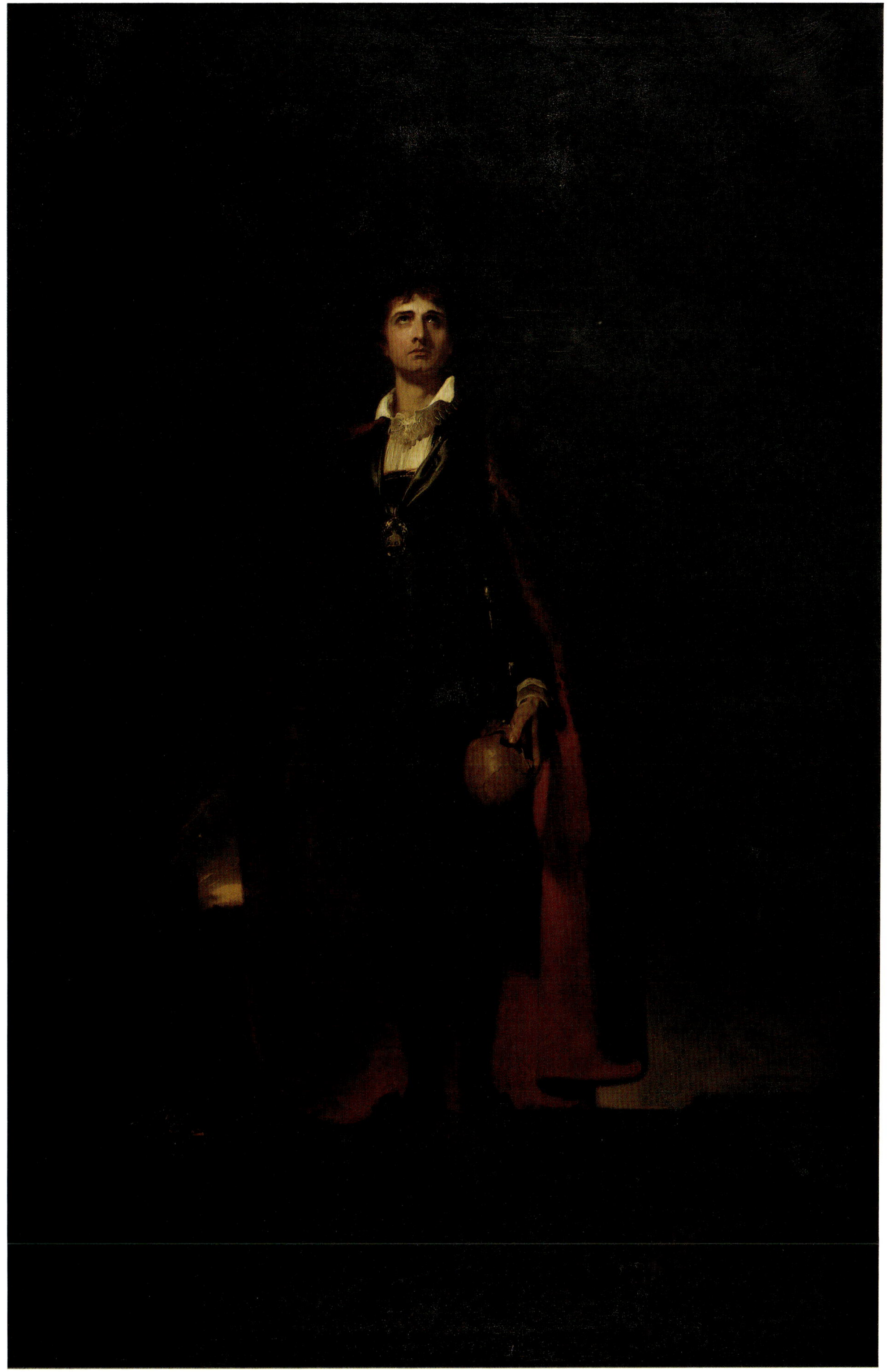

53 **Mrs Siddons** 1803–4

Oil on canvas 254 × 148 (100 × 58$\frac{1}{4}$)
Exh: Royal Academy 1804 (193)
Tate Gallery. Presented by Mrs C. FitzHugh 1843

By the time this portrait was painted, Siddons (see no.37) was nearing the end of her career; she retired from the stage in 1812. Highfill suggests that Lawrence has painted her as she would have appeared during one of her dramatic readings before the King and Queen. A full-length portrait of her as Lady Macbeth by George Henry Harlow (Bob Jones University; small replica Garrick Club) echoes something of the pose and atmosphere of this picture, which also clearly presents the actress as a tragedian, or Muse of Tragedy: she stands in sombre thought, one finger holding open a large volume of plays, with a book beside it titled *Otway* and the name of 'Shakpere' inscribed on an elephant folio volume behind. This may be intended to represent the book of engravings after the celebrated set of paintings of Shakespearean subjects commissioned in the 1780s by Alderman John Boydell for his Shakspeare Gallery. The picture is thus in a sense a reinterpretation of the theme of Reynolds's great portrait of Siddons as the Tragic Muse (no.37). This is the public persona of Siddons: athough she is not strictly shown in character, as her brother is by Lawrence in several pictures (see no.52), the portrait aims to sum up her achievements in tragedies like *Macbeth* and Otway's *Venice Preserved.* The Tate Gallery possesses another portrait of her by Lawrence that gives what is apparently her private character – a modest half-length, in which she is informally dressed with a simple white cap and white dress. The relaxed pose and direct, unassuming expression contradict the traditional idea that it shows her in the role of Mrs Haller in *The Stranger* by Kotzebue. It is in fact a variant of another portrait, of 1797, in a private collection.

Lawrence had been an admirer of Siddons since his youth, and became a close friend. There was even a rumour that the two of them planned to elope together at the time this portrait was painted. He is said to have had love affairs with each of her two daughters, Sally and Maria, in turn, considerably injuring his reputation for gentlemanliness in the process. Dying of consumption in 1798, Maria made her sister vow never to marry him. This domestic tragedy seems to have been forgotton by the date Lawrence came to paint his whole-length of the actress. Her opinion of it was that it was 'more really like me than anything that has been done', but her niece Fanny Kemble thought it looked like 'a handsome cow in a coral necklace' (Whitley 1930, p.218).

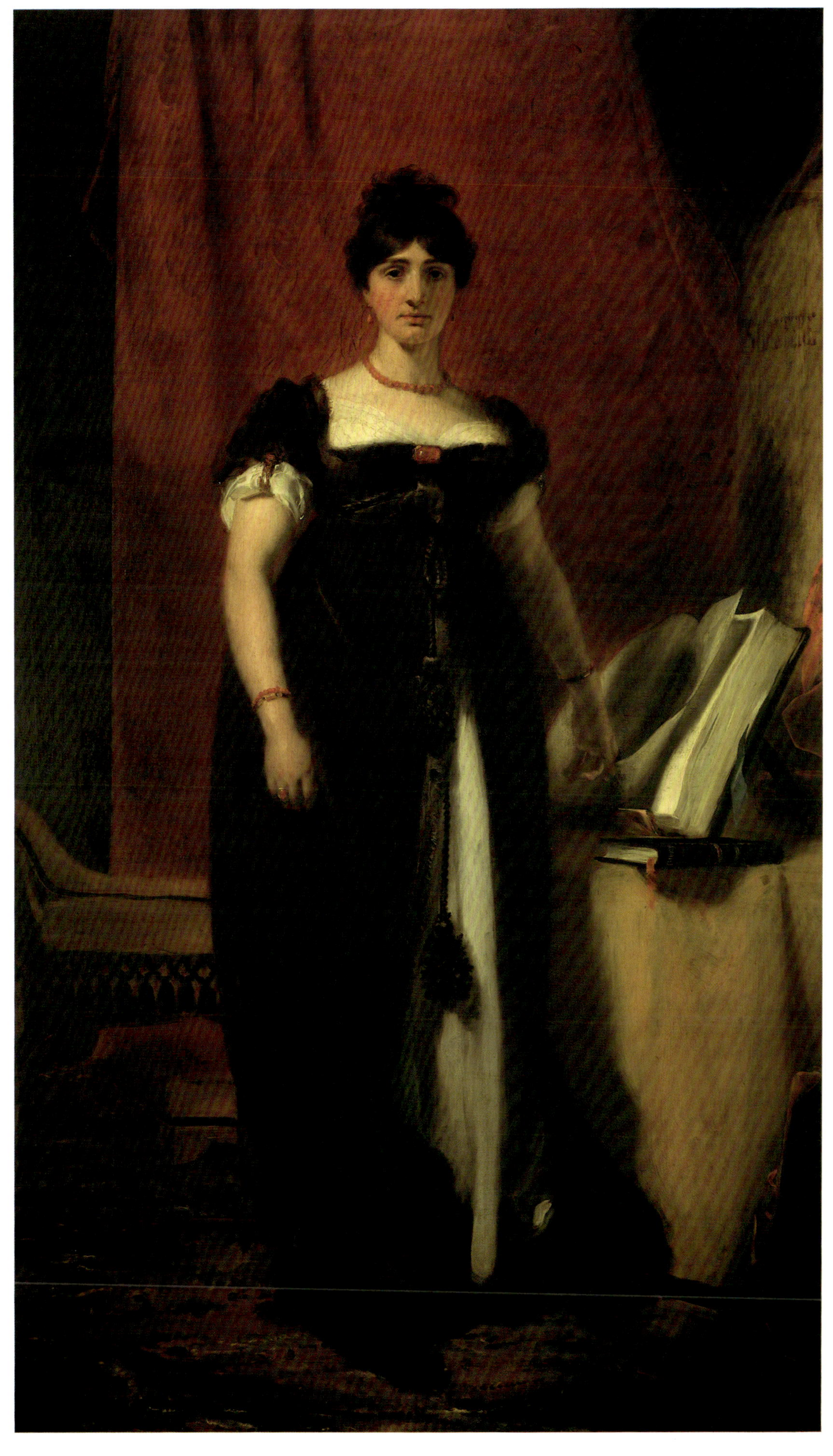

54 Lady Elizabeth Foster, later Duchess of Devonshire, as a Sibyl 1805

Oil on canvas 240 × 148 ($94\frac{1}{2} \times 58\frac{1}{4}$)
Exh: Royal Academy 1805 (195)
The National Gallery of Ireland

It was not Lawrence's habit to present his sitters in allegorical or historical roles as Reynolds had so frequently done. He preferred to suggest drama simply by stormy lighting, or by a theatrical pose. His male portraits often depend on such devices. With female sitters, however, he would occasionally give himself greater latitude, endowing them with the persona of a virtue or a saint – Mrs John Williams as St Cecilia (1804), for instance, or Georgina Maria, Lady Leicester as Hope (1814). This example is a particularly grand conception, in which the sitter becomes one of the Sibyls, utterers of oracular teachings and dire warnings in the ancient world. The Sibyls were originally from Greece and the Middle East, but Italy later claimed two of its own, the Tiburtine and the Cumaean. Lawrence shows his sitter as the Tiburtine Sibyl, resident pythoness of the temple at Tivoli.

There are in fact two temples at Tivoli, one circular, the other rectangular; it is the latter which is more accurately identified as the Temple of the Sibyl, though the former, the Temple of Vesta, on account of its charming shape and dominant site on the cliff-edge, is often given that name and was so identified in Lawrence's day. The sitter's highly eccentric father, the 4th Earl of Bristol and Bishop of Derry, is said to have bought the temple in order to rebuild it on one of his Irish estates. In an early instance of export control, the Papal authorities prevented Bristol from removing the building (Williams I, pp.261–2). The fluted columns that rise broken and gigantic behind the lady suggest the grandeur of an ancient shrine, while the rocky ledge on which she stands looks out over a brooding panorama of the Roman Campagna in which the circular temple can be seen on its cliff-top at the extreme right. This background, and the sitter's elaborately informal, though evidently modern, costume, contribute to an overall effect that is more romantic than classical, and endow her with the attributes of a bardic poet rather than of a revealer of divine truth. In this, she is somewhat like Raeburn's 'Marchioness of Northampton' (no.49).

The Lady Elizabeth was the second of the Earl-Bishop's three daughters. She was already forty-six when this picture was painted, and had been married in 1776 to John Thomas Foster, a member of the Irish Parliament, from whom she separated in 1781. After the breakdown of her marriage she had become the intimate friend of the 5th Duke of Devonshire and his beautiful Duchess, Georgiana, living in a *ménage à trois* with them that occasioned great scandal. After Georgiana's death Elizabeth married the Duke as his second wife in 1809. She herself died in 1824.

Lawrence had already painted another lady as a Sibyl, though in a very different vein: his three-quarter length profile portrait of Mrs Jens Wolff seated reading, of about 1803 (Art Institute of Chicago), contrives to allude to the iconogaphy of Sibylline portraiture without becoming explicitly historical. This is the procedure that Lawrence preferred, and used supremely in another early work, the 'Lady Manners' (no.51), where an attendant peacock suggests that the sitter is posed as Juno, while a fresh rose and a very English flight of steps locate her securely on her home ground.

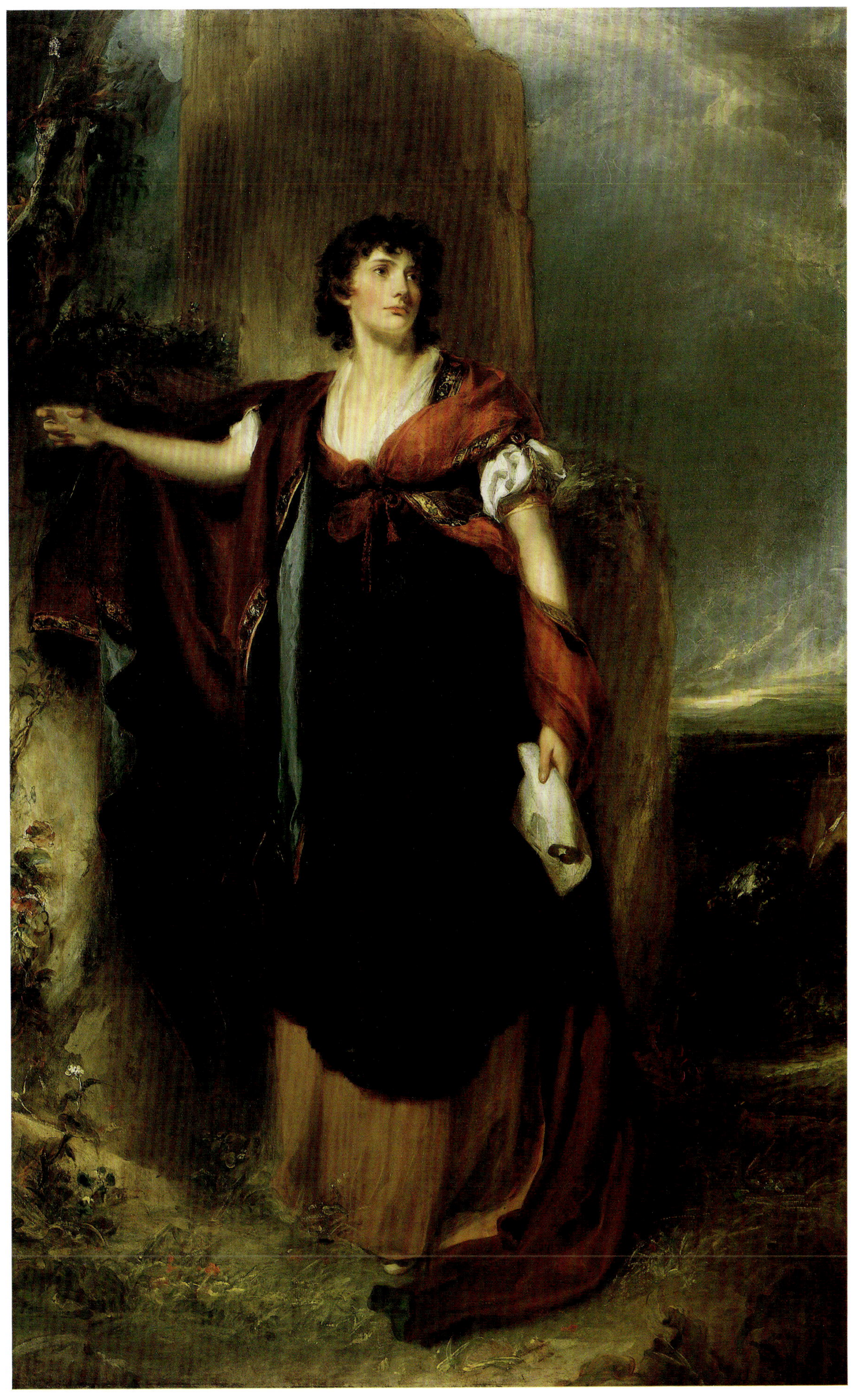

55 The Duke of Wellington Mounted on Copenhagen as at Waterloo 1818

Oil on canvas 396.2 × 243.8 (156 × 96)
Exh: Royal Academy 1818 (165)
inscr. lower right: HANC/ARTHURI DUCIS DE WELLINGTON/IMAGINEM/QUALEM SESE HABUIT IN PROELIO ISTO/APUD WATERLOO,/QUOAD VESTITUM, ARMA, EQUUM, EPHIPPIA,/THOMAS LAURENTIUS EQUES, AEVI SUI PICTORUM FACILE PRINCEPS, FIDELITUR EXPRESSIT, A.S.1818
The Earl Bathurst

If Lawrence was particularly famous for his portrayal of the melting charms of women, he was perhaps at his most original and effective when painting military portraits. The set of likenesses of the allied generals that he painted for the Waterloo Chamber at Windsor is an anthology of his most inventive and romantic works. The example of Reynolds in such pictures as 'Lord Heathfield' (no.38) is carried to new heights of drama and characterisation, with the fullest use being made of smoky skies and stern poses. This canvas is the largest and, in many ways, the grandest of them all, though it does not form part of the Windsor group. It was commissioned by Henry, 3rd Earl Bathurst, Secretary for War and the Colonies at the time of Waterloo, whose portrait Lawrence painted on reciprocal commission for the Duke of Wellington about the same time as this picture.

The title of the picture when it was exhibited at the Academy was 'The Duke of Wellington in the dress that he wore, and on the horse that he rode, at the battle of Waterloo'. The Latin inscription elaborates this. Wellington is seated on Copenhagen, the charger he rode at Waterloo (and buried at his Hampshire home, Stratfield Saye), with the uniform, arms and saddlecloth that he used at the battle. He is not presented, as some of the European generals are, as a commander in the throes of the fight, but as a hero calmly acknowledging his victory.

The grand equestrian portrait has an appropriately distinguished pedigree in Europe, with Titian's 'Charles V on Horseback' (Prado) fathering a long line that includes Rubens's 'Duke of Lerma' (Prado), Velásquez's 'Philip IV' (Prado) and, especially important for England, Van Dyck's great equestrian portrait of Charles I (London, National Gallery). The alternative convention, in which the subject stands beside his horse, was one that Van Dyck had adopted in his portrait of Charles I in the Louvre, and Reynolds made very much his own in idiosyncratic compositions of the Prince of Wales (private collection) and the Marquis of Granby (collection Her Majesty The Queen). The great prototypes, then, were essentially Baroque, and complex movement naturally dominates the compositions of Reynolds's pictures as a consequence. Raeburn's 'William Maxwell of Calderwood' (no.47) illustrates how the romantic potential of the motif could be exploited by artists not necessarily inclined to such flights of rhetoric. Lawrence, on the other hand, who might instinctively have exaggerated the theatricality of the image, deliberately simplifies his design to emphasise the sublime tranquillity of the moment at which the battle is won. Distant fires and a smoke-filled sky ensure that the warlike context is remembered; but this is, for all its romanticism, an almost neo-classical work, evocative of the ancient virtues of fortitude and inspired leadership. It is worth comparing this enormous canvas with the equally ambitious (but unfinished) portrait of Wellington on horseback by Goya, at Apsley House.

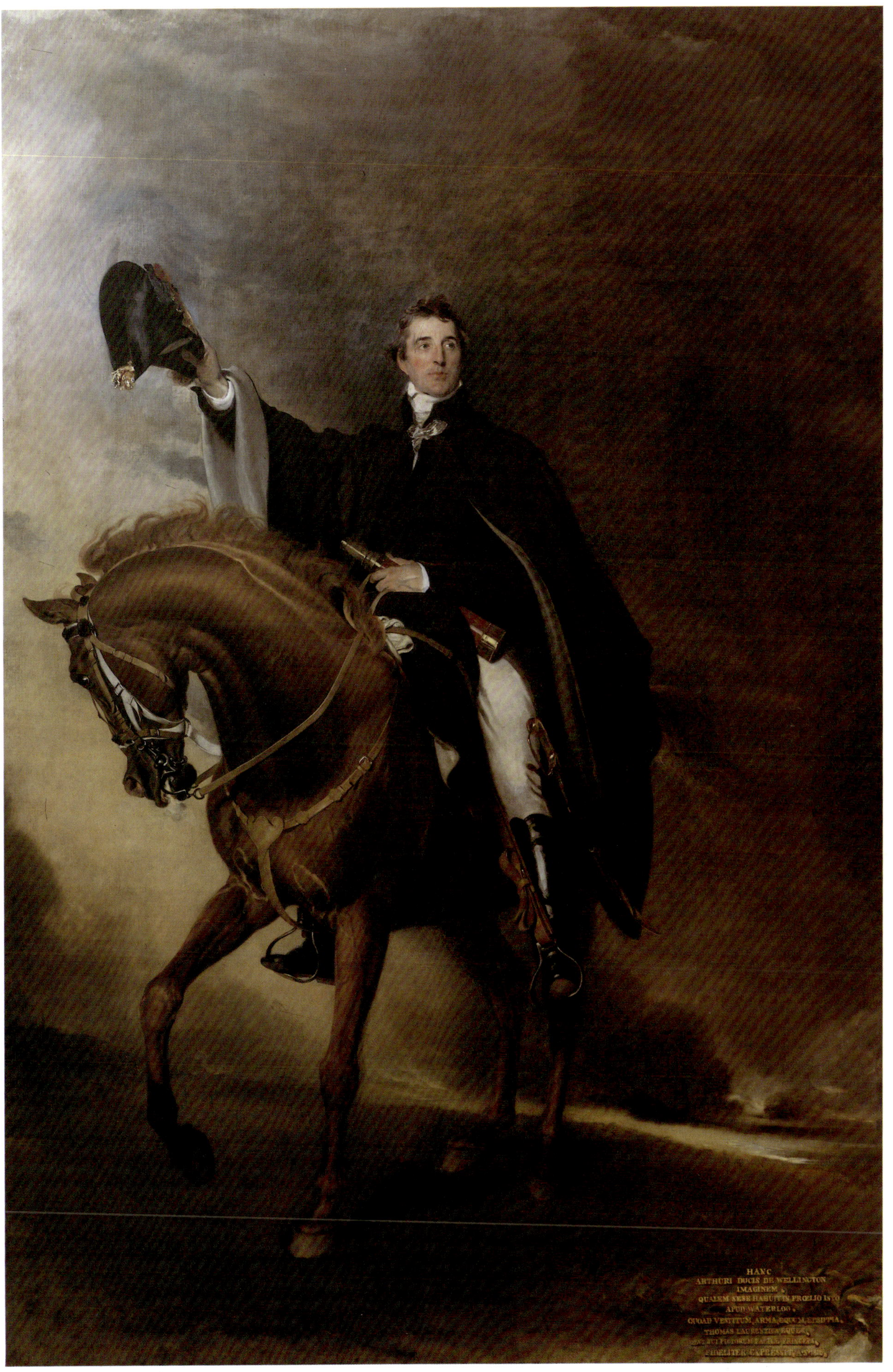
HANC
ARTHURI DUCIS DE WELLINGTON
IMAGINEM,
APUD WATERLOO,

JAMES SANT 1820–1916

56 Captain Colin Mackenzie 1842

Oil on canvas 237 × 145 ($93\frac{1}{4}$ × $57\frac{1}{8}$)
Exh: Royal Academy 1844 (373)
National Army Museum, London, courtesy of the Director

The title given to this picture when it appeared at the Academy in 1844 was 'Captain Colin Mackenzie, Madras Army, lately a hostage in Caubool, in his Affghan dress'. Mackenzie (1806–81) was one of the protagonists of the first Afghan War, which he was lucky and plucky enough to survive. He was appointed assistant political agent under Sir George Clark, and sent to Kabul with a troop of sappers raised by George Broadfoot. During the siege of Kabul fort by the Afghans he led the defence, fighting his way out by night. He was a prisoner with George Lawrence at the famous conference outside Kabul at which McNaghten was murdered. He survived the ill-fated retreat to Jellalabad, but was then chosen as a hostage to Akbar Khan who imprisoned him, intending him to be sold into slavery. Thanks to the arrival of Pollock with some troops he was set free and Akbar Khan fled. He was known among the Afghans as 'The English Mullah' and seems to have had a talent for establishing friendly relations with their leaders. He was later promoted to the rank of Lieutenant-General.

Mackenzie's sympathy with native life, characteristic of many Englishmen in the subcontinent at the time, is epitomised in this stylish portrait, which seems to lift the curtain on the fantasies of the British military man in contact with an exotic and quite alien kind of freedom: he displays the loose and colourfully embroidered costume with an almost exhibitionistic self-consciousness, reminiscent perhaps of Van Dyck's 'orientalist' sitters, the Earl of Denbigh (London, National Gallery) and Sir Robert Shirley (fig.36; Petworth House), whose pose this portrait echoes. In this preoccupation, Mackenzie anticipates that master of oriental disguise, Sir Richard Burton, whom Leighton was to paint in 1875 (London, National Portrait Gallery).

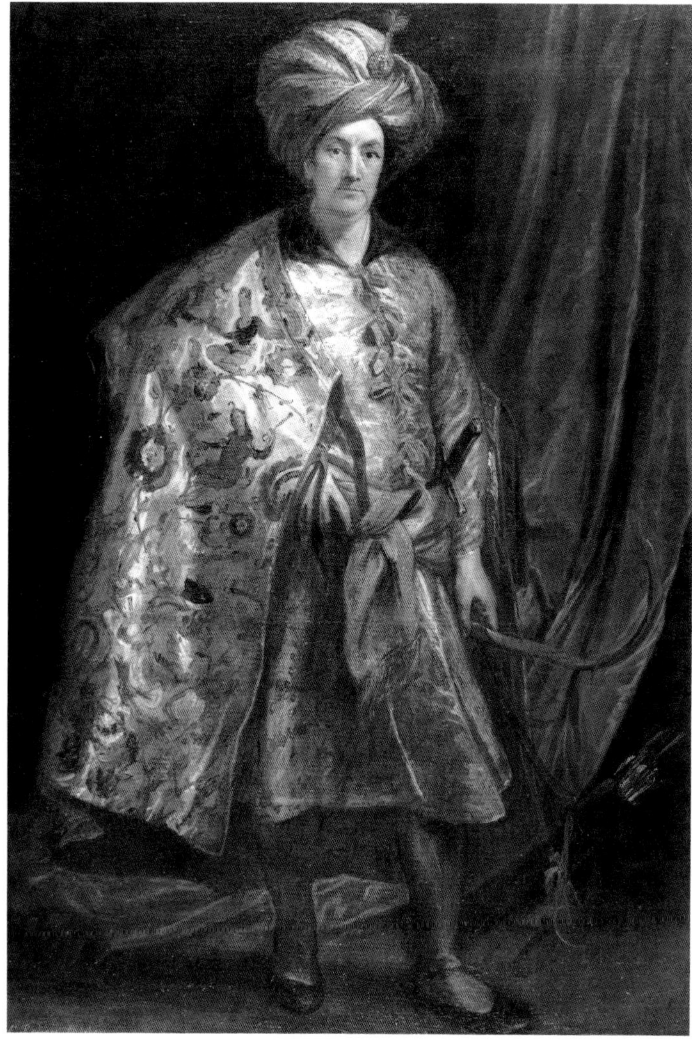

fig.36 Sir Anthony Van Dyck **Sir Robert Shirley** 1622 Oil on canvas
National Trust, Petworth House, Sussex

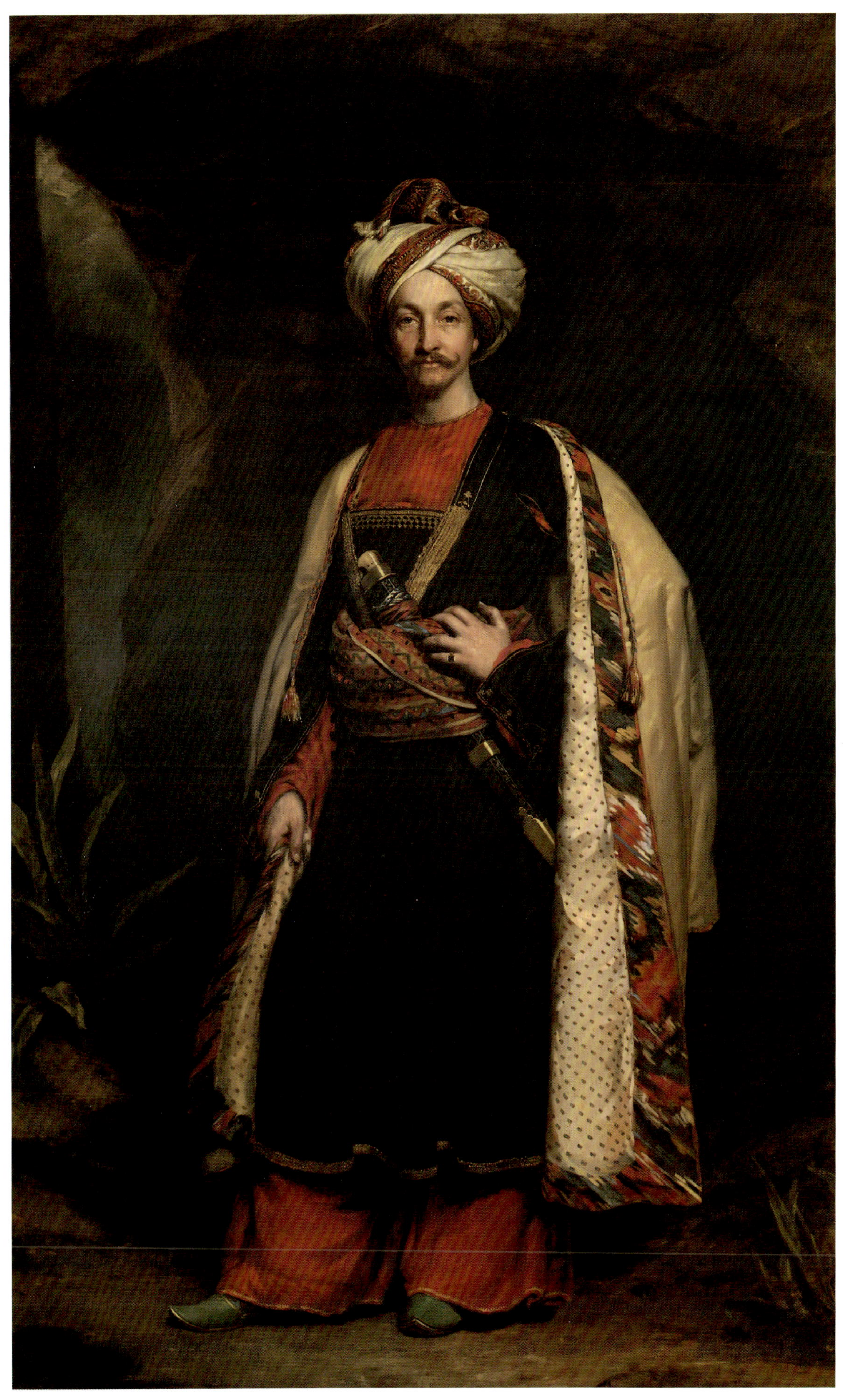

SIR FRANCIS GRANT 1803–1878

57 **Queen Victoria** 1843

Oil on canvas 243.8 × 147.3 (96 × 58)
Crown Estate on loan to the Institute of Directors

Grant was a Scot, who was to become President of the Royal Academy in 1866. He enjoyed the patronage of a wide sector of aristocratic and gentle society, so much so that he must be regarded as the pre-eminent portrait painter of the high Victorian period. He succeeded to the place of Lawrence and Shee, vying with George Hayter for the attention of the rich and celebrated. His national origins and the period in which he lived did not conduce to much rhetoric in his approach to portraiture, but he was capable, especially in his youth, of a kind of nonchalant grandeur which finds its most exalted expression in this state portrait of the young Queen. The traditional trappings of such an image are all in place; indeed, this is a restatement of the theme with few new variations. Grant does not offer to undermine the formality with a flash of intimate revelation as Lawrence had done in his portrait of Queen Charlotte; but he does suggest the somewhat timid girlishness of the sitter, her turned head seeming to imply a diffidence towards the attention she is receiving which is at odds with full-blown state portraiture. In this, he displays a certain insight into his sitter's character, which was indeed a strange, if unsurprising, mixture of imperious confidence and adolescent doubt. She had married Albert in February 1840, at the age of twenty-one, and was deeply in love with him. Lytton Strachey retells an anecdote which, as he says, sums up the central facts of the case: 'When, in wrath, the Prince one day had locked himself into his room, Victoria, no less furious, knocked on the door to be admitted. "Who is there?" he asked. "The Queen of England" was the answer. He did not move, and again there was a hail of knocks. The question and the answer were repeated many times; but at last there was a pause, and then a gentler knocking. "Who is there?" came once more the relentless question. But this time the reply was different. "Your wife, Albert." And the door was immediately opened' (Strachey, p.161). In the thirteen years between 1840 and 1853 she was to bear him four sons and five daughters.

Grant's work often offers comparison with that of Winterhalter, who in fact painted portraits of the Queen and her Consort in this same year, and was to do so at other times in the decade (see no.59). He was also commissioned to paint a portrait of Lord Middleton as a pendant to that of Lady Middleton which Winterhalter executed in 1863 (see no.60).

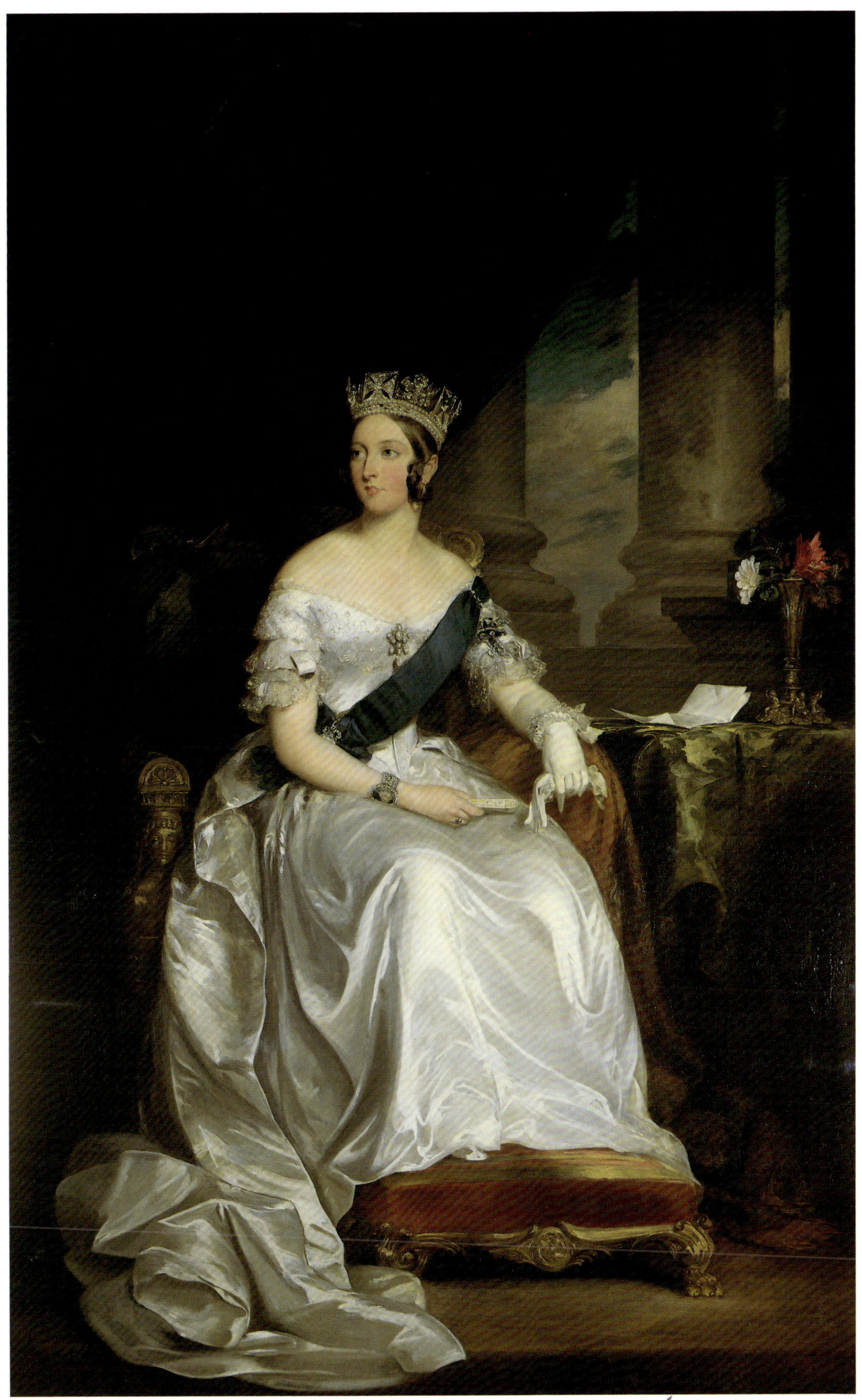

GEORGE FREDERIC WATTS 1817–1904

58 **Augusta, Lady Castletown** *c.*1846

Oil on canvas 208.3 × 143.5 (82 × $56\frac{1}{2}$)
Tate Gallery. Bequeathed by Major W.R.D. Mackenzie 1952

Watts was a prolific portrait painter, and his standard half-lengths in general exemplify the typical virtues of Victorian portraiture: direct, uncluttered, with a strong emphasis on the value of likeness for its own sake as revealing qualities of mind or heart. Such straightforward works derive ultimately from Renaissance prototypes, and count among their forebears the most sober half-lengths of Tintoretto, Moroni and the Dutch. Watts was all his life an ambitious subject painter in the spirit of the grandest of the Old Masters, especially Titian and Tintoretto, and it is surprising how rarely he sought grandeur in portraiture. There are a few exceptions. His group of 'Mrs Cavendish-Bentinck with her Children' (Tate Gallery) echoes Reynolds's 'Lady Cockburn and her Three Children' (National Gallery) of 1773, though it strips away the columns and hangings and splendid parrot that ornament that work, substituting a decidedly homely domestic interior. The parrot and other trappings do occur, however, in this earlier and altogether more impressive piece, which applies to a sitter of the 1840s all the paraphernalia of a grand manner portrait of the 1770s.

Watts first visited Florence in 1843, and was there welcomed by his patron Lord Holland, Minister at the Court of Tuscany between 1839 and 1846. The Hollands' fondness for him was such that a stay intended to last only a few days was extended to years: he did not leave Florence until 1847. Their town residence was the Palazzo Ferroni, and Watts set up a summer studio in the garden of their country retreat, the Villa Careggi. He was a quickly involved in portraiture, and an early likeness of Lady Holland was compared by one Italian guest to Veronese. He was thus soon encouraged to compare himself to the Renaissance masters who remained his models; he also found 'forms and combinations' in the life and scenery of Italy 'that might be adopted without alteration in the grandest composition.' (Watts I, p.68). Naturally, then, some of his largest works date from this time, and he even decorated the Palazzo Ferroni with frescoes. And among the Hollands' innumerable visitors there was no shortage of sitters for portraits.

The subject of this canvas, Augusta Mary Douglas, was born in 1810, the daughter of the Rector of Castle Coote, County Cavan; her maternal grandfather was the 4th Earl of Dunmore. In 1830 she married John Wilson, the illegitimate son of the Earl of Upper Ossory, who was to add to his name by royal licence that of Fitzpatrick in 1842, and who was created Baron Castletown of Upper Ossory in 1869. Their son and heir, Edward Barnaby Fitzpatrick, was born in 1848. Lady Castletown's husband died in 1883; she lived on to the end of the century, dying at the age of eighty-eight.

The picture has a spectacular Baroque frame, which, while not particularly appropriate to Watts's work, is Florentine and was enlarged to accommodate the portrait by Fratelli Pacetti of that city.

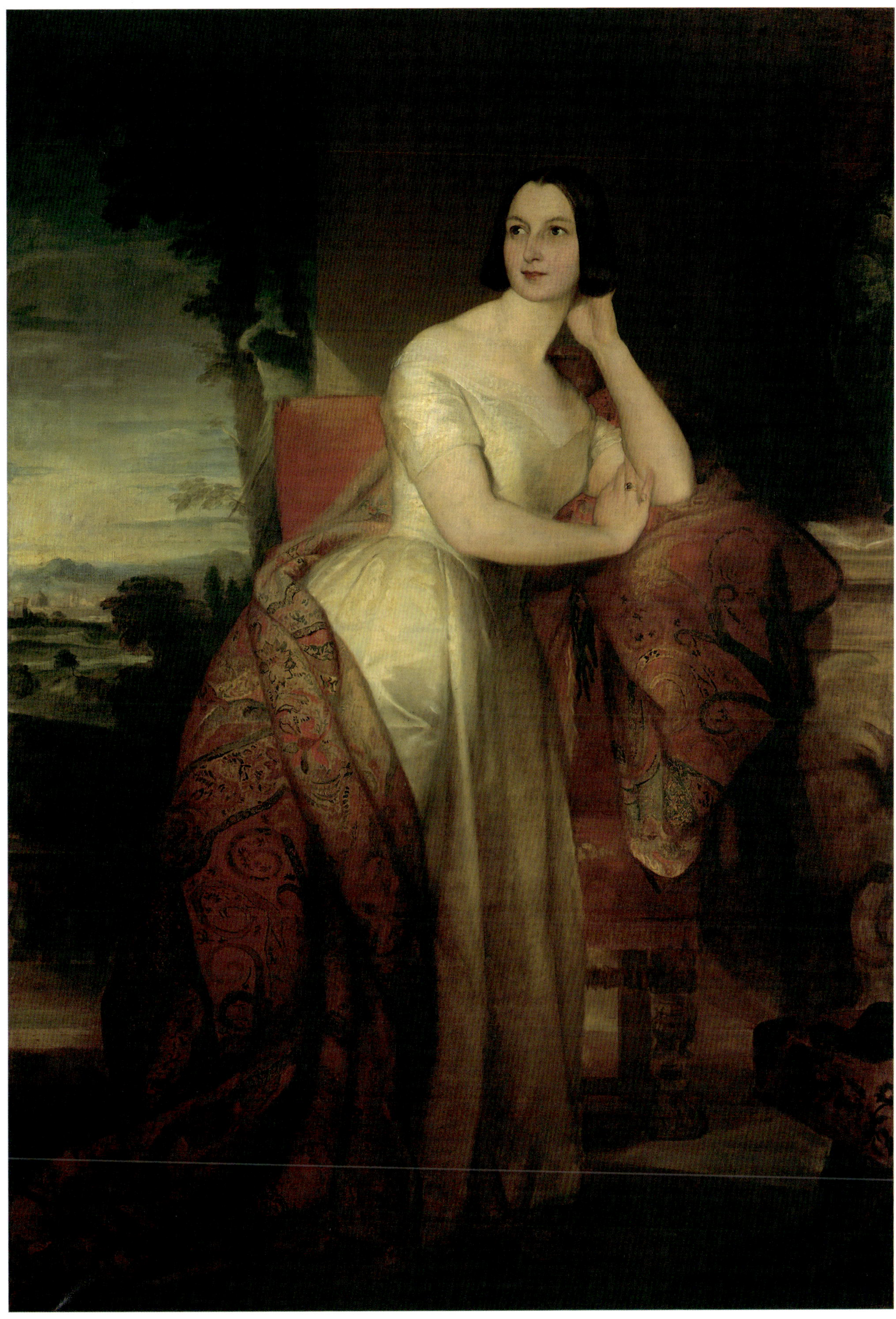

FRANZ XAVER WINTERHALTER 1805–1873

59 **Prince Albert** 1846

Oil on canvas 237.5 × 147.5 ($93\frac{1}{2}$ × 58)
The Trustees of the National Museums and Galleries on Merseyside, Lady Lever Art Gallery

Prince Francis Charles Augustus Albert Emmanuel of Saxe-Coburg Gotha was Queen Victoria's cousin, and three months her junior. They had been childhood friends, and their marriage in 1840 had long been a foregone conclusion for many people. He was a serious, scholarly man who applied himself conscientiously to the duties of his difficult role, and earned himself considerable popularity by his enlightened interest in the arts and industry, which found its most influential expression in the Great Exhibition of 1851 which was largely his brainchild. He died of typhoid fever in December 1861, plunging Victoria into a period of almost total retirement from public life for many years.

This is one of a pair of portraits of Victoria and Albert that were painted at the request of Sir Robert Peel. He asked the Queen that they should be shown 'in that simple attire in which, when he has had the frequent happiness of being admitted to your private society, he has seen your Majesty and the Prince'. It may be the consequent informality of the pictures which led a reviewer to call them 'deficient in refinement'. The perception is an interesting one. The companion portrait of the Queen with the young Prince of Wales (collection Her Majesty The Queen) is considerably more informal than this, and does seem to catch Winterhalter in an uneasy mood, hesitating between formality and intimacy. In his portrait of the Prince Consort, on the other hand, he seems to have resolved the hesitancy into a carefully balanced presentation of the public figure at a private moment, a tension which the whole composition is enlisted to express. Technically, too, the handling is more confident, conveying the smooth good breeding of the sitter by means of a metaphor of paint. The curtains and background, however, are surprisingly generalised, with an almost unfinished appearance. The trappings of the grand formal portrait are all in place, but the pose is deliberately unstable, as Prince Albert rises from the chair – or throne – in which he has been performing his royal role.

The German artist is seen compromising with the typically English requirements of the recipient of the picture, but nevertheless imposes his characteristically elegant interpretation on the whole subject. A comparison with Lawrence's portrait of 'Queen Charlotte' (no.50), which in a very different way is also concerned with the formal as framework for the informal, shows how much more concerned with glamour than with personality Winterhalter is. Nevertheless, the Queen was highly satisfied with the result: 'it is quite Winterhalter's *chef d'oeuvre*,' she declared, 'and is the best likeness ever done of my beloved one'.

In the same year, Winterhalter also painted his large group portrait of the royal family (collection Her Majesty The Queen), in a horizontal format, with the four younger children in the foreground, and the Prince of Wales at his mother's knee. In this work, again, the suave sumptuousness of Winterhalter's handling gives grandeur to a design that compromises in a suitably English way between state utterance and informal record.

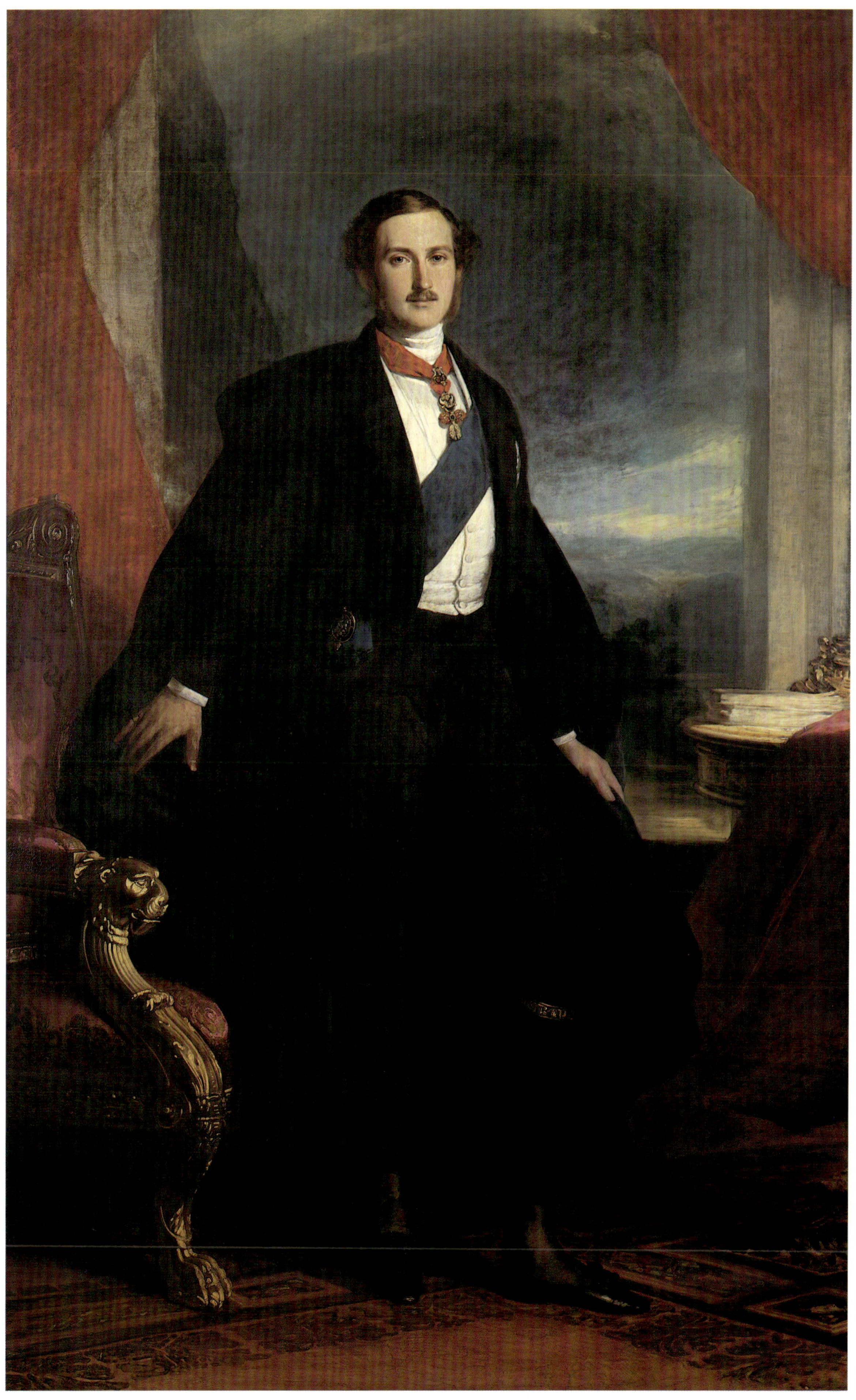

60 **Lady Middleton** 1863

Oil on canvas 239 × 147.5 (94 × 58)
Inscr. lower right: *fr Winterhalter/ Paris 1863*
The Hon. Michael Willoughby

Winterhalter's principal clients were members of the royal houses of Europe; he supplied them with images of a lustre that exactly suited their vision of themselves. But his gloss and sparkle were perceived as spurious and meretricious by other artists, and indeed by much of the general public, who preferred the more unpretentious styles prevailing in mid-century England. His portraits were, in the words of the *Athenaeum*, too 'sensual and fleshy' to be entirely proper among the more modest orders of society. There are therefore relatively few portraits by him of the minor nobility, so that this portrayal of a characterful but not very important country lady is somewhat unusual.

It was painted in Paris, a fact that no doubt explains why its subject is dressed in the height of the French fashion in a gown, probably designed by Worth, in purple velvet with a lace-edged train, appropriate for presentation at the court of Napoleon III and his Empress Eugénie. The viewpoint is low, and the figure fills the space, as Lady Middleton in her enormous crinolines probably did in real life, so that there is room only for a glimpse of drapery and a doorway opening onto a suggestion of wild open country. The cosmopolitan glitter of this grand picture is curiously at odds with what is really one of Winterhalter's most English commissions. It was painted to be presented to Lady Middleton by the 'Tenantry and Professional Gentlemen' on the estate at Wollaton, the Middletons' celebrated Elizabethan house outside Nottingham. Julia Bosville herself was the only daughter of Alexander William Bosville, of Thorpe and Gunthwaite, Yorkshire; she married Henry, 8th Baron Middleton in 1843 at the age of nineteen and bore him thirteen children, one of whom was born in September of the year this portrait was painted. She was an energetic and forceful woman, and a keen rider to hounds. As Winterhalter suggests here, she also had a lively interest in clothes and jewellery, having even designed the kennels at Birdsall, where the Middleton Hunt was housed, so that she could visit them comfortably in her wide skirts. She died in 1901.

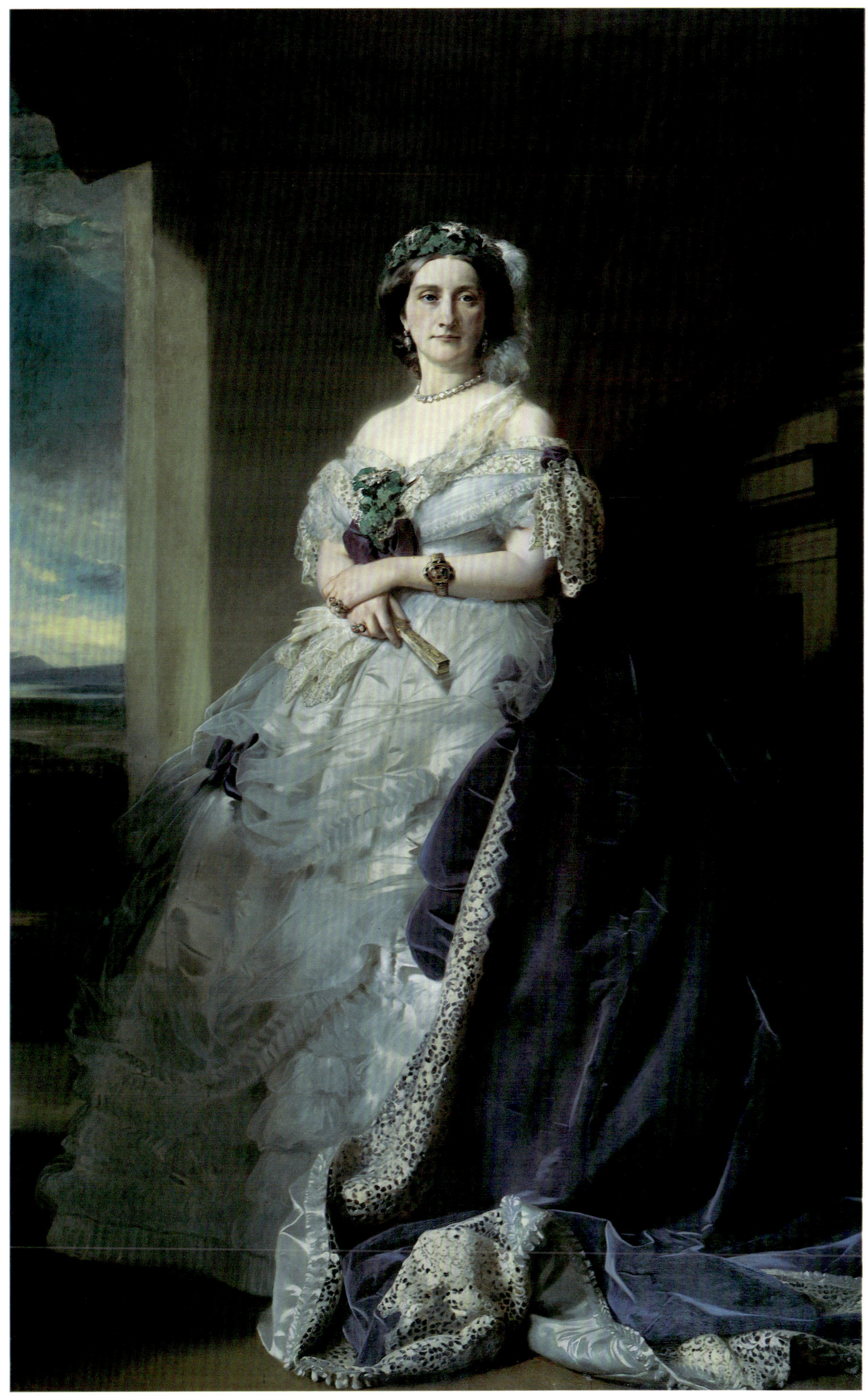

FREDERIC LORD LEIGHTON 1830–1896

61 **Mrs James Guthrie** 1865

Oil on canvas 210.7 × 138.5 (83 × 54½)
Exh: Royal Academy 1866 (7)
Yale Center for British Art, Paul Mellon Collection

The impact on Leighton of a visit to Venice in the autumn of 1865 is reflected in this sumptuous canvas, which he must have painted immediately on his return to England. Mrs Guthrie was at this time the model for the central figure in his picture 'The Syracusan Bride' (1869; private collection). She was born Ellinor Stirling in Perth, Australia, in 1838. Her father was the first Governor of Western Australia, Admiral Sir James Stirling. Brought up mainly in Surrey, she married a young Scottish banker, James Guthrie, in 1856. They had nine children before his death in 1873. Leighton postponed painting the picture because of Mrs Guthrie's poor health between the births of her fifth and sixth daughters. Her languid pose and tired, dreamy look, combined with subtly harmonised blacks and reds, give the picture a flavour of the aesthetic movement, although it predates that development by some years. The presentation is still opulently high Victorian, with a close attention to detail and a ripeness of form that rival Winterhalter (no.59). The handling of paint is, however, rather different, with a softness and sensuousness quite unlike Winterhalter's metallic finish. The comparison is illuminating because Leighton received an important part of his training in Germany – though not in Bavaria like Winterhalter, but the more northern centre of Frankfurt am Main. That essentially Nazarene background accounts for the linear clarity and refinement of Leighton's work, and explains the essential solidity of this composition. Confronted by such an essay in richness we might expect a portrait full of the flowing rhythms of a Veronese or a Genoese Van Dyck; instead Mrs Guthrie remains immobile, the fall of her black taffeta dress restricted to a discreet ripple, her gestures quiet and calculated not to disturb but to stabilise the balance of the design. But it is evident that the particular lushness of the details stems from Venetian painting. The accumulation of textures and colours is deliberately excessive: the lilies and roses in their china vases, which echo the pallid luminosity of the sitter's face; the richly embroidered tablecloth, apparently an altar frontal or cope; the Indian ebony chair inlaid with mother-of-pearl; and the dimly-seen tapestry that forms a backdrop, with its evocative detail of mythological lovers and a cupid with a flaming torch. This last touch is like a veiled hint at the more expansive world that produced the masterpieces of Baroque art that Leighton had recently seen, and perhaps at something in the sitter herself that the circumstances of her life, and the manners of her time, forbade her to express. Indeed, when in 1879 Mrs Guthrie married Forster Fitzgerald Arbuthnot, the friend of Sir Richard Burton and co-translator with him of several famous oriental works of erotica, she may finally have given expression to those hidden aspects of her personality. She died in 1911.

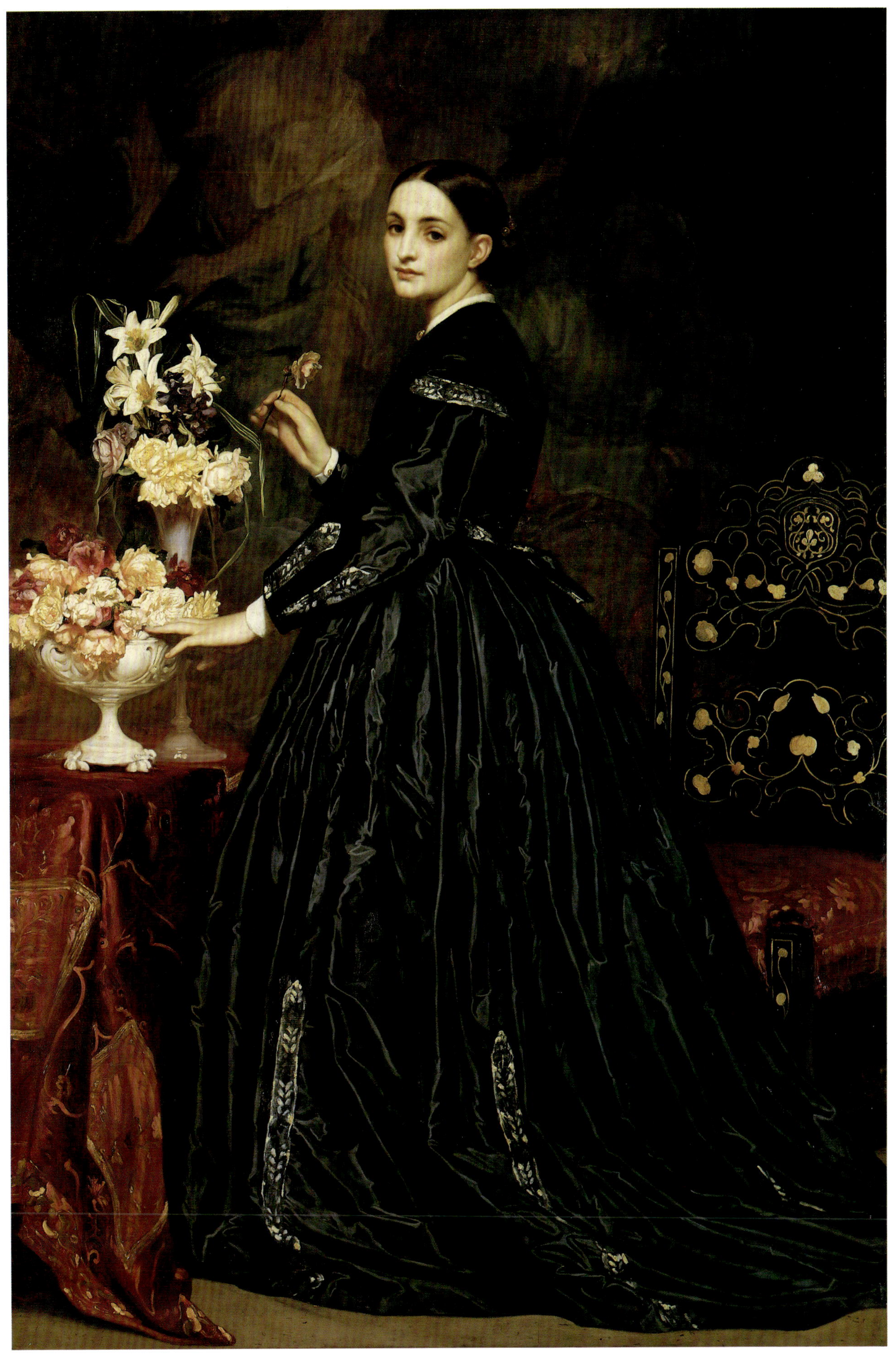

JACQUES-JOSEPH (JAMES) TISSOT 1836–1902

62 Colonel Frederick Gustavus Burnaby 1870

Oil on panel 49.5 × 59.7 ($19\frac{1}{2}$ × $23\frac{1}{2}$)
Inscr. lower left: *J.J.Tissot/70*
Exh: London, International Exhibition 1872 (1282)
National Portrait Gallery

As a Frenchman, Tissot brought to his paintings a Continental refinement of finish that he owed to the training he had received in Paris. But when he practised in England in the 1870s, his sophisticated modern genre subjects struck an agreeably local note, taking up a well-established type of subject matter exemplified in the work of, say, William Powell Frith (1819–1909), and paralleled among his contemporaries by Sir William Quiller Orchardson (1832–1910). Like many immigrant artists, then, Tissot was able to catch an authentically 'English' atmosphere and thus contribute meaningfully to the native tradition. In this portrait he betrays a debt to his friend Edgar Degas (1834–1917), and seems at the same time to be recalling the lounging gentlemen who populate Gainsborough's early pictures, but instead of using the informality of the pose to undercut the rhetoric of the picture, he allows the long, elegant rhythms of the figure to establish their own rather grand presence, making us aware of the superiority of the sitter, both social and physical, rather than bringing us into a close and friendly dialogue with him.

If Burnaby has a dashing air, that exactly reflects his character and life. He was born in 1842 and grew to be a giant of a man, six feet four inches tall and correspondingly well-built. He performed numerous feats of strength, such as carrying a pony under his arm. He was an enthusiastic aeronaut and in 1882 succeeded in crossing the Channel by balloon. In 1859 he entered the army, rising through the ranks of cornet, lieutenant and captain to major in the 3rd Household Cavalry, becoming lieutenant-colonel in 1880 and taking command of the regiment in 1881. He was captain when Tissot painted this portrait (one of his first English works) at the request of Thomas Gibson Bowles, editor of *Vanity Fair*, a magazine Burnaby had helped finance and to which he contributed articles. He travelled extensively, sometimes as correspondent of the *Times* – to South America, Spain and north Africa, Russia and the Middle East. The map of the world hung on the wall behind him in his portrait alludes to these activities. His 1875 'Ride to Khiva' across the Steppes of Russia became a celebrated exploit. Balked of the command of the Blues, who were on their way to Egypt, he went there without orders and volunteered for service under General Baker. Early in 1885 he was killed by a spear during the advance of the forces despatched to relieve Khartoum. An associate of the Prince of Wales, a fine linguist, intrepid, impetuous, sometimes rash, he was very much a type of the Imperial period, and foreshadows in some respects the adventures of Lawrence of Arabia and, perhaps, of George Macdonald Fraser's fictional Harry Flashman. According to the *Dictionary of National Biography* 'his features Jewish and Italian, and his unEnglish appearance led him to resist attempts to procure portraits of him'. Tissot, who seems to have overcome this diffidence, makes little of any such imagined disadvantages, and presents him as a suave and irresistible lion of London society.

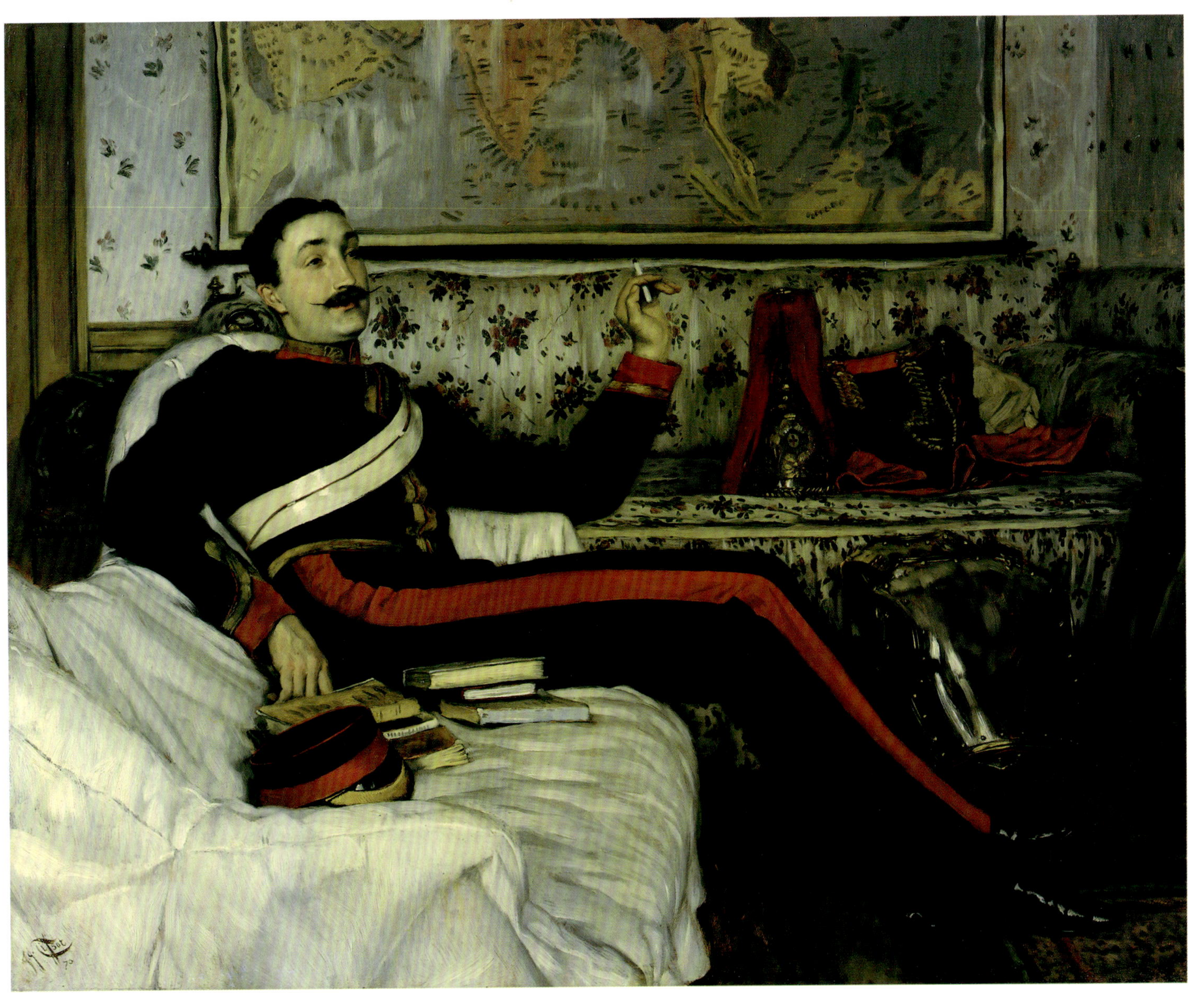

SIR JOHN EVERETT MILLAIS 1829–1896

63 **Hearts Are Trumps** 1872

Oil on canvas 165.7 × 219.7 ($65\frac{1}{4} \times 86\frac{1}{2}$)
Inscr. *JM* (monogram) *1872*
Tate Gallery. Presented by the Trustees of the Chantrey Bequest 1945

The artist's son J.G. Millais recounts the genesis of this picture is his biography of his father (Millais II, p.39): 'In a review of his works it was asserted that, successful as he was in certain branches of his Art, he was quite incapable of making such a picture of three beautiful women together in the dress of the period as Sir Joshua Reynolds had produced in his famous portrait of "The Ladies Waldegrave". He happened to see this review, and at once determined to show the world that such a task was by no means beyond his power, even when handicapped by the ungraceful dress and coiffure of the early seventies. The result was "Hearts are Trumps" in which the three beautiful daughters of Sir Walter Armstrong (now Mrs Tennant-Dunlop, Mrs Secker, and Mrs Ponsonby Blennerhasset) appear, engaged in a game of cards.' The game is apparently dummy whist. The use of 'The Ladies Waldegrave' (fig.37) as a model is significant of the importance Reynolds had for this generation of Victorians. The unassuming domestic activity is more in keeping with the priorities of nineteenth-century realism than the classicising fantasy of Reynolds's other great triple portrait, the 'Three Ladies Adorning a Term of Hymen' (no.35).

The girls' names were Elizabeth, Diana and Mary; Millais himself designed their dresses. Like 'Mrs Bischoffsheim' of the following year (no.64), the picture was immediately likened to the work of Velásquez, and admired for 'keen perception of character, tact, feeling for grace and beauty of a sumptuous kind'. Like 'Mrs Bischoffsheim', too, it was shown at the *Exposition Universelle* in Paris in 1878 and much praised. In particular, one French critic was struck by the '*fortes mâchoires*' of the English girls nurtured on *bifteks* and sandwiches. Inspired as it was by Reynolds's triple portrait, 'Hearts are Trumps' in its turn lies behind Sargent's picture of the three daughters of Colonel Thomas Vickers (1884; Sheffield, Graves Art Gallery). This too was compared, though unfavourably, with Velásquez.

Having been commissioned by Armstrong, the picture passed to his daughter Diana and her husband, J. Herbert Secker, and was acquired by the Tate Gallery in 1945 as a purchase under the terms of the Chantrey Bequest which facilitated the acquisition by the nation on an annual basis of major British paintings.

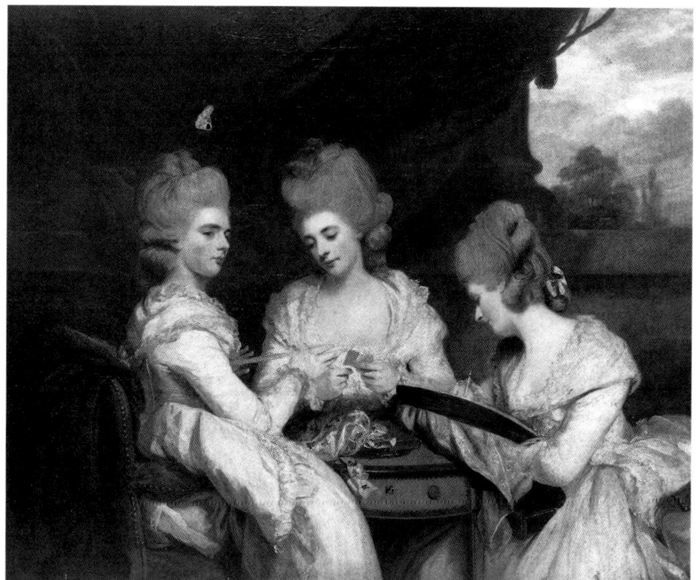

fig.37 Sir Joshua Reynolds **The Ladies Waldegrave** 1781 Oil on canvas
National Gallery of Scotland

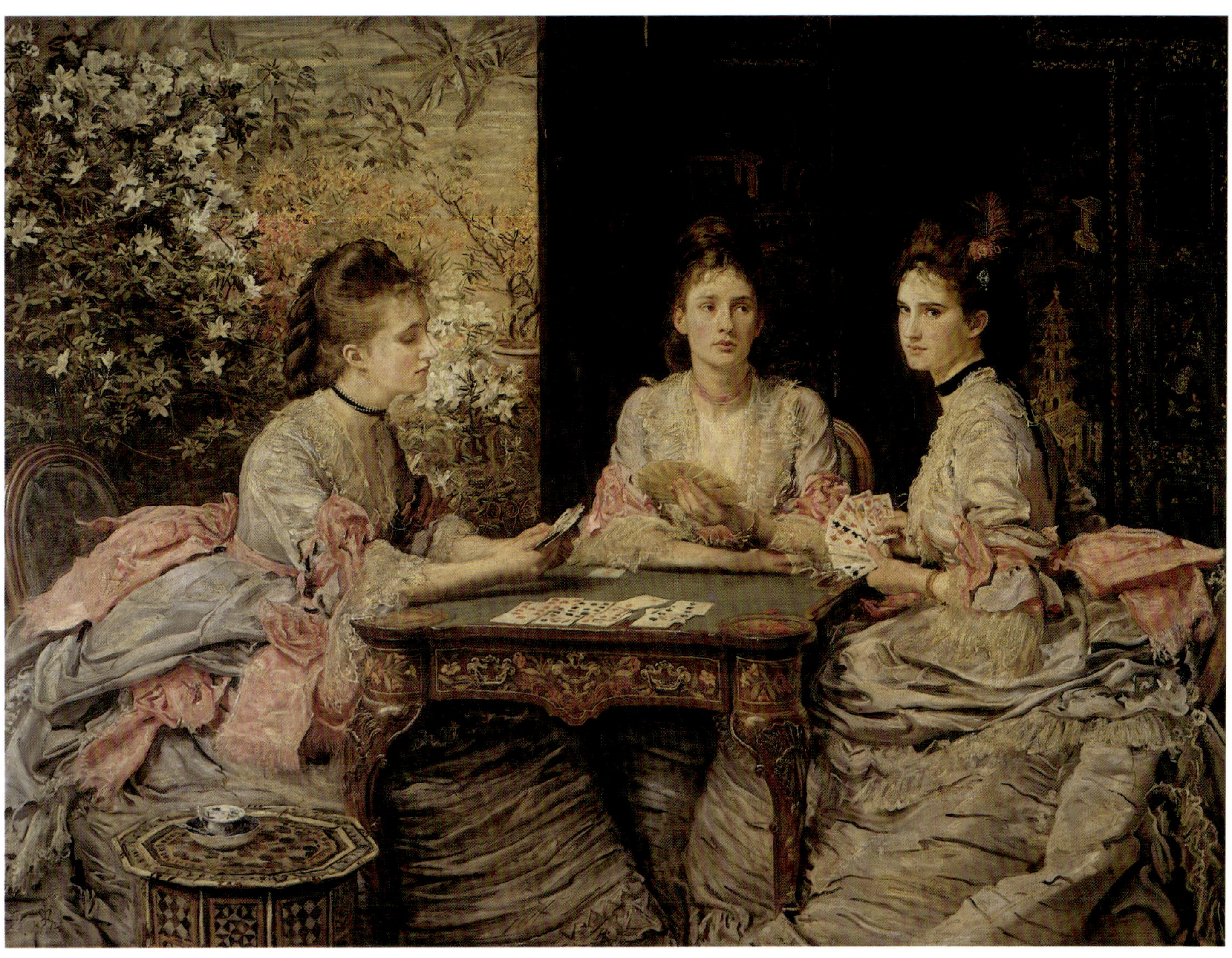

SIR JOHN EVERETT MILLAIS

64 **Mrs Bischoffsheim** 1873

Oil on canvas 130.8 × 90.2 ($51\frac{1}{2} \times 35\frac{1}{2}$)
Inscr. lower left: *JM* (monogram) *1873*
Tate Gallery. Presented by Lady Fitzgerald 1944

The sitter was the wife of Louis Bischoffsheim, of the financial house of Bischoffsheim and Goldschmidt. Throughout the late nineteenth century she was at the hub of the civilised and successful community of central European immigrants in London, entertaining lavishly at the Bischoffsheim's splendid house in South Audley Street (now the Egyptian Embassy) and at The Warren House, Stanmore. As 'Mrs Bisch' she was a kindly maternal influence in the life of the young Ernest Cassel, who was to become the grandfather of Edwina, Countess Mountbatten. Her husband died in 1908; although devastated by that event Mrs Bisch lived on into the 1920s.

Her portrait by Millais was regarded at the time it was painted as a triumph, and that judgement has been endorsed in more recent years (*Millais*, RA, 1967, p.51). Like 'Hearts are Trumps' (no.63) it was compared with Velásquez when first shown, and, with that picture, can perhaps be seen as ushering in the late nineteenth-century tradition of Velásquez-inspired portraiture that was to bring forth Sargent and de Laszló. Millais's sheer technical skill, which was largely responsible for the fashionable comparison, revived something of the panache that had not been seen in English portraiture since the death of Lawrence. But Millais functioned in a world very different from Lawrence's, and his portraits are of a decidedly bourgeois cast. When they are not concerned with the sobriety of the male establishment, they portray the wives and families of prosperous men, not as goddesses but as the wearers of clothes only affordable by such men. If the flowered fabrics and lace flounces are intended to evoke the eighteenth century, they do not succeed in doing so: all is unmistakably of the early 1870s. Compare 'Hearts Are Trumps' as an 'answer' to Reynolds's 'Three Ladies Waldegrave'. The directness of Millais's approach to his male sitters is echoed here in the simple pose and subdued background, but belied by the elaboration of Mrs Bischoffsheim's dress, which parallels the ostentation of mid-eighteenth-century waistcoats in the hands of Hudson and Van Aken (see no.25, for instance). The treatment of the drapery must be the principal reason for the adjectives bestowed on the work: 'The splendour and vigour, the intensity and richness of the painting in this picture, surpass anything even this artist has produced', wrote the *Athenaeum*; and at the Paris *Exposition Universelle* of 1878, as the Munich exhibition in 1879, it was, as Millais's son tells us, 'quite a sensation' (Millais II, p.40).

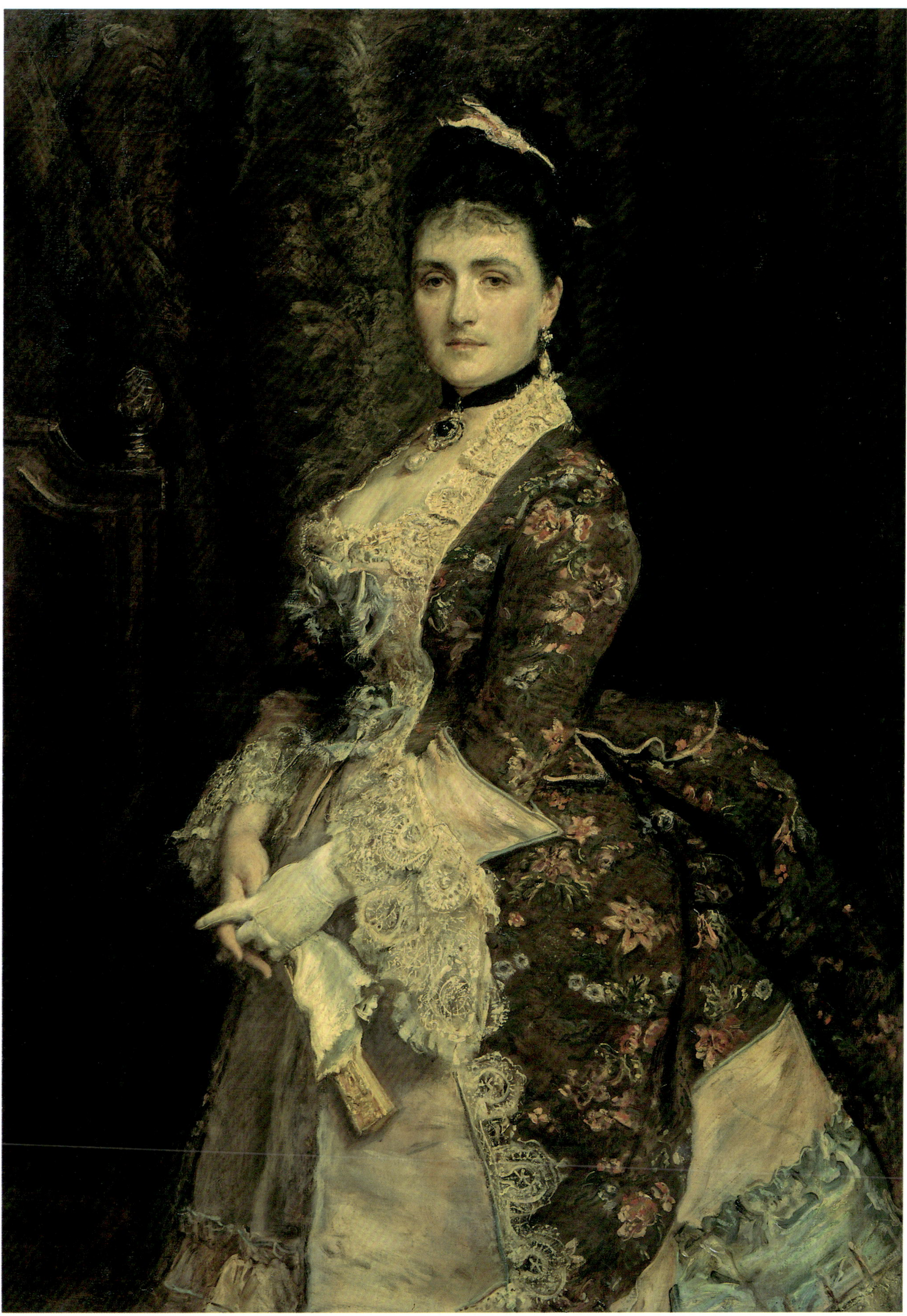

JOHN SINGER SARGENT 1856–1925

65 **Ellen Terry as Lady Macbeth** 1889

Oil on canvas 221 × 114.3 (87 × 45)
Signed lower left: *John S. Sargent*
Exh: New Gallery, London, 1889 (110)
Tate Gallery. Presented by Sir Joseph Duveen 1906

Ellen Alice Terry (1847–1928) was the most famous member of a large theatrical family, and began her stage career at the age of nine. She attracted the attention of G.F. Watts (see no.58) and became his wife, though the marriage was never consummated and was quickly annulled. Watts's portrait of her among roses, called 'Choosing', is in the National Portrait Gallery. Her second husband, Charles Kelly, died in 1885. Meanwhile she was building up a reputation as an actress, and in 1878 became leading lady of Henry Irving's newly formed company at the Lyceum Theatre. It was there that she appeared as Lady Macbeth in 1888, and Sargent almost immediately asked her to sit for him in character. Tragedy was not considered her forte, and she took a little while to agree to this, but did so when it became clear that she had scored a success in the part.

In the event Sargent did not portray her in a specific moment from the play, but instead invented a scene in which she holds a crown over her own head – a Napoleonic gesture which sums up her ambitious purpose. The costume records what she actually wore, however, and the striking 'magenta hair' that especially impressed Sargent. Sittings took place at Sargent's studio in Tite Street, Chelsea, of which Oscar Wilde remarked, 'The street that on a wet and dreary morning has vouchsafed the vision of Lady Macbeth in full regalia magnificently seated in a four-wheeler can never again be as other streets: it must always be full of wonderful possibilities' (Robertson, p.233).

The painting was not universally liked when it appeared, but was recognised as a sensational work. For some, like the *Athenaeum* critic, it was theatrical in the worst sense – 'painting for the pit'; for others it was an ambitious masterpiece. There is a precedent for this kind of picture in Lawrence's 'half-histories' and his presentation of the single figure upright in a composition of very tall format seems to look back specifically at a work like Lawrence's 'Kemble as Hamlet' (no.52).

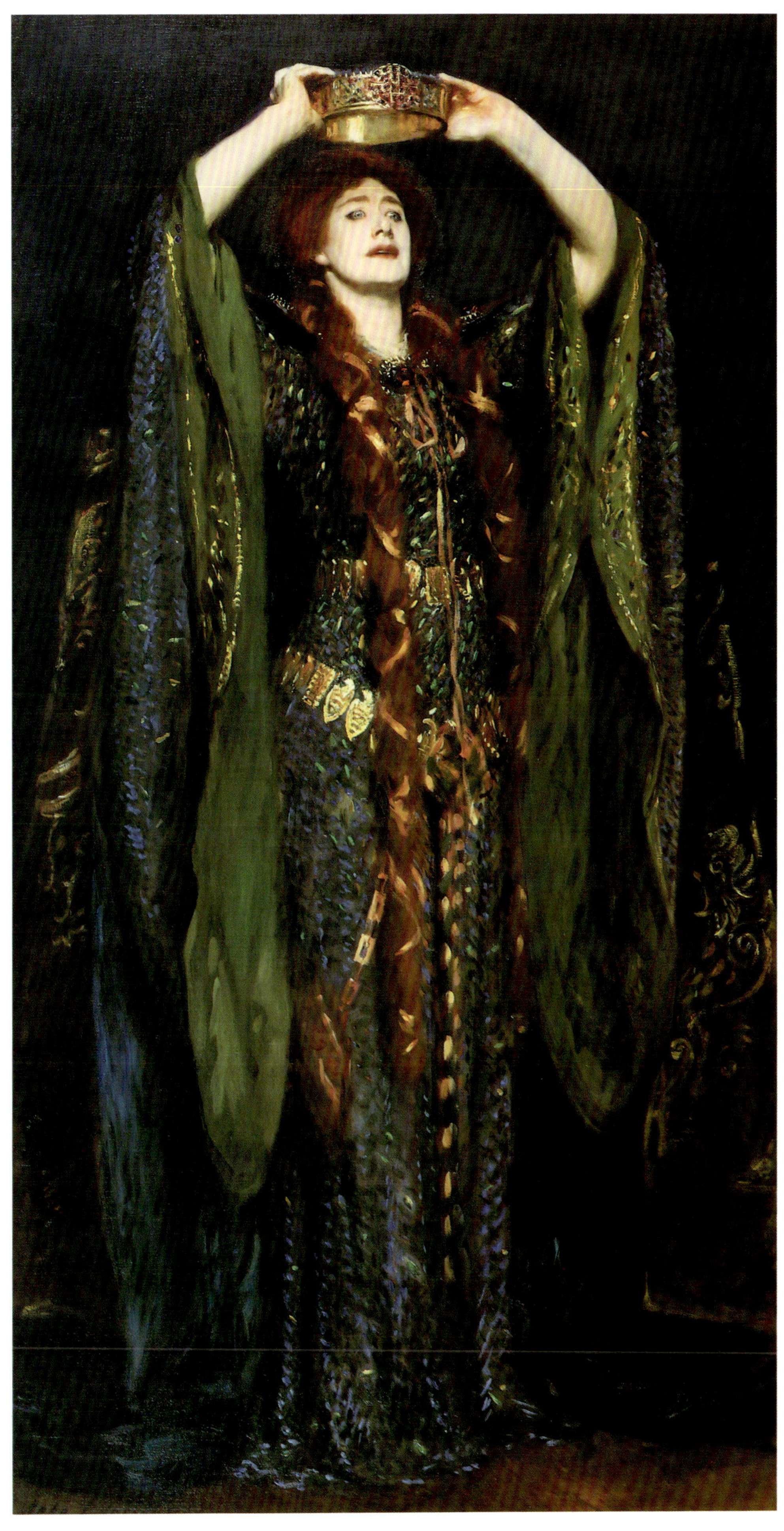

66 **W. Graham Robertson** 1894

Oil on canvas 230.5 × 118.7 ($90\frac{3}{4}$ × $46\frac{3}{4}$)
Inscr. lower right: *John S. Sargent 1894*
Exh: Royal Academy 1895 (503)
Tate Gallery. Presented by W. Graham Robertson 1940

Walford Graham Robertson (1866–1948) was an artist, theatrical designer and collector with a wide circle of interesting and often celebrated friends, but whatever his abilities or qualities as a personality Sargent seems to have been principally motivated to paint this portrait by his slender figure, which he thought would be set off by a long black overcoat Robertson owned. Robertson recalled that the artist 'evidently had the finished picture in his mind from the first and started it almost exactly upon its final lines'. The dominant motif of the whole composition was its astringent verticality: 'It was hot summer weather and I feebly rebelled against the thick overcoat. "But the coat is in the picture," said Sargent. "You must wear it." "Then I can't wear anything else," I cried in despair, and with the sacrifice of most of my wardrobe I became thinner and thinner, much to the satisfaction of the artist, who used to pull and drag the unfortunate coat more and more closely round me until it might have been draping a lamp-post.' (Robertson, p.238). Sargent was also anxious to include Robertson's St Jean de Luz poodle, Mouton, which adds the only soft note in this deliberately austere design. 'Mouton, who, well stricken in years and almost toothless, claimed rather unusual privileges and was always allowed one bite by Sargent, whom he unaccountably disliked, before work began. "He has bitten me now," Sargent would remark mildly, "so we can go ahead"' (p.234). One visitor during the sittings was Sarah Bernhardt, who, according to Robertson, detected a resemblance between her face and his.

In the same year, Whistler's portrait of Comte Robert de Montesquiou was shown at the Paris Salon, and although Sargent saw this, and there is a striking resemblance, he had in fact begun the portrait of Robertson earlier. Even so, the influence of Whistler can hardly be denied. The tall format and restricted palette, mainly of blacks and greys, are typical of many of Whistler's full-lengths. The self-consciously firm vertical of the door-jamb in the background is also very Whistlerian, though uncharacteristic of Sargent.

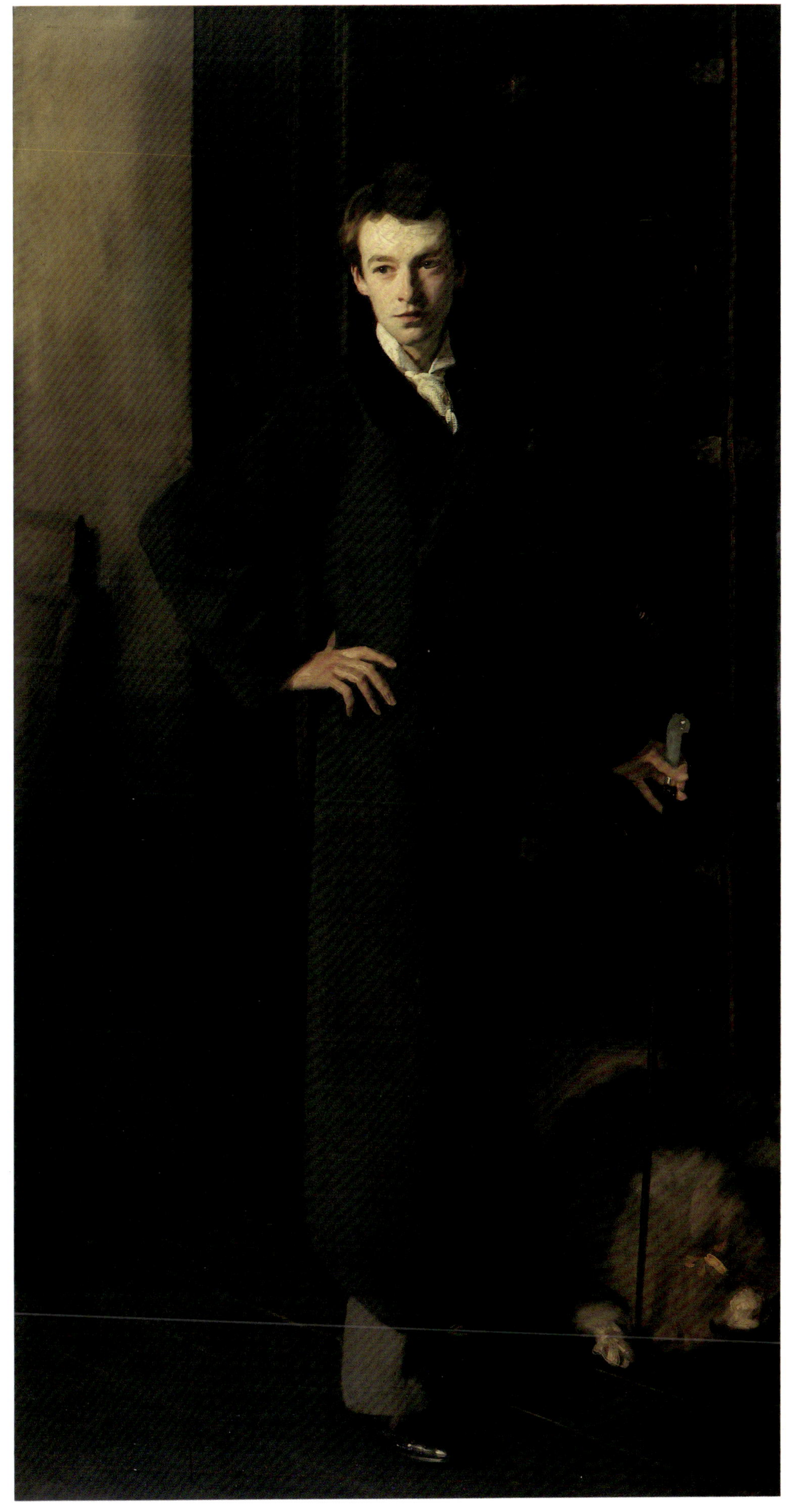

67 **Mrs Carl Meyer and her Children** 1896

Oil on canvas 201.4 × 134 ($79\frac{1}{4} \times 52\frac{3}{4}$)
Inscr. lower left and right: *John S. Sargent 1896*
Exh: Royal Academy 1897 (291)
Private Collection

Carl Meyer was a banker and Chairman of de Beers; his wife was born Adèle Levis. Their children were Frank, who later succeeded to the baronetcy with which Meyer was honoured, and Elsie, who married St John Lambert and, later, Harry Hulbert. In painting them as a group Sargent displays his inventiveness in the matter of composition, adopting here a very different solution from that used in another portrait of mother and children, the *c.*1900 picture of Mrs Cazalet (no.69). He unexpectedly raises the viewpoint above the heads of the sitters, who look up at us as though at something high on the wall above them. It might almost be something menacing, so protective is the mother's gesture as she reaches toward her children, barricaded behind the sofa. The 'bird's-eye' device was to be used again, perhaps in direct emulation of this work, by Boldini in his 1906 portrait of Consuelo, Duchess of Marlborough (fig.38; Metropolitan Museum of Art). The children are pushed to the top and back of the design, but are cleverly brought into prominence by the selective lighting, perhaps that of a fire, by the rhythm of linked arms across the centre, and by the expanse of Mrs Meyer's skirt that fills the lower half of the canvas. The informality of this design, with its figures crammed tightly into the picture-space like a photograph, may have been suggested by the unexpectedly cropped subjects of some of the Impressionists, notably Degas, who often had recourse to the camera in arriving at his compositions.

The dramatic presentation, combined with the delicate interplay of pinks, greys, creams and pale gold ensured that the picture was acclaimed when shown at the Academy in 1897. Sargent's fellow-countryman Henry James, who is often thought of as providing the literary equivalent to his pictures, pronounced characteristically that it was 'so far higher a triumph of painting than anything else in the place that, meeting it early in his course, the spectator turns from it with a grateful sense that the whole message of that art has on this occasion, so far as he is concerned, been uttered' (Olson 1986, p.207).

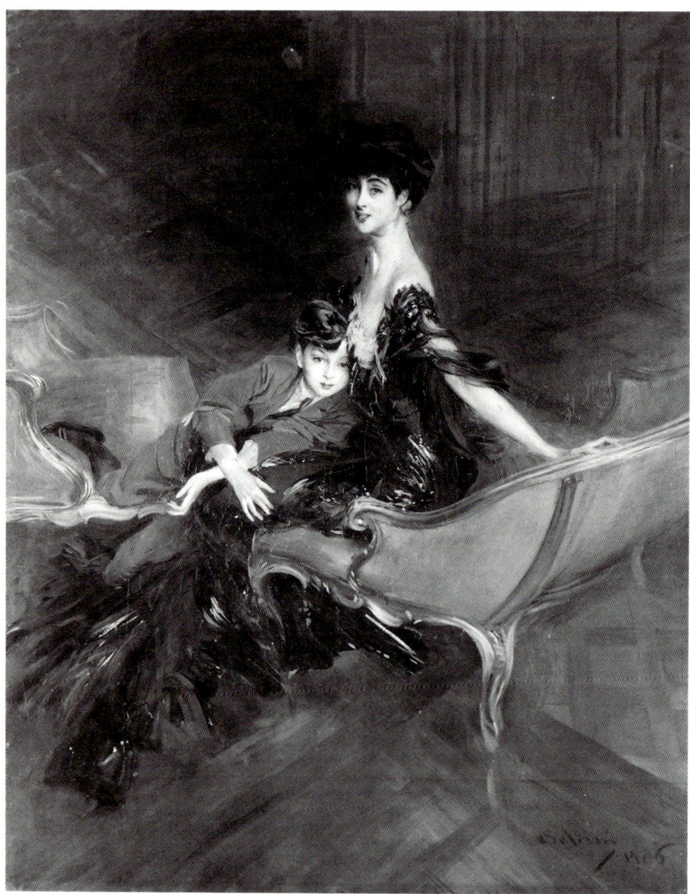

fig.38 Giovanni Boldini **Consuelo Vanderbilt, Duchess of Marlborough and her Son, Lord Ivor Spencer-Churchill** 1906 Oil on canvas *Metropolitan Museum of Art, Gift of Consuelo Vanderbilt Balsan, 1947*

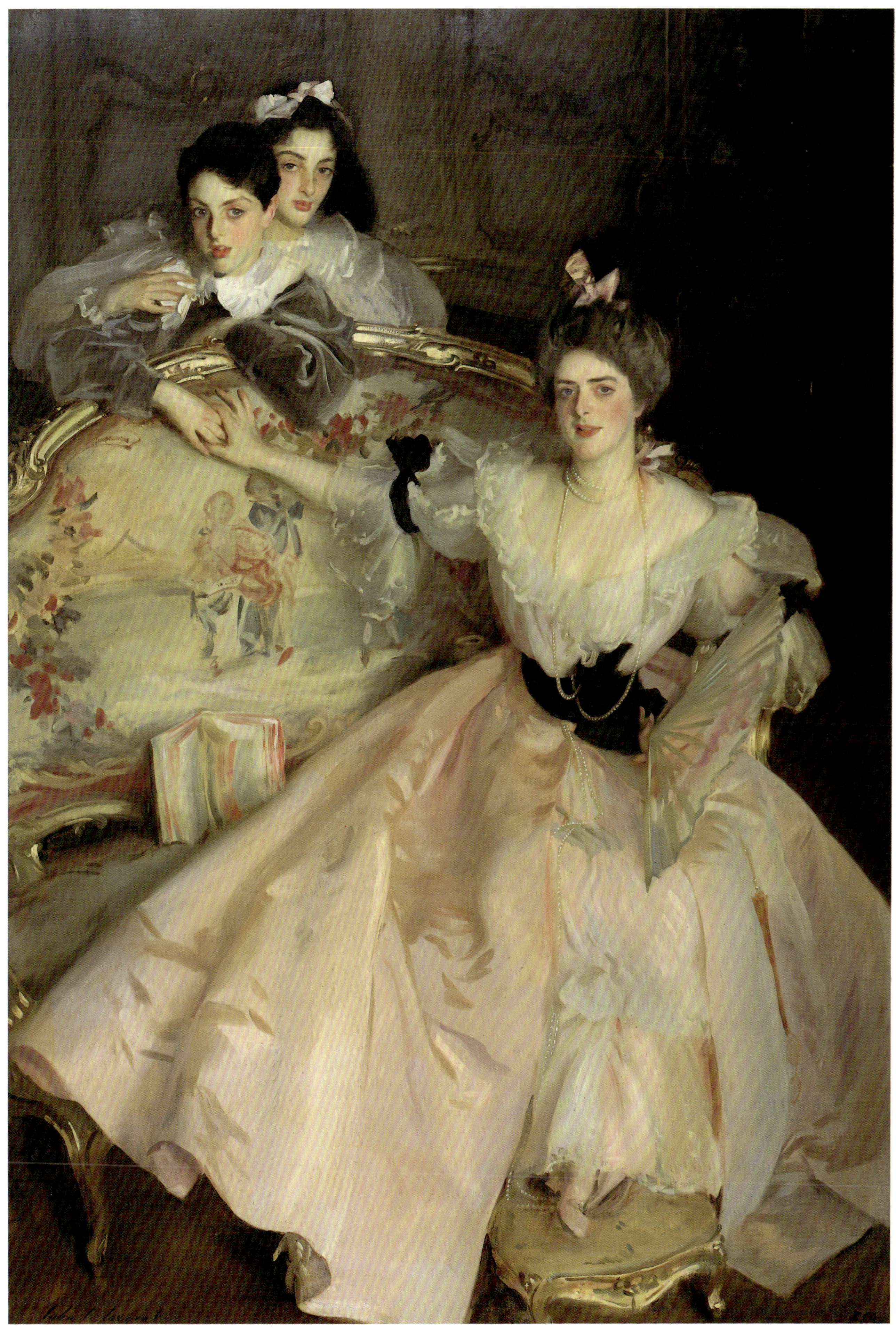

68 **Ena and Betty Wertheimer** 1901

Oil on canvas 185.4 × 130.8 (73 × $51\frac{1}{2}$)
Inscr. lower right: *John S. Sargent 1901*
Exh: Royal Academy 1901 (178)
Tate Gallery. Presented by the widow and family of Asher Wertheimer in accordance with his wishes 1922

In 1898 Sargent was commissioned to paint companion portraits of Asher and Flora Wertheimer for their silver wedding anniversary. Wertheimer was a well-known and successful dealer in Old Masters, furniture and ceramics in London. The artist became a friend of the family, and over the next ten years received a total of twelve commissions from them: a second portrait of Flora (the first was not a success), and portraits of their ten children individually and in groups of two or three. After a showing at the Royal Academy and sometimes in Paris, the gradually accumulating pictures were displayed in the Wertheimer's opulent dining room at Connaught Place, eventually overflowing into the morning room.

Each was planned independently, with its own scale and setting. These two young women were the eldest daughters, born in 1874 and 1877, and were the first to be painted after their parents. They are shown pausing and turning their heads as they walk through the Connaught Place drawing room, where the picture was actually painted, with their father's collections glimmering in the background. The cunningly evoked illusion of detail astonishes, especially in the hands, as does the the contrast of character between the sitters, each apparently painted in the same way. This contrast is pointed up by the accessories: Ena, the taller girl, in white satin, places a hand on the lid of a substantial Chinese vase, while the slighter Betty, in red velvet, holds towards us a transparent fan which is painted as if in movement, opening; by means of these gestures the picture-space is developed through a depth not at first apparent on account of the subdued lighting and dark shadows in which everything but the highlights is muffled. The picture was admired at the Royal Academy in 1901, though it prompted some odd reservations: one critic wrote 'The vivacity – especially in the case of the young ladies – is almost painful' (*Magazine of Art*, 1901, p.388). The *Spectator*, more flatteringly, thought that 'The artist seems to have felt that it was expected of him that he should astonish, and he has done so'.

Ena Wertheimer was to become Mrs Robert Mathias, Betty Mrs Eustace Salaman (Mrs Ricketts *en second noces*). The Wertheimer family portraits were bequeathed to the nation by Asher Wertheimer, remaining with his widow until her death. The National Gallery suspended its rule of not accepting portraits of living people, and displayed the bequest in 1922. The exhibition was extraordinarily popular. *The Year's Art* called Sargent 'that supreme artist of our time'. Evan Charteris, writing the biography of Sargent, claimed that this double portrait was the best of the series and with its 'consummate mastery of colour' counts as 'one of the completest expressions of his art' (Charteris, p.165). Even Roger Fry grudgingly admitted that it was 'in its way a masterpiece', though he went on to dismiss Sargent as not being a true painter.

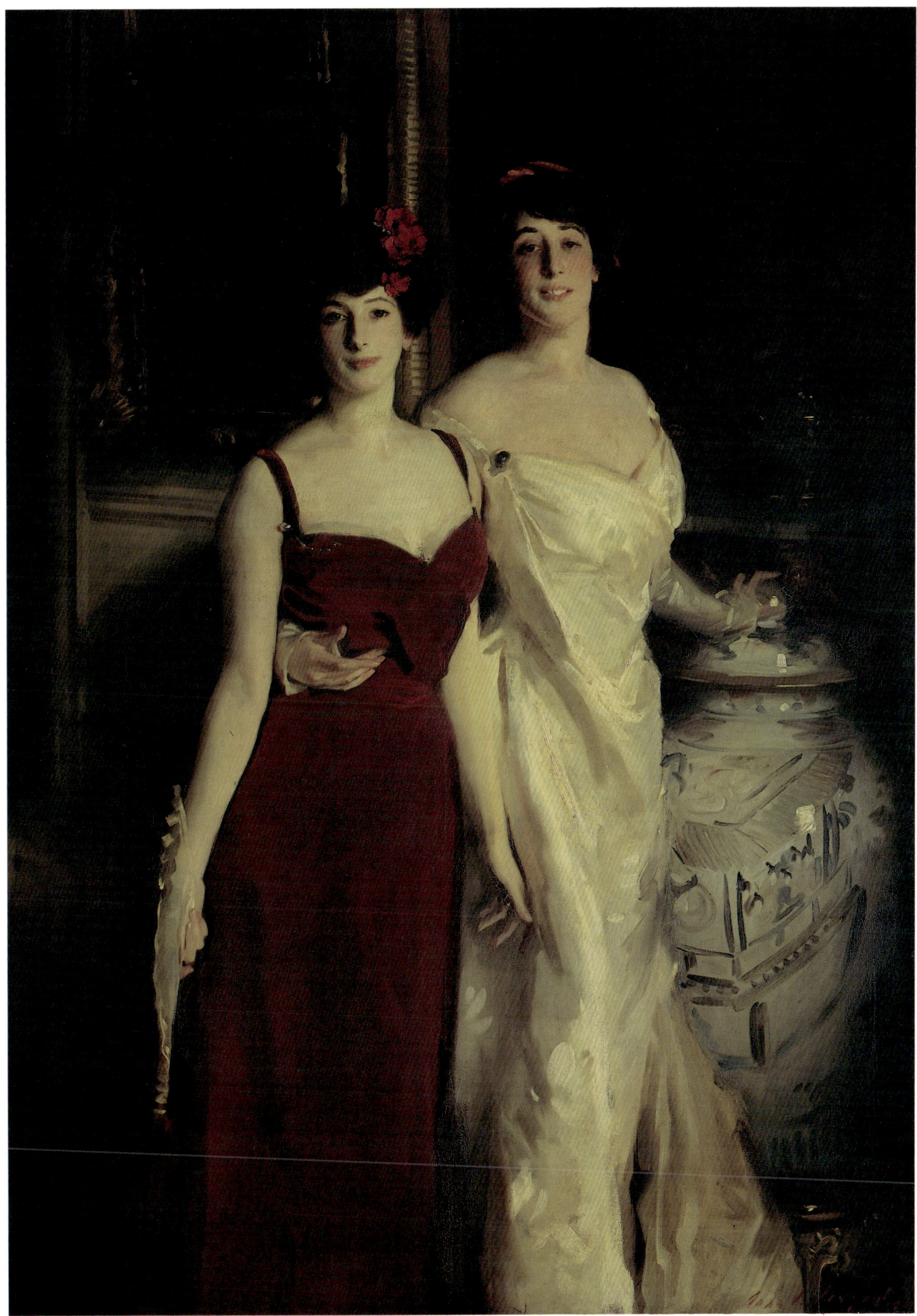

JOHN SINGER SARGENT

69 **Mrs Cazalet and her Children** *c.*1900

Oil on canvas 254 × 165.1 (100 × 65)
Exh: Royal Academy 1901 (103)
Inscr. top left: *John S. Sargent*
Private Collection

This is one of a pair of whole-lengths commissioned by William Marshall Cazalet; the other shows him with his horse in a composition that, as has been pointed out, consciously apes, albeit somewhat stiffly, Reynolds's picture of Captain Robert Orme (National Gallery). Mrs Cazalet was born Maud Lucie Heron, the daughter of Sir John Heron-Maxwell, 7th Baronet of Springkell, and married W.M. Cazalet in 1893. She is shown with the two eldest of her three sons, the six-year-old Edward, who was to die in action in 1916, and the four-year-old Victor Alexander.

There is no stiffness in Sargent's treatment of the mother and children, though they are presented in as dignified and formal a manner as possible. Reynolds did not provide an obvious model for this composition, which seems to look back, in spirit at least, to Lawrence. But a possible source for the composition of standing mother with one child at her feet and the other seated at waist height is Gainsborough's 'Mrs Samuel Moody and her Children', which had been in the Dulwich College Picture Gallery since 1835. By the date of this portrait, Sargent was becoming more dependent on such hints as these, and the shade of Van Dyck, which he had succesfully kept at arm's length throughout the preceding decades, begins to hover palpably in the margins of his canvases. Here there is a very clear debt to Van Dyck in the strong vertical emphasis and shimmering lustre of fabrics, which are calculated to recall his work. The elder boy's vaguely 'period' attire helps to reinforce the allusion.

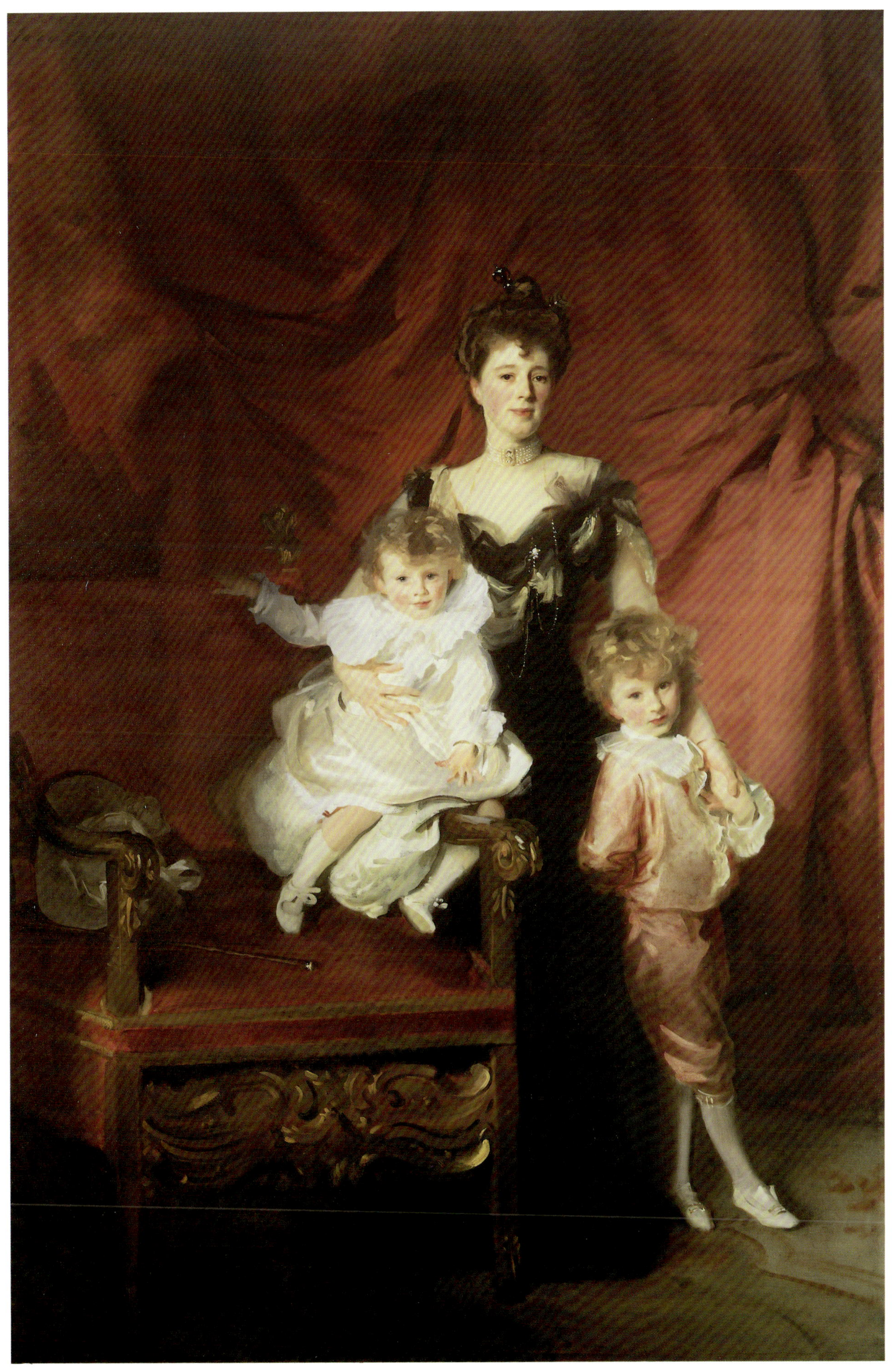

70 **Almina, Daughter of Asher Wertheimer** 1908

Oil on canvas 134 × 101 ($52\frac{3}{4} \times 39\frac{3}{4}$)
Tate Gallery. Presented by the widow and family of Asher Wertheimer in accordance with his wishes 1922

The sequence of Sargent's portraits of the Wertheimer family (see no.68) ended with this dazzling picture of the twenty-two-year-old Almina, who had already appeared in the 1905 group of Hylda, Almina and Conway (Tate Gallery). It is conceived on a relatively modest scale, but is ambitious in its allusion to a famous Van Dyck subject as the basis of the composition, a point that illustrates Sargent's increasing use of Van Dyck as a source of inspiration in the early decades of the new century.

Almina (1866–*c.*1928) wears Persian costume and is shown playing (or pretending to play) a sitar, a lute-like Persian or Indian instrument which belonged to Sargent. It ought to be held vertically. The exotic costume invites comparison with Van Dyck's portrait of Lady Shirley, one of a pair that he painted in Rome when Sir Robert Shirley and his Circassian wife were there in 1622 (fig.39; Petworth House). The figure seated on the floor and the rich fabrics offer a close parallel, reinforced by the circumstance that both sitters have faces turned up to the viewer with an amused smile. But Sargent suppresses the evocative landscape background and tent that lend the portrait of Lady Shirley so much of its atmosphere, preferring as usual a vaguely suggestive area of shadow. Furthermore, his more facile technique and sharp illumination are obviously from a very different world. Sargent's friendship with the Wertheimer family ensures that this, despite its splendid presentation, is really an intimate and affectionate work, directly reflecting the warmth and humour of the sitter's personality.

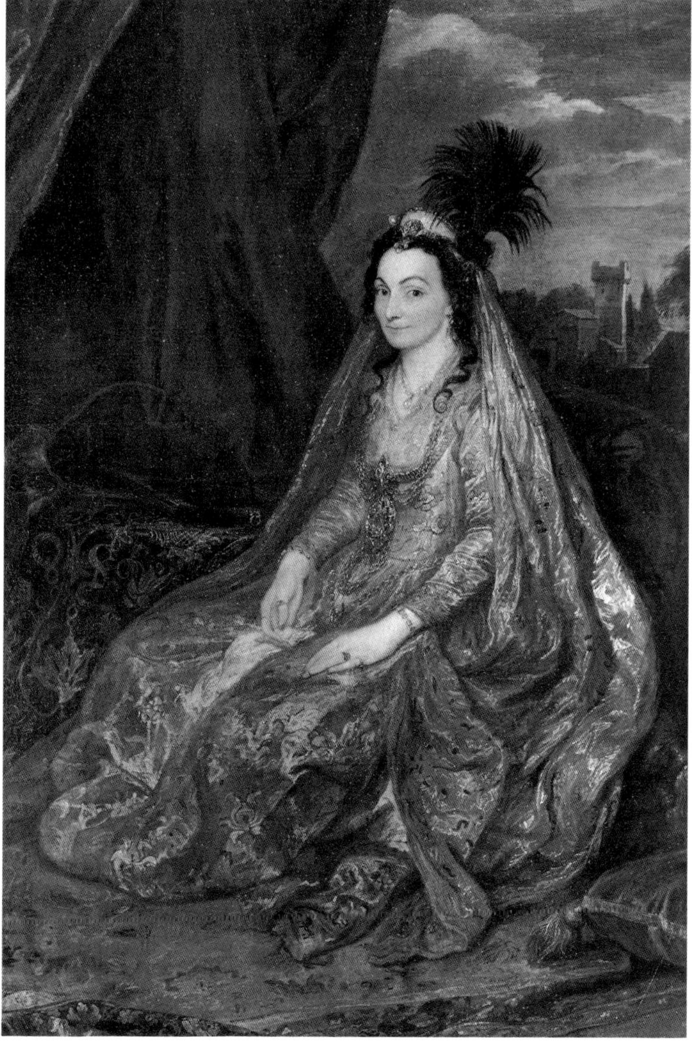

fig.39 Sir Anthony Van Dyck **Lady Shirley** 1622 Oil on canvas
National Trust, Petworth House, Sussex

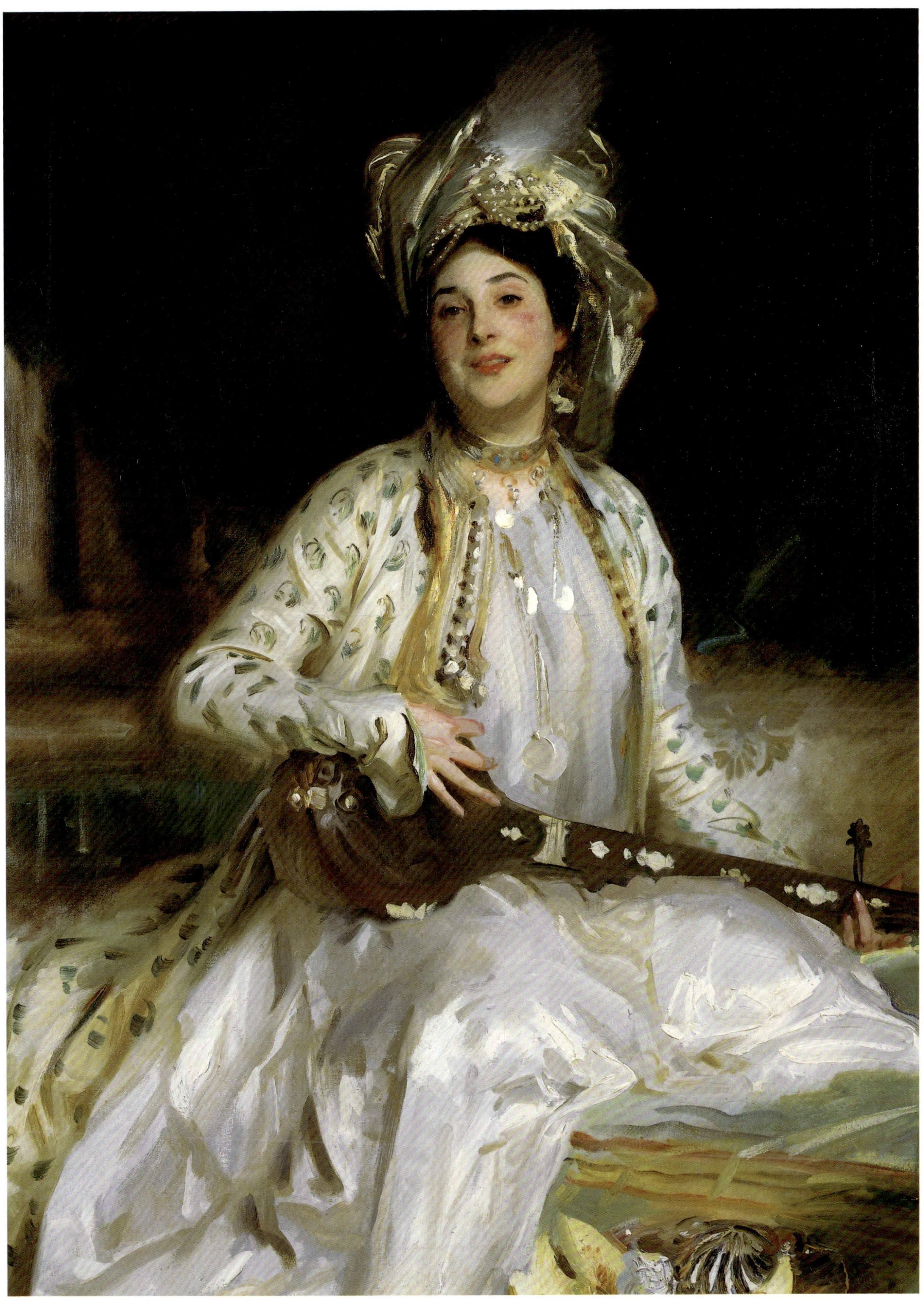

SOLOMON JOSEPH SOLOMON 1860–1927

71 **Mrs Patrick Campbell as 'Paula Tanqueray'** 1894

Oil on canvas 241.3 × 152.5 (95 × 60)
Signed and dated lower left
Exh: Royal Academy 1894 (402)
The Arts Club

Beatrice Stella Tanner (1865–1940) married Patrick Campbell in 1884. Her career began modestly enough in Liverpool in 1888, and it was in the name part of Arthur Wing Pinero's modern drama *The Second Mrs Tanqueray*, at the St James's Theatre in May 1893, that she became an overnight star. At the time the play enjoyed immense notoriety. It is referred to in Hilaire Belloc's cautionary tale *Matilda, who Told Lies and Perished Miserably* (1908):

> It happened that, a few weeks later,
> Her aunt went off to the theatre,
> To see that interesting play
> 'The Second Mrs Tanqueray';
> She had refused to take her niece
> To see this entertaining piece –
> A deprivation just and wise,
> To punish her for telling lies.

The point of this is that the play was considered quite unsuitable for children, and even for most adults, having as its central figure a woman of doubtful morals. Mrs Campbell struck W. Graham Robertson as 'almost painfully thin, with great eyes and slow haunting utterance; she was not exactly beautiful, but intensely interesting and arresting' (Robertson, p.248). In the 1890s and early years of the new century she was a reigning society beauty, famous for her biting wit. The part of Eliza Doolittle in Shaw's *Pygmalion* (1914) was written for her.

Solomon showed regularly at the Royal Academy between 1881 and 1904, interspersing portraits with a number of subject pictures. In composition and palette this work consciously echoes Reynolds's 'Mrs Siddons as the Tragic Muse' (no.37) – even to the dark, bitumenous browns which have developed cracquelure almost worthy of a Reynolds. The grand manner chiaroscuro of Reynolds's great picture is here transformed into the theatrical lighting of a high moment in Pinero's play. Solomon's intention in painting the picture was presumably to capitalise on the sensational success of both play and actress, but he does not seem to have sold it, either at the time of the Academy exhibition in 1894 or later. In due course, but at an unknown date, he presented it to the Arts Club where it now hangs.

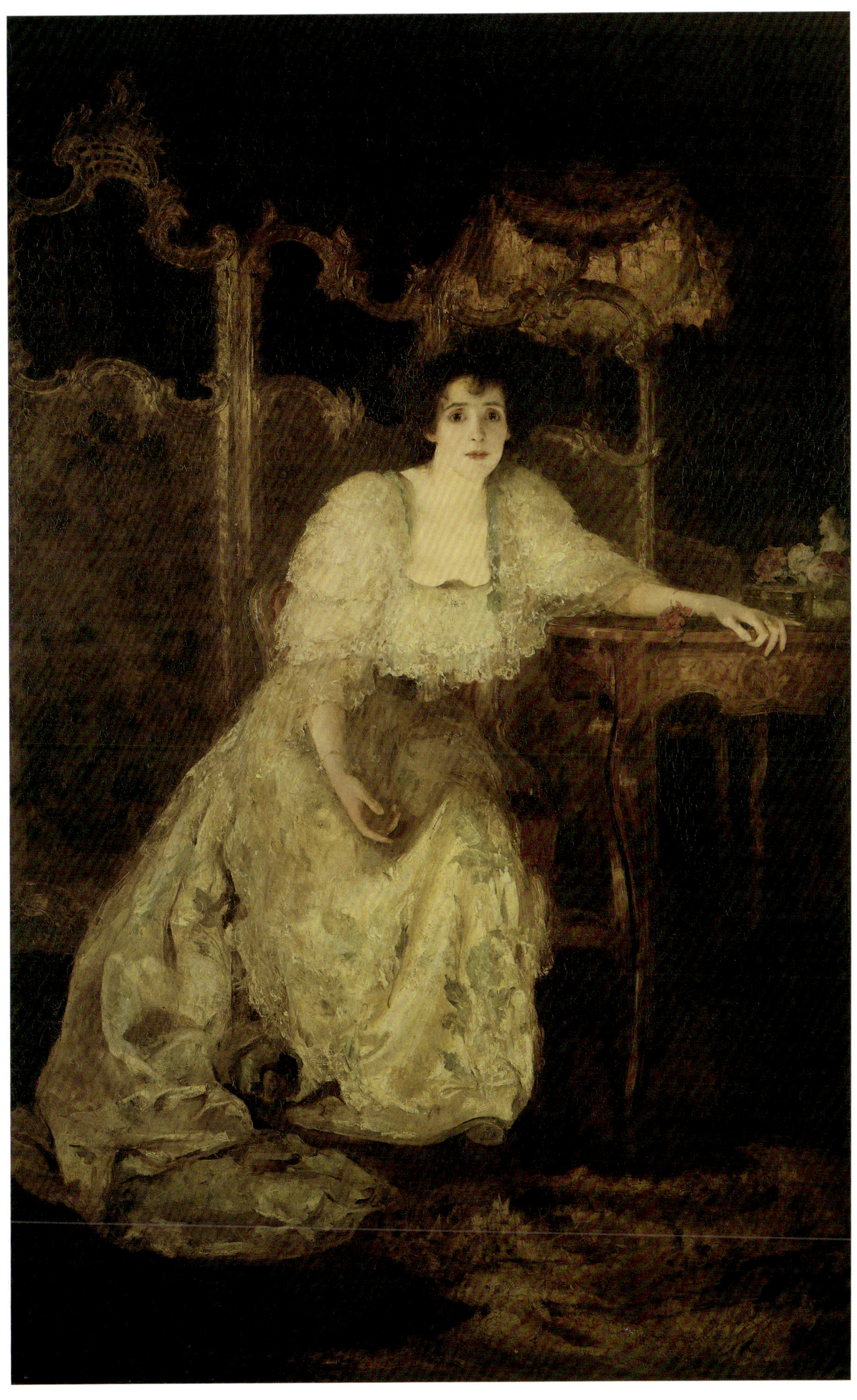

GIOVANNI BOLDINI 1842–1931

72 **Lady Colin Campbell** *c.*1897

Oil on canvas 182.2 × 117.5 ($71\frac{3}{4} \times 46\frac{1}{4}$)
Inscr. Lower right: *Boldini*
National Portrait Gallery

Boldini came from Ferrara in Italy. His career paralleled Sargent's: he studied in Florence and Paris, and worked for a time in London. In the 1890s, while Sargent was the leading society portrait painter in London, Boldini held the same position in Paris, where he occupied Sargent's former studio in the Boulevard Berthier. It was with pictures like this, and perhaps most of all with his celebrated portrait of Consuelo Vanderbilt, Duchess of Marlborough, and her son, Lord Ivor Spencer-Churchill (fig.38 on p.196; Metropolitan Museum of Art), that Boldini earned for himself Sickert's famous accolade describing him as the 'non pareil parent of the wriggle and chiffon school of portraiture'. His sinuous, writhing brushstrokes and outrageous distortions in the interest of extreme slimness and elegance take on the form of what amounts to a parody of Sargent's manner, and indeed of the whole notion of the society portrait. His work is perhaps closer to fashion illustration than to portraiture proper, though it is more accurate to say that he inspired the fashion draughtsmen than that he was influenced by them. The exaggerated stylishness is very un-English; a French equivalent is to be found in the work of Paul César Helleu (1859–1927).

It was in 1881 that the twenty-three-year-old Gertrude Elizabeth Blood married Lord Colin Campbell, the youngest son of the 8th Duke of Argyll and Member of Parliament for Argyllshire. Their marriage ended five years later in a notorious divorce case, a *cause* exceptionally *célèbre*. During the course of the trial, Lady Colin sat several times to Whistler who rushed his work in order to finish before the trial verdict. It was shown at the Society of British Artists' exhibition of 1886–7 amid calls for its removal on account of the scandal attaching to the sitter. At the trial, Lady Colin had alleged cruel mistreatment by her husband, and accused him of adultery with the parlourmaid. He countered by taking out a petition for adultery against her, naming no less than three co-respondents. To be proved adulterous on two separate counts carried with it the stigma of common prostitution, and although she was not convicted the slander stuck and she was ostracised. After 1895, when Lord Colin died, she was able, by the force of her charismatic personality, to regain something of her social standing. She served as art critic for the *Art Journal* and the *World*, and became editor of *The Ladies Field*, publishing in addition a number of books. She died in 1911, when this picture was given by her wish to the National Portrait Gallery.

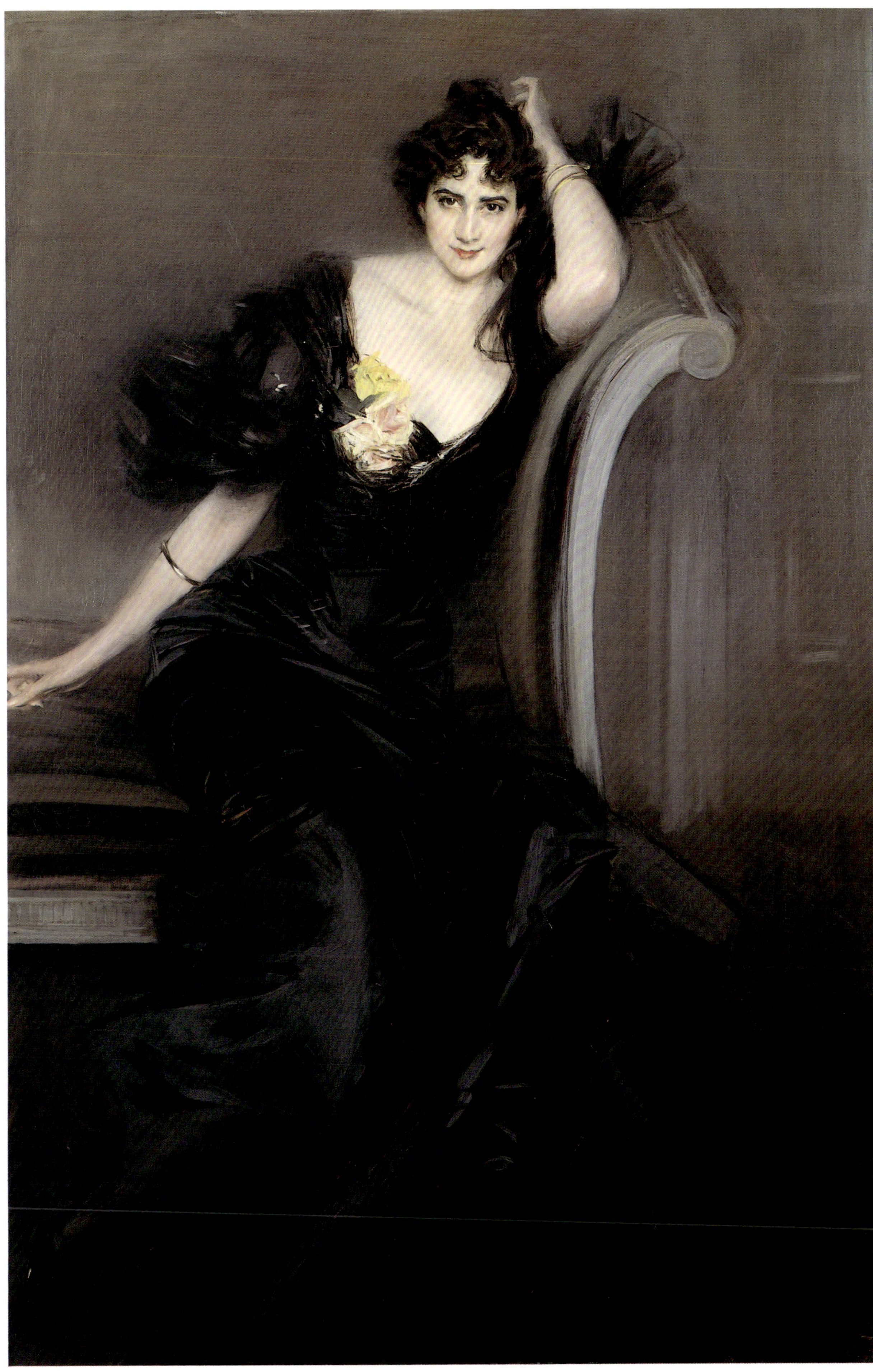

SIR WILLIAM ORPEN 1878–1931

73 **Mrs St George** *c.*1912

Oil on canvas 216 × 119.5 (85 × 47)
Inscr. (on folded edge of canvas): *Orpen*
Jefferson Smurfit Group plc

Howard Hugh St George and his wife commissioned their portraits from Orpen in 1906 but the costume here suggests that Mrs St George was not painted until a few years later. She was a New York heiress, daughter of the banker George Fisher Baker ('The Sphinx of Wall Street'), he a land agent from County Kilkenny. They had met in 1891 and married without Baker's approval. It appears to have been Mrs St George's ambition to gravitate from Irish society to that of London; her patronage of modern art was part of the delicate process of redefinition. Although Orpen was the first of his generation of Slade School students to achieve fame he was barely known in 1906, but Howard St George was a cousin and Orpen, who had known Mrs St George since about 1899, was often in Dublin, where he taught at the Metropolitan School of Art.

This portrait was begun as a three-quarter length, five feet high; a drawing records this composition. During the painting it was enlarged with extra canvas at the base to a full-length of relatively tall proportions. Mrs St George later had the size reduced; a photograph records considerable additional space below the feet and above the plumes of the hat, which were both later repainted by Orpen. At its full length the picture was almost a caricature of the slim Edwardian lady, cylindrical like the best asparagus, the shoulders and bosom tapering up to the proudly held head, the whole figure of an immense height. The type is seen repeatedly in portraits by Whistler, Walter Greaves (1846–1930), Lavery and James Guthrie (1859–1930). Orpen went further in exaggerating the height by means of the background drapery which falls in deep folds reflecting light so sharply that it seems striped, giving an even more astigmatic perspective. The sitter was a tall woman – over six feet – and Orpen, it should be noted, was below average height – 'a young Irishman,' as William Rothenstein remembered him, 'small and shy', with 'grey eyes, thin rather sunken cheeks, and thick brown hair' (Rothenstein, p.333).

The subdued yet glittering palette was an old addiction of the school of Whistler, but it seems to have been Mrs St George's own idea to eschew primary colours here. The dull golds and greys are used here by Orpen to show off the sumptuousness of the costume and his own skill in coping with a variety of textures, though the paint is dry, not applied in fluid glazes like Whistler's. This dry application is a development from Manet, a hero of Orpen's. Advanced French painting of thirty years previously did not disdain the commissioned full length, although Orpen is more liberal in offering specific detail: Mrs St George glides towards us on her golden shoes, holding in her long kid gloves a rabbit fur coat, trimmed in black, over her chenil afternoon gown which is striped black and gold. Her fur boa is ornamented with a huge gold tassel, and she has pearl earrings, a long pearl necklace and ostrich plumes.

At about the time the portrait was painted Orpen and Mrs St George began a prolonged affair; her husband condoned it and their daughter, born in 1912, was brought up as a St George. After the affair became public in that year the couple were known as 'Jack and the Beanstalk'. This was the happiest period of Orpen's life. Mrs St George was his most encouraging patron, demanding pictures of herself and her family, and of the landscapes of their holidays in Ireland. The intimacy may well have been prompted by the connection established during the painting of the portrait; the effect of Mrs St George's striking looks on the painter is already evident enough. They parted in 1921, and Mrs St George died in 1935.

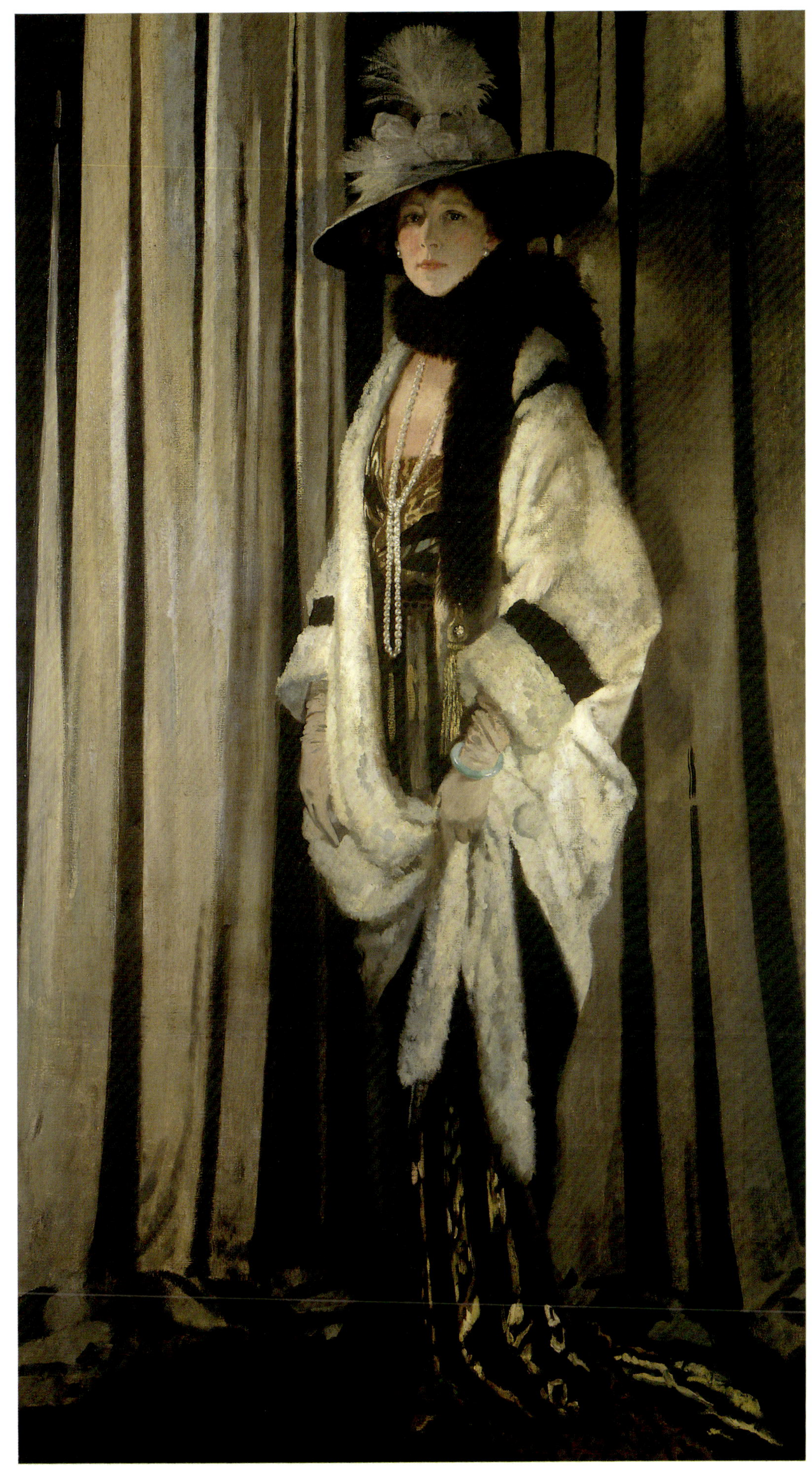

SIR WILLIAM ORPEN

74 **Lady Rocksavage** 1913

Oil on canvas 121.9 × 95.3 (48 × 37½)
Private Collection

Sybil Sassoon, whose long life extended from 1894 to 1989, married the Earl of Rocksavage, later Marquis of Cholmondeley, in 1913. Her father, Sir Edward Sassoon, was Chairman of the banking firm David Sassoon & Sons; he died in 1912. His two children, Sybil and her older brother Philip, both collected works of art (Sir Philip was later to be a distinguished Chairman of the Trustees of the National Gallery), and were interested in the young Orpen. He painted a small double portrait of brother and sister in an interior at Philip's house at 25 Park Lane (private collection); it was a portrait type that he took up from Sargent and made very much his own. This picture of Sybil alone was painted at the artist's request; it was bought by Sir Joseph Duveen who then presented it to the sitter. The picture helped to establish him as a leading painter of society portraits. In 1918 Sybil also bought, among other works by him, the large canvas of 'The Play Scene from Hamlet'. Sybil's pictures were to be added to the already fine collection at the Cholmondeley's Norfolk seat, Houghton Hall. It is for her restoration of Houghton, one of the most lavish yet responsible renovations of a great English country house, that she is perhaps best remembered.

The Sassoon and Cholmondeley portraits can be said to constitute a second generation of swagger, as Sybil's parents had given important commissions to Sargent, and Orpen inherited the connection. His amazing professionalism, his speed and perfect workmanship, all recommended him. He was also personally agreeable, a man of self-deprecatory whim, and a fund of jokes, and Lady Cholmondeley, along with many of his sitters, became a close friend.

Orpen looked to the Old Masters for his exemplars in matters of chiaroscuro, colour and tonal values; but he borrowed his sculptural lighting and ivory finish from the French academic painters of the last century. He was deliberate and businesslike in managing his profession, following procedures remarkably similar to those of the eighteenth century. He charged set fees for different sizes of canvas, and maintained a rapid turnover of work, without second thoughts, using repeated poses and with a researched schedule of clients. The resulting promptness of delivery of course appealed greatly to his patrons. He earned a stupendous income, equivalent at the beginnning of the war to about £200,000 annually today. The more brittle presentations by his successors Philpot, Kelly, Gunn and even Annigoni owed much to his example. Orpen's work is in general more varied than theirs, leavened by his sense of humour and his apparent ease with his subjects. He aimed to show his female sitters as embodying an ideal – albeit very much a current one – of beauty, combining perfect complexion, perfect features, restrained pose and expensive clothes. The relative simplicity of presentation here is lifted to a higher level by the suave assurance with which he offers us these components and by the harmonisation of fabrics – the dress is by Fortuny and is still at Houghton – in a 'symphony' that still owes much of its coherence to Whistler's example.

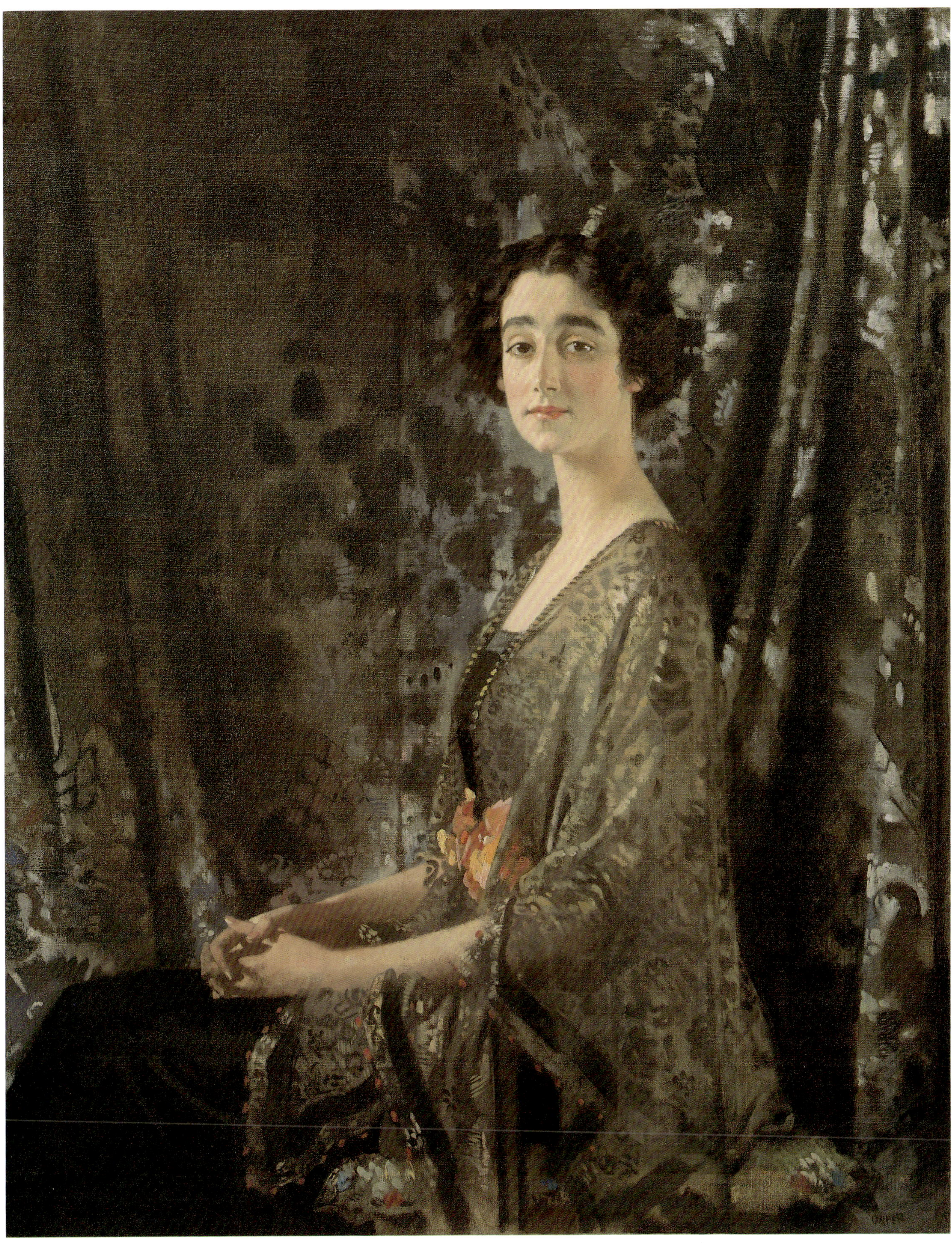

SIR JOHN LAVERY 1856–1941

75 **Hazel in Black and Gold** 1916

Oil on canvas 183.4 × 92.3 ($72\frac{1}{4} \times 36\frac{3}{8}$)
Inscr. lower right: *J Lavery*
Laing Art Gallery, Newcastle upon Tyne (Tyne and Wear Museums)

Lavery's early success was as a *plein-artiste* in the school of Jules Bastien-Lepage (1848–84), and his portraits as much as his genre scenes tended to be painted in bright outdoor light. In his later career he favoured interiors as the settings for his portraits; he sometimes reduced these to a plain black ground, placing against it a single full-length female figure. These, like the pictures by Whistler that they recall, were painted as imaginative works in their own right, only incidentally functioning as portraits; they were not executed on commission, and were subsequently exhibited for sale. The work would not be eligible for inclusion here, however, if Lavery had not specified in his title that the model, as with some other pictures in the series, is his wife. He had married Hazel Martyn, an American artist, in 1910, and she often sat to him; it has been suggested that the picture was a kind of celebration after she had recovered from a serious motor-car accident. But the identity of the sitter is secondary, for she and her clothes are used simply as the vehicle for a study in colour harmonies – the colours that one encounters in a Whistler nocturne. Lavery combines the influence of Whistler with that of Sargent, whose 'La Carmencita' (Paris, Musée d'Orsay) similarly shows a woman with hand on hip in a glittering dress against a dark ground; reviewers were also quick to spot connections with Velásquez. With all these influences very evident, and in its use of modish costume, the picture seems to sum up the mood of fashionable portraiture in the 1910s.

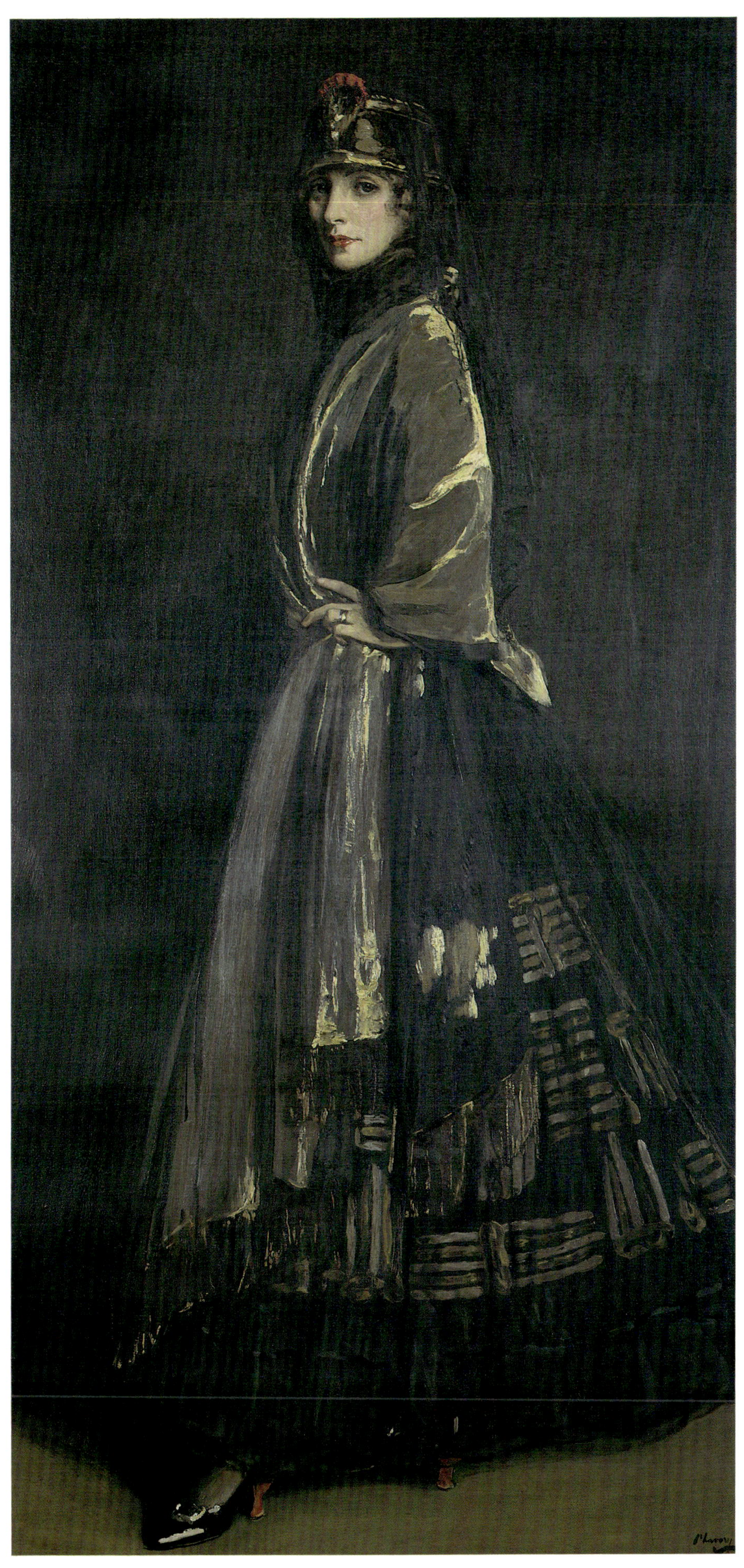

AUGUSTUS EDWIN JOHN 1878–1961

76 **William Nicholson** 1909

Oil on canvas 190 × 145.3 (75 × 57)
The Syndics of the Fitzwilliam Museum, Cambridge

John painted his slightly older and, at the time, more successful fellow artist as a speculation, on a large canvas he had been given by Nicholson himself. He may have intended to throw down the gauntlet to William Orpen (see nos.73–4) who had painted a group of the Nicholson family the year before, and had painted John himself in a similar pose in 1900. For this canvas, destined for the New English Art Club exhibition of 1909, John followed a simple compositional arrangement in which half the canvas above a diagonal cutting it in two contains nothing but the sitter's gloved hand. The device is worth comparing with Reynolds's equally striking use of the figure confined to one half of the design, in pictures like the 'Jane Halliday' at Waddesdon (fig.34 on p.134). This bold composition, and the low-keyed palette, also look back to the royal portraits of Velásquez. John may have agreed this approach beforehand with Nicholson, who cultivated a grand and distinguished manner, and with whom he shared a lively sense of humour. Despite wearing an overcoat (with upturned collar), Nicholson has both his hands balanced on pictures, while his cane rests at an acute angle and he seems to hold his breath and stare in alarm. The pictues he is studying are evidently by John himself.

There is a further, perhaps more important reason for John's choice of a vaguely Spanish style for this picture, although it was only one of his Old Master manners. It was the favoured style of Nicholson himself, whose work through most of his career was dominated by the use of succulent impasto and rich dark colour. The influence of Velásquez on English portraiture can be traced back to the early nineteenth century, when David Wilkie and others went to Spain and encountered his work for the first time in quantity. Millais, Sant and Sargent all paid tribute to him in their work, and he remained a model for much early twentieth-century portraiture. Early as it is in John's output, this canvas has been rated among his finest, 'wonderfully dandified and belligerent', as Michael Holroyd has described it. Certainly, with others of the same year, it set the standards for his career as portrait painter: ambitious, slightly scandalous yet old masterly, respectful of mind and character rather than social rank, and not too serious.

John himself when he entered the Slade in 1899 was an 'arresting figure; he looked like a young faun; he had beautiful eyes, almond-shaped and with lids defined like those Leonardo drew, a short nose, broad cheek-bones, while over a fine forehead fell thick brown hair, parted in the middle. He wore a light curling beard (he had never shaved) and his figure was lithe and elegant . . . he poured out compositions with extraordinary ease; he had the copiousness which goes with genius, and he himself had the eager understanding, the imagination, the readiness for intellectual and physical adventure one associates with genius. A dangerous breaker of hearts he would be' (Rothenstein, p.333).

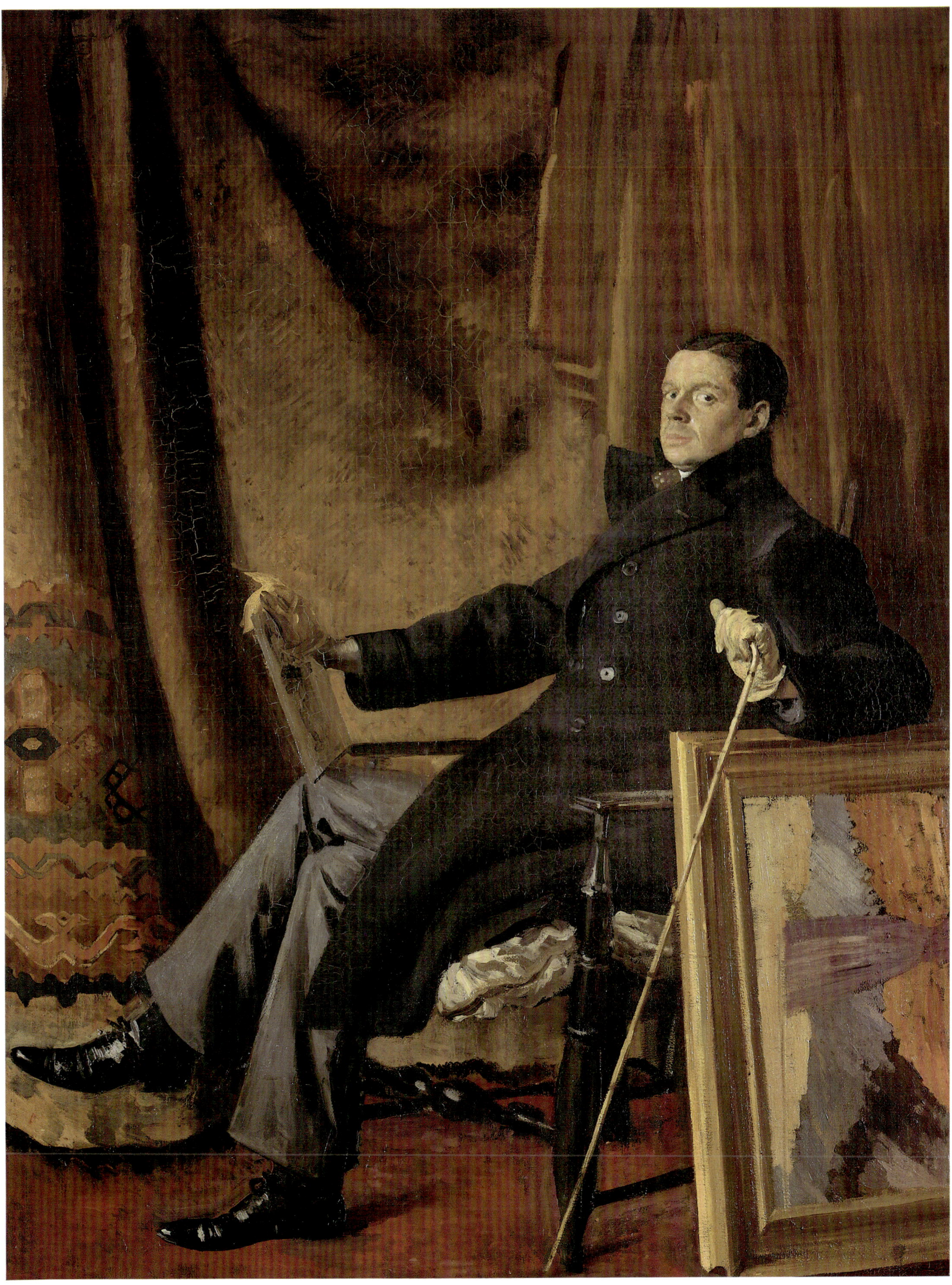

AUGUSTUS EDWIN JOHN

77 **Madame Suggia** 1920–3

Oil on canvas 186.7 × 165.1 ($73\frac{1}{2}$ × 65)
Tate Gallery. Presented by Lord Duveen through the National Arts Collection Fund 1925

The profile portrait is rare, especially as a full length, and has been thought unflattering as it sharpens the features. The two most astonishing nasal profiles in British art belong to the American Madame Gautreau, who posed for Sargent in Paris in 1883, and the Portuguese cellist Guilhermina Suggia, who posed, playing, for John in Chelsea over three years from 1920 to 1922. The intention of each was similar: to create a striking image, and to cause a stir that would promote both sitter and artist. Neither was a commission: both were painted for exhibition and sale.

John had succeeded Sargent before 1914 as the star portrait painter in London, and looked back to his example when in middle age, and after the revolutions of modern art, he sought to revive the scale and authority of the portraits of the *belle époque*. Just as Sargent had tried numerous provocative poses in working out the composition of 'Mme Gautreau' (exhibited at John's own London gallery, the Carfax, in 1909), so the sharp profile of Madame Suggia was arrived at only after many essays from more conventional viewpoints. There are pencil as well as oil studies, one of which showing the sitter in almost the final pose is in an English private collection.

Madame Suggia (1888–1950) was a pupil of Klenzel in Leipzig and later studied with Pablo Casals. At the time of John's portrait she was living in London, which she had made her professional base. She sat to John at his studio in Mallord Street. She was already well known, and at a time when women instrumentalists were still uncommon she attracted further notice by holding the cello between her knees, like a male player, and not in the 'side-saddle' position women were supposed to adopt. She practised during sittings, and committed an immense amount of time to them: she, as well as John, expected the portrait to bring fame. When first exhibited it was bought by an American and requested for the 1924 Pittsburgh International Exhibition where it won a first prize (John had been on the jury the year before). The following year the dealer Joseph Duveen, already a benefactor of the Tate, acquired the picture and gave it to the Gallery.

The loose handling of the cello and the red dress with its lengthy train gives the portrait the air of a rapid creation, flowing as swiftly and easily as the music, and with as subtle cross-rhythms. The reiterated V-shapes in the background drapery, the skirt and even the sitter's neck echo one another to create a unity which lends the work a powerful rhetoric. In fact John had great difficulty with many details of the design and the colour, which as usual with him seems to have been hit on by chance. In earlier versions Madame Suggia wore yellow-gold, then white. An oil sketch shows her in blue, with sequins. The red dress was made specially for the painting, and was even lengthened in the course of the sittings.

Many of John's best portraits are of writers or artists, and Suggia counts among these although he was not himself particularly fond of music. In such cases he would generally make the initial proposal, and his portraits of W.B. Yeats, James Joyce, W.H. Davies, George Bernard Shaw, Matthew Smith, Joseph Hone and Thomas Hardy suggest his imaginative involvement with those creative minds. He was no snob, but believed in a nobility of the arts, and hence that an ambitious scale was appropriate to a performer and interpreter like this outstanding cellist. In the end, although the picture ranks as perhaps the finest of all John's portraits, it is in a sense not a portrait at all, but a subject-picture, dealing with the nature of genius and the expressive power of art.

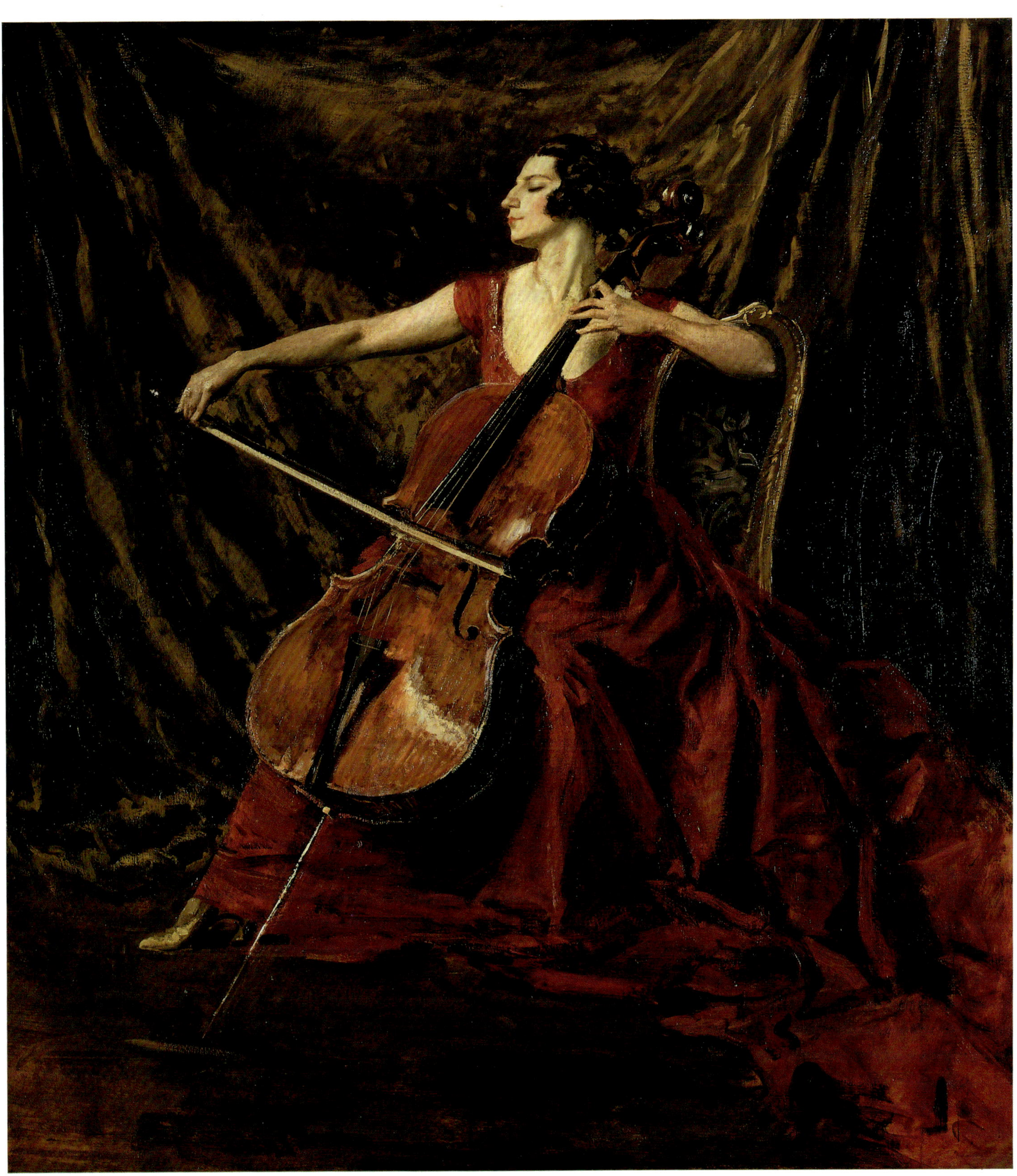

PHILIP ALEXIUS DE LASZLÓ 1869–1937

78 Countess Fitzwilliam, Wife of the 7th Earl Fitzwilliam 1911

Oil on canvas 243.9 × 119.4 (96 × 47)
Inscr. upper right: *PA László/1911/Wentworth*
The Trustees of the Rt Hon. Olive, Countess Fitzwilliam's Chattels Settlement, by permission of Lady Juliet de Chair

The 7th Countess Fitzwilliam was born Lady Maud Dundas, sister to the Marquis of Zetland who was Governor of Bengal, where the family fortunes had been amassed in the eighteenth century. The embroidered gown and drapery that she is here shown wearing were acquired on one of her periodic visits to her brother in India. De Lazsló's instinctive facility in the presentation of his sitters as glamorous and fashionable is unmistakably un-English. He was Hungarian by birth and trained in Budapest, at the National Academy of Arts, before working in Paris, Munich and Dresden. His approach to portraiture was thus formed on the Continent of Europe, and he brought to England qualities that enabled him easily to step into Sargent's shoes.

This picture was painted at the Fitzwilliam family seat, Wentworth Woodhouse in Yorkshire, where the splendid collection of British and Contintental pictures, begun in the eighteenth century, hung until the house was sold in the 1950s. De Laszló's sitter's book indicates that work on the portrait was begun on 18 October 1911; it was apparently finished in the following month. This is one of the most characterful of his female portraits, conveying at once the vitality of the sitter and her unforced authority. The influence of Van Dyck is evident, but the artist's early facility can be appreciated here separately from the tendency to ape Sargent's manner which increasingly affected his style, especially after the older artist's death in 1925. In 1911 the new fashion for hobble skirts had recently modified the line of women's clothes to something distinctly less flowing than the S-bend styles of the Edwardian years (the fashion of an intermediate phase is to be seen in Orpen's portrait of Mrs St George, no.73), and the curious rhythms of this canvas, characteristic of this moment, are dictated by that circumstance. In 1912, the year after this picture, de Laszló painted a portrait sketch of the Countess's son, Viscount Milton, at the age of two.

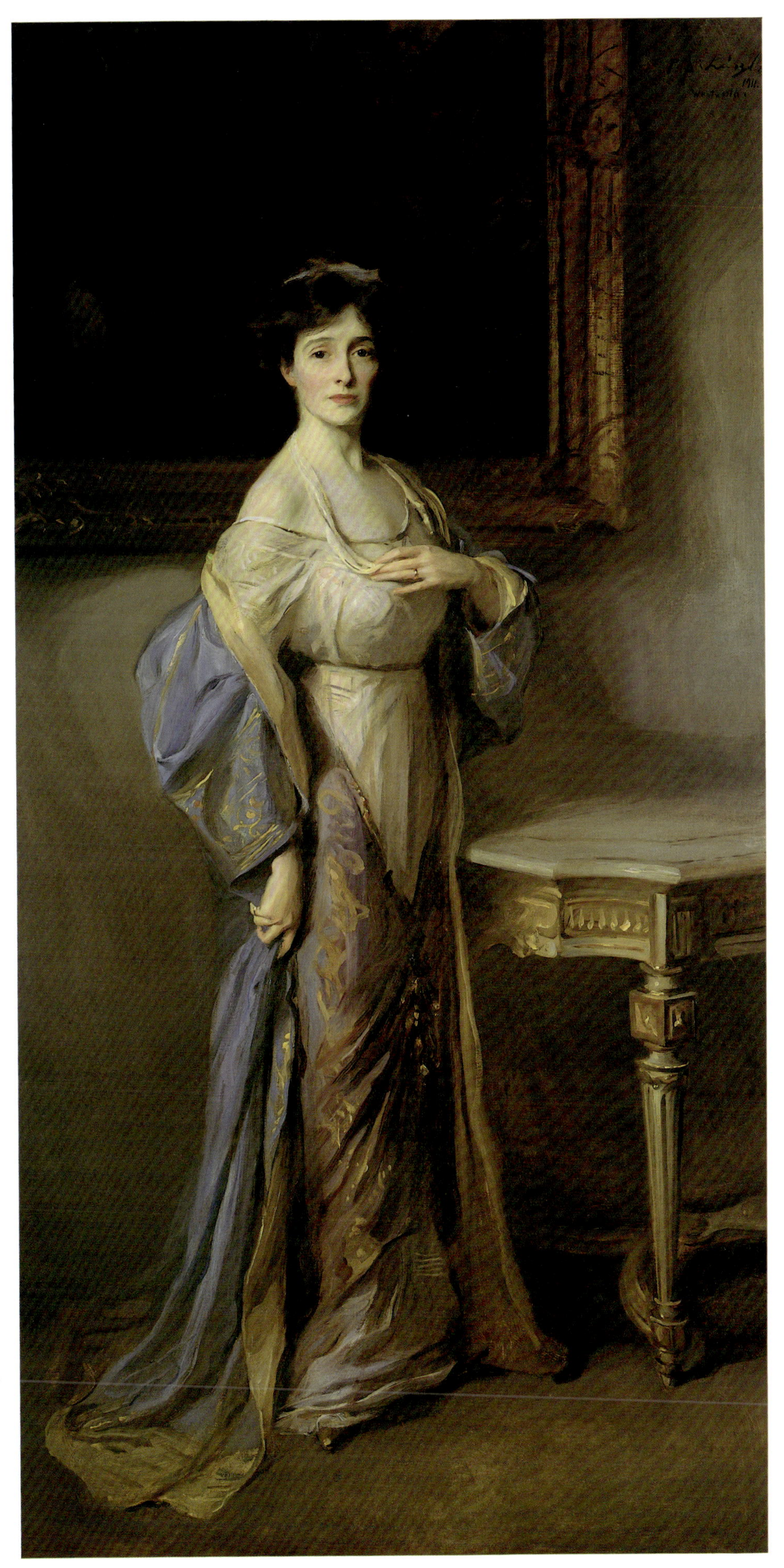

79 Archbishop Randall Davidson 1926

Oil on canvas 251.5 × 139.7 (99 × 55)
Inscr. lower right *de Laszló/ Lambeth Palace 1926*
The Corporation of the Church House

Davidson was Archbishop of Canterbury from 1903 to 1928; he had previously been Bishop of Rochester (1891–95) and of Winchester (1895–1903). De Laszló's sitter's book notes that sittings began on 20 May 1926. 'My aim,' he wrote, 'was to express in the portrait the high office which he held, in all its picturesqueness, and at the same time to portray himself, and all that he stood for – his alert expression, his vigorous personality, the fighter for the freedom of the Church, not the dreamer but the man of action.' (Rutter, p.362)

Davidson was a moderate, ecumenical Archbishop, a far from flamboyant figure, with a strong Scottish Presbyterian background, who did much to bring together the disputing sections of the Church into something like a peaceful communion, though he retired, after a quarter of a century at Canterbury, during the heated debates that preceded the final ratification of the revised Prayer Book of 1928. An early biogapher epitomised him as 'a strong man, sincere, steadfast, perhaps limited in sympathy, certainly incapable of always understanding the significance of novel movements and unusual demands, but never failing in his eagerness to serve the nation and the Church' (Dark, p.vii). De Laszló's own perception of him seems to corroborate this assessment: 'I do not think the Archbishop is blessed with great imagination, but he is an honest man, conscious of his responsibilities, thorough and business-like, the best type of Scotsman – rather dry, nearer materialism than idealism, cautious and well balanced' (Rutter, p.362).

These comments suggest that the artist enjoyed the ironically dramatic treatment he gave the Archibishop. The Primate himself, he records, was afraid the picture would be 'too artificial', and worried that the size of the picture would be 'too showy'. This is one of de Laszló's grandest works, and surely one of the most flamboyant of all British ecclesiastical portraits. It is curious but perhaps no accident that de Laszló, a portrait painter known particularly for his stylishness, enjoyed many commissions from the Church of England in the 1920s. The idea of showing the Primate enthroned is, of course, in the best tradition of state portraiture, and as such the picture is important in the history of the ecclesiastical portrait. Its sheer scale is unusual, as is the baroque sweep of the drapery and the theatrical presentation. According to de Laszló, the throne is 'a Gothic chair, formerly used by the late Archbishop Tate at the coronation of Queen Victoria, and by Dr Davidson at the coronations of Edward VII and George V'. He added rather surprisingly, 'I could have chosen a more picturesque chair, and at first intended to use one of my own red Renaissance chairs, but finally decided to have this one, on account of its great historical importance' (Rutter, p.361). The echoes of Reynolds's 'Mrs Siddons as the Tragic Muse' (no.37) are perhaps accidental, although de Laszló cannot have been unaware of that picture. The reference, intentional or not, reinforces the irony inherent in the portrayal of an Anglican primate in this way. But it is also a reflection of an entirely apt theatricality that is intrinsic to the Archbishop's role.

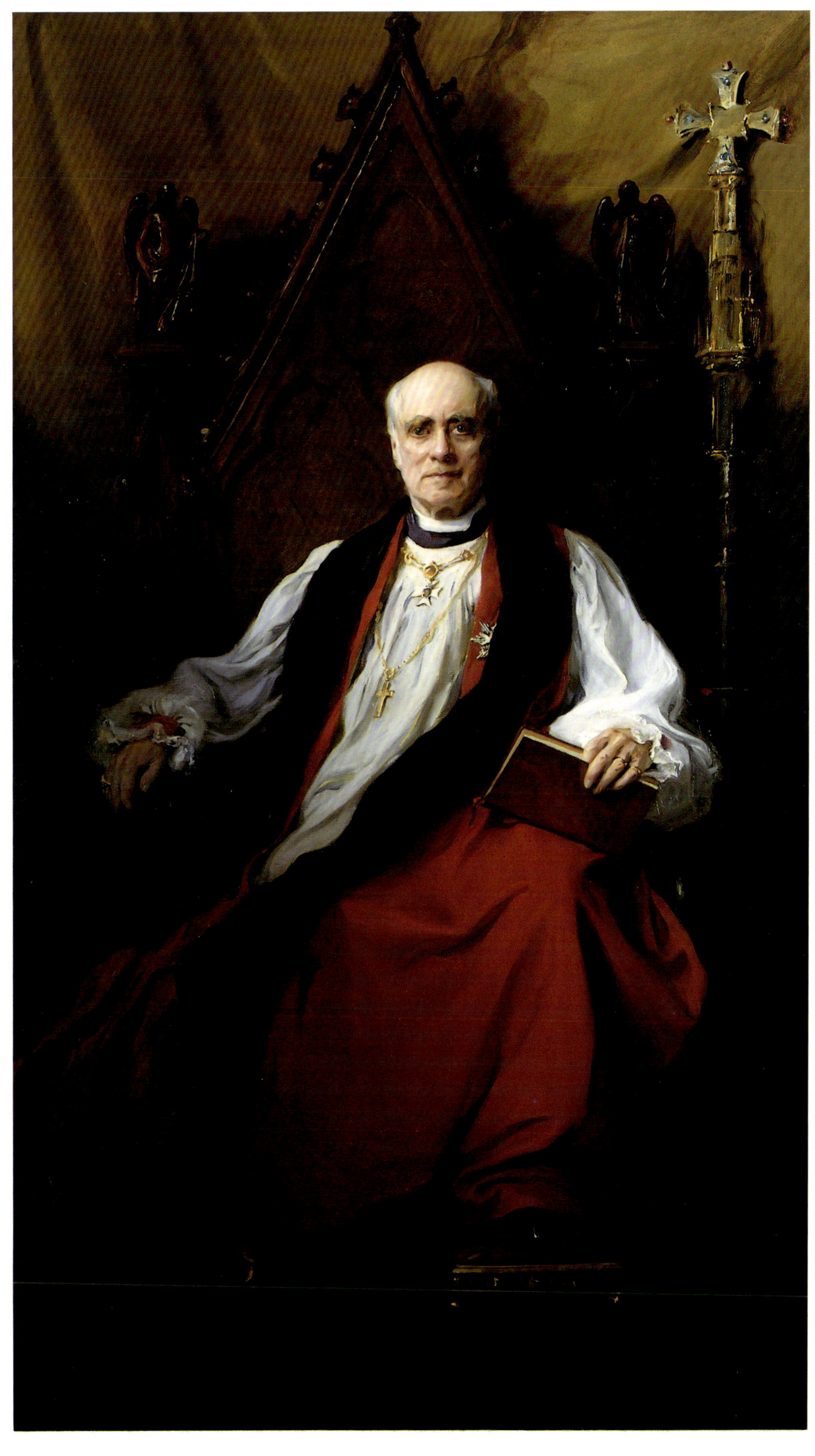

Bibliography

All books published in London unless otherwise stated

The Age of Charles II, Winter exh. cat., Royal Academy 1960–1

Archer, Mildred, *India and British Portraiture 1770–1825*, Oxford 1979

Arnold, Bruce, *Orpen: Mirror to an Age*, 1981

Ashton, Geoffrey, *Catalogue of the Garrick Club Collection* (forthcoming)

Baker, C.H. Collins, *Lely and Kneller*, 1922

Barrell, John, *The Political Theory of Painting from Reynolds to Hazlitt 'The Body of the Public'*, New Haven and London 1986

Beckett, R.B., *Lely*, 1951

Bindman, David, *Hogarth*, 1981

The British Face: A View of Portraiture 1625–1850, exh. cat., P. & D. Colnaghi & Co. Ltd 1986

Brown, Christopher, *Van Dyck*, Oxford 1982

Buckeridge, Bainbrigge, *An Essay towards an English School of Painting* (1706) 1969

Burke's Peerage, 102nd ed., 1959

Cannon-Brookes, Peter, (ed.), *Paintings from Tabley*, exh. cat., Heim Gallery 1989

Caw, James L. (introduction), *Portraits by Sir Henry Raeburn*, Edinburgh 1909

Charteris, The Hon. Evan, *John Sargent*, 1927

Clark, Anthony M. in Edgar Peters Bowron (ed.), *Pompeo Batoni: A Complete Catalogue of his Wörks with an Introductory Text*, Oxford 1985

C[okayne], G.E. (ed.), *Complete Baronetage*, 5 vols., 1900–9; Microprint ed., Gloucester 1983

Cunningham, Allan, *The Lives of the most Eminent British Painters and Sculptors*, 5 vols., New York 1834

Dark, Sidney, *Archbishop Davidson and the English Church*, 1929

De Laszló, Philip, *Painting a Portrait, Recorded by A.L. Baldry*, London and New York 1934

Dictionary of National Biography

Einberg, Elizabeth, *Manners and Morals: Hogarth and British Painting 1700–1760*, exh. cat., Tate Gallery 1987

Emmons, Robert, *The Life and Opinions of Walter Richard Sickert*, 1941

Farington, Joseph, *Diary*, ed. Kenneth Garlick and Angus Mackintyre, and Kathryn Cave, 16 vols., New Haven and London 1979–84

Fothergill, Brian, *The Mitred Earl, an Eighteenth-Century Eccentric*, 1974

Fry, Roger, *Reflections on British Painting*, 1934

Garlick, Kenneth, *Sir Thomas Lawrence: A Complete Catalogue of the Oil Paintings*, Oxford 1989

Gaunt, William, *Court Painting in England from Tudor to Victorian Times*, London 1980

Gibson, Robin, *Catalogue of Portraits in the Collection of the Earl of Clarendon* (privately published) 1977

Haskell, Francis and Nicholas Penny, *Taste and the Antique: The Lure of Classical Sculpture 1500–1900*, New Haven and London 1981

Hayes, John, *Thomas Gainsborough*, exh. cat., Tate Gallery 1980

Hayes, John, *The Portrait in British Art*, exh. cat., National Portrait Gallery 1991

Hazlitt, William, *The Conversations of James Northcote Esq., R.A.*, 2 vols., 1830, ed. Frank Swinnerton 1949

Hickey, William, *Memoirs*, ed. Peter Quennell, 1984

Highfill, Philip H., Jnr., Kalman A. Burnim and Edmund A. Langhans, *A Biographical Dictionary of . . . Stage Personnel in London 1660–1800*, 16 vols. (2 forthcoming), Carbondale 1973–

Hogarth, William, *The Analysis of Beauty, with the Rejected Passages from the Manuscript Drafts and Autobiographical Notes*, ed. Joseph Burke, Oxford 1955

Horsley, J.C., *Recollections of a Royal Academician*, 1903

Hume, David, *A Treatise of Human Nature* (1739) Oxford 1833

Ingamells, John, *The English Episcopal Portrait 1559–1835* (privately published) 1981

Johnson, Edward Mead, *Francis Cotes: Complete Edition with a Critical Essay and a Catalogue*, Oxford 1976

Judson, J. R., *Gerrit van Honthorst: A Discussion of his Position in Dutch Art*, The Hague 1959

Kerslake, John, *National Portrait Gallery: Early Georgian Portraits*, 2 vols., 1977

Knowles, John, *The Life and Writings of Henry Fuseli, Esq. M.A. R.A.*, 3 vols., 1831

Konody, P.G., and Sidney Dark, *Sir William Orpen* 1932

Larsen, Eric, *L'Opera Completa di Van Dyck 1626–1641*, Milan 1980

Leslie, Charles Robert, *Autobiographical Recollections*, ed. Tom Taylor, 2 vols., 1860

Leslie, Charles Robert and Tom Taylor, *The Life and Times of Joshua Reynolds*, 2 vols., 1865

Lewis, W.S., and others, *The Yale Edition of Horace Walpole's Correspondence*, 48 vols, New Haven and Oxford 1937–83

Lockhart, J.G., *Life of Sir Walter Scott*, library ed., 2 vols. 1878

Maas, Jeremy, *Victorian Painters*, 1969, new ed., New York 1988

Macaulay, Lord, *The History of England from the Accession of James II* 2 vols., popular ed. 1906

McConkey, Kenneth, *Sir John Lavery R.A. 1856–1941*, exh. cat., Ulster Museum Belfast and Fine Art Society 1984

McConkey, Kenneth, *Edwardian Portraits: Images of an Age of Opulence*, 1987

Mackintosh, Iain, assisted by Geoffrey Ashton, *The Georgian Playhouse*, exh. cat., Hayward Gallery 1975

Macmillan, Duncan, *Painting in Scotland: The Golden Age*, exh. cat., Edinburgh, Talbot Rice Art Centre and London, Tate Gallery (Oxford) 1986

Malone, Edmund (ed.), *The Works of Sir Joshua Reynolds, Knight*, 3 vols., 3rd ed. 1801

Mannings, David, Review of Renate Prochno, *Joshua Reynolds*, in *Burlington Magazine*, March 1992, p.192

Matyjaszkiewicz, Krystyna (ed.), *James Tissot*, exh. cat., Barbican Art Gallery 1984

Miles, Ellen G., *Thomas Hudson 1701–1779, Portrait-Painter and Collector*, exh. cat., Kenwood 1979

Millais, John Guille, *The Life and Letters of Sir John Everett Millais, P.R.A.*, 2 vols. 1899

Millais, PRB, PRA, exh. cat., Royal Academy of Arts, 1967

Millar, Oliver, *The Later Georgian Pictures in the Collection of Her Majesty The Queen*, 2 vols., Oxford 1969

Millar, Oliver, *The Age of Charles I: Painting in England 1620–1649*, exh. cat., Tate Gallery 1972

Millar, Oliver, *Sir Peter Lely 1618–80*, exh. cat., National Portrait Gallery 1978

Millar, Oliver, *Van Dyck in England*, exh. cat., National Portrait Gallery 1982

Newall, Christopher, *The Art of Lord Leighton*, Oxford and New York 1990

Nisser, Wilhelm, *Michael Dahl and the Contemporary Swedish School of Painting*, Uppsala 1927

Northcote, James, *The Life of Sir Joshua Reynolds*, 2 vols., 1818

Olson, Stanley, *John Singer Sargent: His Portrait*, 1986

Orgel, Stephen, and Roy Strong, *Inigo Jones: The Theatre of the Stuart Court*, 2 vols., University of California 1973

Ormond, Richard, *John Singer Sargent: Paintings Drawings Watercolours*, 1970

Ormond, Richard, *National Portrait Gallery: Early Victorian Portraits*, 2 vols., 1973

Ormond, Richard, and Carol Blackett-Ord, *Franz Xaver Winterhalter and the Courts of Europe 1830–70*, exh. cat., National Portrait Gallery 1987

William Orpen: A Centenary Exhibition, exh. cat., National Gallery of Ireland, Dublin 1978

Pepys, Samuel, *Diary and Correspondence*, ed. Lord Richard Braybrooke, 4 vols., 1858

Piper, David, *The English Face*, 1957 rev. ed. 1992

Pilkington, M., *A Dictionary of Painters from the Revival of the Art to the Present Period*, 1770, rev. ed. (by Fuseli) 1810

Pinnington, Edward, *Sir Henry Raeburn, R.A.*, 1904

Richardson, Jonathan, *Essay on the Theory of Painting*, 1715, new ed. 1773

Robertson, W. Graham, *Time Was*, 1931

Rogers, Malcolm, 'The Meaning of Van Dyck's Portrait of Sir John Suckling', *Burlington Magazine*, Nov. 1978, pp. 741–5

Rogers, Malcolm, *John Closterman, Master of the English Baroque*, exh. cat., National Portrait Gallery 1981

Rogers, Malcolm, 'John and John Baptist Closterman: A Catalogue of their Works', *Walpole Society*, vol. XLIX, 1983, pp.224–76

Rogers, Malcolm, *William Dobson 1611–46*, exh. cat., National Portrait Gallery 1983

Rothenstein, William, *Men and Memories*, Cambridge 1931

Rutter, Owen, *Portrait of a Painter: The Authorized Life of Philip de Laszlo*, 1939

Sackville-West, Vita, *Knole and the Sackvilles*, 1922, new ed. 1991

Shaftesbury, Earl of, *Characteristicks of Men, Manners, Opinions, Times*, 1711

Shaftesbury, Earl of, *Second Characters, or, the Language of Forms*, ed. Benjamin Rand, Cambridge 1914

Shawe-Taylor, Desmond, *The Georgians: Eighteenth-Century Portraiture and Society*, 1990

Simpson, Percy, and C.F. Bell, *Designs by Inigo Jones for Masques and Plays at Court*, Oxford 1924

Smart, Alastair, *The Life and Art of Allan Ramsay*, 1952

Solkin, David, 'Great Pictures or Great Men? Reynolds, Male Portraiture and the Power of Art', *Oxford Art Journal*, vol.9, no.2, 1986, pp.42–9

Stewart, J. Douglas, *Sir Godfrey Kneller and the English Baroque Portrait*, Oxford 1983

Strong, Sir Roy, and others, *The British Portrait*, Woodbridge 1991

Treasures of Fyvie, exh. cat., Scottish National Portrait Gallery 1985

Vertue, George, 'Note Books', *Walpole Society*, vol.XVIII, 1930; vol.XX, 1932; vol.XXII, 1934; vol.XXIV, 1936; vol.XXVI, 1938; vol.XXX, 1955

Walpole, Horace, *Anecdotes of Painting in England, with some Account of the Principal Artists*, rev. ed., Ralph N. Wornum, 3 vols., 1888

Wark, Robert R., *Ten British Pictures 1740–1840*, San Marino 1971

Wark, Robert R., ed., *Sir Joshua Reynolds, Discourses on Art*, New Haven and London 1975

Waterhouse, Ellis, *Painting in Britain 1530–1790*, Harmondsworth 1953

Waterhouse, Ellis, *Gainsborough*, 1958, new ed. 1966

Waterhouse, Ellis, *The Dictionary of 16th and 17th Century British Painters*, Woodbridge 1988

Watts, M.S., *George Frederick Watts, The Annals of an Artist's Life*, 2 vols., 1912

Wendorf, Richard, *The Elements of Life: Biography and Portrait-Painting in Stuart and Georgian England*, Oxford 1990

West, Shearer, 'The Half-History Portraits of Thomas Lawrence', *Art History*, vol.14, no.2, June 1991, pp.225–49

Whitley, W.T., *Art in England 1821–1837*, 1930

Williams, D.E., *The Life and Correspondence of Sir Thomas Lawrence, Kt.*, 2 vols., 1831

Biographical Details of Artists

BATONI, POMPEO

1708–1787

Born in Lucca in 1708, the son of a goldsmith. Trained first in his father's workshop before moving to Rome in 1727 to study painting under Sebastiano Conca. Influenced by Raphael and the Antique he initially became known as a painter of religious and historical subjects before turning to portraiture. Sitters included popes and princes of Europe but he was most popular among English visitors to Rome on the grand tour. Elected to the Accademia di S. Luca in 1741. Died 1787, probably in Rome.

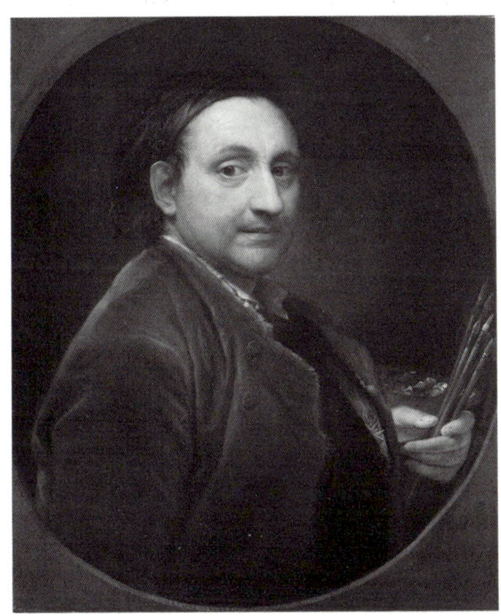

Pompeo Batoni **Self-Portrait** 1765 Oil on canvas *Bayerische Staatsgemäldesammlungen*

BEECHEY, SIR WILLIAM

1753–1839

Born in Burford, Oxfordshire, in 1753, Beechey came to London in 1774 and studied at the Royal Academy Schools under Zoffany. In Norwich between 1776 and 1787 he established a successful portrait practice, gradually increasing the scale of his canvases. Moved to London in 1787 and became portrait painter to Queen Charlotte in 1793, his sitters including the Royal Princesses and the King. Elected ARA 1793, RA in 1798, the year of his knighthood. Died at Hampstead in 1839.

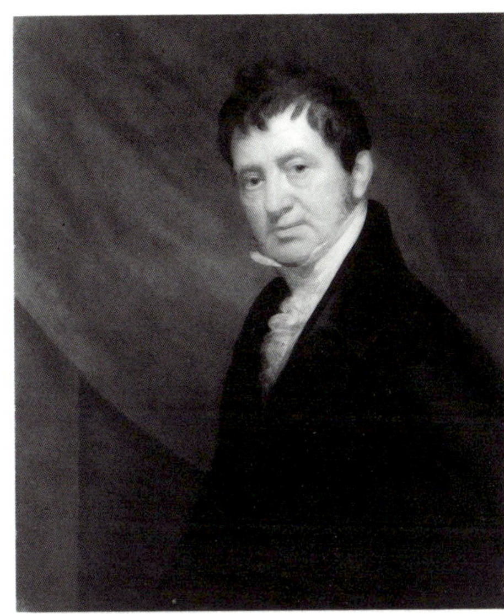

Sir William Beechey (finished by John Wood) **Self-Portrait** *c.*1836 Oil on canvas *National Portrait Gallery, London*

BOLDINI, GIOVANNI

1842–1931

The son of a painter and restorer, Boldini was born in Ferrara in 1842. Went to Florence in 1862 and worked at the Accademia delle Belle Arti. Associated with the radical Macchiaioli group. In 1867 he visited the *Exposition Universelle* in Paris and he moved there in 1871. First exhibited at the Salon in 1874 and went on to win numerous awards over the next two decades. In 1897 he travelled to the USA. Around this time he was becoming known as a society portrait painter, his sitters including the Infanta Eulalia of Spain, writers and actresses. Lived in Nice and London during the First World War. Returned to Paris in 1918, where he died in 1931.

CLOSTERMAN, JOHN

1660–1711

Born in Osnabrück, Germany in 1660. Received his initial training from his father. Studied for two years in Paris in the studio of the history painter and portraitist François de Troy before coming to England in 1681. Worked first as a drapery painter in partnership with the established portrait painter John Riley. Established his own practice by mid-1680s and was well known by the 1690s as a painter of middle-class intellectuals, with a particular talent for group portraits. Painted the Spanish Royal Family in Madrid on his way to Rome in 1698, returning to England in 1700. He seems to have stopped painting in 1706 and concentrated on a career as an art dealer and collector.

COPLEY, JOHN SINGLETON

1738–1815

A highly ambitious painter, born in Boston, Massachusetts in 1738, Copley established a lucrative portrait practice in his home town by the mid-1750s. Came to England in 1774 to gain experience,

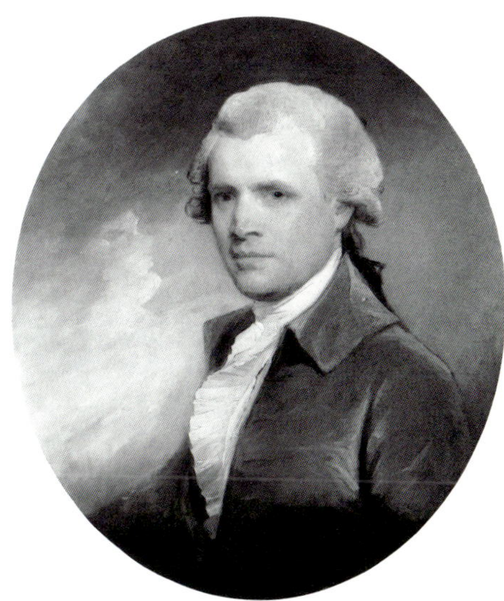

Gilbert Stuart **John Singleton Copley** *c.*1784 Oil on canvas *National Portrait Gallery, London*

encouraged by Reynolds who had seen one of his portraits at the Royal Academy. He travelled via Paris to Rome before settling in London in 1775 with his family who had by then fled the political unrest in Boston. Had some success in England painting portraits and scenes from recent history but never quite made the mark he had hoped, with few commissions from the nobility and the Royal Family. He became an ARA 1776 and full member in 1779 but was involved in controversy at the Academy in the 1790s which did little for his reputation. Suffered ill-health, loss of ability and financial difficulties in the fifteen years before his death in London in 1815.

COTES, FRANCIS
1726–1770

Cotes was born in London and went on to become one of the most important portrait painters of his day. He trained under Knapton in the 1740s and began producing portraits in pastel from *c.*1747. Over the next decade he moved into oil painting and produced his first portrait of the Royal Family in 1767. In the mid-1760s he shared the services of the drapery painter Peter Toms with Reynolds. In his numerous pastel portrait busts he was influenced by Liotard. Was primarily concerned with producing a good and elegant likeness of his sitter with little emphasis on character. Died in London in 1770.

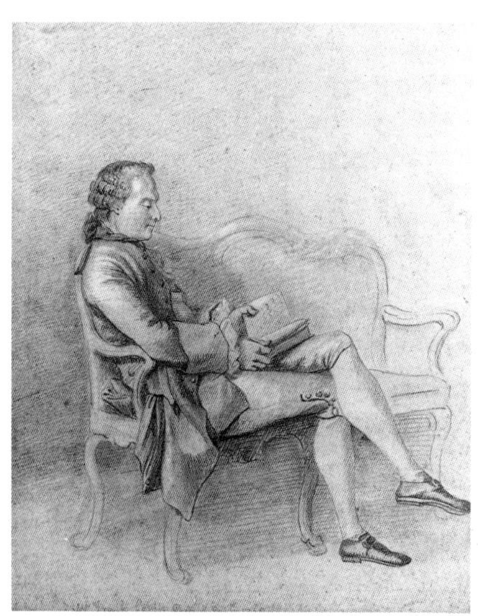

attributed to Paul Sandby **Francis Cotes** 1755 Pencil and chalk *Castle Museum and Art Gallery, Nottingham*

DOBSON, WILLIAM
1610/11–1646

Born in London in 1610/11, the son of the principal servant to Francis Bacon, Dobson was soon forced to find a career as his father frittered away the family fortune. Choosing to become an artist, he studied under William Peake, an engraver and dealer, and Francis Cleyn, a decorative painter and the designer of woven tapestries for Charles I at Mortlake. Dobson had access to the Royal Collection and was clearly influenced by Venetian and Netherlandish styles. Best known for his allegorical portraits, influenced by Cleyn. In 1642 he gained employment in the court set up by Charles I in Oxford during the Civil War, replacing Van Dyck as court painter. In 1646, following the collapse of the royalist cause, he returned to London where he fell into debt and was imprisoned. He was released shortly before his death in London in 1646.

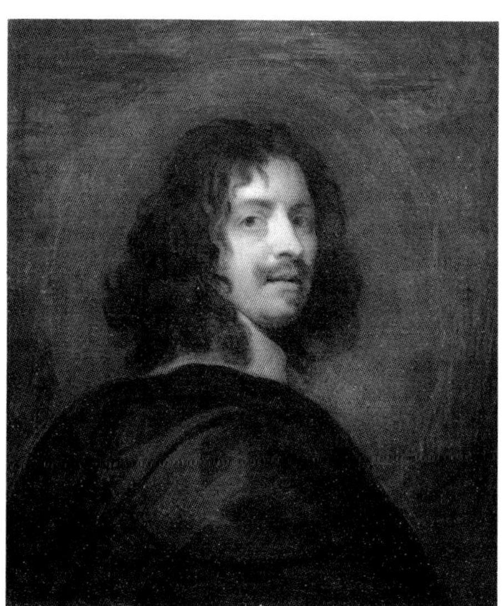

after William Dobson **Portrait of the Artist** *c.*1642–6 Oil on canvas *National Portrait Gallery, London*

GAINSBOROUGH, THOMAS
1727–1788

A child prodigy, Gainsborough was born in Sudbury, Suffolk in 1727 and was already working professionally at age thirteen. He studied at the St Martin's Lane Academy and under Hayman and Gravelot from 1740–8. He returned to Suffolk and made a living painting portraits in Ipswich from 1751/2 until 1759 when he moved to Bath, where he was an instant success. Although always devoted to the painting of landscape, he made his reputation and living as a fashionable portrait painter. He visited London annually, exhibiting at the Society of Artists, and moved there in 1774. His portrait practice was second only to that of Reynolds, his greatest rival. Employed by the Royal Family from 1776. Unlike Reynolds, he was not interested in history painting but from around 1781 he developed a new style of fancy picture influenced by Murillo. In 1784 he quarrelled with the Royal Academy and ceased to exhibit there, using his studio instead. Died in London in 1788, and was eulogised by Reynolds in his Discourse to the Academy that year.

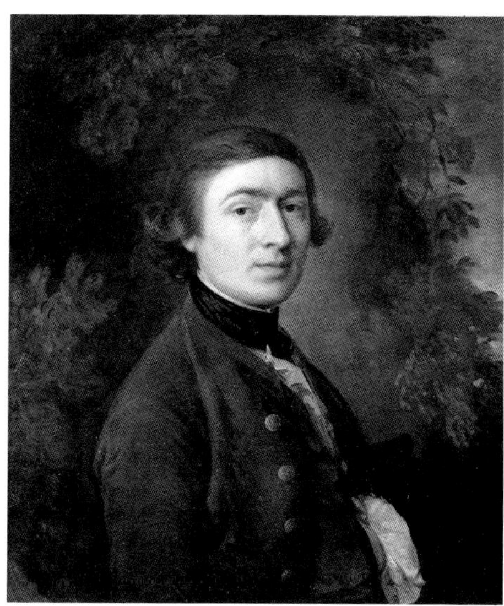

Thomas Gainsborough **Self-Portrait** *c.*1759 Oil on canvas *National Portrait Gallery, London*

GRANT, SIR FRANCIS
1803–1878

Despite receiving no artistic training, Grant went on to become one of the most successful portraitists of his time. Born at Kilgraston in Perthshire in 1803, he first began painting as an amateur. Turned to painting professionally after he had spent his inheritance. A keen hunter himself, he became known for his hunting scenes, and his portraits often include horses and dogs. His success was assured when Queen Victoria approved his painting of her riding at Windsor (exh. 1840). His success can partly be attributed to his high social connections and tendency to flatter his sitters. In 1866 he became President of the Royal Academy and was knighted. Died 1878 in Melton Mowbray.

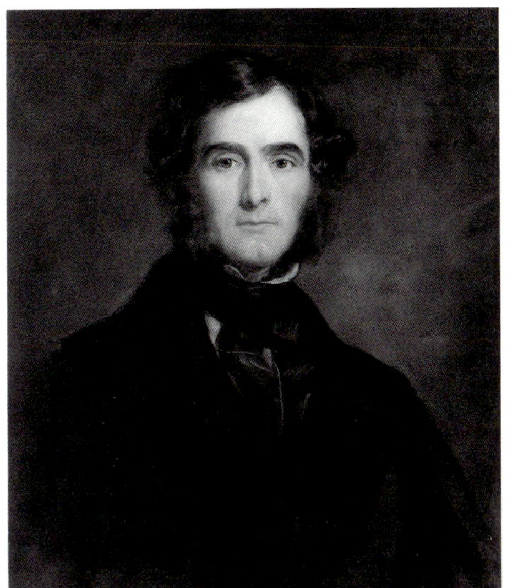

Sir Francis Grant **Self-Portrait** *c.*1845
Oil on canvas *National Portrait Gallery, London*

GRISONI, GIUSEPPE
1699–1769

Born Pierre Joseph Grison in Mons 1699, Grisoni went to Florence and trained as a pupil of Tommaso Redi. Met John Talman in Rome who persuaded him to come to England in *c.*1720. Painted a number of history paintings and portraits, including the 1st Earl of Macclesfield, but his main work was a ceiling at Canons, now destroyed. Most of his work was decorative, but there are several altarpieces in Florence and a number of portraits, some of them allegorical in style. Teacher of William Hoare, who accompanied him on his return to Italy in 1728. Died in Florence 1769.

HOGARTH, WILLIAM
1697–1764

Born in London in 1697, Hogarth was apprenticed to the engraver Ellis Gamble in 1713, studied at Vanderbank's Academy in 1720 and worked first as an engraver of satirical prints. From around 1728–9 he began painting seriously with a scene from *The Beggar's Opera*, moving on to conversation pieces and portraits. In 1732 he produced 'The Harlot's Progress', the first of his series of pictures on moral subjects. His engravings were as popular as his paintings and in 1735 he was instrumental in the passing of the Copyright Act to protect his prints from being copied. In 1734 he founded the Academy in St Martin's Lane, an anti-academic school of art. He encouraged artists to present works to the Foundling Hospital, established in 1746. By his death in London in 1764, Hogarth had failed in his ambition to become a great history painter like his father-in-law Sir James Thornhill but he had no rival in contemporary genre painting.

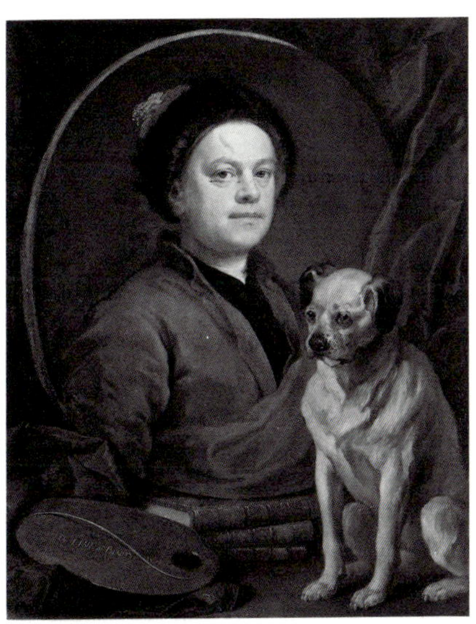

William Hogarth **The Painter and his Pug** 1745
Oil on canvas *Tate Gallery*

HUDSON, THOMAS
1701–1779

Born in Devon in 1701, Hudson trained under Jonathan Richardson, whose daughter he married in 1725. He divided his time between London and the West Country until 1740 when he settled permanently in London. He inherited many of Richardson's clients on his retirement in 1740. Influenced by the Baroque style of Van Dyck and Lely, Hudson also experimented in the manner of Rembrandt. His rather conservative approach appealed to older sitters and he became the most fashionable portraitist in London from 1742 until the return of Reynolds from Italy in 1753. He visited the Low Countries in 1748 and Italy in 1752. Taught Reynolds from 1740–3 and Joseph Wright of Derby in 1751. From 1751–7 he concentrated on large-scale group portraits, moving out to Twickenham in 1755. Produced very few paintings after 1760 and died in 1779.

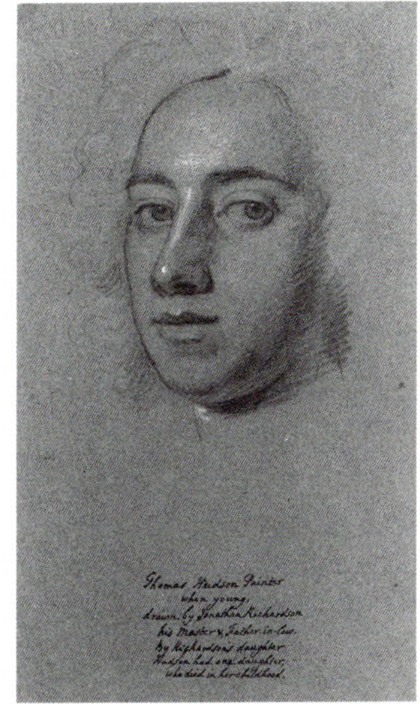

Jonathan Richardson **Thomas Hudson**
Chalk *Trustees of the British Museum*

HUYSMANS, JACOB
*c.*1633–*c.*1696

A Flemish painter of portraits, religious and historical subjects who came to England shortly after the Restoration. He was born in Antwerp in *c.*1633 and was apprenticed to Wouters in 1649 or 1650. Settled in London in 1662 and, as a Roman Catholic, found favour with the Queen, Catherine of Braganza. He worked in the grand Continental Baroque manner, packing his portraits with allegorical details. His popularity made him Lely's most serious rival. His later work includes a large number of portraits of children and some religious subjects. He died in London in *c.*1696.

JOHN, AUGUSTUS EDWIN
1878–1961

A flamboyant character with considerable technical skill, John was born in Tenby, South Wales in 1878 and came to London to study at the Slade from 1894–8. From

1899 he showed regularly with the New English Art Club. He taught at an art school in Liverpool from 1901–2 and from 1903–7 was co-principal of the Chelsea Art School with Orpen. In 1911 he was elected to the Camden Town Group. Visited Modigliani in Paris in 1913 and returned there in 1919 as an official war artist. Appointed a Trustee of the Tate Gallery in 1933. Died at Fordingbridge, Hampshire, in 1961.

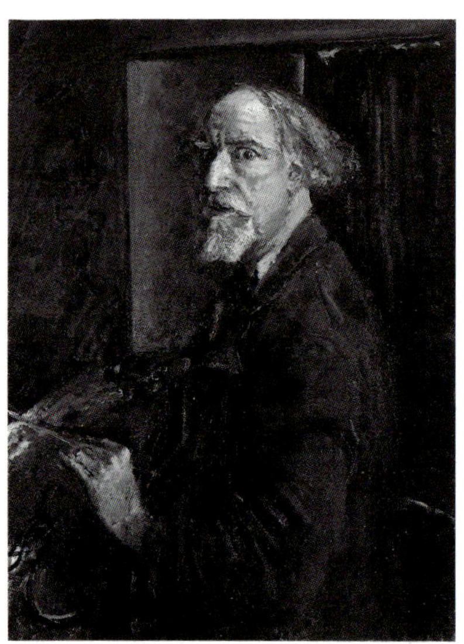

Augustus Edwin John **Self-Portrait** *c.*1935–45 Oil on canvas *The Metropolitan Museum of Art, Bequest of Stephen C. Clark, 1960*

KETTLE, TILLY
1734/5–1786

Kettle is probably best known for his portraits of the British ruling classes in India and of native princes and Nabobs. Born 1734/5 in London and trained at St Martin's Lane Academy, studying in the 3rd Duke of Richmond's Gallery, he had turned professional by *c.*1760. Travelled around the Midlands painting portraits from 1762–4 and established a busy portrait practice in London from 1764–9. His decision to set up business in India from 1769–76 made his fortune but he found few commissions on his return to England. Attempts to revive his career in Dublin and Brussels were unsuccessful and he died on his way back to India in 1786.

KNELLER, SIR GODFREY, BT
1646/9–1723

Born Gottfried Kniller in Lübeck, Germany. He was a pupil of Ferdinand Bol, and probably Rembrandt for a brief period in the 1660s. Spent 1672–5 in Rome and Venice, briefly returned to Lübeck and finally settled in England in 1676. Here he was highly successful and ran a huge studio producing replicas and copies. His high Baroque manner set the style for the next decade. Knighted in 1692 and made a Baronet by George I in 1715. In 1688 he was appointed principal painter to William and Mary, a post which he held jointly with Riley and continued to hold until his death in 1723. He was Governor of the first London Academy in 1711.

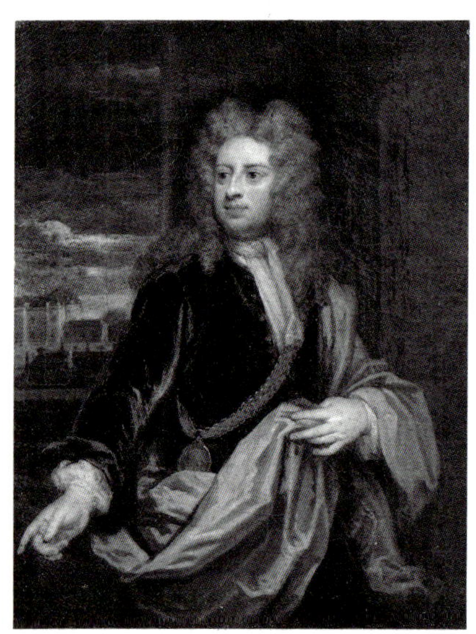

Studio of Sir Godfrey Kneller Bt **Sir Godfrey Kneller** *c.*1706–11 Oil on canvas *National Portrait Gallery, London*

LASZLO (DE LOMBOS), PHILIP ALEXIUS DE 1869–1937

One of the most fashionable artists working in the Austro-Hungarian Empire. De Laszló was born in Budapest and commenced his artistic training there. He went on to study at the Académie Julien in Paris and also in Munich. His skill at promoting himself and his art brought him considerable success. In 1900 he married into the Guinness family and began to find employment in England and Ireland. He moved to London in 1907 where he enjoyed success painting in a free style influenced by Sargent. Visited the USA in 1908 where his sitters included Roosevelt. Died in London 1937.

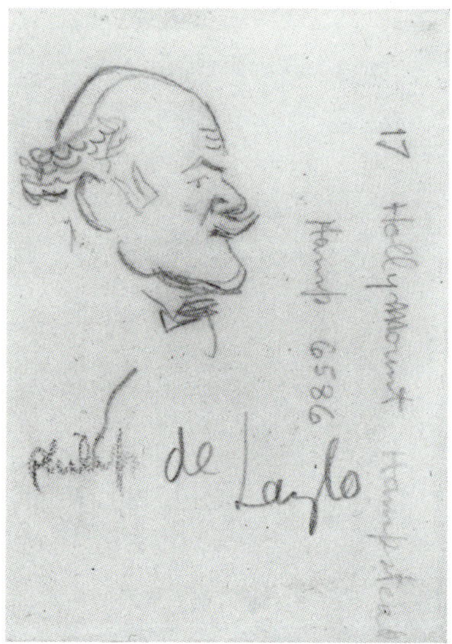

Sir David Low **Philip Alexius de Laszló de Lombos** Pencil *National Portrait Gallery, London*

LAVERY, SIR JOHN
1856–1941

Born in Belfast in 1856, Lavery first showed an interest in art around 1872. Moving to Glasgow in *c.*1874 he was apprenticed to J.B. MacNair, an artist photographer, before training at the Haldane Academy of Art. Set up his studio at Glasgow in 1878 and remained there until 1896, with brief interludes in London (at Heatherley's Art School) in

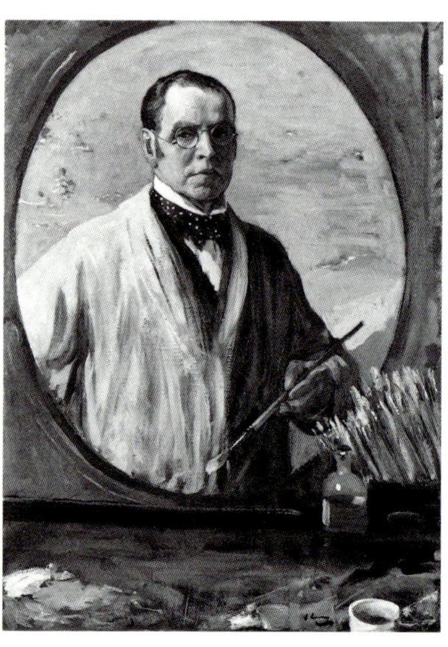

Sir John Lavery **Self-Portrait** 1928 Oil on canvas *Ulster Museum, Belfast*

1879 and in Europe in 1892. Moved to London in 1896, where he became President of the Royal Society of Portrait Painters. Appointed official war artist in 1917 and was knighted in 1918. Travelled to California in 1936 and died five years later in Kilmagenny, County Kilkenny.

LAWRENCE, SIR THOMAS 1769–1830

A child prodigy who largely taught himself to paint, Lawrence was born in Bristol in 1769. In 1780 his father's business failed and the family moved to Bath. By age fourteen he was supporting his family as a painter of portraits in pastels. Moving to London by 1786 and studying at the Royal Academy Schools in 1787, Lawrence shot to fame in 1789/90 when he was asked to paint Queen Charlotte at Windsor. Appointed 1792 as Painter in Ordinary to the King. Became an ARA 1791 and full member in 1794. In the 1790s he became involved in the theatre and painted a number of portraits of the actor J.P. Kemble. He rarely attempted true history painting. Commissioned in 1818 by the Prince Regent to travel to France and Italy and paint portraits of the allied military leaders and heads of state after the defeat of Napoleon. On his return to England in 1820 he was made President of the Royal Academy. Painted mainly portraits of fashionable ladies and leading public figures in the ten years before his death in London in 1830.

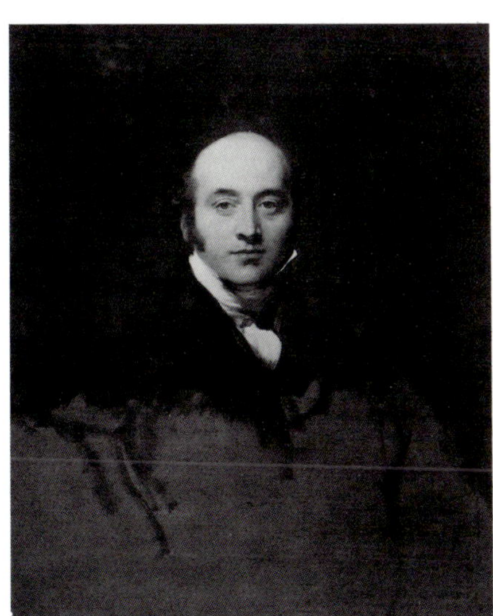

Sir Thomas Lawrence **Self-Portrait** *c.*1825 Oil on canvas *Royal Academy of Arts, London*

LEIGHTON, FREDERIC, LORD LEIGHTON OF STRETTON 1830–1896

Born in Scarborough to a family almost constantly on the move throughout Europe. Between the ages of ten and seventeen he studied at various places in Italy and Germany, including the Academy in Florence and the Städelsches Kunstinstitut in Frankfurt. His travels exposed him to many artists and styles and he was influenced by the Nazarenes, Bouguereau, Gérôme, Italian Renaissance painting and classical sculpture. He was knighted in 1878, was made a Baronet in 1886 and in 1896 became the first British artist to be raised to the peerage. In the 1850s he had studios in Rome and Paris before returning to London in 1858. In 1864 he commissioned the building of Leighton House and was elected ARA. Elected RA in 1868 and became President in 1878. Died 1896 in London.

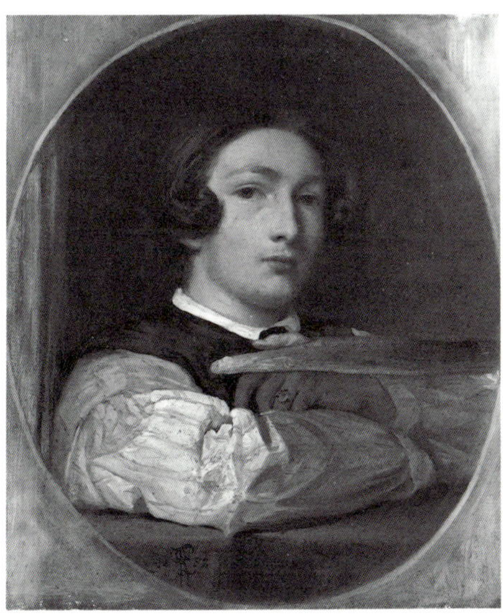

Frederic Lord Leighton **Self-Portrait with Palette** 1852 Oil on canvas *Städelsches Kunstinstitut, Frankfurt*

LELY, SIR PETER 1618–1680

Born Pieter Van der Faes in Soest, Westphalia. Of Dutch parentage, he trained under Franz Pietersz. de Grebber in Haarlem, becoming a Master of the Haarlem Guild in 1637. Around 1643 he came to England, initially painting pastoral scenes of a slightly erotic nature. However, these did not appeal to English taste and from 1647 he took up portraiture. Patronised by the Duke of Northumberland, whose collection of paintings by Van Dyck and Dobson were to influence his style. He painted the Royal Family during their imprisonment at Syon House and Petworth and in 1661 was appointed principal painter to Charles II. He ran a busy studio, mainly painting noble families prominent during the Restoration, although he also painted Cromwell. Also known as a collector. He was knighted in the last year of his life, dying in London in 1680.

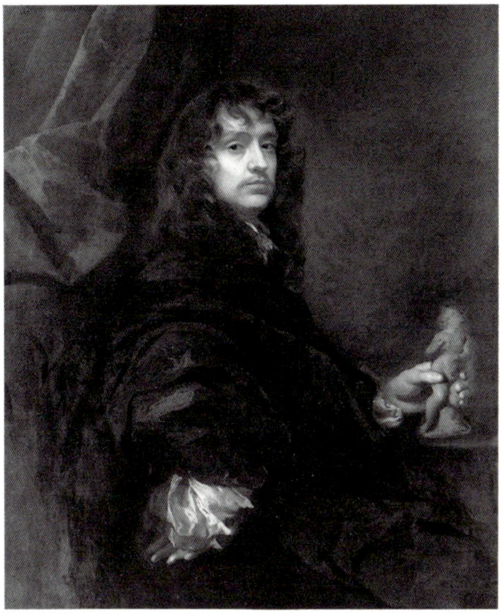

Sir Peter Lely **Self-Portrait** *c.*1660 Oil on canvas *National Portrait Gallery, London*

MILLAIS, SIR JOHN EVERETT, BT 1829–1896

Born in Southampton in 1829, he spent his youth in Jersey and Dinan. Youngest ever pupil at the Royal Academy Schools at the age of eleven. There he met Holman Hunt, and together with Rossetti they founded the Pre-Raphaelite Brotherhood in 1848. In 1853 he spent a holiday in Scotland with Ruskin and his wife Effie. He married Effie in 1855 following the annulment of her marriage, and they settled in Perth. In 1861 he returned to London, becoming very rich and successful with his portraits of important figures of the day. His later work includes sentimental pictures of children and large-scale modern genre subjects. From 1870 he took to painting Scottish landscapes. Made a Baronet in 1885. Elected President of the Royal Academy in 1896 but died later that year in London.

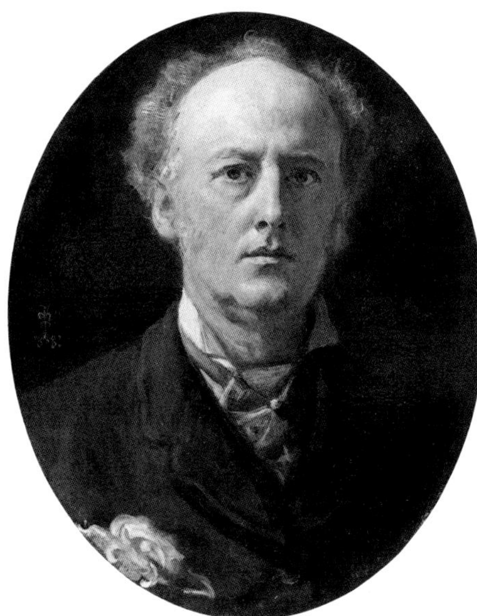

Sir John Everett Millais **Self-Portrait** 1883 Oil on canvas *City of Aberdeen Art Gallery and Museums Collection*

ORPEN, SIR WILLIAM NEWENHAM MONTAGUE

1878–1931

One of the most popular portrait painters of the post-Victorian period. Born at Stillorgan in County Dublin and trained at the Dublin Metropolitan School of Art 1890–7. He went on to train at the Slade from 1897–9 and from 1902 shared a teaching studio with Augustus John.

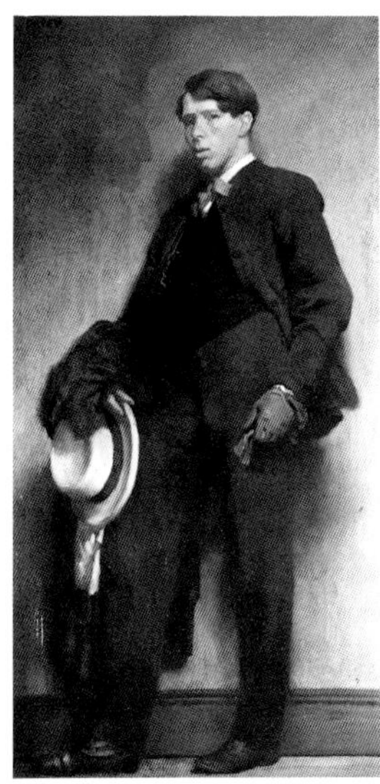

Sir William Orpen **Self-Portrait** *c.*1901 Oil on canvas *Glasgow City Art Gallery and Museum*

Elected ARA 1910 and in 1911 became a founder-member of the National Portrait Society. Appointed official war artist from 1917–19, he later donated his war works to the Imperial War Museum. He was knighted in 1918 and became an RA in 1920. He died in London in 1931.

RAEBURN, SIR HENRY

1756–1823

Born 1756 in Stockbridge, Edinburgh, Raeburn was mainly self-taught. Encouraged by Reynolds, he travelled to Rome via London in 1784–6. From 1787 he established himself in Edinburgh with only occasional visits to London. Beginning with miniatures he soon began to paint life-size portraits and was the leading portrait painter in Scotland by 1797. His earlier portraits have elaborate backgrounds but he gradually adopted a simpler format, concentrating on dramatic effects of light and shade rendered with great breadth. Elected to the Royal Academy in 1815 and knighted in 1822. He became the King's Painter for Scotland in 1823, dying later that year in Edinburgh.

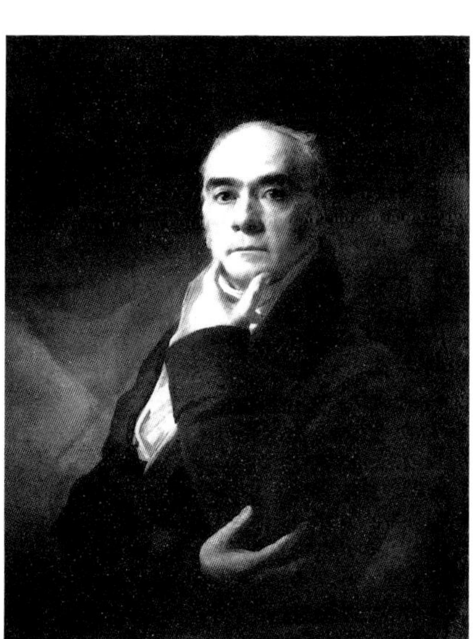

Sir Henry Raeburn **Self-Portrait** *c.*1815 Oil on canvas *National Gallery of Scotland*

RAMSAY, ALLAN

1713–1784

Born in Edinburgh in 1713, Ramsay became the pupil of Hysing in London from 1732–3. He studied under Imperiali and Solimena in Italy from 1736–8, and also drew at the Académie in Paris. On his return to London in 1738 he found patrons among the Scottish nobility and kept a summer studio in Edinburgh until 1755. His portraits in the Continental manner, using Van Aken as his drapery painter, were very fashionable. A second visit to Italy in 1754–7 prompted a more delicate style of painting. In 1761 he was appointed Painter to George III, giving up private commissions to concentrate on his portraits of the Royal Family. Following a visit to Paris in 1765, his work shows the influence of de la Tour. He injured his right arm in 1773 but his busy studio continued to produce replicas under his supervision. Died at Dover on his way home from another trip to Italy in 1784.

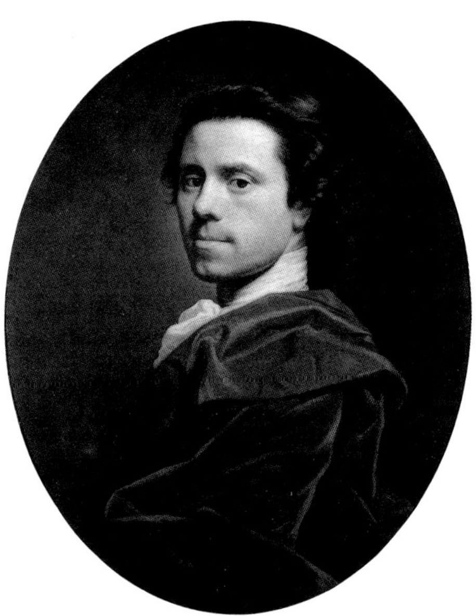

Allan Ramsay **Self-Portrait** *c.*1739 Oil on canvas *National Portrait Gallery, London*

REYNOLDS, SIR JOSHUA

1723–1792

Born at Plympton in Devon in 1723. In 1740 he was apprenticed to Thomas Hudson, buying his way out in 1743 and working independently in Devon and London. Travelled in Italy from 1749, spending 1750–2 in Rome. Settled in

London in 1753 where he became the dominant influence on British portraiture until his death in 1792. He ran a busy studio with much of the work on drapery and backgrounds being carried out by assistants. He aimed to elevate the status of portraiture by basing it on classical sculpture and Old Masters. His attempts at history painting were not entirely successful. His experiments with new media often had disastrous results, and many of his paintings are now ruined. He was greatly interested in art theory, promulgating his ideas in the series of Discourses that he delivered annually at the Academy in his capacity as first President. Died 1792 in London.

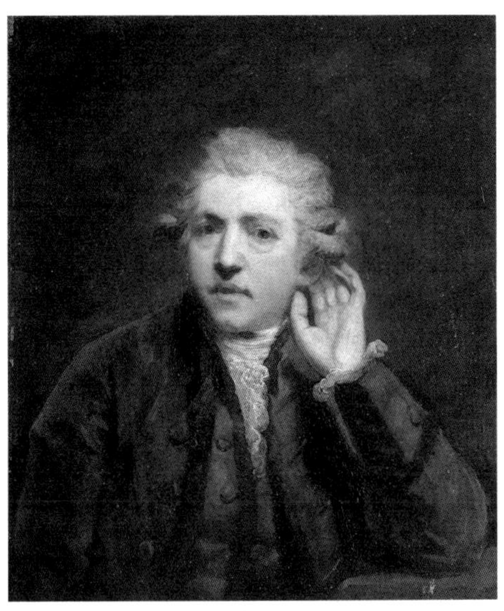

Sir Joshua Reynolds **Self-Portrait as a Deaf Man** *c.*1775 Oil on canvas *Tate Gallery. Bequeathed by Miss Emily Drummond 1930*

RICHARDSON, JONATHAN
*c.*1665–1745

A portrait painter and influential writer on the subject of art and literature. Richardson was born in London and studied under Riley from 1688–91. He became very popular as a portrait painter, and worked prolifically 1700–40, the link between Kneller and Hudson. Also known as a collector and connoisseur of Old Master drawings. In 1711 he helped Kneller and others to found the first London academy of art. 1715 saw the publication of his *Theory of Painting*. Teacher of Thomas Hudson, who had married his daughter in 1725.

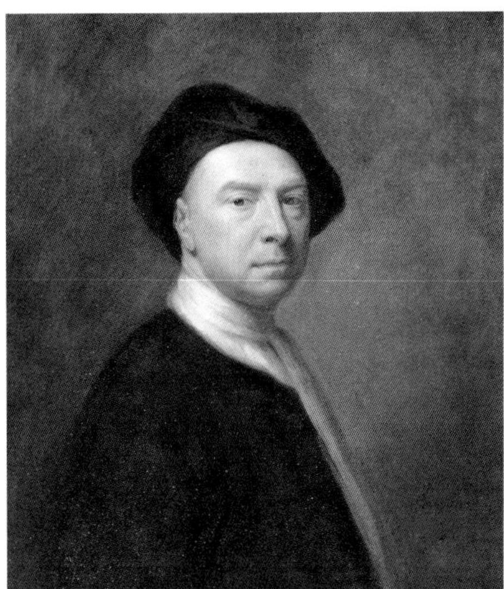

Jonathan Richardson **Self-Portrait** *c.*1729 Oil on canvas *National Portrait Gallery, London*

SANT, JAMES
1820–1916

A prolific painter of portraits, landscape and genre. Born 1820 in Croydon and trained under John Varley and A.W. Callcott before attending the Royal Academy Schools. Exhibited regularly from 1840 and was elected ARA in 1861 and RA in 1869 before retiring from the Academy in 1914. He received many portrait commissions and was appointed Painter to the Queen in 1872. Died in London in 1916.

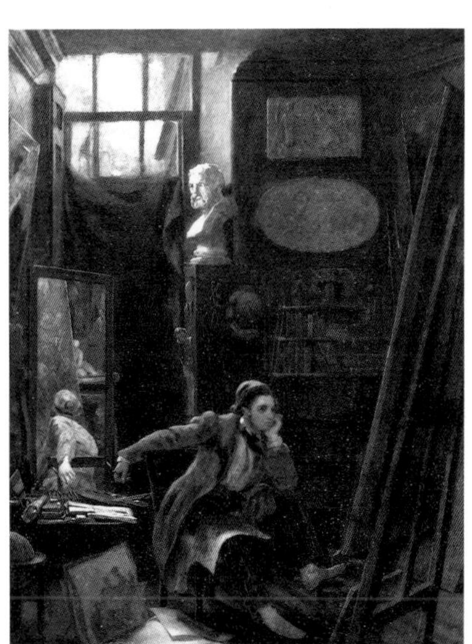

James Sant **Self-Portrait** *c.*1840 Oil on canvas *National Portrait Gallery, London*

SARGENT, JOHN SINGER
1856–1925

Born 1856 in Florence of American parents, he began his training in the studio of Carl Welsch in Rome at age twelve. This was followed by studies in Dresden and Florence (at the Accademia delle Belli Arti) 1871–4. Moving to Paris in 1874 he studied under Carolus-Duran and at the Ecole des Beaux-Arts. In 1876 he travelled to the USA and visited Europe and North Africa during the late 1870s. Came to England in 1884 and settled in London in 1886, exhibiting at the Royal Academy and the New English Art Club that same year. Elected ARA 1890 and RA 1891, but declined to become President. Had great success as a society portrait painter, working largely on commission in both Europe and the USA. His associates include Whistler, whom he met in Venice, and Monet whom he visited at Giverny in 1889. His most important public commissions were for decorations of the Boston Public Library and Museum in the USA (begun in 1890). In 1918 he travelled to France as an official war artist along with Henry Tonks. He died in London in 1925.

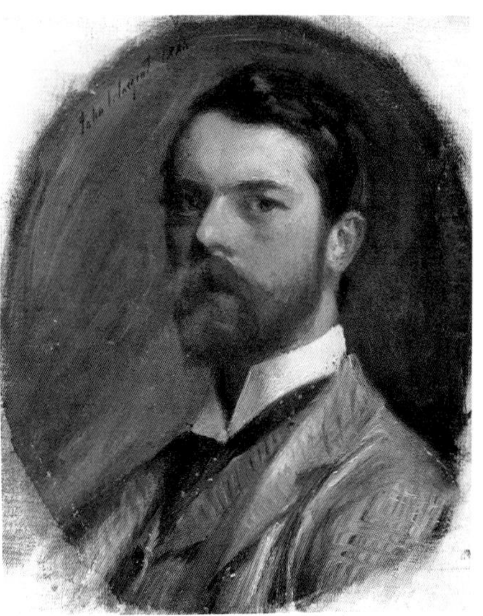

John Singer Sargent **Self-Portrait** 1886 Oil on canvas *City of Aberdeen Art Gallery and Museums Collection*

SOLOMON, SOLOMON JOSEPH 1860–1927

Was born in London 1860 and attended Heatherley's Art School in 1876 before going on to the Royal Academy Schools in 1877 where he was taught by Millais and Sir Lawrence Alma-Tadema. Also studied at the Ecole des Beaux-Arts in Paris and the Academy in Munich. From 1880–92 he travelled in North Africa, Spain and Italy with the painter Arthur Hacker. Became ARA 1896 and RA 1906. During the First World War, played an important role in the development of military camouflage techniques, helping to set up the British camouflage section with assistance from the French.

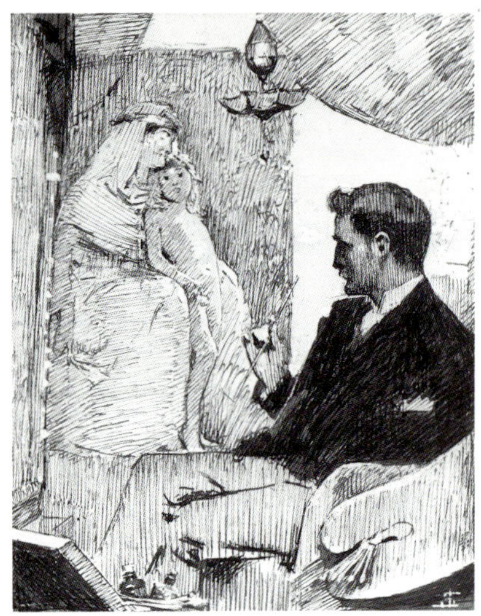

Solomon J. Solomon **Self-Portrait at the Easel** Pen and ink *National Portrait Gallery, London*

TISSOT, JACQUES-JOSEPH (JAMES) 1836–1902

Painter of fashionable society at leisure, awkward social situations, private family moments and religious subjects. Tissot was born in Nantes and received an academic training in Paris under Lamothe and Flandrin. Debut at the Salon in 1859 with paintings on medieval themes. Found more success in the 1860s with images of modern society. The collapse of the Second Empire in Paris under the strain of the France-Prussian War prompted him to come to England in 1871. Showed regularly at the Royal Academy from 1864–81. Returned to Paris in 1882 following the death of his beloved mistress and model Kathleen Newton. Increasing interest in spiritualism and the Church caused him to give up secular subjects around 1885. Travelled to the Holy Land in 1886, making 365 studies on the life of Christ. Died 1902 at Buillon.

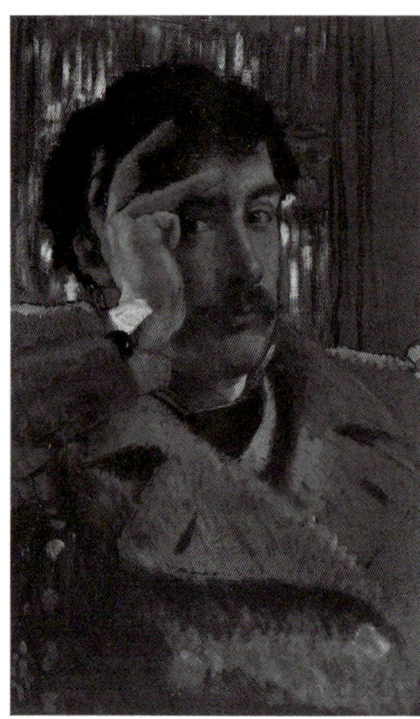

James Tissot **Self-Portrait** *c.*1865 Oil on canvas *The Fine Arts Museums of San Francisco, Mildred Anna Williams Collection, 1961.16*

VAN DYCK, SIR ANTHONY 1599–1641

Born 1599 in Antwerp and at age ten became a pupil of Hendrik van Balen, Dean of the Artist's Guild in Antwerp, becoming a Master in 1618. Despite having his own studio by 1616 he continued to train under Rubens, acting as leading assistant to him for the decorations of S. Charles Borromée in Antwerp. The Earl of Arundel, a great collector and patron, encouraged him to come to England in 1620 where he was granted a court pension. Travelled to Italy in 1621 with the Countess of Arundel and remained there until his return to Antwerp in 1628. His reputation as a portraitist was already established and he became painter to the courts of Brussels and The Hague. Returning to England in 1632 he was appointed Principal Painter to their Majesties and granted a large pension, two residences and a knighthood by Charles I. In 1635 he painted the head of the King in three positions, to enable Bernini to sculpt a bust. Divided his time between England and Antwerp during 1634–41, mainly painting portraits of prominent figures. In 1640 he became ill on a trip to Antwerp and Paris and died in England in 1641.

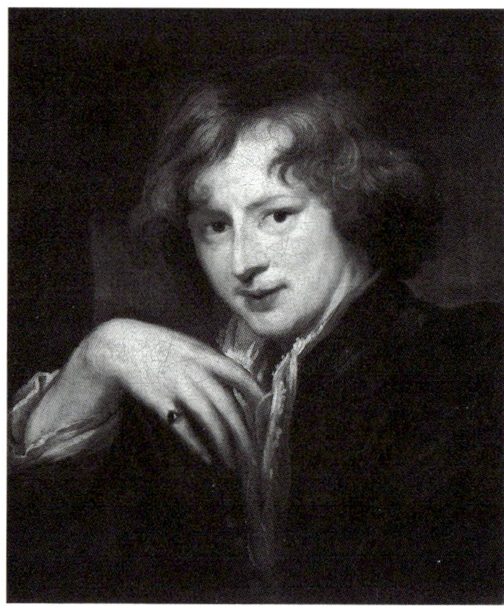

after Van Dyck **Portrait of the Artist** *c.*1621 Oil on canvas *Trustees of the National Gallery, London*

WATTS, GEORGE FREDERIC 1817–1904

Preferring history and allegorical painting, Watts moved on to portraiture reluctantly. Born in London in 1817 and apprenticed to a sculptor before training at the Royal Academy Schools (in 1835) and the school of the artist and cricketer 'Felix'. Travelled

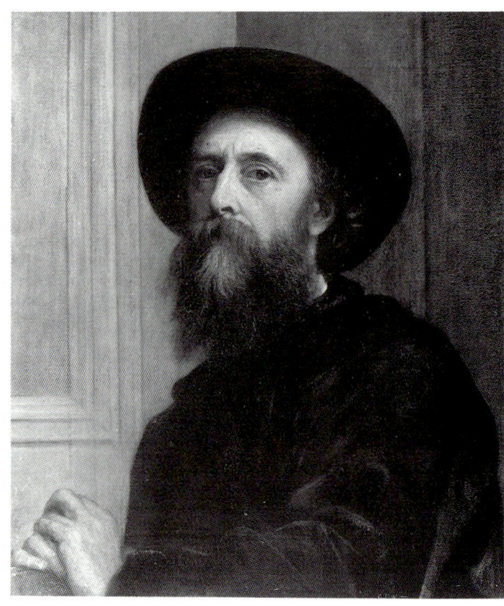

George Frederic Watts **Self-Portrait** 1864 Oil on canvas *Tate Gallery*

in Italy via Paris, from 1843–7. From 1851 became permanent guest of his patrons the Prinsep family at Little Holland House. Brief marriage (from 1864–5) to Ellen Terry, then aged sixteen. Elected ARA and RA in 1867. Moved to the Isle of Wight with the Prinseps in 1875 but was forced to return to maintain his portrait practice. Received Order of Merit in 1902 but twice declined a baronetcy. From the 1880s onwards he painted portraits of famous Victorians, interspersed with allegorical pictures. From the late 1860s his interest in sculpture revived. Died at Compton near Guildford in 1904.

WINTERHALTER, FRANZ XAVER
1805–1873

Renowned for his sumptuous portraits of European court society. Born at Menzenschwand in the Black Forest in 1805 and trained as an engraver in Freiburg before studying painting in Munich. He settled in Karlsruhe in 1828 but from 1835 to 1870 much of his time was spent in Paris. In 1841 he was recommended to Queen Victoria and quickly became her favourite, returning to London occasionally on new commissions. Worked extensively for the courts of Europe, including Germany, Austria and Russia, setting the style for the period. Died in Frankfurt in 1873.

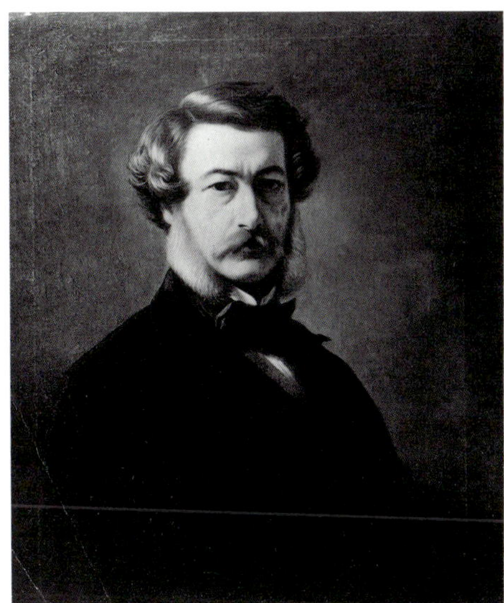

after Franz Xaver Winterhalter (copy by Enrico Belli) **Portrait of the Artist** 1874 Oil on canvas *Her Majesty The Queen*

WET, JACOB DE
1640–1697

Best known for his decorative history paintings, de Wet was born in Haarlem, son of the painter Jacob Willemz. de Wet. In 1685 he moved to Scotland where he was commissioned to work at Holyrood House on a ceiling and 110 portraits of real and legendary kings. His other works include portraits and decorations at Glamis Castle. Died in Amsterdam in 1697.

WRIGHT, JOHN MICHAEL
1617–1694

Portraitist, connoisseur and antiquary popular in the Restoration court. Born probably in London 1617 and trained in Edinburgh 1636–41 as apprentice to George Jameson. Travelled to Rome in 1640s, where he probably converted to Catholicism and became an authority on antiquities. Attended the Accademia di S. Luca in 1648. Returned to England in 1656 leaving his family behind in Rome. Found employment with Charles II and was successful as a portraitist by 1659. Also painted the ceiling in Charles II's bedroom at Whitehall Palace. Spent 1679–80 in Dublin. In Rome 1686–7 with James II's embassy, but his career suffered after the expulsion of the King. Ceased to paint for the court in 1688, and ended his life in relative poverty in London in 1694.

ZOFFANY, JOHAN
1733–1810

Born Zauffaly in Frankfurt in 1733, son of the court cabinet-maker and architect to the Prince von Thurn und Taxis. Apprenticed to Martin Speer and received some training on a visit to Rome in 1750. Worked for Benjamin Wilson on his arrival in London in 1760. Garrick helped him to establish himself as a painter, commissioning him to paint portraits of actors and theatrical scenes. The years 1772–8 spent in Florence painting a view of the Tribuna of the Uffizi. Was less successful on his return to England and in 1783 decided to go to Bengal to seek his fortune. The Governor General, Warren Hastings, became a major patron and Zoffany was wealthy enough to retire from painting by 1800. Returned to England in 1789, dying in London in 1810.

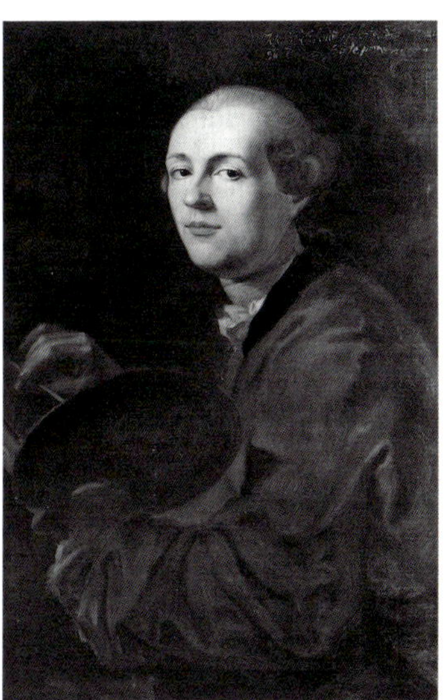

Johan Zoffany **Self-Portrait with Palette** *c.*1759 Oil on canvas *Mainfränkisches Museum Würzburg*

Index of Works

Lenders

Numbers refer to the catalogue entries

PUBLIC COLLECTIONS

Calke Abbey, The Harpur-Crewe Collection (The National Trust) 31
Cambridge, Fitzwilliam Museum 7, 76
Cardiff, National Museum of Wales 11
Charlecote, The Lucy Collection (The National Trust) 28
Cleveland Museum of Art 51
Dublin, National Gallery of Ireland 54
Edinburgh, National Gallery of Scotland 46
Edinburgh, National Trust for Scotland 30, 47
Edinburgh, Scottish National Portrait Gallery 16, 39
Ickworth, The Bristol Collection (The National Trust) 40
Liverpool, Walker Art Gallery (The National Museums and Galleries on Merseyside) 17
London, Thomas Coram Foundation for Children 24
London, Dulwich Picture Gallery 37
London, National Army Museum 56
London, Iveagh Bequest, Kenwood (English Heritage) 36
London, National Gallery 38, 43, 50
London, National Portrait Gallery 2, 21, 62, 72
London, Royal Academy of Arts 45
London, Tate Gallery 8, 33, 35, 42, 52, 53, 58, 63, 64, 65, 66, 68, 70, 77
New Haven, Yale Center for British Art 61
Newcastle upon Tyne, Laing Art Gallery (Tyne and Wear Museums) 75
Port Sunlight, Lady Lever Art Gallery (The National Museums and Galleries on Merseyside) 59
The Powis Estate Trustees, Powis Castle 14
York City Art Gallery 32

PRIVATE COLLECTIONS

Her Majesty The Queen 44
The Arts Club 71
The Duke of Atholl 19
The Earl Bathurst 12, 55
The Earl of Clarendon 10
Viscount Coke and the Trustees of the Holkham Estate 29
The Corporation of the Church House 79
Crown Estate 57
The Duke of Devonshire and the Chatsworth Settlement Trustees 34
Dunvegan Castle 27
The Trustees of the Rt Hon. Olive, Countess Fitzwilliam's Chattels Settlement 1, 3, 4, 78
Garrick Club, London 23
Grimsthorpe and Drummond Castle Trust 26
Jefferson Smurfit Group PLC 73
Mrs Kitty Lemos 20
The Duke of Marlborough 6
The Duke of Norfolk 13
The Marquess of Northampton, 48, 49
The Duke of Northumberland 5
Private Collections 15, 18, 22, 25, 67, 69, 74
University of Manchester, Tabley House Collection 9
The Hon. Michael Willoughby 60
The Marquess of Zetland 41

Photographic Credits

Aberdeen Art Gallery; Bayerische Staatsgemäldesammlungen; Birmingham Museums & Art Gallery; Museo Boldini; British Museum; The Burrell Collection; Castle Museum & Art Gallery, Nottingham; Christie's Colour Library; Cleveland Museum of Art; A. C. Cooper; Courtauld Institute of Art; Prudence Cuming Associates Ltd; Dulwich College Picture Gallery; Ursula Edelmann; Mark Fiennes; Fitzwilliam Museum; Städelsches Kunstinstitut Frankfurt; Frick Collection, New York; Glasgow City Art Gallery; Photo-Verlag Gundermann; English Heritage; Les Golding; Hamilton Colour; Angelo Hornak; Christopher Hurst; John Kellett; Laing Art Gallery; Sam de Laszlo; Layland Ross; Mainfränkisches Museum Würzburg; Jack McKenzie (A.I.C. Photographic Services); Metropolitan Museum of Art, New York; Studio Morgan; National Army Museum, London (Courtesy of the Director); National Galleries of Scotland; National Gallery, London; National Gallery of Ireland; National Maritime Museum; National Museum of Wales; National Museums and Galleries on Merseyside; National Portrait Gallery, London; National Trust Photographic Library; National Trust for Scotland Photo Library; Sydney W. Newbery; Plymouth City Museum and Art Gallery; Simon Reynolds; Royal Academy of Arts; Royal Collection; The Fine Arts Museum of San Francisco; Glen Segal Tate Gallery Photographic Department; Ulster Museum; John Webb; Jeremy Whitaker; Derrick E. Witty; Yale Center for British Art; York City Art Gallery

Ways of Giving to the Tate Gallery

The Tate Gallery attracts funds from the private sector to support its programme of activities in London, Liverpool and St Ives. Support is raised from the business community, individuals, trusts and foundations, and includes sponsorships, donations, bequests and gifts of works of art. The Tate Gallery is recognised as a charity under Inland Revenue reference number x78055/1.

DONATIONS

There are a variety of ways through which you can make a donation to the Tate Gallery.

Donations All donations, however small, will be gratefully received and acknowledged by the Tate Gallery.

Covenants A Deed of Covenant, which must be taken out for a minimum of four years, will enable the Tate Gallery to claim back tax on your charitable donation. For example, a covenant for £100 per annum will allow the Gallery to claim a further £33 at present tax rates.

Gift-Aid For individuals and companies wishing to make donations of £400 and above, Gift-Aid allows the Gallery to claim back tax on your charitable donation. In addition, if you are a higher rate taxpayer you will be able to claim tax relief on the donation. A Gift-Aid form and explanatory leaflet can be sent to you if you require further information.

Bequests You may wish to remember the Tate Gallery in your will or make a specific donation *In Memoriam*. A bequest may take the form of either a specific cash sum, a residual proportion of your estate or a specific item of property, such as a work of art. Certain tax advantages can be obtained by making a legacy in favour of the Tate Gallery. Please check with the Tate Gallery when you draw up your will that it is able to accept your bequest.

American Fund for the Tate Gallery The American Fund was formed in 1986 to facilitate gifts of works of art, donations and bequests to the Tate Gallery from United States residents. It receives full tax exempt status from the IRS.

INDIVIDUAL MEMBERSHIP PROGRAMMES

FRIENDS OF THE TATE GALLERY

Since their formation in 1958, the Friends of the Tate Gallery have helped to buy major works of art for the Tate Gallery collection, from Stubbs to Hockney.

Members are entitled to immediate and unlimited free admission to Tate Gallery exhibitions with a guest, invitations to previews of Tate Gallery exhibitions, opportunities to visit the Gallery when closed to the public, a discount of 10 per cent in the Tate Gallery shop, special events, *Friends Events* and *Tate Preview* magazines mailed three times a year, free admission to exhibitions at Tate Gallery Liverpool, and use of the new Friends Room at the Tate Gallery, supported by Lloyd's of London.

Three categories of higher level memberships, Associate Fellow at £100, Deputy Fellow at £250, and Fellow at £500, entitle members to a range of extra benefits including guest cards and invitations to exclusive special events.

The Friends of the Tate Gallery are supported by Tate & Lyle PLC.

Further details on the Friends may be obtained from:

Friends of the Tate Gallery
Tate Gallery
Millbank
London SW1P 4RG

Tel: 071–821 1313

PATRONS OF THE TATE GALLERY

The Patrons of British Art support British painting and sculpture from the Elizabethan period through to the early twentieth century in the Tate Gallery's collection. They encourage knowledge and awareness of British Art by providing an opportunity to study Britain's cultural heritage.

The Patrons of New Art support contemporary art in the Tate Gallery's collection. They promote a lively and informed interest in contemporary art and are associated with The Turner Prize, one of the most prestigious awards for the visual arts.

Annual membership of the Patrons ranges from £350 to £750, and funds the purchase of works of art for the Tate Gallery's collection.

Benefits for both groups include invitations to Tate Gallery receptions, an opportunity to sit on the Patrons' acquisitions committees, special events including visits to private and corporate collections and complimentary catalogues of Tate Gallery exhibitions.

Further details on the Patrons may be obtained from:

The Development Office
Tate Gallery
Millbank
London SW1P 4RG

Tel: 071–821 1313

CORPORATE MEMBERSHIP PROGRAMME

Membership of the Tate Gallery's Corporate Membership Programme offers companies outstanding value-for-money and provides opportunities for every employee to enjoy a closer knowledge of the Gallery, its collection and exhibitions.

Membership benefits are specifically geared to business needs and include private views for company employees, free and discount admission to exhibitions, discount in the Gallery shop, out-of-hours Gallery visits, behind-the-scenes tours, exclusive use of the Gallery for corporate entertainment, invitations to VIP events, copies of Gallery literature and acknowledgment in Gallery publications.

TATE GALLERY CORPORATE MEMBERS

Partners
Agfa UK Ltd
Barclays Bank PLC
The British Petroleum Company plc
Glaxo Holdings p.l.c.
Manpower (UK) Ltd
THORN EMI
Unilever

Associates
Bell Helicopter Textron
Channel 4 Television
Debenham Tewson & Chinnocks
Ernst & Young
KPMG Peat Marwick
Lazard Brothers & Co Ltd
Linklaters & Paines
Smith & Williamson
S.G. Warburg Group
Vickers plc

CORPORATE SPONSORSHIP

The Tate Gallery works closely with sponsors to ensure that their business interests are well served, and has a reputation for developing imaginative fund-raising initiatives. Sponsorships can range from a few thousand pounds to considerable investment in long-term programmes; small businesses as well as multi-national corporations have benefited from the high profile and prestige of Tate Gallery sponsorship.

Opportunities available at Tate Gallery London, Liverpool and St Ives include exhibitions (some also tour the UK), education, conservation and research programmes, audience development, visitor access to the Collection and special events. Sponsorship benefits include national and regional publicity, targeted marketing to niche audiences, exclusive corporate entertainment, employee benefits and acknowledgment in Tate Gallery publications.

TATE GALLERY LONDON: PRINCIPAL CORPORATE SPONSORS
(alphabetical order)

Barclays Bank PLC
1991, *Constable*
The British Land Company PLC
1990, *Joseph Wright of Derby**
The British Petroleum Company plc
1990–3, *New Displays*
Channel 4 Television
1991–3, The Turner Prize
Daimler-Benz AG
1991, *Max Ernst*
Pearson plc
1992–5 Elizabethan Curator Post
Reed International P.L.C.
1990, *On Classic Ground: Picasso, Léger, de Chirico and the New Classicism, 1910–30*
Tatle & Lyle PLC
1991–3, Friends Relaunch Marketing Programme
Volkswagen
1990–2, The Turner Scholarships

TATE GALLERY LONDON: CORPORATE SPONSORS
(alphabetical order)

Agfa Graphic Systems Group
1992, *Turner: The Fifth Decade**
Beck's
1992, *Otto Dix*
Blackwall Green Ltd
1991, International Conference on the Packing and Transportation of Paintings
Borghi Transporti Spedizioni SPA
1991, International Conference on the Packing and Transportation of Paintings
James Bourlets & Sons
1991, International Conference on the Packing and Transportation of Paintings
British Steel plc
1990, *William Coldstream*
Carroll, Dempsey & Thirkell
1990, *Anish Kapoor**
Clifton Nurseries
1990–2, Christmas Tree (in kind)
D'Art Kunstspedition GmbH
1991, International Conference on the Packing and Transportation of Paintings
Debenham Tewson & Chinnocks
1990, *Turner: Painting and Poetry*
Digital Equipment Co Ltd
1991–2, *From Turner's Studio*
Gander and White Shipping Ltd
1991, International Conference on the Packing and Transportation of Paintings
Gerlach Art Packers & Shippers
1991, International Conference on the Packing and Transportation of Paintings
Harsch Transports
1991, International Conference on the Packing and Transportation of Paintings
Hasenkamp Internationale Transporte
1991, International Conference on the Packing and Transportation of Paintings
The Independent
1992, *Otto Dix* (in kind)
KPMG Management Consulting
1991, *Anthony Caro: Sculpture towards Architecture**
Kunsttrans Antiquitaten
1991, International Conference on the Packing and Transportation of Paintings
Lloyd's of London
1991, Friends Room
Martinspeed Ltd
1991, International Conference on the Packing and Transportation of Paintings
Masterpiece International Ltd
1991, International Conference on the Packing and Transportation of Paintings
Mat Securitas Express AG
1991, International Conference on the Packing the Transportation of Paintings
Mobel Transport AG
1991, International Conference on the Packing and Transportation of Paintings
Momart plc
1991, International Conference on the Packing and Transportation of Paintings
Propileo Transport
1991, International Conference on the Packing and Transportation of Paintings
Rees Martin Art Service
1991, International Conference on the Packing and Transportation of Paintings
SRU Limited
1992, *Richard Hamilton**
TSB Group plc
1992, *Turner and Byron*
1992–5, *William Blake* display series
Wingate & Johnston Ltd
1991, International Conference on the Packing and Transportation of Paintings

*denotes a first-time sponsorship in the arts, recognised by an award under the Government's Business Sponsorship Incentive Scheme, administered by the Association for Business Sponsorship of the Arts.

TATE GALLERY LIVERPOOL: CORPORATE SPONSORS
(alphabetical order)

AIB Bank
1991, *Strongholds*
Barclays Bank PLC
1990, *New Light On Sculpture*
BASF
1990, *Lifelines*
British Alcan Aluminium plc
1991, *Dynamism*
1991, *Giacometti*
British Telecom plc
1990, Outreach Programme
Concord Lighting
1990, *New Light On Sculpture*
Cultural Relations Committee, Departments of Foreign Affairs, Ireland
1991, *Strongholds*
English Estates
1991, Mobile Art Programme
Granada Television plc
1990, *New North*
Korean Air
1992, *Working with Nature* (in kind)
The Littlewoods Organisation plc
1992–5, *New Realities*
Merseyside Development Corporation
1990, Outreach Programme
1992, *Myth-Making*
1992, *Stanley Spencer*
Mobil Oil Company Ltd
1990, *New North*
Momart plc
1990–2, The Momart Fellowship
NSK Bearings Europe Ltd
1991, *A Cabinet of Signs: Contemporary Art from Post-Modern Japan*
Ryanair
1991, *Strongholds* (in kind)
Samsung Electronics
1992, *Working With Nature*
Volkswagen
1991, Mobile Art Programme (in kind)

TATE GALLERY BENEFACTORS
London, Liverpool and St Ives

FOUNDING BENEFACTORS (date order)

Sir Henry Tate
Sir Joseph Duveen
Lord Duveen
The Clore Foundation

PRINCIPAL BENEFACTORS
(alphabetical order)

American Fund for the Tate Gallery
Calouste Gulbenkian Foundation
The Henry Moore Foundation
National Heritage Memorial Fund
National Art Collections Fund
The Nomura Securities Co., Ltd
Dr Mortimer and Theresa Sackler Foundation
The Wolfson Foundation and Family Charitable Trust

BENEFACTORS (alphabetical order)

The Baring Foundation
Gilbert and Janet de Botton
Mr Edwin C. Cohen
John S. Cohen Foundation
The John Ellerman Foundation
Esmée Fairbairn Charitable Trust
The Getty Grant Program
Granada Group plc
John and Olivia Hughes
The Leverhulme Trust
John Lewis Partnership
Museums and Galleries Improvement Fund
Ocean Group plc (P.H. Holt Trust)
The Pilgrim Trust
GEC Plessey Telecommunications
The Eleanor Rathbone Charitable Trust
Mr John Ritblat
The Sainsbury Family Charitable Trusts
Save & Prosper Educational Trust
SRU Limited
Bernard Sunley Charitable Foundation
Weinberg Foundation

TATE GALLERY DONORS

LONDON (alphabetical order)

Professor Abbott
Hurry Armour Trust
Sir Richard Attenborough CBE
BAA plc
Friends of Nancy Balfour OBE
The Hon. Robin Baring
Mr Tom Bendhem
Michael and Marcia Blakenham
Miss Mary Boone
Botts & Company Limited
C.T. Bowring (Charities Trust) Ltd
Christie, Manson & Woods Ltd
Mr R.N. Collins
Mrs Dagny Corcoran
Anthony d'Offay Gallery
Miss W.A. Donner
Evelyn, Lady Downshire's Trust Fund
Mr Paul Dupee
Elephant Trust
European Arts Festival
Roberto Fainello Art Advisers Ltd
Gabo Trust for Sculpture Conservation
The German Government
Mr and Mrs David Gilmour
Goethe Institut
The Worshipful Company of Goldsmiths
Sir Nicholas and Lady Goodison Charitable Settlement
Richard Green Fine Paintings
Gytha Trust
Mr Robert Horton
Idlewild Trust
The Italian Government
Sir Anthony and Lady Jacobs
Mrs Gabrielle Keiller
Knapping Fund
The Helena and Kenneth Levy Bequest
Mr and Mrs Lawrence Lowenthal
Midland Bank Artscard
Mr and Mrs Robert Mnuchin
Peter Moores Foundation
Mr Peter Nahum
Old Possum's Practical Trust
Mr William Pegrum
Phillips Fine Art Auctioneers
Reed International P.L.C.
Mrs Jill Ritblat
Mrs Jean Sainsbury
The Hon. Simon Sainsbury
Schroder Charity Trust
The Swan Trust
Tate Gallery Publications
Mr Barry and the Hon. Mrs Townsley
U.K. Charity Lotteries Ltd
Waley-Cohen Charitable Trust
The Andy Warhol Foundation for the Visual Arts, Inc.
Mr Mark Weiss
Willis Faber plc
Thomas and Odette Worrell
Mrs Jayne Wrightsman

and those donors who wish to remain anonymous

LIVERPOOL (alphabetical order)

The Baring Foundation
David and Ruth Behrend Trust
Ivor Braka Ltd
The British Council
British Telecom plc
Calouste Gulbenkian Foundation
Mr and Mrs Henry Cotton
English Estates
European Arts Festival
Mrs Sue Hammerson OBE
Mr John Heyman
Liverpool Council for Voluntary Services
Merseyside Development Corporation
Momart plc
The Henry Moore Foundation
Ocean Group plc (P.H. Holt Trust)
Eleanor Rathbone Charitable Trust
Tate Gallery Liverpool Supporters
Bernard Sunley Charitable Foundation
Unilever
Visiting Arts

and those donors who wish to remain anonymous

ST IVES (alphabetical order)

Donors to the Appeal coordinated by the Steering Group for the Tate Gallery St Ives and the St Ives Action Group.

Viscount Amory Charitable Trust
Barbinder Trust
Barclays Bank PLC
The Baring Foundation
BICC Group
Patricia, Lady Boyd and Viscount Boyd
British Telecom plc
Cable and Wireless plc
Carlton Communications
Mr Francis Carnwath
Christie, Manson & Woods Ltd
Mr Peter Cocks
John S. Cohen Foundation
Miss Jean Cooper
D'Oyly Carte Charitable Trust
David Messum Fine Paintings
Dewhurst House
Dixons Group plc
The John Ellerman Foundation
English China Clays Group
Esmée Fairbairn Charitable Trust
The Worshipful Company of Fishmongers
The Foundation for Sport and the Arts
J. Paul Getty Jr Charitable Trust
Gimpel Fils
Grand Metropolitan Trust
Ms Judith Hodgson
Sir Geoffrey and Lady Holland
Mr Bernard Jacobson
Mr John Kilby
Lloyds Bank plc
Lord Leverhulme's Trust
The Manifold Trust
The Mayor Gallery
Marlborough Fine Art
The Worshipful Company of Mercers
Mercury Asset Management plc
Meyer International plc
The Henry Moore Foundation
National Westminster Bank plc
New Art Centre
Pall European Limited
The Pilgrim Trust
The Joseph Rank (1942) Charitable Trust
Mr Roy Ray
The Rayne Foundation
Royal Bank of Scotland
The Sainsbury Family Charitable Trusts
Mr Nicholas Serota
Mr Roger Slack
Trustees of H.E.W. Spurr Deceased
South West British Gas
South West Water plc
South Western Electricity plc
Sun Alliance Group
Television South West
The TSB Foundation for England and Wales
Unilever
Mrs Angela Verren Taunt
Weinberg Foundation
Wembley plc
Western Morning News, West Briton, Cornish Guardian and The Cornishman
Westlake & Co
Mr and Mrs Derek White
Mr and Mrs Graham Williams
Wingate Charitable Trust
Mrs Monica Wynter

and those donors who wish to remain anonymous